# The History of African Cities
# South of the Sahara

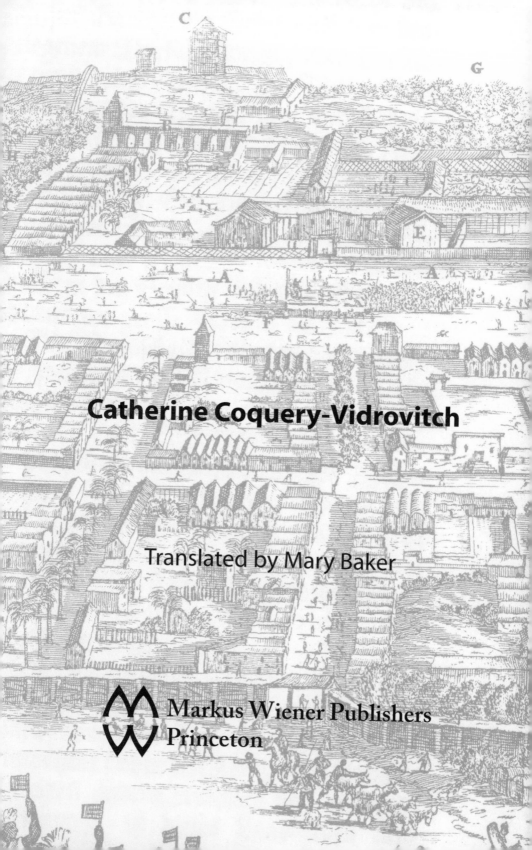

# Catherine Coquery-Vidrovitch

## Translated by Mary Baker

**Markus Wiener Publishers**
Princeton

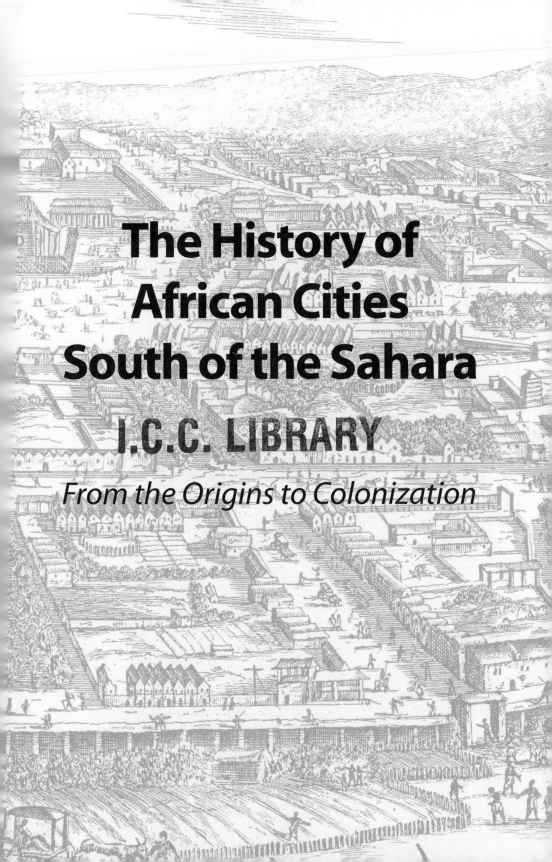

# The History of African Cities South of the Sahara

*From the Origins to Colonization*

Copyright © 2005 by Markus Wiener Publishers for the English translation.

For information write to:
Markus Wiener Publishers
231 Nassau Street, Princeton, NJ 08542
www.markuswiener.com

First published in French under the title *Histoire des villes d'Afrique noire: Des origines à la colonisation*
Copyright © Éditions Albin Michel S.A., 1993, for the French edition

*Cet ouvrage, publié dans le cadre d'un programme d'aide à la publication, bénéficie du soutien du Ministère des Affaires étrangères et du Service Culturel de l'Ambassade de France aux Etats-Unis.*

This work, published as part of a program of aid for publication, received support from the French Ministry of Foreign Affairs and the Cultural Services of the French Embassy in the United States.

Cover and book design by Wangden Kelsang, HeartBridge Communications

Library of Congress Cataloging-in-Publication Data

Coquery-Vidrovitch, Catherine.
    [Histoire des villes d'Afrique noire. English]
    The history of African cities south of the Sahara : from the origins
to colonization / Catherine Coquery-Vidrovitch ; translated by Mary Baker.
        p. cm.
    Translation of: Histoire des villes d'Afrique noire.
    Includes bibliographical references and index.
    ISBN 1-55876-302-3 (hardcover : alk. paper)
    1. Cities and towns--Africa, Sub-Saharan--History. I. Title.
    HT148.S8C6713 2004
    307.76'0967--dc22
                                                            2004022622
    ISBN 1-55876-303-1 (paperback)

Printed in the United States of America on acid-free paper

# Contents

List of Maps . . . . . . . . . . . . . . . . . . . . . . . . . . . . vii
Preface to the American Edition . . . . . . . . . . . . . . . ix
Introduction to the French Edition (1994) . . . . . . . . . . . xiii
Note on the Transcription of Proper Nouns . . . . . . . . . . . . . xv
Acknowledgements . . . . . . . . . . . . . . . . . . . . . . . . xvii

1. Cities in Africa . . . . . . . . . . . . . . . . . . . . . . . 1
   *African Urbanization?* . . . . . . . . . . . . . . . . . . . . . . 3
   *Precolonial African Cities: An Attempt at Definition* . . . . . . 12
   *An Attempt at Periodization* . . . . . . . . . . . . . . . . . . 26

2. Ancient Cities . . . . . . . . . . . . . . . . . . . . . . . . 29
   *East Africa and the Meroitic Heritage* . . . . . . . . . . . . . 33
   *Western Sudan and the Interior Delta of the Niger* . . . . . . . 42
   *Conclusion* . . . . . . . . . . . . . . . . . . . . . . . . . . 49

3. Bantu Cities . . . . . . . . . . . . . . . . . . . . . . . . . 53
   *Zimbabwe and the Stone Ruins of Southern Africa* . . . . . . . . 55
   *The Capitals of the Small Kingdoms of Central Africa* . . . . . 65
   *The Capitals of Central West African Kingdoms* . . . . . . . . . 77

4. Islam and African Cities . . . . . . . . . . . . . . . . . . . 89
   *From Ancient to Islamized Cities* . . . . . . . . . . . . . . . . 93
   *West Africa* . . . . . . . . . . . . . . . . . . . . . . . . . 100
   *Swahili Cities* . . . . . . . . . . . . . . . . . . . . . . . . 126

5. The Atlantic Period: From the Sixteenth Century to the
   Eighteenth Century . . . . . . . . . . . . . . . . . . . . . 135
   *Before the Slave Trade* . . . . . . . . . . . . . . . . . . . . 138
   *The Slave Trade Period* . . . . . . . . . . . . . . . . . . . . 169

6. The Nineteenth-Century Urban Revolution . . . . . . . . . . 205
    *Ports and Markets in East Africa* . . . . . . . . . . . . . . . . 212
    *The Urban Revolution in Sudanese Africa* . . . . . . . . . . 229
    *From North to South: The Colonial Transition* . . . . . . . . 277

Conclusion . . . . . . . . . . . . . . . . . . . . . . . . . . . . 317
    *The Importance of Economics* . . . . . . . . . . . . . . . . . 318
    *Different Types of Cities* . . . . . . . . . . . . . . . . . . . . 323
    *Urbanization and Colonization* . . . . . . . . . . . . . . . 326
    *Culture and Cities* . . . . . . . . . . . . . . . . . . . . . . . 330

Notes . . . . . . . . . . . . . . . . . . . . . . . . . . . . . . . 333
Bibliography . . . . . . . . . . . . . . . . . . . . . . . . . . . . 379
Index of Cities and Peoples . . . . . . . . . . . . . . . . . . . 413
About the Author . . . . . . . . . . . . . . . . . . . . . . . . . 422

# Maps

1. Urban Tropical Africa Today; Yoruba and Igbo Cities . . . . 10

2. Ancient Cities of East Africa . . . . . . . . . . . . . . . . . 37

3. Ancient Cities of West Africa and Main Trade Routes . . . . 48

4. Shona Lands and Cities in Zimbabwe . . . . . . . . . . . 58

5. Royal Cities and Estates in Burundi under the Reign of
   Mwezi Gisabo (ca. 1852–1908) . . . . . . . . . . . . . . . 70

6. Cities of Ancient Kongo and Trade Routes . . . . . . . . 79

7. Hausa City-States and Their Neighbors . . . . . . . . . . 121

8. The Hinterland of the Gold Coast to the West of the Volta
   in the 17th Century . . . . . . . . . . . . . . . . . . . . . 152

9. Slave-Trading Cities on the Slave Coast East of the Volta
   in the 18th Century . . . . . . . . . . . . . . . . . . . . . 177

10. Formation of Abomey's Historical Quarters . . . . . . . . 187

11. Kumasi: The Old City . . . . . . . . . . . . . . . . . . . . 196

12. Cities in Yao Country, Central East Africa (End of the 19th
    Century) . . . . . . . . . . . . . . . . . . . . . . . . . . . 217

13. Cities and Caravan Routes in the Sudan (19th Century) . . . 232

14. Ethiopia's Main Capital Cities from the 4th to the 20th
    Century . . . . . . . . . . . . . . . . . . . . . . . . . . . . 268

15. Location of Freetown in the 19th Century . . . . . . . . . 291

16. Senegal and Southern Rivers in the 19th Century . . . . . . 302

17. St. Louis Island and Surroundings in 1789 . . . . . . . . . . 303
18. The Urban Network in Southern Africa at the End of the
    Colonial Period . . . . . . . . . . . . . . . . . . . . . . . 312
19. The "Colonial" City from the Cape to Today's City Center . . 315

# Preface to the American Edition

It is probably presumptuous, twelve years after the publication of this book in French, to publish a translation that is only partially updated. Yet, it seems worthwhile because until recently there has not been comparable material available in English, other than collections of essays. Interestingly, the bibliography of this edition contains many recent works in that language because much research on African urbanism, particularly pertaining to independence, has been published since this book first appeared. For example, the forthcoming summary of urban history by Bill Freund[1] is eagerly anticipated, but it focuses on the nineteenth and twentieth centuries. Earlier periods have received less attention from recent researchers. Indeed, the state of current research is such that much older books on precolonial cities by Basil Davidson and Robert Hull are republished or to be republished.[2]

In London in 1996, a major international conference on Africa's Urban Past breathed new life into research in this area and resulted in the partial but high-quality publication of papers presented at that event; 17 articles were selected from 104.[3] The groundbreaking introduction to the collection summarizes key points, in particular the fact that residential segregation was not invented by colonizers but often existed before the arrival of the Europeans. A minority of articles selected concern the period prior to the twentieth century (colonization and independence). Most of the articles provide incisive analyses of specific points by focusing on a city or group of cities (cities in Ghana, for example). The scope of the work is sufficiently broad to provide an overview of current research on political, economic, and cultural urban history, with a full range of concordant and opposing viewpoints on urbanism, space, and social issues. However, the monographic bias hinders the development of a thematic understanding of the problems, though this thematic does reappear in the case studies (e.g., women in Ghanaian cities, burial customs at Accra, the land problem in Bahir Dar, and the question of urban heritage in Zanzibar). Rare exceptions aside, however, the authors overlook French-language publications despite the fact that this is one of the areas where French-speaking historians have done the most work. One of the goals of the present book is thus to provide English speakers with a basis for comparison.

Since the publication in France, the bibliography has been updated and sometimes fine-tuned, such as in the case of details provided by the McIntoshes in the decades following their major archeological discovery in 1980 concerning the ancient city of Jenne-Jeno in Mali. Our recent knowledge is mainly enriched by case studies, including that by Jonathon Glassman on the history of the east coast and especially the city of Pangani in the nineteenth century, and the book on the sultanate of Geledi in a similar period.[4] However, there do not seem to have been any major developments in the field comparable to the explosion of research on the history of ancient urban Africa that occurred in the 30 years preceding the first publication of this work. Progress has instead been made in our knowledge of the growth and change of modern cities and colonial urbanism. While in principle the period covered by this book ends at the dawn of colonization, the bibliography includes a number of works on modern and colonial times because they often refer to the period preceding their specific focus.

Naturally, this book is based on my own research and a great deal of fieldwork. Virtually every year from 1965 on, I was involved in research projects and teaching assignments in various African countries, mostly in locations mentioned in the book. It seemed to me essential to gain some familiarity with as many cities as possible, because their foundations and structures are so different from those we are used to in the West. However, given the scope of the project, the book is also based on the work of many other observers, travelers, missionaries, and researchers. I am in debt to so many of them that it would be inappropriate to mention only a few. Please see the exhaustive list of what I have read in the bibliography. Of course, others need to be added; a work that claims to be a summary necessarily leaves out as much as it contains. All of the books and articles used are not of the same caliber. Besides excellent works there are others that are useful mainly because they provide testimony about a world that no longer exists. Many have to be read carefully to identify what pertains to Africa and what pertains to an observer, most often a foreigner, whose views were biased by his or her own cultural heritage. How many narratives hesitate to call what is being described a "city" or a "true city"! I have tried to understand what was meant and separate the wheat from the chaff. How few, for example, wondered what the local people called their habitat in their own language and thus whether the concept of "city" was as universal as they thought. The "colonial library" has long wreaked havoc, and continues to do so.

This book therefore has two goals. The first is to retrace the major stages and key characteristics of the history of urban Africa, which played a much greater role in the general process of African history than the size of the urban population might lead one to believe, since it remained so small for so long. In ancient times, as in the twentieth century, and often for analogous reasons, cities were key players in all aspects of history: political processes, military interventions, economic networks, cultural dissemination, and ideological change. In this respect, this book was originally designed to combat a trend at a time when research was focused on rural Africa and Africans were generally seen as peasants and "strangers to the city."[5] This book shows that this was not the case, and that city life was a constant in Africa, as elsewhere, but differently.

The second goal is not only to provide a narrative and report findings but also to identify the general cadence of urban change in each location and time. The history of each city is specific to its time and place. However, in Africa as elsewhere, there has also been an urban rhythm, with constants and variables. The history of these cities has to be studied from a comparative standpoint. Until recently, books and articles have focused on cities alone. This book tries to situate the phenomenon of urbanization in the general flow of the complex evolutionary processes that cities both reveal and disseminate. This thread is constant throughout the work, though it is especially strong in the beginning and conclusion.

Catherine Coquery-Vidrovitch<br>
October 2004

# Introduction to the French Edition (1994)

This extended summary of urban history has required a perhaps inordinate amount of work because it is intended to touch on all aspects of *longue durée* history of Africa, from the origins to the dawn of the twentieth century. This undertaking is both quixotic and perilous when the topic is a continent characterized by huge differences of every order: ecological (from desert to rainy forest), political (from the least centralized kinship-based societies to great slave-trading states), and economic (from ground-level, low-tech subsistence economies to major international trades).[6] I could be reproached for overreaching my supposed specialty (modern Africa); this book is based on an analysis of a huge number of documents in archeology, on traditions, and in varied languages. I also studied a multitude of specific historical publications and issues, for this work is based on both an attentive review of existing materials and on my own fieldwork. In addition, I visited most of the cities I speak of.

The scope of this summary should not lead to false impressions, however. To begin with, historians of Africa have written little about cities, particularly ancient cities. (I prefer the adjective "ancient" to "precolonial" because it is paradoxical to define a society by what happened later.) Historians have left the topic to a few mainly English-speaking anthropologists and, concerning the colonial period, to French geographers. Africa was long considered a continent immured in rural life. For the most part, I do not dispute this. My goal is not simply to "reestablish" a forgotten urban Africa. The great majority (over 95 percent if not 99 percent) of the sub-Saharan continent was populated by peasants. Yet, despite their small numbers and minority status, there have been cities in Africa, as elsewhere, throughout the continent's history. Moreover, they played, and continue to play, an essential role as melting pots and cultural disseminators, and as engines of social and political change. In a way, their influence was far out of proportion to their apparent size. I therefore want to at least show, first, that cities have existed in all parts of Africa for a very long time, although the dates vary depending on the location, and second, that cities have played dynamic key roles. The fact that African development seems to lag so far behind that of other continents is partly because there were not enough cities, and generally the cities were not very big.

This is no longer true today. For a series of demographic and historical reasons, the continent of Africa is now probably more urbanized than China, relatively speaking. In 1990, the populations of thirty cities reached a million,[7] yet there were only three that size at the time of the independences: Cairo, Ibadan, and Johannesburg. Since then, they have acquired features shared by most urban centers in the third world.

In the past . . . the past is a very different story, and that is the history I intended to write.

Concretely, the work is based on research conducted over a number of years to compile the most exhaustive possible bibliography on the history of urbanization in sub-Saharan Africa, from the origins of cities to the eve of colonialization.[8] At the same time, under the auspices of the CNRS[9] Institute, which I headed for fifteen years, from 1981 to 1996,[10] I conducted research, organized conferences, and edited collective works on the theme. The teamwork and fieldwork that went into those collective activities contributed to many aspects of this book.[11]

I am greatly indebted to my African friends and colleagues, whose lucidity, knowledge, and humor showed me the extent to which the Africa they live in differs from the Africa that was taught to them as well as to us as part of their Eurocentric intellectual heritage. While not denying the obvious distinctness of a specific history, it is time to renounce the "customary authenticity," the "Negro soul," and other commonplaces of a "tradition" that we now know to be largely an invention and stereotype.[12] In this sense, to reconstitute the history of African cities is also to try to give back to that part of the world the share of the universal that it has so long been denied.

# Note on the Transcription of Proper Nouns

Since this book concerns the whole Sub-Saharan subcontinent, transcription is a sensitive problem, and there does not seem to be any truly satisfactory solution. Almost every author uses either a transcription system close to his or her own language (usually English, French, or Portuguese and often borrowed from colonial usage), or, in the case of African specialists and meticulous researchers, a transcription system close to national languages. In the latter case, the transcription tries to express the original pronunciation, which was often, if not always, distorted by the Western ear. Sometimes the transcription system employed is the official system of a modern African state. The problem is that such legal transcription systems vary from country to country. The same applies for words in Arabic, which, in order to make reading easier, are not transcribed in the strictly official manner.

In this book, which is based in large part on documents written in English, I have generally used the simplified international transcription employed by English-language authors. A few phonemes are controversial, such as *dj* (in French). *Jenne-Jeno* designates the ancient city that is now known as Djenné in French and Jenne in English. Other less known towns keep their French spelling (such as Bobo Dioulasso). Peul in French becomes in English Fulani (singular) and Fulbe (plural). One of the most difficult words to transcribe is *diula* (*dyula, djula, Jula,* and others): there are simply too many options. Jula probably is the more accepted English translation today. The transliteration of Arabic names is still more problematic, all the more so if the choice, as it is here, is not to adopt the official transcription, little understandable for non-Arabic-speaking people. The spelling of geographical names more or less enshrined by usage and maintained to the present by atlases (also inherited from colonial times) has been used so as to avoid disorienting readers unfamiliar with the (justified) obsessions of historians and linguists. The names of local peoples are generally invariable.

Stating intentions and carrying them out are two different things. I have tried to maintain this pragmatic approach throughout the work, but I may not have succeeded. I beg the reader's indulgence. It may well be impossible to succeed in satisfying specialists and readers when attempting to impose a general unified spelling all over Africa, where there are so many languages and such varied rules and uses of transcription.[13]

# Acknowledgements

I would like to thank the institutions that, thanks to their warm and efficient welcome, encouraged and then helped me to compile the required documentation and discuss some of my hypotheses: the Joint Committee on African Studies of the SSRC/ACLS (Social Science Research Council) USA, of which I was a happy member for several years; the Woodrow Wilson Center for International Scholars, Washington, D.C., where I began this research thanks to a six-month grant in 1987; the Shelby Cullom Davis Center at Princeton University, where I spent a semester in 1992; and the State University of New York at Binghamton, where I have been teaching six weeks a year since 1981.

I also express my gratitude to all the researchers who, whether they realized it or not, provided me with the friendly help I needed to complete the undertaking, notably when I began to explore this field of research on the occasion of an overview paper commissioned in 1989 by the Joint Committee on African Studies. The comments of the Committee's members, then and later, and the reviews of the French version of this book, were very helpful.

There are so many people to thank that I hesitate to cite them all. My thanks go especially to Natalie Zemon Davis, Hélène d'Almeida-Topor, Florence Bernault, Odile Goerg, Françoise Héritier, Faranirina Rajaonah, Marcia Wright, Marc Augé, Adrien Benga, Pierre Boilley, Fred Cooper, Mamadou Diouf, Toyin Falola, Alain Forest, Bill Freund, Prosser Gifford, Didier Gondola, Allen Isaacman, Bogumil Jewsiewicki-Koss, Anthony D. King, Pierre Kipré, Doulaye Konaté, Tom Lodge, John Lonsdale, Paul Lovejoy, Alan Mabin, Issiaka Mande, Elikia Mbokolo, André Miquel, Valentin Mudimbe, Richard Roberts, Richard Stren, Ibrahima Thioub, Dale Tomich, Jean-Louis Triaud, Jan Vansina and Immanuel Wallerstein. I was happy enough to visit a second time Old Zimbabwe in 1985 with Peter Garlake as a guide, and to discuss with Graham Connah, when I was a fellow at the Humanities Research Centre, Australian National University (ANU) in summer 1995. Many others should also be mentioned here.

I am indebted to the doctoral students in my research seminars, at Binghamton, New York; in Paris; and in diverse francophone universities in Africa, as well as the undergraduates on whom I "tested" my initial theories for several years. Finally, nothing was more important to me than the understanding of my African friends, who let me travel freely with their warm hospitality on their continent. Many thanks also to the ACCT, today AIF (Agence internationale de la Francophonie) for providing the support needed to speed publication of this book, and to the French Ministry of Culture for providing a grant for the translation.

I wish to give special thanks to the librarians at Binghamton University for their patience and efficiency, and to underscore the exceptional quality of their collections concerning the South questions. I thank Mary Baker, my translator, for her understanding and patience; Willa Speiser for her intelligent and rigorous editing; and Susan Lorand, whose attentive and gentle help clarifying numerous details proved invaluable in the final editorial stages before printing. Finally, I would like to express my deep gratitude to my publisher, Markus Wiener, for his jovial stubbornness and friendly humor.

# 1

# Cities in Africa

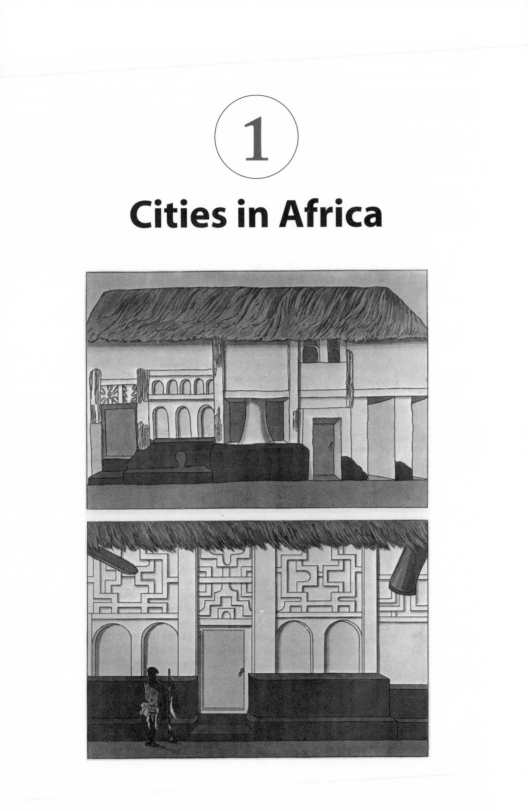

The oldest house in Coomassee (above)
Part of the quarters of the mission (below)

T. Edward Bowdich, *Mission from Cape Coast Castle to Ashantee* (London: J. Murray, 1819).

*Chapter One*

# Cities in Africa

## African Urbanization?

African city or city in Africa? In other words, is the topic primarily African history, or is it urban history? Of course it is both, since urbanization is universal. However, it takes specific forms depending on the case, not because a city is located in Africa but because it developed in a specific social and technological context. At a certain level of generality, the context suggests a set of cultural and political convergences. These features are themselves difficult to define because the concept of city, like that of civilization, includes a number of aspects, such as *space, society, economics,* and *collective mentality.*[1] *Space?* From the confines of the desert to the rain forest, from the high plateaus of the eastern and central savanna to the Mediterranean climatic areas, either in Maghreb or on the shores of South Africa, the ecological contrasts are enormous and their range seems too vast to encompass a single identity. *Society?* Ingenious ethnological fieldwork has shown the extraordinary variety of social and political organizations, which range from decentralized lineage organizations based on the links of social rather than biologi-

3

cal kinship to strict hierarchies based on caste systems, slavery, and the power of military or merchant aristocracies over the territory. *Economics?* Here again, thanks to economic anthropology, there is a wide range of possibilities more or less related to the other possibilities, e.g., societies that are foraging, pastoral, agricultural or linked (or not) to more or less predatory long-distance trade. *Collective mentality?* This is where a kind of African identity appears. Despite the ecological, social, economic, and political diversity, a specific history and culture have marked all parts of the continent. They are related to thousands of years of contact among Bantu, Nilotic, Saharan, and other peoples and languages. Onto this broadly shared cultural (that is, linguistic) foundation was grafted a history that was often marked by dramatic episodes revealing the unrelenting process of the creation of dependency. The experience of all the peoples of Africa south of the Sahara—for example, the slave trade to the north and to the Indian and Atlantic Oceans, later colonization, and then the power of its antidote, panafricanism—contains shared features that have helped to forge a feeling of African cultural identity.

When it comes to cities, what is shared is a historical rhythm. The beginnings of urbanization were generally late and incomplete. With the exception of a few interior urban crossroads along river or land routes, urban growth was located on the coasts of the huge continent (desert ports and market towns of the Sahel, Swahili cities on the Indian Ocean, and trading ports on the Atlantic coast). Over the centuries, this was conducive to the diffusion of various cultural influences directly or through series of networks. Finally, the virtually continent-wide rupture caused by the shock of colonization was decisive in contemporary African urbanism. It resulted in the emergence of cities characterized by the apparent juxtaposition, and inevitable interpenetration, of two apparently contradictory models: the ancient local model, or models, which were already largely culturally mixed, and a specific colonial/white/metropolitan model. For a long time this was the only visible element of generally very modest colonization, even in colonies considered to be settlements. For example, in Nairobi in 1933, settlers—some 7,500 Europeans, almost half (48 percent) of the total European population of Kenya—officially made up only 20 percent of the city's population but more likely actually made up 10 percent.[2]

To what extent do geo-cultural form and heritage allow us to distinguish today's African cities from third-world cities in general? In both cases the majority of the urbanites are poor (and mostly new to the city, given increasing urban migration), and urbanism is distorted. Urban areas are divided into one or more recent, high-status centers (such as business and administrative districts) and a spreading, sometimes immense, dirt-poor habitat that is poorly served and under-integrated. The absent or mediocre maintenance of the latter areas accelerates deterioration, which is all the more rapid because some of the housing and furnishings integrate poorly into the lifestyles of new city dwellers, who use them (for example, canals, roads and plumbing) without care or understanding. The inadequacy of the transportation infrastructure leads in many places (such as Ouagadougou or Cotonou) to a permanent daily spectacle in the form of hordes of pedestrians and overloaded, antiquated, and rickety minibuses, in addition to a sea of motor scooters, and before that a sea of bicycles. Finally, all of these features, along with the animation of vast, noisy, colorful daily markets, are amazingly similar from one end of the continent to the other. In what ways do these features differ from those of the poor quarters of any large modern, not necessarily tropical, city? According to René de Maximy, the difference lies in the fact that these cities were and remain peopled by Africans, in other words, by individuals, groups, and peoples who react in accordance with a specific historical and cultural heritage.[3]

In both time and space, these cities express not a static state but a constantly evolving spatial and social dynamic. The relations between the urban population and its environment are structured in accordance with a certain number of political and social desires and ecological, technological and ideological constraints. The contemporary process that began in colonial times is Africa's passage from a generally rural civilization to an urban society. The phenomenon can be understood in two ways, both of which are in constant interaction with each other. First, what were the causes and conditions of increased urbanization and the factors that could create and change the urban environment? From this Western point of view, the city is a dependent variable resulting from a specific process: the societal system as a whole—precolonial, colonial, and postcolonial. Second, how has the urban reality in turn affected the elements that determine its structure? This turns the urban context into an independent variable. City life changes forms of behavior (with respect to birth, life, death, work, and neighborhoods), social processes (mobility, acculturation, class consciousness, and political awareness), values, and the status of groups and individuals.

## Urbanization: A Revolutionary Process

Africa's urban revolution was different from that of the West, where urbanization is older and occurred in a very specific context of both increased agricultural production (the "green revolution" has not yet occurred in Africa) and industrialization, in other words, parallel to economic development. However, we must not forget how slow European urbanization was in earlier times. Cities certainly played a driving role in developing the medieval economy, but at the time they were few and small. At the beginning of pre-modern times, no more than 5 to 10 percent of Europe's population was urbanized. In the sixteenth century, the only places where 15 to 20 percent of the population lived in urban agglomerations were northern Italy and the Netherlands, and the cities in those regions would be considered small today: a city of 20,000 was exceptional. Counting Constantinople, there were yet only nine cities with 100,000 or more inhabitants (a sound criterion for urbanization) in Europe; five of the cities were in Italy. They contained 1.6 percent of the population of Europe in 1600, 1.9 percent in 1700, and only 2.2 percent in 1800.

In 1800, no more than 2.4 percent of the world population of 900 million lived in cities of 2,000 inhabitants or more, and most city dwellers lived in the "big" cities (half of all city dwellers lived in 44 cities). Nonetheless, Europe was the most urbanized continent in the world, with 18 percent of the world population, 30 percent of the world's city dwellers, and 21 cities with over 100,000 inhabitants. Asia came next, with 19 big cities into which crowded over 60 percent of the continent's urban population.[4] It is very difficult to suggest figures for Africa. While in 1000 there probably was in Europe no city to be compared to Cairo (Fustat), the number south of the Sahara certainly was smaller, even though one of the goals of this book is to show that there has been exaggeration of the nonurban nature of sub-Saharan Africa. To begin with, 80 to 95 percent of the population worldwide lived and worked in the countryside or in small towns with fewer than 10,000 citizens. On the eve of the Industrial Revolution, the European continent, like other parts of the world, remained almost completely agricultural.[5] As in ancient Africa, the problem for most people, including city dwellers, remained subsistence.

The urban revolution was spectacular. Industrial metropolises were born in northwestern Europe in an area that had been very rural until then. Perhaps it was precisely the absence of prior urbanization that was conducive to the bond with industrialization. In 1801, fewer than 10 percent of the people in England and Wales lived in cities with more than 100,000 inhabitants. This proportion doubled over 40 years and again in the following 60 years. England was relatively well urbanized in 1900. Generally, the later industrialization occurs, the more quickly the country is urbanized. The process took 79 years in England, 66 in the United States, 48 in Germany, 36 in Japan, and 26 in Australia. Does this foreshadow the speed of the contemporary urban boom in Africa? There is a major difference: in the developed countries, there was a close link between urbanization and economic development. However, there are other contrasts. In the nineteenth century in the West, the death rate in cities overcrowded with poor workers was much higher than that in the countryside. Rural migrations determined both the growth of the cities and the emptying of the countryside. Today, urban migration is finally slowing down and there are fewer differences between the urban and rural populations. The urban rate of growth increasingly matches the general rate of growth, and there is an absolute and relative decline in the number of farm workers.

Today, urbanization is not occurring in Africa in the same way that it did elsewhere in the past. Even if we were to find in precolonial urban history some features common to all preindustrial societies, the contemporary change in the process is clear. Despite the surge in migration, urban growth remains largely the result of absolute growth of the population, which is faster in the cities than in the countryside, even though agricultural areas are increasingly overpopulated. Between 1940 and

1950, the average annual urban growth in sub-Saharan Africa was 4.7 percent (7 countries) compared with 4.7 percent in Asia (15 countries) and 4.2 percent in Latin America (12 countries). In Europe at the end of the nineteenth century, at the time of maximum urbanization, it did not exceed 2.1 percent. The growth has continued and the rates are now the highest in the world. Africa's urban population increased 69 percent from 1950 to 1960. Between 1960 and 1990, 1960 being when the independence movements exploded (unfortunate coincidence or cause?), Lagos (in what is now Nigeria) grew 12 percent a year and Kinshasa (in what is now Congo) 14 percent. At the beginning of the 1970s it was estimated that by the end of the twentieth century more than 300 million Africans would be living in cities of more than 20,000 inhabitants, compared with 36 million in 1960.[6] Even though this prediction turned out to be exaggerated (the urban population was around 200 million in 1990) and urban growth seems to have begun to stabilize, cities now account for most of the demographic growth, which continues at full tilt. In the 1990s, projections (excluding deaths from AIDS) were that Africa's urban population will have increased tenfold between 1950 and 2025. Because of the demographic explosion, which was and remains brutal, the ratio between rural and city dwellers now is on the verge of becoming inverted. The phenomenon can only continue to accelerate for some time, no matter what the future of rural areas. Either increased poverty in farming areas will lead to an even more massive flow of poor people to the city, or a marked improvement in agricultural techniques and production will have the same result through a correlated increase in rural underemployment. Since in sub-Saharan Africa urbanization is independent of industrialization and the process began the latest and is lasting the longest, the continent is now unable to deal with the increasing poverty in the overpopulated countryside or carry out the urban planning required by the cities' massive growth.

Africa is different from Southeast Asia, which, regardless of a few enormous cities and some major exceptions (Singapore), remains overall a largely rural area; today barely a quarter of China's population lives in cities. While it is arbitrary to generalize on this scale, in Asia agriculture is often modernized and some industries are experiencing strong growth. Africa is also different from Latin America, where colonization and the initial virtual eradication of aboriginal populations, through elimination or absorption (Brazil), marginalization (Andean countries), or relative absence prior to colonization (Argentina), favored the formation of urban civilizations with a highly mixed metropolitan origin: these new people, having suppressed most of the autochthonous people, were to become the foundation of today's civil society.

In Africa, colonial powers promoted the city as the key component of a largely indigenous economic and political society. Does this mean that the urban fact did not exist beforehand? Rather, its very existence was an uncontrolled threat that had to be domesticated and made to benefit the West. Indeed, colonial urban history seems to have been a special transition point. No doubt it was a new departure, but it was grafted onto existing urban features, the heritage of which has to be understood. To what extent is there a difference in degree or nature between the cities of precolonial historical Africa and the urban civilization in gestation today and tomorrow? While the colonial intrusion into Africa may have resulted in an urban revolution, it was neither the first nor the only such revolution.

## How Should We Understand "Urban Revolution"?

It is less a sudden flow of migrants than a cumulative process of cultural upheavals caused by the city. The urban lifestyle transforms the habits and mentalities of even non–city dwellers, who then become subject to the power of urban institutions and culture. That power increases as improvements are made to transportation and access to the city.

The archaeologist V. Gordon Childe launched the idea that in antiquity, urban growth and "civilization"[7] were inseparable. According to him, the city transcends or even opposes the accepted ideas, customs, and laws of the surrounding rural environment, thereby acquiring a dynamic strength that can properly be called revolutionary. This argument was meant to apply specifically to the Mesopotamian-Mediterranean civilization. However, the process is renewed every time social and political changes to the whole produce new urban forms: unceasingly, a new city emerges, not *the* civilization, but a new form of civilization

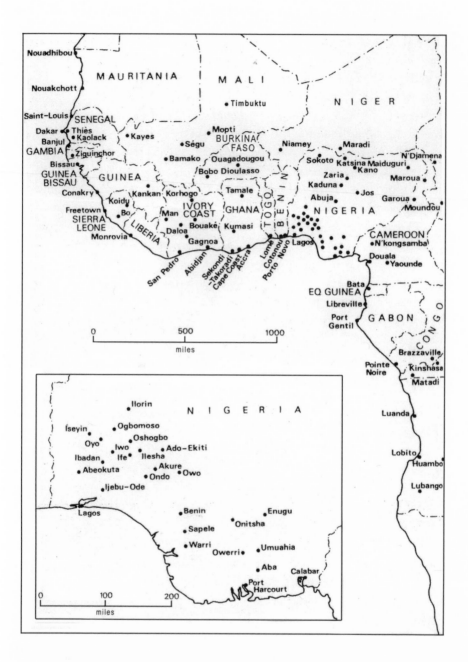

**Map 1.** Urban Tropical Africa Today (Inset: Yoruba and Igbo Cities)
Based on: A. O'Connor, *The African City*, London: Hutchinson, 1982, pp. 12–13

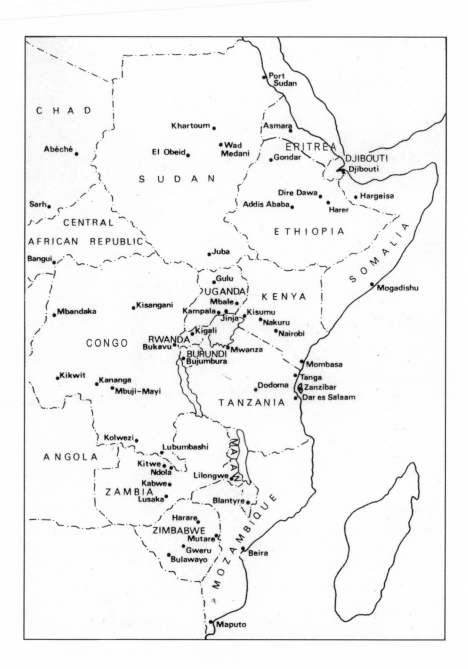

constantly remodeled by the very process of urbanization. Since the city is a growing thing and not an instantaneous creation, the new forms of life to which it gives rise do not obliterate those that used to dominate. On the contrary, they absorb them, digest them, and sometimes even revive them, a tendency that is all the stronger when the urban population recently came from the existing rural environment.[8] The city's function as a cultural melting pot is obviously enormous today and increased by the city's role as the focal point of the surrounding civilization, thereby extending the urban lifestyle far beyond municipal boundaries. Yet cities have always existed in Africa. The purpose of this book is to chart their genesis.

## Precolonial African Cities: An Attempt at Definition

In recent decades, many worthy books and articles on urban history and sociology have been published.[9] However, most of the research has been done on western cities and urbanism, from cities of antiquity to industrial metropolises, from medieval towns to modern centers of commercial capitalism. In contrast, the history of urban Africa has been the subject of only two summaries, both in English (aside from a series of monographs). The first, by Basil Davidson, is innovative and warm but also shaped by the period when it was published (1959) and its author's militant temperament.[10] It is a passionate argument for rehabilitation in favor of the forgotten or neglected grandeur of the cities and, more generally, ancient civilizations of Africa. The second, published more than fifteen years later (1976), focuses more on a comparative study of ancient urban social features and is based on the philosophy of the "noble savage" ideology; it contrasts the humanity and serenity of the semi-rural towns of the past to the excessive and "anti-nature" character of contemporary industrial metropolises.[11]

Actually, these two authors' irritation toward the European contempt for "rural Africa" is understandable when we see how western urbanists tend to postulate the "modern" colonial or contemporary city as an innovation in Africa and how, in contrast with superb works on the history of cities and urbanism, general historiography has expounded a number of truisms and, in fact, several foolish hypotheses about extra-European contexts. The reason for this is that, consciously or not, but always implicitly, there is a presupposition that the only fully developed urban model is the Western standard of reference. Until the late 1990s, only sociologists were interested in urban change in Africa. Works on urban history (of which many were written between 1950 and 1960) were notable for their virtually complete lack of any reference to sub-Saharan Africa. For example, Gideon Sjoberg's book on preindustrial cities,[12] which had a high profile at the time, compares examples from Europe, the Americas (the Maya of the Yucatan), all of Asia, and Egypt. Africa is written off in a relatively vague line according to which "Dahomey, the Ashanti and the Yoruba" had, strictly speaking, only "semi-urban" centers. Things began to change with two comprehensive books, the only ones until now to attempt an universal and comparative urban history, the second of which goes so far as to give, in a nonetheless slightly paradoxical manner, more space to African cities than to cities in the Arab world.[13]

## African Vocabulary for Cities

For further demonstration of the existence of African cities in the past, what could be better than to examine African languages themselves? Depending on the language and culture, the words used to designate cities take different forms and refer to different key concepts. However, generally, a distinction is made between the rural and the urban.

Curiously, it is in Arab countries that the contrast is least clear. In the Sudan, in street Arabic, there is linguistic confusion between the concepts of "urban quarter" (typical of Muslim cities) and "village." The word *hilla*, which is more commonly used today for "village" than the classical *quarya*, designates both locations, but other words, such as the classical *hagy*, are now used to refer to urban quarters.[14] In contrast, a very definite distinction is made between the traditional city and some urban innovations of the nineteenth century since the term *dem* (plural: *dayum*) is used to designate both the nineteenth-century slave trading posts at Bahr el Ghazal and the poor, rundown quarters of former colonial cities. The precolonial Islamization of the cities of western Africa also resulted in a differentiation based on culture. A distinction is drawn between the *koire-boro* (city dweller with some education) and the *gand-ji-boro* (Songhai peasant), and between the *galo-dougou* (administrative and cultural center) and the Bambara *badiadougou* (village) in Mali.

However, at the time of independence, other Sahel countries had not yet found a specific noun to designate the city, which was barely distinguished, at the level of vocabulary, from the village: *deuk* in Wolof (Senegal), *kut* in Bobo, *tengha* (land, village in general, city) in Moore (Burkina Faso). In other cases a compound noun was invented based on the term designating a village. For example, among the Bamum, where the population was grouped into *nzu* (residential units of various sizes), the city, which was made up of a multitude of nzu, was designated by a descriptive paraphrase: *nti nsom* ("inside the wall").[15] This is similar to the Hausa conception of the city: *birni*, a Hausa common noun, initially conveyed the idea of walls and fortifications, in contrast with village enclosures made up only of plant debris or "dead hedges." The meaning was thus extended to what was contained within the defensive wall, that is, the city. The differentiation, when it occurs, can also refer to the notion of size: *donguba*, "big village" in Bambara, *tyo-pio* in Gurunsi (Burkina Faso); or to the city as a seat of power: the Mosi capital is *Na-tengha*, in other words the residential city of the Mogho-Naba, the Mosi chief. Sometimes, in contrast, the vocabulary makes explicit reference to a recent aspect of the notion, for example *gomma-glo*, "White man's village," among the Bete of Ivory Coast.[16]

In Ethiopia, the concept of "city" refers to its origin and primary function: *t'eyent* (in Gueze) and *kätäma* (in Amharic) are virtually synonymous and designate an urban settlement, but originally meant a military camp, with the associated idea of political importance.[17]

In southern Africa, the name *Zimbabwe* is known to be ancient; in 1506 the Portuguese were already speaking of *Zunbanhy* to refer to the ruins near Fort Victoria and again in 1552 of *Sambaed*, which seems very likely to have come from descriptions gathered from Swahili traders in Sofala.[18] The term also refers to the city's origins; it seems to have been derived from *disbar woe*, "venerated house" (sanctuary), or from *disbar daze Maybe*, a contraction of "stone houses." There also seems to be another form of description of the *kibuga*, which evokes "an active, industrious place."[19] In Madagascar, the notion of quantity seems to have been most striking to contemporaries. Tananarive seems to come from *tanana* (city) and from *'arive* (thousand), which therefore means a city with a thousand inhabitants (or else "a thousand cities"?). Likewise, Fenoarivo seems to mean "full of a thousand inhabitants," and Arivoni-mamo a "thousand Imamos."[20]

However, in West Africa we sometimes find the most explicit aware-ness of the specific concept of "city." In Pular, *misside* (village) is distin-guished from *sarè* or *tunfundé* (city). In Akan country (former Ivory Coast), as in Yoruba country, the key concept is both social and political and thus distinct from classical European meanings. This makes it dif-ficult to translate without resorting to paraphrase. Among the Akan there are two entities. First, *afamu*, which refers to a regional geo-graphical unit with neither political nor ethnic connotations. It could be fairly safely translated as a geographical and sociocultural region or sub-region, but in the fluid context of the seventeenth century, it could contain a number of *oman* (plural: *aman*). The latter term, which refers to a political unit, was translated by Europeans as "city" even though the Asante made another distinction between *kuro* and *akura* (village). A kuro was not fortified but had a collective defense organization made up of young people, as well as a marketplace, a council of the chiefs of the various lineages with certain forms of autonomous power, such as to levy taxes and see to certain works in the common interest (road main-tenance). The council also had a say in the semihereditary election of the chief of the community, the *ohene*. In the ohene's house there was a special space, the *adampan*, that was used basically as a communal home, and the ohene was the institutional link with the oman.[21]

Given these nuances, the old dictionaries were cautious. In 1881, Basle suggested distinguishing in oman "the inhabitants of a city as a political body" and "the inhabitants of a country united under the same government." In 1916, Rattray suggested that the original meaning was "a city and the people of that city."[22] By extension, that included the land and settlements around the city and its administra-tive, political and, of course, economic hinterland. Thus it was normal that in the seventeenth century the same term (including the root "oman") designated the city and the area that it controlled. Eguafo-*man* was the capital of the Eguafo political area (Great Kamenda), Abor*aman* (Abraman) was both the name of the city and its province and, around 1660–62, near the Danish fort of Frederickburg, we find *Aman*fro (Manfro), etc.[23] The same kind of distinction existed among the Fon in Dahomey, between *coudji* or *codji* (village) and *to* or *éto* (city). These people were familiar with an ancient, very specific administrative hierarchy.

The Yoruba have a concept that is different but belongs to the same way of thinking: *ilù*. *Ilù* designated more a form of government than a city because it was used to refer to both the settlement as a location and the council of chiefs who, in cooperation with the *oba*, or sacred king, made up the settlement's government. In modern language, the word has taken on a general meaning: that of nation, for example; England has become *ilù oyinbo*, in other words, the Europeans' *ilù*. However, in earlier times, since every city controlled its own area as a city-state, *ilù* was instead used to establish a kind of distinction, similar to that in ancient Greek cities, between citizens and noncitizens. Members of the ilù might or might not live in the city, but they were part of it because the unit governed by the institutions did not stop at the walls of the city.[24]

This topic has not yet been researched systematically. However, these notes show that a style of settlement and habitat distinct from that of rural areas did indeed exist in many parts of ancient Africa.

## A Universal Definition

Obviously, the first thing we have to do is define what we are talking about: What do we mean by urbanization? This should also help to answer the question that historians have of course asked: since when has the urban phenomenon existed in sub-Saharan Africa, and in what form?

First, it is a spatial process, "whereby human beings congregate in relatively large number at one particular spot."[25] It concerns a specific location that is fairly well defined (we go "to town"), a humanized place with buildings, where powers converge, confront one another, neutralize one another, and merge. Thus it is also a social process; in other words, it has socially determined structures. In 1938, the sociologist Louis Wirth defined the city as "a relatively large, dense and permanent settlement of socially heterogeneous individuals."[26] The heterogeneity can be multiple and thus generate dynamics and contradictions among ethnic, linguistic, occupational, class, and other groups. There is also a set of multifunctional features that extend beyond the city's boundaries through the political or administrative power that it wields and the region that it controls; for when one speaks of a city, one speaks of an urban network. This social dimension is also cultural. The city is a center, a place where both population and civilization are concentrated. It attracts and combines, and blends cultures and memories. Yet it is more: a city is also a center for cultural sharing and dissemination.[27] A metropolis could be defined by its ability to spread its institutions. Not only does it absorb, integrate, and blend contributions from the outside to create new cultures (such as Swahili culture), it in turn conveys the result to the outside world. In medieval times, Timbuktu and Jenne spread their ideologies and architecture throughout all of western Sudan. They became the prototypes of many Sahelian communities.

Are the urban phenomenon and the process of urbanization universal? Certainly, in the very general sense that we have just described. That is not to say that the same periodized schema has always occurred everywhere in the same way. That would amount to identifying urbanization and modernization, modernization and industrialization, and, in Africa, modernization and colonialism. Turning this into a universal archetype would be to favor the Western pattern born out of the industrializing nineteenth century, posited both as the ultimate stage and therefore what is to be achieved elsewhere. Yet it is far from clear that twentieth-century Africa's forms of urbanization are analogous to of Victorian England, for example. Could not the industrial city be considered instead as a variation, a major variation certainly but not necessarily a unique one, of the urban process?[28]

## Determining Criteria for Urbanization

A definition that is too general may not be useful in practice. The approach requires greater precision, and several authors have tried to identify the criteria of urbanization.

First, let us agree on what the criteria do not need to be. As in Europe, size is not a criterion. There can be cities of 1,000 to 2,000 inhabitants and villages of 50,000. This has been said again and again in reference to Europe.[29] It is true of the agrovilles in southern Italy in the twentieth century. It is also true for many settlements in Africa, before and after colonization. There can be small cities and huge villages. Large, extremely compact villages grew up and were able to defend themselves effectively against attacks. There were fortified villages and island villages. The "land of rivers" in central Congo was an amphibious, thoroughly waterlogged area covered with large fishing villages. At the end of the nineteenth century, the first foreign observers estimated that 5,000, 10,000, 20,000, or more people lived in the communities.[30] Despite the intense regional trade with cassava farmers and canoemen from the upper Alima, and despite the fact that the villages were way stations on the great river road for dyewood, ivory, and, especially, slaves from upstream and products of trade with the Europeans (e.g., cloth and utensils) from downstream, life there was neither organized nor structured differently than elsewhere. Households supported themselves through their own subsistence activities (e.g., spear fishing, catching fish with a net, and basket and pottery production). Communities were exclusive, with admission based on kinship and slavery. There was no centralized leadership, and the balance between centrifugal and centripetal forces was constantly readjusted. Centrifugal forces stemmed from rivalry between households, while centripetal forces sprang from the cultural and linguistic (i.e., ethnic) consistency of the whole, based on basic principles of residential kinship and uniform cultural groupings by age. While all we know about these agglomerations (which sleeping sickness eliminated without a trace over a period of about twenty years at the turn of the century) comes from reports by the first explorers (including Stanley and Brazza), apparently they were simply very large villages.

The existence of cities was also not related to the density or number of inhabitants in the region. A well-known example is Igboland in southern Nigeria, which had more or less the same population as Yorubaland in the southwest but was twice as densely populated. Yet it did not give rise to a precolonial urban civilization, though this did occur among the Yoruba. While Umor in Igboland had more than 10,000 inhabitants, it remained only a village of farmers.[31] The very notion of density is completely relative: Foumbam, the capital of the Bamum kingdom in Cameroon, was probably not much more densely populated than the rural hills of Buganda. Rwanda, which was nearly totally rural until very recently, is now one of the most densely populated countries in Africa (with some 600 inhabitants per square kilometer). Today, there are vast districts in the urban periphery where residential areas (of mainly British heritage) are very spread out, which can result in densities not far from or even lower than those of neighboring rural settlements.

Urban spaces in Africa also sometimes included numerous enclosed areas (residential compounds, *kraals* or paddocks, and vegetable gardens) inside the city walls for a population that was still largely dependent on agriculture. Perhaps 70 percent of the inhabitants of the ancient Yoruba cities continued to farm, as did the inhabitants of ancient Sumer and those of the Mayan cities in the Yucatan. Note that the percentage of city dwellers who farmed was also high in the cities of medieval Europe. There are many reports of "garden cities" in Africa. In the Kingdom of Kongo, the capital was so green that "a slightly nearsighted missionary could have crossed the whole city without seeing a single house."[32] Even in colonial times, Kibuga, capital of the Kingdom of Ganda and twin city of Kampala, looked less "like a city than an immense garden."[33] Similarly, only around 1980, before the use of cement became widespread, Poto-Poto, a huge working-class quarter of Brazzaville, still looked like a big village. Cities also looked like villages because that was often how they had begun (as did many European cities, where we can still see the traces of one or more primitive rural hubs). Benin City in southern Nigeria dates from the twelfth century, but archaeological digs show that it resulted from the merger of a number of earlier neighboring villages.[34]

Three other more convincing criteria have been suggested with respect to ancient cities of central Africa, which were probably the least "urbanized" in Africa.[35] The cities in question are Zimbabwe, capital of the eponymous medieval empire and abandoned around 1450; Mbanza, capital of Kongo and visited by a Portuguese traveler in 1491; and Musumba, capital of the Lunda empire (western Katanga), first described by a European observer in 1847. The three criteria are:

1.  The way the agglomeration's inhabitants were fed, which was not based exclusively on their farming activities. As we will see later, this criterion cannot be avoided anywhere and comes into play very early.

2.  The existence of specialized craftsmen associated with residence rather than kinship. In a city, division of labor and specialization is inevitable.

3.  Finally, the monumental architecture of the main buildings, even when ordinary houses were simply modeled after rural homes, which was all the more frequent since permanent building material was often rare (except in East Africa). This criterion is probably universal since the city is the center of civil and religious power, and this is symbolized in its city planning, though there can be pre-urban and nonurban monuments, such as forts, temples, and funerary monuments.

Specialists of western preindustrial urbanization have been much more demanding. Actually, they have always used the specific type of city that they have studied as a reference point. Gordon Childe, a specialist of the Antiquity, states no less than ten criteria, enumerated in a disorderly fashion.[36] He insists, and most historians of European cities follow his example, on the adoption of writing, which allows information to be recorded and transmitted, and on arithmetic, indispensable for measuring weight, time, and space. However, could we not object that peasants, more than any others, had to have the sense, if not the science, of space and time? A more persuasive argument would be that these discoveries imply the existence of a group of highly specialized nonfarmers with enough leisure time to develop such elaborate techniques. This would be a consequence rather than a cause of urbanization. Here, we come back to the inseparability of cities and civilization.

Fernand Braudel insisted on the universal nature of the city, which "is always a city, no matter where it is located, in time or space,"[37] and on the need to suggest a definition that is sufficiently general to cover all urban phenomena. He nonetheless finds the quintessence of the city in modern mercantile society, therefore in a monetary economy. Thus, he emphasizes the importance of monetary instruments and the use of money, to which he gives a relatively narrow definition.[38]

These examples are intended simply to show how difficult it would be, according to these authors who all have the western Mediterranean model in mind, to speak of cities in Africa before colonial times.[39]

If we could employ only one criterion, it would certainly not be writing but, as Max Weber proposes, the fact that in a city (a highly economic entity), not every one depends directly on farming.[40] A whole series of observations follow from this, in particular concerning the heterogeneous nature of the urban population, with respect to origins (not based exclusively on kinship), activities, resulting social status, even religion (in the case of foreign colonies of Muslim traders) and, finally, culture. The idea of a city not populated only by farmers can be expressed in a manner more focused on exchanges, with emphasis on the criterion of accessibility:[41] a true urban society is a society open to the outside. People, products, and ideas of various origins converge toward it and come out of it, which implies trade, markets, and exchange of nonagricultural products (e.g., artisanal products) for the supplies required by the agglomeration to survive.

Instead of criteria, we should therefore speak of the conditions required for urbanization, in other words, for the specialization of functions. At least three conditions must be met.[42]

1. The possibility of a surplus of agricultural production able to feed nonproducers. Until modern times, when new intercontinental transportation technology revolu-

tionized supply, a city could not be imagined without an agricultural hinterland (which shows the relevance of the concepts of regions and urban networks). However, given the low productivity of preindustrial agriculture, which was limited in Africa to the tract of land that an individual man or woman armed with a hoe could work (a maximum of 5 acres per person per year, just enough to ensure the subsistence of the producers), an agglomeration of any size required innovations in farming methods. While there was no true technological innovation, the introduction of new plants was used to provide foodstuff for a growing population. Cassava and corn introduced by the Portuguese certainly helped capitals in central Africa to emerge (e.g., Musumba and Mbanza-Kongo). A large city could not rely only on its immediate hinterland. Thus it had to obtain tribute from a wider area and engage in greater interregional trade for supplies.

2.  Trade was therefore an integral component of the city and involved the presence of a class of merchants that specialized in collecting and redistributing supplies, with groups specializing in storage, transportation, and accounting, including: marketwomen and men carrying goods and maintaining communication and transportation. For example, in Cairo in the twelfth century, there were 36,000 boats and 30,000 people renting mules and donkeys.[43] Markets as an institution were part and parcel of the city. There were periodic markets outside of cities (particularly in western Africa and near the Pool on the lower Congo River), but there was never a city without a market. The importance of long-distance trade can be seen in the growth of cities everywhere and at all times in history (e.g., all around the Mediterranean Sea and in the storage depots of southern Arabia).

Sub-Saharan Africa has many examples of these long-distance networks of trade, which, as we will see, are far from always being linked to the extension of Arab networks. Because of the high cost of transportation in terms of danger and many kinds of needs (camels, porters, subsistence goods), long-distance trade was limited to goods of high value, and thus to the richest traders, who were often foreign. They were honored but regulated by local authorities. In Asante, the sovereign confiscated the goods of subjects who were too enterprising and closely monitored the colony of Muslim traders from the north.

3.  This all implied the presence of a political authority, in other words, a class of officials able to organize the use of surpluses by nonproducers. On one hand they imposed a degree of stability that promoted the production and circulation of supplies. On the other hand, they controlled and coordinated the relations among the social and occupational groups living in the city, thereby also ensuring the maintenance and livelihood of artisans located there in service to the ruling aristocracy. This required the services of a public administration and a police force that could meet the needs of the city and the state as a whole, for example with respect to defense. This was paid for through tribute and in food, raw materials, and manufactured goods, the redistribution of which simultaneously reinforced the power of the sovereign. Likewise, military strength could enrich a city through conquests and by ensuring the security of the whole, as illustrated by the abundance of city walls and entry fees and the frequent inflow of rural citizens when in danger. This reinforced the scope of the city's organization and its political authority over its surroundings. Power went hand in hand with ideol-

ogy and religion: the city often included a holy place, although there could be specialization among cities, with some being political and others military or religious (e.g., in Yorubaland, the religious power was in the secondary city of Ife rather than in Oyo, the political capital). Finally, the city ensured ideological consistency through education; such as through *madrasas* (Muslim universities), which played a political and intellectual role in medieval Muslim cities. In short, the city reflected the power of its leader; a city prospered with the power of its chiefs and declined when that power diminished. For these reasons, there would be little chance of cities emerging in societies said to be "stateless," in other words, where organization and balance rest exclusively on kinship-type lines. In this case, there were no cities, but a network of village chiefs essentially with subsistence. In cases where there is a city without a state, the city becomes the state. City-states, such as the Hausa cities from the sixteenth to seventeenth centuries, controlled their own business, external affairs and, necessarily, the immediate rural neighborhood, or hinterland.[44] In such cases the urban network is no longer simply an economic structure; it is also a network of more or less equal trade among neighboring yet independent city-states that have grown without merging. A case in point is that of the Hausa "mother cities" of Daura, Kano, Zaria (Zazzau), Gobir, Katsina, Rano, and Birain, which dominated the secondary network made up of numerous, fairly regularly spaced (between 10 and 30 miles apart) small centers, at least from the beginning of the nineteenth century, according to detailed descriptions by travelers at the time.[45]

This density was well adapted to the transportation capacity at that time; the distance could not be much greater if a city was to be a market town, for production was generally limited, per capita income low, and communications rudimentary.[46]

In contrast, when a city's power extends far into the surrounding region, it becomes a political and religious metropolis with control over a wide area, as was the case with Old Oyo (Katanga) in Yorubaland; at its zenith Old Oyo was the head of four provinces, each administered by a main center. The province where Oyo was located thus had its own regional capital (Ikoyo), which itself governed a network of small secondary centers (Kishi, Igboho, Irawo, Iwere, Igbomosho, etc[47]). However, when rivalries arose, the dissident could leave to establish another capital city somewhere else, as did Afonja, a military leader from Oyo who left in 1817 to settle at Ilorin.[48]

The notions of network and hierarchy are thus inherent to the process of urbanization. Since a city is by definition open to the outside, it is never alone. The interregional network to which it belongs implies a hierarchy of flows and powers. Depending on the circumstances and the time, the predominance of certain centers can either impede or boost the potential growth of subordinate or competing centers. As soon as one city has taken the lead in any way, such as by developing better (particularly military) technology, taking advantage of an event (e.g., an epidemic or famine), achieving greater growth, or gaining control of valuable long-distance trade, it incorporates the others into its system, if only by recruiting needed labor from them through slavery or tribute. The network becomes a long-lasting structure and has been a force from the precolonial era to the present. For example, the Yoruba cities, Bobo Dioulasso, and towns and markets in Asante country established their influence over specific areas at least as far back as the seventeenth century.[49] However, the urban colonial rupture generally substituted one urban network for another, particularly by giving precedence to coastal centers at the expense of those inland, which used to dominate.

In summary, a city can be defined as a center of dense human population and cultural diffusion; and the conditions for its existence are the inseparable economic and political means by which production and exchange are organized.

## An Attempt at Periodization

Given their historical depth, it is not convincing to propose a typology to classify African cities in accordance with their origin or dominant features at a given point in history. This is what O'Connor tried to do in the early 1980s when he identified six types of African urban settlements:[50] 1. indigenous cities (such as the Yoruba cities and Addis Ababa, even though the latter was founded by imperial decree only at the very end of the nineteenth century); 2. Muslim cities (such as the Hausa cities and desert ports); 3. colonial cities founded by administrative order (such as Cotonou, Bangui and Libreville); 4. European cities created through legal segregation, such as Nairobi, Lusaka, and Salisbury (now known as Harare); 5. twin cities composed of two distinct original groups (such as Khartoum/Omdurman in Sudan and Kampala/Kibuga in Uganda); 6. hybrid cities that are supposed to combine several of these previous features more or less harmoniously (such as Kumasi in Ghana and St. Louis in Senegal).

This hypothesis appears unworkable. All African cities are hybrids and have sometimes developed over a very long period. Instead of a typology, the most we could propose would be a chronology of African urbanization, while keeping in mind the fact that such a schema is necessarily reductionist. Periodization implies long intermediary phases of transition/interpenetration between the various models, and a temporal succession implies that the various kinds of cities could have a cumulative relationship. A possible chronology follows.

1.  Ancient cities, which emerged with the expansion of agriculture, depending on the location. Examples of this extend from the city for which the most ancient archaeological records are available (Jenne-Jeno, dating from the beginning of the first millennium CE), to the fortified cities of the interlacustrine area (dating from around the eighth century), to the obviously fascinating example of the stone builders in the Shona cultural area, whose most famous city was Great Zimbabwe, which disappeared around 1450.

2. Cities that were created through contact with Islam and the Arab world of long-distance trade. They already seem more classical and familiar, both along the eastern coast and in western Sahelian Sudan. Their function as commercial and cultural links is clear. However, we know little about the phases and degrees of transition through contact that was sometimes direct but more often diffuse and indirect.

3. Starting in the second half of the fifteenth century, the Portuguese model, and then more generally the European model, was introduced. Thus the European model appeared very early and does not date only from the colonial period. This point is relevant to our argument, especially since there is also the problem of interference with the preceding models, i.e., ancient and Islamized cities. Nonetheless, European-style cities (aside from the exceptional case of early Portuguese colonization in Mozambique and on the Angolan coast) developed in accordance with local conditions, without the political and legal dependency on the West characteristic of the colonial period.

4. Obviously, the colonial period brought about a divide, but it did not necessarily destroy the earlier urban centers. Colonial cities used, completed, and competed victoriously with existing settlements. The colonial period also determined the future of the cities, no matter how long their past was. Again, as within the previous phases, we must distinguish a number of stages within the colonial period, from military and administrative coercion to metropolises with economic power and strategically important ports. Yet one thing is sure: even when they were created from scratch by decree (e.g., Cotonou and Kampala), all colonial cities were complexes to which the typology proposed

by O'Connor does not apply. They were economic, political, social and cultural melting pots in which new societies were created through an ongoing process of synthesis of old and new.

This explains the immense complexity of the urban issue at the modern period of the independences.

# 2

# Ancient Cities

Pyramids at Nuri

*Chapter Two*

# Ancient Cities

If we assume that the first cities appeared at the same time as agriculture, then the question is when this great undertaking began in Africa. In fact, there was a great deal of variation and there is no precisely dated or datable "Neolithic revolution" applying to the whole continent. The change was remarkably slow and dispersed. For example, there is limited archaeological evidence (e.g., polished stone artifacts) that agriculture was practiced in the western savanna in the third millennium BCE. At that time, the Sahara was in the final stages of desertification and herders were withdrawing to the south. There is also evidence of copper work in Niger and Mauritania at the end of the second millennium BCE (though it began to flourish only between 850 and 100 bce[1]). Clearly, agriculture was reasonably well established virtually everywhere in this area by the first millennium BCE, although this cannot be claimed of all locations prior to that.[2]

Farther south, in the forest, however, no botanical or archaeological evidence has yet been found to show when the yam was domesticated. Yams may have been gathered as early as the fifth millennium BCE. The Proto-Bantu were mainly people of the rivers, and therefore fishermen. Knowledge of iron metallurgy was irregularly adopted. Bantu-speaking people probably spread farming techniques as they moved, but there is no proof of this except that the dates of the beginnings of both processes are very close together. Among some hunter-gatherers, the process of change lasted at least until 500 CE (e.g., in Sierra-Leone and Liberia[3]) and even into the tenth century. Often, even after the partial adoption of metallurgy, stone tools (chipped flint) continued to be used. The arrival of the Iron Age in a given society is characterized by the *everyday* use of a technology that previously might have been used only a little or occasionally, although for a long time.[4] We know very little about this because data are scarce, and there are too few archaeological digs and not enough research. Much of what has been found from the late Stone Age, which in some places lasted as late as the eve of colonialization, has not yet been dated satisfactorily, even though the remains are abundant and can even be found on the surface in many parts of Africa (e.g., on the Teke Plateau in the Congo). However, archaeological discoveries are progressing quickly, although they often remain confidential, hidden in highly specialized publications and, even more often, in unpublished theses.

Cities were able to develop because, thanks to agriculture, they became the centers or partial centers of nonagricultural activities, particularly trade. The earliest known proto-urban settlements in ancient sub-Saharan Africa were indeed interregional or even international centers for their areas. For example, there were the cities on the eastern coast, the desert "ports" in the west, and the settlements in central Africa at the crossroads of two ways of life (e.g., where herders came into contact with farmers, and near mineral deposits as in Katanga and at Zimbabwe). In every case, an urban commercial and cultural network anchored meeting points that, no matter how small, were characterized by the relative social and cultural heterogeneity that characterizes a city.

Each time we acquire a few details about their origins, we are also struck by the role of colonizer played by the first cities. The settlements were by definition new developments in Neolithic or even pre-Neolithic times, when hunters, gatherers, and farmers were almost entirely self-subsistent. Cities thus adopted areas of conquest, which explains their protective and defensive roles, as shown by fortifications and even walls. New cities also gave rise to new activities, and so spread new lifestyles. There is evidence that urban culture was disseminated early, as can be seen in the cases of the Yoruba, the Shona centers, and the interlacustrine kingdoms.

The first archaeological evidence of urbanization in sub-Saharan Africa, both on the eastern coast and in the western Sahel, is very old, dating from well before the influence of Arab urban culture.

## East Africa and the Meroitic Heritage

### From Ancient Egypt to the South.
### Meroë and Axum: The Nubian Filiation

Ancient Egypt was familiar with gold and copper long before it adopted iron metallurgy around or even after 1000 BCE. This was well after the Mesopotamian civilizations, which were smelting iron at the end of the Neolithic era, around 5000 BCE. In Egypt, iron was rare and valuable, reserved for tools and weapons owned and distributed by public entities. Farm tools, which were developed in the third millennium BCE, were made of hardwood and flint rather than bronze or iron.[5] Yet, while Egypt was relatively slow and cautious when it came to adopting technological innovations from the outside, it was urbanized very early. Indeed, urbanization spread along the Nile Valley from Egypt. The transition zone was Nubia, a junction and conduit for dissemination from upper Egypt and the first cataract (Assuan), up the Blue Nile toward Ethiopia and the Red Sea, through the plains of Kordofan and Darfur to the Lake Chad Basin, and from there toward the Niger Basin and finally the Atlantic Ocean.

In the late Neolithic (i.e., the early third millennium BCE), almost all of the Middle Nile region seems to have been abandoned because of ecological deterioration.[6] However, at the time of the New Kingdom, the Kushite kings of the twenty-fifth dynasty (around 750 BCE ) united Nubia (now northern Sudan) with Egypt. It did not last long. After the rupture, the Kush kingdom developed separately from Dakka (in Upper Egypt) to Sennar (on the Blue Nile). The capital was initially at Napata, but in 600 BCE was transferred much further south, to Meroë.[7]

It was a river civilization, characterized by a narrow band of sedentary shoreline settlements that grew broader only in the south, where there is more rain. A series of sites has been identified from north to south: the most northern traces have been found at Dakka (formerly Pselchis).[8] At Faras on Sudan's present-day border, a huge cemetery has been found with more than 2,000 tombs from the Ptolemaic era (first and second centuries CE). While the main urban center has not been identified, a few official buildings have been uncovered: a "western palace" built out of dried bricks (dating from the first century CE) and buildings later reused in Coptic Christian structures. Further to the south, Kawa is located across from the modern city of Dongola. Remains of temples can be found there, as well as clear evidence of a major city dating back to the New Kingdom, thus to pre-Meroitic times, but survived long beyond that era. A number of the temples show that the site was inhabited at least until the end of the third century BCE, when it seems the city was seriously damaged by fire. Recent research at the Amir 'Abdullah cemetery has shown that it was used in the fourth to second centuries BCE. Pottery similar to that found farther south suggests that populations were gradually moving toward the north, and that they continued to do so, since the same kinds of pottery fragments appeared in lower Nubia two or three centuries later.[9]

The site of the first capital, Napata, has not yet been identified. However, the royal cemeteries and temples have been found: the Kurru cemetery is located six miles upstream from the modern city of Karima, on the opposite bank. It contains eighty-two tombs, most of which are in the form of small pointed pyramids, similar to the private pyramids that had long existed in Ancient Egypt. In front of the cemetery, the city was nonetheless probably on the left bank, just to the north of the present city of Merowe, where there are traces of occupation (a temple and a cemetery). To the south, after the Nile and Atbara meet, the plain broadens into a wide area known as the Island of Meroë. This was the true center of the Meroitic civilization, which bloomed because the rainfall in the area was favorable to agriculture and herding beyond the riverbanks.

Meroë, the capital city, was the royal residence from the sixth century BCE to the fourth century CE. It was spread out over a wide area on the eastern bank, where temples, cemeteries, and pyramids (burial sites of kings and their families) have been found. Meroë's fame results mainly from the discovery of six piles of debris from iron metallurgy, though controversy has arisen concerning earlier digs between 1909 and 1914. Because few iron tools were found on the site, it had been suggested that the slag heaps were the remains of metallurgy other than that of iron.[10] The controversy continues, although in 1977 other researchers discovered nearby furnaces used to melt iron ore.[11] Was Meroë indeed the "Birmingham of Africa," as it was proposed in the 1970s, and did it convey its discoveries to the whole sub-Saharan continent? The question is not yet solved. Today it seems that iron metallurgy did not appear in Meroë before the fourth century BCE, and that it flourished mainly around the first and second centuries CE, after the technology had been established, along with other forms of technology, at Nok (at the Taruga site) in Nigeria. The Nok civilization, famous for its clay figurines, seems to have acquired iron technology from Carthaginian sources from the north, possibly via the "chariot route" across the central Sahara (so named for the rock paintings of horse-drawn chariots, such as at Tassili-n-Adjer and Adrar of the Iforas, and also farther south, at Tondia in present-day Mali, dating from the end of the first millennium BCE).

In any case, it seems certain that Meroë was a "big" city, as Herodotus noted (II, 29). It was a capital city with a huge royal residence located in the center; it was surrounded by suburbs and perhaps encircled by fortifications. Located at the crossroads of caravan routes and the river route, it was unquestionably both an administrative city and a crucial link for trade with Egypt. The royal city had palaces, royal baths, temples, pyramids, and cemeteries. Excavations carried out by the universities of Calgary and Khartoum between 1972 and 1975 uncovered the "royal city." Meroë was a center not just for trade, but also for artisans, which meant it had the tradespeople required for construction and commerce. Remarkably fine and skillfully decorated pottery has been found there. There were two traditional forms of pottery: that turned on wheels by men, with a wide variety of styles and decorations and constituting a separate art produced for sale, particularly to the upper classes and perhaps the middle class; and that made by women, which was simpler, rooted in the rural African tradition and similar to pottery found elsewhere in Sudan and the rest of Africa, even today. The royal tombs also contain gold and silver jewelry with semiprecious stones of many different origins and styles, such as local and Egyptian, with animal motifs (including giraffes, rhinoceroses, and ostriches). There were talented woodworkers in Meroë, as shown by remains of various pieces of furniture, such as beds and chests, and musical instruments found in the tombs. Linen and cotton were woven and leather was tanned. The city probably reached its height at the beginning of the Hellenic period. Ptolemean demand made this southern empire a strategic center for the supply and export of rare goods and exports of gold, incense, ivory, ebony, oils, semiprecious stones, ostrich plumes, and leopard skins. Many of these items came from the south and were destined for Egypt or perhaps southern Arabia. The surrounding area is full of the traces of caravan trails pegged out with wells. The city's decline probably followed that of the Roman Empire. In short, its path was analogous to that of the later medieval Saharan/Sahelian empires in the west, which saw the flow of Sudanese gold reduced to a trickle with the decline of the Mediterranean world. Attacking nomads destroyed trade. The vestiges described above found in tombs suggest that when Meroë faded, no major changes occurred in the local economy. However, Meroë's demise meant the end of royal power and trade. Urban "civilization" sought refuge further south.[12]

The next stop, namely Axum and its "royal vassals," was located at the crossroads of northern Ethiopia, Sudan, and southern Arabia. The first known mention of Axum and the Red Sea port of Adulia (the latter described as an "official counter") is found in the *Periplus of the Erythrean Sea*, which dates to the second half of the first century CE, rather than the beginning of the third century CE as was previously thought. The *Periplus of the Erythrean Sea* was probably the work of an officer of the Roman Empire living in Egypt who wrote all of it aside from later additions concerning the eastern coast. Its author was thus an eyewitness to the strategic economic importance of the coastal area.[13] Axum's growth in the second century CE was based on tribute and international trade. It was Christianized in the fourth century CE (Ezana was converted in 330), and provided the foundations of the Ethiopian Empire. Protected from raiders by the surrounding mountains, it was a commercial power

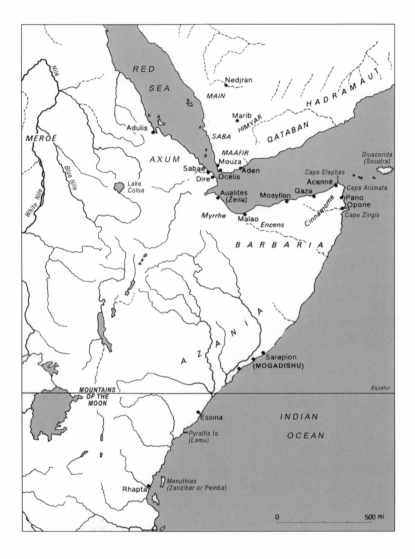

**Map 2.** Ancient Cities of East Africa

Based on: *General History of Africa*, vol. 2: *Ancient Civilizations of Africa*,
Paris: Unesco/Berkeley: University of California Press, 1980, p. 146

and controlled the routes linking the Roman world to India, and Arabia to Africa. Until its decline in the seventh century CE, it was also a cultural power that reflected a blend of northern Africa and southern Arabia, and it passed Meroë's culture on to the Horn of Africa.[14] Evidence of this can be seen in its coins, monumental stelas, varied items such as glass beads, which show influences from the pre-Muslim Middle East (Syria, Iraq, and Iran) and, to a lesser extent, Egypt and Nubia.[15]

## The Eastern Coast of Africa:  Ancient Ports

What sometimes escapes our eyes as westerners focused on the Atlantic Ocean is that the Red Sea and the north of the Indian Ocean were long an arena of expansion for the Roman Empire, partly as a result of the influence of Greek traders in Egypt. However, there was vigorous competition from pre-Muslim Arabs based in the Arabian Peninsula, which could not be avoided by those engaging in cabotage between the African and Indian coasts. Pliny mentioned the importance of the Arabian Peninsula, India, and China in supplying the Mediterranean world at the time of Augustus. For example, incense and myrrh came from Arabia, and ivory, pepper, and (already!) cotton fabric were exported by India.[16] Before the *Periplus,* Romans seem to have ignored the coast south of Cape Gardafui (off the Horn of Africa). Thus it was Arab and even Indian sailors who, through their knowledge of the reversal of the monsoon, had a virtual trade monopoly in the area. Evidence that the Romans wanted to compete with the Arabs by setting up a direct sea route to India can be found in the few sources from that time, such as, in addition to the *Periplus*, Ptolemy's *Geography* (mid-second century CE) and Costas Indicopleustes's *Christian Topography* (early sixth century CE). The latter provides some information about Ethiopia and the Persian supremacy in western India at the time of the decline of the Roman Empire.

The Persian period began in the fourth century. Unfortunately, we know little about it. There is no continuity between Roman documents and those of the beginning of Islam (ninth century), and the great poverty of archaeological evidence from the period does not help. Until

very recently we had only a few numismatic "treasures," such as varied
and ill-matched collections of mostly Greek and Roman coins that were
poorly identified and dated, and thus of little use even though some date
to the first centuries CE and others are from the twelfth, fourteenth,
and even sixteenth centuries. The gap of knowledge was closed by the
discovery of Sassanian pottery, imported from the Gulf area, all along
the African coast, in the north (at Ras Hafun, just south of the Horn of
Africa) and on the coast of Mozambique. Since the pottery dates from
the first century BCE to the fifth century CE, it is especially valuable as
proof of the age of pre-Islamic intercontinental trade.[17]

We know that the Persians monopolized trade with India in the
sixth century and with China in the seventh century. At the beginning
of the seventh century, they conquered southwestern Arabia, possibly
dominated the south of Egypt, and controlled Ethiopia. Their empire
fell to the Muslim conquest around 635, but they were able to maintain
control over maritime trade in the area. This was how the tradition of
Shirazi migrations (from the name of the city Shiraz, in Persia) from
the Persian Gulf to the coasts of Arabia and East Africa originated,
and it continues to the present day. Nonetheless, those who founded
Kilwa in the twelfth century may simply have moved south from long-
populated, partially "Bantu-ized" areas on the African coast of Benadir,
between Shungawaya and Mogadishu.[18]

Was the origin of coastal cities therefore mainly, as was once claimed,
the result of foreign settlers? Perhaps foreign settlers used the coast only
for handy anchorage along shipping routes with destinations far beyond
Africa. The mercantile cities were long considered foreign enclaves
rather than nearby, coastal, or insular cabotage stations, and they were
thought to be ports open to the world between the African coast (from
present-day Kenya to Mozambique and Madagascar) and the coasts of
Southeast Asia, India, and Indonesia, passing by the deserts of the Horn
of Africa and the Arabian coast. It was probably not so simple. To assert
that the fortunes of these cities owed nothing to the local people is to
ignore the presence on the world markets of the time of at least three
African products: gold, ivory, and rock crystal. For them to be imported
into the Mediterranean region, there had to be not only extensive
shipping networks but also producers. Ivory, which at the time passed

almost exclusively through East African ports, was used widely in antiquity. Many objects carved in ivory date back to the time of Roman, then Byzantine empires in the first through sixth centuries CE. Later, until the Swahili renaissance, between the twelfth and the eighteenth centuries, that resulted from Islamization, the sources of production dried up, both from the Maghreb and from the Indian Ocean. From the three centuries separating the decline of the Byzantine Empire and the emergence of the Swahili culture, only a few rare pieces of ivory can be found in Europe. During that time, craftspeople used substitutes, such as bone, walrus, and narwhal tusks, and even the tusks of fossil mammoths from Siberia.[19]

Suppliers to the Mediterranean world in the first centuries of our era, the African inhabitants of the nearby hinterland must have been attracted by the ports of transit along the coast. We know very little about the Africans of that time and place except that (as mentioned in the *Periplus*) they were tall. This refers perhaps to Sanye and Mbugu hunters and perhaps to people of Kush origin, in other words, people who had come down from the highlands of Kenya. The microliths they left are evidence that they were in the Stone Age and did not yet know how to work iron. This knowledge was, however, acquired as a result of the rapid Bantu infiltration from the south. Still, it seems that these people were not seafarers and used only small pirogues, not open sea dhows.

We do not know much about the cities, either. The *Periplus* describes them as a series of emporia, or small city-states, each with its own chief and market. It notes a number of them on the Somalian coast, relatively few of which have been identified in the field; two that have been identified are Essina and Sarapion (possibly north of Mogadishu) and Nikon (probably Port Dunford). Bur Gao, then called Shungawaya, seems to have been the first city where Arabs settled permanently.[20] The Pyralean Islands have been identified as the Lamu Archipelago in northern Kenya. Lamu, officially founded in the eighth century, would thus date back to that time. To the south, "two day's sailing" from Lamu, was Menouthias Island, initially thought to be Zanzibar and then identified as Pemba (*Periplus*, para. 15[21]). The *Periplus* mentions only one emporium on the southern coast, again at two days by sea from

Menouthias, thus somewhere between Dar es-Salaam and Pangani, perhaps on the Pangani River: the emporium of Rhapta. Rhapta was a good means of penetrating into the hinterland. Theoretically controlled by southern Arabia, it was for all practical purposes independent and ended up essentially as the Roman outpost on the Indian Ocean. It is described as extremely busy, and links were established with the interior, which was said to be mountainous (perhaps referring to the peaks of Kilimanjaro[22]). Archaeological discoveries dated to approximately 500 CE have been reported not far from there, at Gonja (Pare Hills). The finds, which include seashells and shell beads, confirm the links with the coast.[23] Producers in the immediate hinterland just inland from the coast have long met the demand for ivory, rhinoceros horns, and tortoise shells. The export of coconut oil was also noted at the time of the Periplus (coconut trees were introduced from Asia), which implies that manufacturing was carried out. Goods were exchanged for iron goods, particularly weapons, which could have affected internal power relations. A little wine and wheat were also imported, "not for trade, but to serve for getting the good-will of the savages" (Periplus, 16, 17).

In other words, these cities were not only visited by foreign sailors but were inhabited and visited by Africans. Children of mixed blood certainly resulted from local contact with outside trade. The first such children were probably, as elsewhere, the children of African slave women. As early as the seventh century, there is mention of Zanj slaves on the Arabian coast; these slaves were soldiers, servants, and farm workers involved in the reclamation of marshy areas in southern Iraq. There was a slave revolt at the end of the seventh century early in the Islamic period, but it was perhaps not the first.[24]

On the African coast, a specific urban group probably was at the origin of this traffic. The role of female slaves used locally as concubines and domestic slaves employed by city-dwellers must have been a determining factor. It was the beginning, if only to a limited extent, of the mixing of ancient cultures that is characteristic of later Swahili cities: this mixing of cultures is revealed by the Swahili language, which derived from Bantu languages and borrowed part of its vocabulary from Persian and, later (mainly in the nineteenth century), Arabic.

## Western Sudan and the Interior Delta of the Niger

### Tichitt: Villages or Cities?

Paradoxically, it is in West Africa, where Egyptian heritage is very distant, that urban remains are perhaps the most ancient, or at least the most deeply rooted. The first evidence dates back to the Neolithic: remains found in Mauritania along the line of the Tichitt-Walata escarpment, on the cliffs of Dhar Tichitt and Akreijt. There are around 500 fortified villages, each containing 20 to 300 compounds, along approximately 250 miles. The 127 largest settlements, which have been identified using aerial photographs, have two communal cemeteries, which means a total population of around 6,000 people, not all of whom were necessarily contemporaries.[25] The series of settlements date from 3800 to 2300 bp[26] and are located mainly on the peaks overlooking the former lake of Aouker, relatively far from areas suitable for cultivation, which is initially surprising. Logically, farmers should have settled at lower altitude, around the lakes that existed in the area at the time. Indeed, a two-part organization can be seen; it may have involved the same people, because the chronology of settlements in both locations is analogous. Most of the houses are made from stone and built on the cliff, indicating rainy-season settlements that concentrated mainly on livestock and millet production. However, there are also traces of temporary dry-season camps below, in the dips between the dunes. The main activities seem to have been livestock production, fishing, and foraging. At least one large site can be identified, extending over fifteen hectares (seven acres).[27] The area shows traces of what could very well have been one of the distinctive features of such ancient African habitats: a functional division of space into different sectors that were occupied in succession by a single urban population composed of a number of groups that moved to the uplands during the rainy season and the lowlands in the dry season.[28] The habitat was clearly divided into separate enclosures that touched one another, or were separated by nonorthonogal passages. The organized living spaces suggest the possibility of a sociopolitical change toward the end of the period. A defensive system of fortifications appears, and there are traces of more diversified economic activities, such as agriculture, hunting, and artisanal production. This was probably fostered by the decline of activities (such as fishing) that had become less dependable owing to the climate. These clues indicate a sphere of power in the process of overtaking the previous tribal and patriarchal organization. Were they purely villages or were they proto-urban? We do not know. These sites were abandoned very early (between 400 and 200 BCE), undoubtedly because the area became increasingly dry.

Elsewhere, notably in the Aïr (northern Niger), traces of local industry (e.g., stone tools, pottery, millstones for grain, and local copper work) from the same period have been found, but there are no signs of comparable human settlements.[29] The first contact with Arabs, perhaps at the end of the seventh century but at least by the twelfth century CE, resulted in the establishment of urban settlements to serve caravans passing through the area (through Kawar, in the Aïr, to the north of Bornu). However, it seems that there was no continuity between these two stages, again probably because the land was drying up. In the ancient period, which interests us here, perhaps this was already the beginning of a network of contacts spreading around the first sites. Although we can see that the Tichitt set of settlements is located just to the north of the site presumed to be the capital of the ancient kingdom of Ghana, there is a gap of several centuries for which there is no evidence of intermediary links. The many ruins identified but not yet investigated may help to fill in what is missing, but we cannot rule out the possibility that desertification resulted in a real break at the beginning of the Christian era.

## In the South, a Culture without Cities?

### Nok

The Nok lived more to the south, between Niger and Benue, on the Jos Plateau in present-day central Nigeria, a little to the south of Hausaland. In the course of 35 years of research (begun in 1928 and later conducted by the archaeologist Bernard Fagg), more than 200 earthenware statuettes were found in a number of sites, particularly in the Nok and Jemaa regions. Many were small, with the smallest measuring 4 inches in height; the largest, according to the fragments found, might have been 45 inches high. Some were, and still are, attached to pottery vases. Almost all of them are of people, although at least one depicts an animal. Carbon 14 dating shows the statuettes to date from between 790 BCE and the first centuries of the common era at the latest. Everything suggests that the pottery techniques are those still commonly used today in Nigeria: a clay matrix containing grains of quartz, mica, and granite; and rapid baking for two hours in an open fire at a temperature not exceeding 800° Celsius, with the residual humidity in the earth eliminated first through heating before being put in the fire. This technique probably reflects the mining activity in the area, which apparently was intense. In the Taruga Valley, about sixty miles southwest of Nok, a three-acre site has been discovered. Four campaigns of archaeological digs have discovered the vestiges of thirteen low-blast furnaces in the midst of iron slag. The smelters seem to have operated mainly in the fifth to third centuries BCE and apparently are the earliest example of metallurgy in West Africa. Since the dates and styles of the furnaces are older than the iron industry in Meroë, the modern hypothesis is that the technology was either native or, more likely, imported from Punic North Africa.

This raises two types of issues. First, was there at Nok a culture (in V. Gordon Childe's sense)? In other words, was this a site where a civilization emerged? There certainly are artistic similarities among all the pottery, and there was indeed repeated reproduction of a set of objects that can be considered the concrete expression of the social traditions of a community. Can this be taken further, though? Were there the beginnings of an "urban" culture around the mining and artistic activities (which can also be considered religious, since the figurines symbolized for their sculptors supernatural forces on which they wished to act, such as with respect to casting iron or ensuring the prosperity of the harvest)? So far, only one Nok settlement has been excavated, at Samun Dukiya in 1969. Lack of funding has prevented further excavation. At the site, there are a few crags. According to a tradition that has been perpetuated up to the present (though it is not clear from when it dates), the prehistoric inhabitants built their huts on the peaks. Remains testifying to their presence have accumulated at the foot of the crags, from which they seem to have fallen or been thrown. Digs at the settlement have been fruitful. Angela Fagg, the daughter of Bernard Fagg and a great specialist herself, has uncovered fragments of earthenware figurines and shards of pottery, shaped and broken stones, lithic beads and inlay work, and many pieces of iron objects (e.g., hooks, bracelets, knife fragments, arrowheads, spearheads, and a cylinder made out of a rolled band of metal). A stone axe and a large, deeply grooved stone have also been found. This allows us to conclude that, as in southern Africa, people who had already mastered iron metallurgy continued to use Stone Age technology relatively late. This suggests a concentration of activities and even trade, possibly linked with a population density that was relatively high for the place and time. This is all the more remarkable in that later climatic vicissitudes and politics have tended to empty the area of its inhabitants. Nevertheless, since there is no concrete evidence at this point, we are in no position to make further claims.[30] There is no proof of a relationship between the Nok and the urban tradition in Nigeria, although such a relationship could be suggested by the lost-wax works produced a number of centuries later at Ife and Benin City prior to the arrival of Europeans.

## Igbo-Ukwu

The southernmost discovery in West Africa is Igbo-Ukwu in southeastern Nigeria, about twenty-five miles from Onitsha, in Igbo country. Igbo-Ukwu seems to date back to the ninth century, and its style appears to be unrelated to the Nok.[31] Finds indicate trade with the north through middlemen: products commercialized by Arabs probably traveled all the way down to Igbo-Ukwu. Direct influence is out of the question, however. At most, we can simply show the role played by long-distance trade in the emergence of an exceptional and possibly urban location because, in three sites and dating two centuries before the emergence of Ife's art, a treasure that includes 685 bronze and copper lost-wax objects and 165,000 beads has been discovered. This treasure indicates a concentration of considerable societal wealth based on technology developed by specialized artisans but of clearly local inspiration (evidenced by the use of forms such as the calabash). This suggests the institution of a chiefdom able to control long-distance trade, since the closest sources of copper were in the Aïr, in Niger (near Takedda), and at Nioro, in Mali. Otherwise, it had to come from North Africa.

## Jenne-Jeno: The First City of Western Sudan

More significant are the discovery in 1977 of the Jenne-Jeno site between Timbuktu and Jenne and the excellent resulting book by two American anthropologists, the McIntoshes. So far, it is the only settlement on the interior delta of the Niger that has yielded considerable urban remains from before 1000 BCE.[32] Before it dried out, the area was covered by a broad lake that gradually shrank around 4000–3500 BCE. Until 1000 BCE, the floodplain of the river was wider than it is today. Only temporary fishing and herding settlements could be established even in the driest months. However, between 250 BCE and 700–800 CE, a severe drought began in western Africa, and permanent settlements became possible. This was the origin of Jenne-Jeno, located in a slightly raised area, safe from the floodplain itself.

According to the McIntoshes, whose proposals have been discussed since 1990, the agglomeration seems to have begun developing around 250 BCE. Iron was known from the beginning, whereas copper appeared only in the fifth century CE. It seems that by 200 CE, the settlement covered more than twenty-five acres and, basing our calculations on the population of present-day sites of comparable size (an approximate but suggestive method), could have had up to 4,000 inhabitants. The population grew strongly between 400 and 900 CE. At its largest, the site was encircled by a 1.3-mile wall. The stratiography shows increasing complexity. Apparently, the lifespan of the round or rectangular houses could be as long as several centuries. The cylindrical sun-dried bricks, so characteristic of Jenne, seem to date back to the seventh or eighth century CE. There were large cemeteries, proof of a growing population that began to decline before the end of the first millennium. The site seems to have been completely abandoned in the fifteenth century. However, at its height, between 750 and 1150 CE, it covered at least 80 acres, perhaps even 100 acres around 900 CE, plus 22 acres in the Hambarketolo suburb located just to the north and linked to the main center by an earth dike.

This discovery is exciting, for it proves the existence of a city around the beginning of the common era in West Africa. It shows that there was pre-Arab interregional trade, made possible because the city was located at an exceptional crossroads: in a floodplain at the junction of two ecosystems, namely the dry savanna and the Sahel, and therefore conducive to complementary exchanges. Although the area has no stone or iron (the closest iron deposit is in the Benedugu, about forty miles to the southwest), iron was used and there is evidence of the early appearance of stone beads, the origin of which is unknown but certainly outside of the interior delta of the Niger. Trade involving travel of distances greater than ten miles required the establishment of a complex organization, involving night way stations, household division of labor, and commercial institutions. Trade with the north clearly also began early, even though there is direct evidence only as far back as the fourth century CE. Copper of Saharan origin has been found, and, while salt does not keep, we know that it was actively traded for copper as early as the fifth century CE.[33]

The logistics of trade were simple: the great waterway was the most efficient means of transportation for heavy and bulky goods. In addition to seasonal navigation, there was the agricultural potential of the floodplain, which could sustain a relatively large population with dried fish and cereals, thanks to fishing and the farms in the hinterland. The existence of Jenne-Jeno shows that the incentive for development in the area was not just north-south long-distance trans-Saharan trade. Initially, there was local and regional trade focusing on river ports along the long, narrow east-west band of the Sahelian border. This suggests the rise of complex interregional relations extending from western Senegal (where vestiges of settlements have also been found[34]) to close to the Chad basin. It was not the Arab intrusion that created trade. On the contrary, the prior existence of regional networks accounts for the otherwise inexplicable rapidity with which the Arab merchant and urban civilization became established in the area.

Was Jenne-Jeno the only regional metropolis at the time? Was it the only place where a long political balance, resulting from the successful symbiosis of groups of various origins, enabled a dense population to develop? Or, conversely, did the density of the population favor administrative centralization that, in turn, provided a stable environment for the exchange of goods and services? These questions cannot be answered yet. Perhaps the city grew because it was a link between the east-west and north-south axes. Perhaps too the initial settlement was a

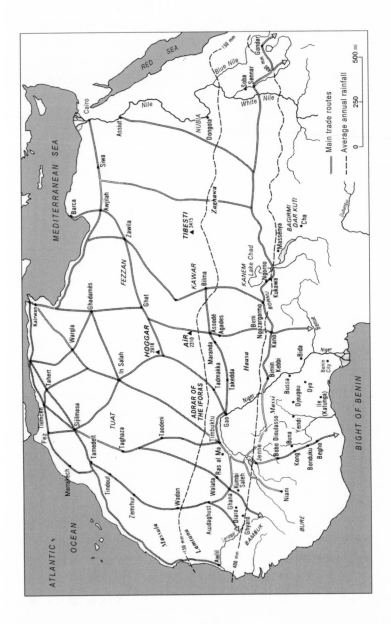

**Map 3. Ancient Cities of West Africa and Main Trade Routes**
Created with assistance from the CNRS, Paris

hub that branched out into other, sometimes only seasonal, sites to form a network. After all, As-Sâdi says that, according to tradition, the Jenne territory used to include 7,077 villages that were so close to one another that messages could be conveyed by calling from village to village. This is corroborated by many finds.[35]

In any case, Islam was apparently the major cause of the decline of the city's original site. Oral records ascribe abandonment to demographic pressure, which is not a very convincing argument when we consider that the later city of Jenne is located less than two miles away. A more likely explanation is that the Muslims, whether new arrivals or locals converted in imitation of their king toward the end of the thirteenth century, felt the need to create a sanctified city and desert the ancient pagan site. The inhabitants of Jenne-Jeno, who were fishers, farmers, and craftspeople, were rapidly attracted by the new center. The abandonment of the old city coincided with Islamization of the area.

## Conclusion

The evidence converges to suggest that West Africa did not wait for the influence of the Arab world to give birth to the first urban agglomerations.[36] Since the late 1960s, French research has concentrated on the site at Tegdaust, thought to be the location of Awdaghust, the famous location of Saharan salt production. The site was first occupied prior to the eighth century CE, thus prior to the penetration of Islam. Here again, the human settlement seems to have had two locations. The older one dates back to a time when the threat of water in the sandy bowl was still too great to allow a permanent settlement. The people therefore settled on sandstone terraces, thirty to forty feet above flood level. The establishment of stable enclosures on lower ground dates from the seventh and eighth centuries CE. The huge enclosures, separated by mud brick or stone walls, marked out apparently collective and technologically advanced spaces that were used for work more than for accommodation. Relatively elaborate copper metallurgy (lost-wax molds and alloys) developed there beginning in the second half of the eighth century. The continuity of Sudanese artisanal production, not only of metalwork but also of cotton weaving, is also shown by the presence of spindle heads from before the eighth century. In the same century, the presence of a few imported objects made out of ceramic and glass suggests the first contacts with North Africa. Everyday life and activities were technologically and culturally rooted in the black world, however. Evidence of this lies in the later changes in the landscape and in the lifestyle of urban dwellers, which are clear from the tenth century on and obviously resulted from the arrival of people from the Maghreb.[37]

Elsewhere, even though the lower levels have not been explored systematically, other sites seem to have been occupied for a very long time. Yet at Kumbi-Saleh, presumed to be the site of the ancient capital of Ghana, all that has been found is the Islamized business center and no traces of the aboriginal royal quarter or of those for services (such as stables), which were described by Al-Bakri. The site is thought to have been settled, at least in a pre-urban fashion, in 500 CE. Likewise, Polish-Guinean digs have proved that the presumed site of Niani, capital of the Mali Empire (though this title remains controversial because the remains show little resemblance to the opulent descriptions of Ibn Battuta[38]), had been occupied since the sixth century CE.[39] Consolidation of the urban space began with major trans-Saharan trade here as well.

Another case is the site of Maranda, mentioned by six Arab authors between 872 and 1154 as a major center located on the caravan route between Egypt and Gao and thought to be present-day Marandet in the Aïr. Not only has much evidence of copper metallurgy been found, but the first carbon 14 datings place the site's occupation between 550 and 640 CE, plus or minus a hundred years. This again would have required a network of aboriginal trade onto which Arab caravans could have been grafted. The grafting would have had to be early because, according to one source, albeit a controversial one, the first expedition crossed the Fezzan in 666, less than 50 years after the Hegira.[40]

As more and more archaeological discoveries are made, there is increasing evidence of urban life that was not only ancient but also aboriginal. The urbanism reflects what we suspect, based on later sources, about the culture of African societies. The urban planning contradicts

the centralized vision and carefully mapped view of the Western medieval city tucked behind walls and crammed around monumental
buildings, such as churches, palaces, markets, and, later, bell towers.
In Africa, city dwellers used many different locations, depending on
the season and function (that is, work or rest). The absence of private,
individual ownership of the land made it possible to extend and vary
human settlements, including cities. The market, meeting place par
excellence, could also be a space on its own, and not especially close
to the city; this is still often seen today throughout the Sahel. The arrangement of juxtaposed enclosures corresponded to family communities that set aside spaces for traffic and communal activities. Thus, this
arrangement was not simply the transposition of a rural habitat. Rather,
the urban habitat expressed a specific social organization, based on the
extended family. The space belonging to kin stopped where that of the
neighboring lineage group began. Sacred spaces, such as altars maintaining links with ancestors, were also scattered, both inside inhabited
spaces and in the countryside. Yet, as they are today, people were still
"linked together by invisible obligations that every individual is supposed to know and fulfill. Divided and even scattered, the religious
space of the African community is perfectly known and perceived."[41]
The same applied to all urban spaces, which could spread out although
they were divided into areas of production, worship, brush, sacred
woods, and stocks of firewood and supplies. They were limited only
by a fragile balance between "the spread of settlement" and the "ability of the environment to sustain."[42] Construction materials, primarily
mud, adobe, and unbaked bricks, were not permanent and this helped
to make the environment flexible, inhabitants mobile, and monuments
temporary. The ephemeral quality of these materials contrasts notably
with stone, which was promoted later, mainly by the Arabs. Stone
authorized and even imposed more monumentality, and thus also
centralization, on a habitat that had until then been disjointed. The
contrast is striking at Awdaghust, between Jenne-Jeno and Jenne, and
in the Swahili cities.

In summary, the organization of urban space in ancient, pre-Muslim
times was such that we can speak of cities. This means, however, that
we have to abandon the Mediterranean Arab and/or Western model.

Instead, despite clear differences owing to ecology, we find a configuration that is in some respects comparable to that of the ancient Bantu cities in the rainy forests and forest savanna of the center and south of the continent. This is because we are dealing with shared cultural characteristics, such as kin-based social organization and the absence of the notion of private property.

# 3

# Bantu Cities

Part of the temple of Great Zimbabwe

Leo Frobenius, *Kulturgeschichte Afrikas* (Zürich: Phaidon-Verlag, 1933).

# Chapter Three

---

# Bantu Cities

As surprising as it may seem with such contrasting geographical and historical areas, there could be, a millennium apart, a point of convergence between the emergence of proto-urbanization in western and central Africa. At least in the Rift area, from the interlacustrine states to the South African veld, we find a similar association of farmers and herders, and the same predominance of the latter. At the time when colonizers asserted that Africans were unable to create cities by themselves, it used to be suggested that the herders had migrated far from the north or even from Asia, but today these fanciful theories are rejected.

## Zimbabwe and the Stone Ruins of Southern Africa

Basil Davidson was right to point out that Great Zimbabwe was no exception, and that other great cities existed in East Africa.[1] The city of Zimbabwe, famous for its colossal stone ruins, seems to be the most perfect and most centralized achievement by peoples in this area that were at more or less the same level of economic and social achievement. With the exception of vague and rare allusions in Arab texts, the only clues we have to the time prior to the fifteenth century are archaeological vestiges, such as the remains of pyramids, rock paintings, and ruins of stone buildings. The Stone Age probably prevailed from the highlands of Kenya to South Africa, but in conjunction (especially in mining areas) with gold, copper, and, later, iron metallurgy, particularly between the fourth and twelfth centuries.

Archaeological sites rich in stone ruins have been found virtually everywhere. Swept away by his enthusiasm for his discovery of African history in the late 1950s, Basil Davidson saw this as evidence of a multitude of cities that had disappeared as a result of trade and conquest. Today we interpret these archaeological remains more cautiously. Most of the ruins show traces of an agricultural civilization that seems to have flourished mainly between the twelfth and the sixteenth or even eighteenth centuries, depending on the location. This civilization would have been broken by the Arab intrusion from the coasts, which generated slave raiding, and also by migrations of warriors and nomad herders who came down from the Horn of Africa in the north perhaps as early as the beginning of the first millennium CE and who later, in the early nineteenth century, began coming up from the south at the time of the Zulu migrations (so-called *Mfecane*).

A relatively late (possibly seventeenth century) example of this urban culture is Engaruka, which was discovered in 1935 on the border between Kenya and Tanzania, on the escarpment of the rift to the southwest of Natron Lake. It was initially studied by L. S. B. Leakey, who counted about 6,300 stone houses, plus 500 others in the valley, which justified the hypothesis of a city of 30,000 to 40,000 inhabitants.[2] This was seen as evidence of the emergence of an aboriginal urban civilization, known as the "Azanian civilization," among the local Mbulu population. This Azanian civilization was raided and destroyed by Masai invasions. Hamo Sassoon has disproved this hypothesis: he has shown that on the approximately 1,500 acres at Engaruka, there was an extensive, semi-itinerant agrarian civilization. There is no proof that all the buildings are from the same period. Only 2,000 to 4,000 rural dwellers would have been sufficient to cover the area with traces of their compounds and kraals.[3] Sutton has suggested the same thing concerning Vudee to the northeast, where terrace farming is practiced even today, and especially with respect to the south of the country, where he noticed very few archaeological finds one generation ago.[4]

Are Inyanga ruins urban or rural? Inyanga covered a hilly area of a completely different scale: 2,500 square miles in Zimbabwe behind the port of Sofala, not far from the Mozambique border. The Inyanga flourished mainly between the sixteenth and eighteenth centuries, living outside the urban area and outside the control of the Shona, who had migrated toward the north (and whom the Portuguese knew as the Monomotapa, or Mutapa). The Inyanga were in an area where active relations with outside traders were possible, but it seems there was no direct contact between the Inyanga and Shona cultures. As at Engaruka, traces of walls surrounding groups of dwellings have been found. Were these cities or villages? The economy was based on subsistence farming of grain and livestock. The hilly terrain was systematically terraced using loose stones, with irrigation ditches, small dams, and wide stone basins that served as enclosures for livestock or storage for grain, although the first European settlers interpreted them as "slave enclosures."[5] The population was probably no denser than at Engaruka. The people had honed simple technologies to meet their needs. Rapid soil depletion required shifting cultivation, and frequent relocation could explain the remarkable extent of the terraced countryside. Some of the wealthier families of chiefs had larger compounds. However, the parallel existence of an urban civilization is dubious because, unlike at Zimbabwe, the traces of material culture show extreme poverty and very low development: simple pottery and beads, very few iron objects, and little copper jewelry.[6] Construction techniques were rudimentary, employing only local granite gathered in the surrounding hills. Dry blocks of stone were placed on the outside, and the interstices were filled with smaller debris. Groups of houses were spread along terraces built along the hills. All of this suggests subsistence, or even survival, agriculture and the daily life of ordinary people—the absence of an aristocracy or political class. The fortified aspect of this stone civilization, that is, the traces of walls and forts perched on the hills, certainly shows communal effort, but for purposes that were more agricultural than military. The structures served to defend small communities that rarely included more than a dozen

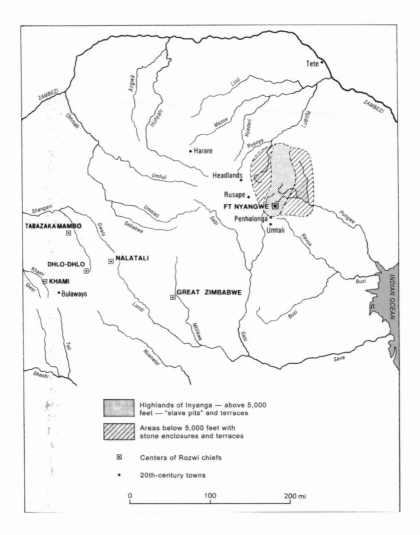

**Map 4.** Shona Lands and Cities in Zimbabwe
Based on: P.E.N. Tendall, *History of Central Africa*, London: Longman, 1967, p. 58

men, with a maximum of perhaps 20 including adolescents, to protect harvests and livestock from slave raids from the eastern coast. It is also possible that these small groups were better able to protect themselves after the trade in firearms and the influence of the Portuguese military model spread into the hinterland.

Thus, it seems that we cannot yet speak of an urban civilization in this case. Though separated by 1,000 years, the emergence of the fortified villages seems, in the end, comparable to what may have happened on the edge of the Sahara, along the Tichitt escarpment.

Zimbabwe, dating from several centuries earlier, is a completely different case. Whitty's categorical statement that "[n]either Zimbabwe nor Inyanga reached a stage of development approaching 'true urbanization'"[7] seems at the very least debatable and to have terribly Eurocentric connotations. Owing to its political centralization and the wealth of its artisanal production, Zimbabwe was certainly the center of an urban civilization. It is the largest of the approximately 150 sets of ruins found in the shaley granite terrain between the Zambezi and the Limpopo. Another 50 have probably completely disappeared. These were all built more or less at the same time, between the eleventh and fifteenth centuries. The culture was similar everywhere, characterized by the same kinds of dwellings, pottery, and ironwork, and by small numbers of gold and glass beads; pillage was frequent, particularly beginning in the nineteenth century. Most of the sites are relatively small: no more than 30 people would have lived at each site. Thus, the sites were rural and the subsistence economy was based on semi-transhumant herding, evidenced by the fact that the houses typically had animal enclosures. Some of the inhabitants probably left the site for several months of the year in search of better pastures; this would have been true of Great Zimbabwe at its height also. The luxurious ceramics that have been found there reveal a considerably more sophisticated culture that has been seen nowhere else in the neighborhood, however.

Toward the end of the twelfth century the location stopped being an ordinary village and became the seat of an elite population. The elite had taken control of the pastoral community and routinely employed a differentiated partially slave workforce made up of specialized craftspeople, such as stonecutters and carriers, masons, potters, jewelers and sculptors, and perhaps ironworkers. Why did the change occur? It was not the result of a conquering force, for the architecture is not military. We know that Zimbabwe's ruins are made up of two parts: an acropolis and the remains of fairly colossal walls encircling some of the dwellings, which are probably the vestiges of the royal residence located in the heart of a relatively large central basin framed by hills. The acropolis was in the past mistakenly thought to be a fortress, but there are no defenses on the rear flank, which is on an easy slope. Originally, there was probably a sanctuary on the summit, a little like the arrangement at Delphi. Evidence for this is the presence of monoliths, platforms probably used for sacrifices, and soapstone birds, a number of which have been found. The royal rulers lived at the foot, under the protection of the "rain making" sanctuary.

Zimbabwe's origins probably had to do with control over commercial livestock, which stimulated outside trade. Zimbabwe had a monopoly over the gold trade based on the output of nearby mines, especially those in Ndebele country; the mines were not necessarily under Zimbabwe's direct control, however, which suggests the possibility of "domestic" gold panning, perhaps also carried out using slave labor to a limited extent. The enterprise was probably similar to the system described a little later by the Portuguese with respect to Monomotapa: the Mwene Mutapa, or "lord of the plundered lands," did not own the mines himself either but, at least symbolically, purchased the production using livestock. Prosperity depended on peace and stability in the area, which extended between the mining regions and the coast. The Swahili and then the Portuguese took over from there in the port of Sofala. It was probably not by chance that Kilwa began flourishing in the fifteenth century, specifically with the decline of Zimbabwe, for at the time of the northern coast's "gold age," Kilwa built its wealth on trade with the south.

There is no doubt that the gold was swallowed up by the Indian Ocean. Despite the pillaging that occurred after Cecil Rhodes discovered the region, the traces of lively trade between the twelfth and fifteenth centuries have been pieced back together. In 1903, a remarkably rich cache was found, containing pearls and some Chinese porcelain (a dozen pieces of celadon ware). The business quarter has been identified by the 30,000 pearls that have been found there. The presence of cowry shells, copper wire, and many iron objects (hoes and iron braid) seems to suggest a flourishing artisan class, although we do not know whether the objects were imported or made locally.

Zimbabwe peaked in the thirteenth century. Vassals and dependents provided the court with gold, livestock, ivory, iron, and cloth. Artisanal and commercial activities based on gold, copper, and bronze ornaments, weaving, glass beads, and imported ceramics were at their height. The stone architecture tells us about local construction techniques. Except for the monumental royal architecture, walls were thick, curved, and too long to support a roof. Generally mortarless and twice as high as they were wide, they were made of large stone blocks and *daga* (gravel mixed with red or gray clay), and were used to delimit livestock enclosures. Homes were circular and made of *daga* alone, with openings only for doors and water drainage. The royal wall shows the century-long development of more refined and elaborate techniques, which seem to have been the local response to local and regional opportunities and problems.

How many people were brought together under the aristocracy? This is not easy to calculate. According to P. Garlake, if we estimate that there were six or seven adults per compound, the total population could have been 1,000 to 2,500 adults, plus 750 more from "secondary courts," whose presence is indicated by more distant ruins. According to the latest aerial surveys of the 1980s, the population in the compounds was much denser than originally suspected, and it has been suggested that the original figures be doubled,[8] which would place the total population at 11,000 to 18,000. This is all the more plausible given that the monumental construction of the wall would have required the simultaneous labor of not more than 400 men for a number of decades.[9]

Thus both the agglomeration and the dominant aristocracy were limited and belonged to a framework still largely dependent on a subsistence economy. Everything indicates that the reason Zimbabwe was abandoned in the middle of the fifteenth century was not that there was an unprecedented disaster such as war or fire that left no traces. It was simply that, at the height of Shona power, the urban population probably became dangerously dense, or at least too dense for the means available to the society. The soil, on which agriculture made excessive demands because adjuvants were not employed, gradually became depleted. Thus, environmental constraints were probably the reasons that the Shona rulers decided to move some 200 miles to the north to found the short-lived Monomotapa kingdom, which did not last much later than the sixteenth century.[10] However, the site of old Zimbabwe was not totally abandoned. The return to archaeological research in the late 1970s has uncovered Chinese porcelain from the sixteenth century.[11] In fact, at least some of the priests of the Zimbabwe sanctuary remained there, the last of whom seem to have been killed at the time of the *Mfecane* (so-called Nguni migrations northward from South Africa, partly led by chiefs opposed to Shaka) by invaders headed by Mugabe just before the Nguni army's invasion of Zwangendaba.

In short, Zimbabwe seems to be a particularly thought-provoking example of an ancient city that was well adapted to its ecological, economic, and social environment in an area that was still largely dominated by open subsistence farming and where market and industrial towns remained small but no less "urban" than many small centers in the Middle Ages in the West.

In the north, the Monomotapa was followed by Rozwi domination. Farther west and in closer contact with the gold mines in Ndebele country, the Rozwi occupied Khami and Dhlo-Dhlo in the eighteenth and early nineteenth centuries. Both settlements are situated near Bulawayo in present-day western Zimbabwe and seem also to have been the residences of chiefs.[12] The Rozwi were there before the Nguni and may have been the descendants of Changamire, who rebelled against the Monomotapa toward the end of the seventeenth century. Some of them seem to have left the Zimbabwe area, by then completely ruined, only in the nineteenth century. In any case, their culture appears related to that of Zimbabwe. For example, soapstone birds have been found. Did they also inherit an urban tradition from Zimbabwe? Khami hill, which was terraced, and the ruins of Dhlo-Dhlo, also made up of two enormous platforms (the smaller of which covers 1,000 square yards), are imposing, and they do not seem to have been simple military fortifications. Ivory objects, bronze and iron weapons, pottery, and gold and glass beads have been found at Khami, although in relatively small quantities. However, research has not yet proved urbanization in the area.

In the south, the spectacular site of Mapungunbwe, at the top of a hill in the Transvaal on the southern shore of the Limpopo, is likely evidence of the area covered by Shona urban culture. Mapungunbwe seems to have reached its height in the twelfth century and may have been used as a defensive post on the southern border. It appears to have been destroyed in a great fire around 1400.[13] R. Summers considered it to be of Zimbabwe heritage, but ten years later the chronology was reversed, and it is now considered "the first capital of Zimbabwe culture."[14] The site, like other less prestigious sites along the shores of the Limpopo, includes many in tombs (26 were excavated in the 1980s), and a wealth of funerary treasures has been uncovered. So far, however, there are hardly any traces of a thriving city. It is possible that the habitat was abandoned long before the funerary rites took place.

In South Africa, research was long hindered by the apartheid government, which wished to perpetuate the myth that the whites were the first to settle in the area; all the same, a significant number of stone ruins has been found; the ruins cover a wide area around 1,000 miles in length and 150 to 300 miles wide, from the Zambezi River to the Orange River, between Kimberley and the Drakensberg chain. All, or almost all, of the ruins are located to the west of the Rift, at an altitude of about 1,000 to 1,500 yards. Groups of 10 to 20 sites are about 10 to 25 miles apart—one or two days' journey on foot, which is a reasonable distance between small centers in a premodern civilization. The most impressive site is in the eastern Transvaal and has walls about five feet high. Nevertheless, the fact that several thousand miles of stone terraces have been found is a sure sign of an agrarian civilization.

The first sites seem to date back to the beginning of the common era, and the latest were abandoned recently, not so long before colonialism, most often voluntarily, which suggests a relation to ecology similar to that at Zimbabwe. The most impressive sites were rarely abandoned or destroyed before the Mfecane (1820 to 1830), the huge military conquest that came up from Natal following Shaka's Zulu revolution and destroyed most of the tribal patriarchal societies previously living in the area, along with their proto-urban settlements.[15] Pillage and raiding did the rest. About twenty sites are of European origin, showing traces of Portuguese influence in the sixteenth and seventeenth centuries. The use of mortar illustrates this clearly.[16] It should not be forgotten that the Portuguese, who arrived in 1498, were active on the Mozambique coast for at least a century. Before 1512, they sent Antonio Fernandes from Sofala to the interior, charged with finding the route to the capital of the Monomotapa. He probably undertook two trips and recorded the distance between settlements in terms of days of travel. The Portuguese therefore had early influence on the construction of forts, although no evidence has yet been found of continuity between the ruins in the hinterland and Sofala. Research is still in its infancy!

One of the sites is particularly intriguing: Kurrichane in the western Transvaal.[17] Kurrichane, which has completely disappeared, was a prosperous center around 1820. It was described at that time by John Campbell, a Scottish missionary of the London Missionary Society, as the capital of the Hurutse tribe of the Tswana group and a settlement of about 16,000 inhabitants—at least as large as Great Zimbabwe—located on the top of the highest hill in the area and surrounded by a stone wall with narrow doors. Campbell left behind a series of sketches done on the spot. In the sketch, each home was made up of a large circular hut surrounded by auxiliary buildings and was located inside an enclosure surrounded by a circular stone wall that could be used as a pen for livestock. The houses were painted bright colors, such as yellow and red, and had sculpted clay pillars with figures painted in various colors, particularly on the face of the wall that faced inside. The walls of the houses, which were also made of stone, were generally cylindrical, and the thatched roofs were conical. Some of the more elaborate constructions had covered passageways from one terrace to another. It was an industrious Iron Age community; Campbell saw a furnace and a large, busy crowd.[18] Although he did insist on the density and vitality of the population, Campbell did not mention monumental architecture. Agriculture remained essential, and the farm terraces extended far beyond the urban settlement properly speaking (which can explain, once again, the remarkable area covered by the ruins).

Alas! Nine years later, in 1829, another missionary, Robert Moffat, also visited the site not far from where he met the Zulu (Ndebele) chief, Mzilikazi. He also says that there were many "cities" but that they were all in ruins.[19] All of them had stone walls and clay decorations on the walls and over the doors. They had been destroyed only one or two years before by the Mfecane, specifically, the Koloko and Matabele campaigns.

Thirty-five years later, another traveler went to the site and also reported ruins. He asked shepherds about their origin, but the inhabitants of the area no longer knew anything about them.[20] They had come from elsewhere and had no memory of the cities that had disappeared.

Were there in southern Africa other cities comparable to Zimbabwe? It is not impossible.

## The Capitals of the Small Kingdoms of Central Africa

Despite assertions to the contrary, it is not certain that the three main interlacustrine groups (so-called Bwata, Hutu, and Tutsi/Hima), which are today exaggeratedly antagonistic for political reasons, can assign chronologically distinct dates to the origins of their disputes. In any case, researchers refused to take a position on the point because there is no scientific certainty regarding how the area was originally populated.[21] The problem is that the history is so old that memory of it has been lost; Jean-Pierre Chrétien called it an "enigma."[22] Nonetheless, it is still possible that the oldest group is the Batwa (pygmies), who provide evidence of an earlier society with a lifestyle based on hunting and gathering. The gap that progressively increased after the sixteenth or eighteenth centuries resulted from the early meeting of two complex groups: this meeting would have taken place some time around 2,000 BP. During the first millennium CE, the Bantu expansion seems to have resulted in the proliferation of sedentary groups with agricultural activities that could have been related to the development of iron metallurgy. Originally, the cultural and economic differentiations between these varied groups were minimal, as the herders possibly coming from the northern plateau had also settled as cultivators of cereals, and the cultivators were also cattle herders. Therefore differences between herders and cultivators were related more to lifestyle than to a remote different geographical origin. In the interlascustrine area, varied oppositions grew with social and political processes. In Burundi, there are no origin myths that say that people emerged by arriving from elsewhere. However, we do find genealogical histories that describe the rise to power of new dynasties related to the supremacy of semi-transhumant herders over more sedentary farmers.

Apparently, beginning in the fourteenth century, Hima herders in present-day northern Uganda and northeast Rwanda took power by establishing the Chwezi kingdom, which was governed from the fortified cities of Bigo and Kabengo, which were encircled by defensive ditches that were carved in rock or made of dried earth. The religious center of the kingdom was Mubende, about 100 miles west of present-day Kampala. Dating by archaeologists places Mubende in the fourteenth and fifteenth centuries, which corresponds to the time of the origins calculated using the genealogies of the Bunyoro kings.[23]

The first capital cities, which were sometimes more than a mile wide, were built around the royal palace and kraal (stockyard). Between the royal land and the ramparts there was a habitat that was not yet very urban, since it was broken up by large livestock enclosures. Starting in the fifteenth and sixteenth centuries, other groups of herders took power in turn, successively forming small kingdoms, such as Bunyoro, Ankole, Buganda, Rwanda, and Burundi. These kingdoms were dominated by herders whose wealth and power depended on cattle, but it fell on the farmers' shoulders to ensure the community's subsistence.

The later wealth of some of these kingdoms resulted from trade contacts with the eastern coast. Thus, around 1750, Buganda engaged in major trade via Karagwe and Nyamwezi country, where ivory hunting and trade, and later the slave trade, developed. There is reason to wonder whether international economic relations played an important role in the distribution of the cities. Long-distance trade, which involved luxury goods that were costly because they came from afar and were rare, made the fortunes of the ruling aristocracies who had the monopoly on such goods. The capital cities of these influential chiefs could only benefit from this. Therefore there was often a conjunction of two favorable currents in these cities. First, there was regional activity based on agriculture and/or herding, which supplied food to an unusually large agglomeration and provided the chief with a power base that was reinforced through military raids and even conquests at the expense of neighboring settlements. This only strengthened the impact of the capital city. Second, the presence of an exceptional resource could facilitate longer-range action. This is clear in the case of gold and copper mining. When the king controlled this sort of production and had a monopoly over its trade, the capital city was certain to flourish. This was the case for Musumba, capital of the Lunda in Katanga and for Zimbabwe in Shona country. Could control over iron have played the same role? Meroë's size seems to suggest this, but the archaeological evidence in central Africa is still too scanty for a conclusion to be drawn. For now, it seems that long-distance trade, which fosters the growth of a city, is not a necessary condition for the emergence of a city.

Yet, without major trade, was Meroë strictly speaking a city or only a fortified camp? What makes such a capital different from a village is that it was a remarkably grouped and organized habitat in a society made up of farmers and herders, almost all of whom were scattered and survived on subsistence production along with limited exchanges of food. The human settlement did not exist by itself, but in the framework of semicolonization, which implies, in particular, a military force and a relatively heterogeneous population. The presence of a political class (the king and his court) made the royal capital a centralizing power that appropriated a share of all the activities in the surrounding area to benefit a privileged group. Social differentiation, specialization, and urbanism were therefore present, even though they still seemed to be in their infancy in some respects. The classical plan of the capital city was that of straight roads converging at the palace or royal compound in the center and connected by circular streets, similar in pattern to a spider web. The roads led to the quarters where the compounds of the various chiefs spread out in the direction of the provinces they controlled. The city was also full of spaces, made up of series of compounds (houses and livestock enclosures or even lands side by side) that simply reproduced the rural architectural model on a larger and more widely spaced scale. It was, as R. Hull says, a city that minimized urbanity in order to maximize urban space, e.g., market spaces, meeting spaces, agricultural spaces, and living spaces.[24] All known descriptions and interpretations of ancient Bantu cities portray more or less this schema.


## In Burundi

At the time of Mwezi Gisabo (1852–1908), when Burundi's contacts with the outside were still minimal if not nonexistent, the kingdom's urbanity was closely linked to its political system. Oscar Baumann, the first European explorer to visit the country, did not arrive until 1892.[25] At that point in Burundi, there was not one capital city, but a network of cities, or "royal hills" (*ikirimba*), scattered throughout the country wherever the king decided to move his home or compound. The many capitals were therefore not successive but simultaneous, and their populations swelled periodically depending on the king's movements. The king had a whole series of estates, that is, the royal hills, where he lived during his frequent travels. The homes changed with each reign because, in addition to the compounds inherited from his predecessors, where he had to build his own residence in a location slightly different from that of the preceding king, the king established new residences himself. Thus, E. Mworoha counted a total of 51 royal hills. He distinguished the political capitals, properly speaking, where the king celebrated the national seeding festival (the *Muganuro*), from the secondary political centers, where he had a queen; he visited the latter often and they were important for internal management of the area. There were also ritual centers that were under royal authority but occupied by political-religious dignitaries (for example, Kiyange, home of the king's sister-queen, and Mugera, the compound where the king was born). Finally, there were the economic centers, with compounds for farming and for use as stockyards. These were often abandoned political residences and would therefore be more accurately described as major rural enterprises than as cities. The feature common to all these settlements of widely varying size was that they concentrated at least periodically an exceptionally high population in this rural country, and their relatively diversified habitat mirrored the corresponding social hierarchy.[26] Every settlement had a succession of residential quarters (*insago*) made up of a temporary and often provisory settlement occupied by chiefs and the province's subjects when the king himself was living in the compound. Then there was the public square (*imama*) located in front of the compound, which was where the king met and had contact with his people. Inside the compound, which was enclosed by a high fence with two main entrances, the royal compound, or city of the king, included three large courtyards that were assigned specific functions. One was for herders and herds, one was the sanctuary in the middle of which was located the royal palace, which was itself surrounded by a fence, and one was the housekeeping (kitchens and granaries) area governed by the queen. The royal compound did not contain many more than twenty houses. This "urban" framework perhaps lasted for centuries in most parts of central-southern Africa; in fact, the description of her husband's royal cities by Christina Sibiya, a Zulu chief's wife in the mid-twentieth century, still largely fits this description.[27]

## In Rwanda

Nyanza was a royal capital of ancient Rwanda. Like the Burundi cities, it was composed of the king's residence (*Ibwami*), the hill on which the residence was built, and the surrounding hills occupied by permanent or temporary residents. Attempts, too Eurocentric-minded to be convincing, have been made to show that the temporary agglomerations were only proto-urban beginnings.[28] Certainly, the choice of site was voluntary and corresponded to specific rituals, which were used by oracles to designate locations suitable for permanent or less temporary settlements. The court oracles took a few pinches of earth from the hill under consideration and mixed them with the king's saliva and cow's milk. This mixture was then fed to a young bull, which was then killed and eviscerated. If the entrails were read as favorable, they were buried with the animal's carcass and a sacred fig tree was planted on the grave. The descriptions that we have of the city are unfortunately late, dating to the early twentieth century, but there is good reason to think that the buildings were not fundamentally different from what they would have been

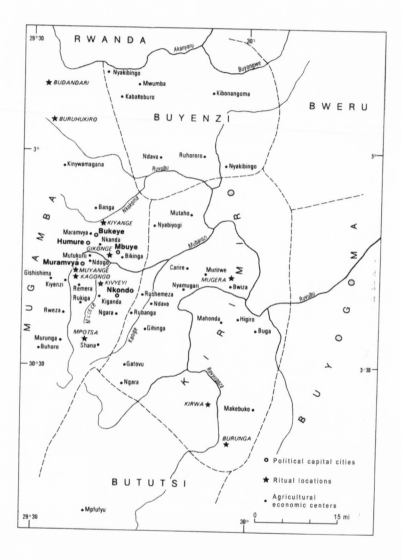

**Map 5.** Royal Cities and Estates in Burundi under the
Reign of Mwezi Gisabo (ca. 1852–1908)
Based on: Émile Mworoha, *Peuples et rois de l'Afrique des Lacs*,
Dakar-Abidjan: Nouvelles Éditions Africains, 1977, p. 146

in earlier centuries. The agglomeration consisted of a large complex of round huts with big yards and high hedges to mark out compounds that spread along the hills.[29] The *rugo*, or royal compound, was made up of circular reed fences around thatched houses with walls made of branches supported by wooden stakes. The houses were carpeted with mats and had a clay hearth in the center for the king, his wives and his entourage.[30] The royal residence was simple but large, perhaps 200 by at least 100 yards, and gave the impression of a huge maze of interlaced huts and granaries, with a single doorway to the outside, opening onto the large public square (*karubanda*). The square was used by the king's many court-iers and also as the seat of the council, where the king rendered justice on his subjects. In more or less concentric circles surrounding the square and royal compound were the compounds of dependents, built along the same lines but more modestly, so as to avoid wounding the king's pride. The king's wives lived in the inner circle; each wife had her own herd and compound. Next came the compounds of dignitaries, and then, far-ther out, more dispersed, and simpler, were the homes of less important inhabitants. These gradually thinned out toward the surrounding hills, which were used as grazing lands for the herds of the court.

The city contained all of the dependents who, in one way or another, supplied and supported the royal house. These included slaves and ser-vants responsible for food, clothing, pleasure, and religion; guardians of the treasure; and craftsmen such as blacksmiths, weavers (of fig bark), mat-makers, basket makers, potters, tanners, and butchers. The city also depended on rural inhabitants, who were controlled by provincial chiefs and required to deliver agricultural taxes to the royal residence in the form of beans, millet, sorghum, maize, and peas; these goods were stored in the granary area and were the responsibility of royal officers. Herders paid their taxes in livestock, which allowed the king to distribute them to his dependents and subjects to demonstrate his wealth and generosity.

The interlocking compounds gave an overall and accurate impres-sion of concentration of population, although the density remained low and the total population could vary considerably depending on the time of the year. All capitals were based partially on war and emptied during military campaigns, which were regulated by the alternating dry and wet seasons and the periods when the farmers returned to the fields.

The general organization of the seat of royal power seems very similar to that of the other capitals of which we have descriptions. This applies across the whole continent, from Ethiopia to southern Africa and from Abomey to the Congo. It lasted as late as in the twentieth century, for example in Foumbam, capital of the Bamoum. Of course, there were obvious regional variations related to construction materials (wood, adobe, earth, stone, and, later, cement), building techniques, and the shapes of houses and compounds (round or rectangular).

The precolonial capitals nonetheless kept some of the features of temporary agglomerations, the economic functions of which were limited to keeping, storing, and, at festivals that were sometimes opulent, redistributing the products of royal taxes and forced labor. Artisans' products were exclusively for consumption by the king and those close to him. These products were not commercialized, and the people who lived in the capital, which was supported by a wide range of tribute, produced virtually nothing.

## Ankole

Is this generally static model of temporary and limited cities, as described by European travelers who began visiting them at the end of the nineteenth century, really revealing of earlier centuries? Roland Oliver suggests instead that the fragility of these cities, which was linked to their mobility, tended to increase in the nineteenth century because of growing insecurity caused by heavy imports of firearms throughout most of the continent. Basing his arguments on the findings of archaeological digs on the sites of ancient Ankole capitals, he considers that the capital and palace of the *Mugabe* was a true city in previous centuries, and not just a parasitical compound. According to oral traditions, there have been twenty kings since the fifteenth century. There are archaeological reasons to think that first four, who are undated and more or less legendary, each had two or three capital cities. However, from Ntare the First[31] there was only one capital city per reign. Later, the frequency with which the principal residence was changed even by the same reigning king (every ten years at the beginning of the nineteenth century) very clearly sped up when political instability increased (and was reduced to one or two years at the most at the end of the century.[32]

A jump was made to production and trade when complementarity increasingly linked the city not only with the immediate hinterland but also with more distant areas. The local vocabulary reveals the meaning of the words used to speak of these cities: the word in Ganda that means "capital" (*kibuga*, or "royal city") seems to be derived from the verb *ok-webuga*, which literally means "walk in every direction." Thus, *kibuga* could be translated as "a very busy, industrious place," in other words, a city.[33] Similarly, farther south, a possible origin of the name of the city of Zimbabwe could be *Dzimba dza Mabwe*, which is a contraction meaning "stone houses."[34] This expression was used before the arrival of the Portuguese, since the first Portuguese visitor to speak of the city, in 1506, called it *Zunbanhy*, which seems to have been based on the description by Swahili traders in Sofala.[35] In other words, the term itself refers in both cases to a description of a habitat and population density that are exceptional compared with the surrounding countryside.

## Musumba, Capital of the Lunda Empire

Musumba also was an exceptional settlement, as early as in the sixteenth century. It was the capital of the ancient Lunda Empire, west of present-day Katanga (southwestern Congo). Unfortunately, we have hardly any specific information about its population because the earliest *de visu* description dates only from 1842, when, despite its decline, Musumba still had 20,000 inhabitants.[36] Originally, the population had become dense, and a government was emerging thanks to the introduction and spread of cassava and corn imported by the first Portuguese. It was also a nonagricultural center, as a result of the Luba chiefs' control of copper-producing areas. This combination of circumstances, along with active trade, brought the empire to its height in the seventeenth and eighteenth centuries. Copper played an important role: when the Europeans arrived, small copper bars were widespread currency in central Africa.

There was also diversified internal trade, however, owing to the extent and capacity of the corn fields, and to salt produced in the Kolwezi area, ivory obtained through hunting (which led the Chokwe people, who specialized in ivory, to flourish in the eighteenth century[37]), and slaves in demand in both the east and west, toward the lower Zambezi and the Atlantic. The slave trade finally replaced all the other trades in the eighteenth and nineteenth centuries, causing the definitive decline of the chiefdoms previously in power. In the nineteenth century, Musumba was displaced by Kazimbe, capital city of the realm of the same name. Antonio Galitto, who led a Portuguese expedition there in 1831, described Kazimbe as "perhaps the largest city in central Africa."[38] Here, as elsewhere, the conditions required for a city were met: an agricultural surplus, greater than before; a political class; and a group of merchants that could attract producers (farmers and hunters) located at less than a day's walk from the city. However, Musumba and Kazimbe remained "mobile" cities because each new king erected a new compound facing a great wide space that was used as a meeting place and market.

## The *Kibugu* of the Ganda Kingdom

This degree of mobility was not the case, at least in later years, for an active center like the *kibuga* of Buganda, the Ganda kingdom. The site of the royal city was typical of interlacustrine capitals, which were always located on top of a hill. This was a strategic position that enabled the city to be well protected against attacks while giving the king (*kabaka*) the possibility of strategic retreat. For many years, the king moved his seat relatively often from one hill to another, and the change became compulsory at the death of the king, when his successor acceded to the throne. From at least the eighteenth century on, the kibuga (or royal city) always moved, though within a relatively limited space in the center of the kingdom near the shore of Lake Victoria on Murchinson Bay. At the end of the nineteenth century, this mobility became extreme; between the death of King Sunna II in 1856 and the arrival of the British officer Lugard in 1890, the site seems to have changed at least ten times. Unfortunately for historians, the first European did not visit it until 1862. Stanley visited the capital in 1875, but it was then at Rubaga. In 1875, Wilson saw it in the same location, but the king was simultaneously occupying another palace at Nabulagala (Kasubi) nearby. Finally, around 1885, the royal compound settled at Mengo Hills, next to Makerere Hill, which became its final location. Water came from wells and a number of surrounding rivers.

The first detailed description dates from 1911 and is based on the traditions gathered at the time, which referred to the reigns of Suna (c. 1832–1857) and Mutesa (1857–1884).[39] The capital was divided into as many quarters as there were provinces. Each chief built dwellings in his compound for his wives, slaves, and dependents, as well as lodging for visitors. Mobility remained the rule within the city, since a chief who was promoted or deposed had to leave, along with all his family and dependents, within a few hours.[40] He was surrounded by dependent chiefs from his province; the quarter, located in the direction of the province and surrounded by a reed fence, also included empty spaces reserved for peasants who periodically came to serve as forced labor on the government's public works projects. There was a relatively large amount of land reserved for agriculture, including banana plantations and fruit trees, which complemented the supplies provided by the rest of the country. In principle, the people from each individual province were grouped together and the city radiated in all directions. In 1889, missionaries spoke of a knot of wide, well-maintained roads, which were very clean near the houses. These roads made it possible to summon people from anywhere in the realm whenever they were required. It should be noted that a very similar description, term for term, could be given of a twentieth-century realm: Foumbam, capital of Bamum, in the Cameroon interior.[41]

What was the population of the city? Here again, unfortunately, the earliest figures date only from 1907–1908, in other words, the colonial period. It goes without saying that they are not very enlightening about ancient times. Nonetheless, around 1850–58, at the time of R. F. Burton's travels, the explorer estimated that the royal city was nearly one and a half miles long (and in 1911, Roscoe added that it was more than half a mile wide). The whole kibuga was very spread out since it took a day to go from one end to the other, lengthwise. (Roscoe specified that it was five to seven miles long by at least one and a half miles wide.) It was in fact an administrative unit under the direct control of the *katikoro* (the prime minister, one of the three principal dignitaries of the state recognized by the 1900 British Protectorate Agreement). Other reports, from 1907–1908, attribute about 25 square miles to the kibuga, in other words, an area that remained virtually constant until the beginnings of independence in 1962. Cardinal Lavigerie estimated in 1866 that there were 400 to 500 dwellings; Roscoe's informants counted 496 in the royal compound alone, plus 100 for the katikoro and about 370 for other dignitaries. In all, estimates seem to indicate that at the turn of the twentieth century, the kibuga had a population of around 70,000. While Burton mentioned a royal harem of 3,000 in 1858, Roscoe, referring to traditions, speaks of a total of 3,000 people living in the royal compound; one of Gordon's agents, who passed through in 1875, estimated that there were 10,000 people in the crowd surrounding his party when they arrived. An official census in 1911 found 32,000 inhabitants, but Church Missionary Society reports of virtually the same date put the population at only a little over 15,000.[42] It would be presumptuous to consider that they are valid for the eighteenth century, but it is obvious that in the nineteenth century, the urban nature of the settlement was no longer controversial, if only because of the heterogeneity of the population: slaves from neighboring societies, Swahili soldiers, the approaching arrival of Indian and Sudanese traders, and Muslims (though the majority of the inhabitants would follow the kabaka's example and convert to Catholicism even before the beginning of colonization).

The Ganda king's ability to maintain and even develop his capital in the nineteenth century probably resulted from the combination of a favorable ecological and subsistence environment and controlled international relations, at least until colonial submission. These factors also provided the country with some shelter from an exclusive, destructive slave trade. This was not the case in the west, where the ravages of the trade quickly destroyed preexisting networks.

# The Capitals of Central West African Kingdoms

## In the Kongo Kingdom

In the west, the primary example of cities is clearly the Kongo kingdom capital, Mbanza-Kongo, or São Salvador, as it was later called. Kongo cities displayed the same constants that we have seen elsewhere: the compound and dwelling of the king (at Mbanza-Kongo) or the regional chief (at Soyo), which were built by dependents at the center of the agglomeration. Since the area was wooded, the residences appeared more rustic and the huts were loosely laid out on the land (in colonial terms, "concession" in French and "compound" in English), separated by winding footpaths through thickets.[43] Soyo, a provincial town, had a circumference of "five leagues." Loango was described by Father Proyart in the eighteenth century as "divided into as many little hamlets as there are families, and each family has near its hamlet a piece of land that it farms for subsistence."[44]

In these centers, which were at least somewhat multifunctional, the buildings were not much different from those in villages: usually cob on wickerwork and a light frame, with a thatched roof. This form of construction seems to have become more popular than wood and straw in the time of Lorenzo da Lucca (in the early eighteenth century). The capital, Mbanza-Kongo, was undoubtedly the only real city before the Portuguese arrived. "Several thousand inhabitants" lived in the generally proto-urban agglomeration, which had a residential hierarchy.[45] The dwellings of notables were larger and better cared for. A large open space in front of the palace was used for the king's political, religious, and legal functions. The palace itself was surrounded by a fence that was nearly one mile in circumference and made of stakes tied together with vines. Inside, another fence and maze, apparently characteristic of the residences of Kongo princes, encircled the royal home itself for protection and defense. The residence had a side for men (the king's quarters) and a side for women (the quarters for the queen, the other wives, and their slaves).

It is difficult to distinguish between the ancient city and that which developed, if not under European influence, then at least at that time, because King Afonso converted to Christianity when the Portuguese arrived in 1491 and immediately began building a cathedral. The king had a thousand men gather the stones needed; the task was completed in three months. The church was "very beautiful and very large . . . with three naves, pillars made of handsome beams and a roof lined with wood and covered in straw."[46]

Antonio Pigafetta[47] credited the same king with the construction of a surrounding wall, which apparently encircled the Portuguese city and the palace, each of which measured nearly one and a half miles in circumference. Other reports seem to indicate that the ramparts were discontinuous. There were not yet any two-story homes, and everything fell into ruin very quickly. Following a period of incessant civil wars (1645–72), the ruined city was almost abandoned. When Father Lorenzo da Lucca arrived in 1706, all that could be seen were the remains of an "ill-fated city" consisting of a temporary settlement near a palace made of "stakes and straw" not far from ancient buildings, including churches and Portuguese houses, that were falling down and invaded by brush.

How many people lived in the city at various points in its history? Pigafetta gives the highest estimate of over 100,000 inhabitants on the whole plateau where the capital was located. Yet around the same time, in 1604, missionaries estimated São Salvador's population to be 30,000—about 2,000 households (at 15 people per household). It is possible that this figure remained more or less stable for two or three generations. John Thornton suggests there were 60,000 inhabitants in the mid-seventeenth century.[48] The data for the end of the eighteenth century vary widely, however. There were still 35,000 inhabitants in 1760, but the population dropped to 5,000 in 1770 and 3,000 two years later.[49] The site was almost completely abandoned in 1795, with only 100 people and 22 huts.[50] The number of dwellings climbed back up to 3,000, with 18,000 inhabitants, by 1845, but fell to only 200 buildings in 1879 following a violent smallpox epidemic, and there were only 600 "poor, beaten" souls in 1881. What ecological or political vagaries caused these variations? The population had risen to 3,500 around 1889 when a new batch of missionaries arrived. A few secondary centers apparently

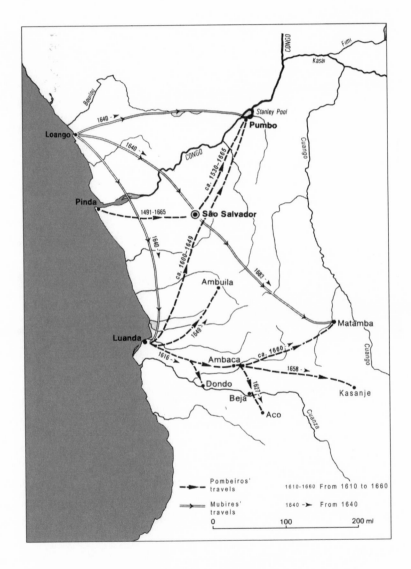

**Map 6.** Cities of Ancient Kongo and Trade Routes
Based on: W.G.L. Randles, *L'Ancien Royaume du Congo des origines à la fin du XIXᵉ siècle*, Paris, The Hague: Mouton, 1968, p. 175

bore up better thanks to the slave trade. Soyo, São Salvador's rival city, took advantage of its fall and doubled in population between 1645 and 1700, attaining at least 12,000 and over possibly more than 30,000 inhabitants. Loango seems to have still had 15,000 inhabitants in 1787.[51] These were clearly no longer centers linked with a European presence.

To their surprise, the Portuguese who reached the Congolese coast at the end of the fifteenth century found a political structure that had been centralized for at least a century.[52] As in other central African capitals, Mbanza-Kongo's subsistence depended largely on the immediate hinterland. Slaves tended nearby plantations, and the local aristocracy governed production and distribution; the latter's control over regional trade in iron, salt, ivory, cloth, and slaves, which were already traded between regions, ensured its power. The Portuguese brought Christianity to the capital, Mbanza-Kongo, which was located away from the coast and renamed São Salvador when it became the seat of the episcopate, Christianity, and Atlantic trade. In 1491, King Nzinga a Nkuwu was baptized João the First, and his son Afonso established the state religion. In the sixteenth century, economic activity still centered essentially on the abundant copper in the area, which was used as the local currency, and on ivory and slaves. The latter trade was based on the re-export of people gathered through expansionist wars conducted by the king along the eastern borders of his empire. For at least a century, this did not directly threaten the stability of the kingdom (although the long-term war economy finally did) and did not attack the bone and sinew of the country, as it did later. In short, as elsewhere on the west coast of Africa, the Portuguese remained along the coast, in the settlement at Luanda; unlike their other posts, they occupied Luanda continuously until Angola became independent in 1975. Inland, especially until the end of the sixteenth century, the Kongo kingdom remained politically autonomous and poorly known outside the area. Its external affairs long remained aboriginal; African civil wars between chiefdoms reflected the complexity of local alliances and rivalries until the eighteenth century.[53]

There was already a fundamental distinction between the *mbanza*, or cities—that is, groups of people with relationships not based on lineage—and the *mabata*, or little villages, in the surrounding hinterland. While each settlement had its own economy, the settlements were linked by relationships of domination and dependence. The cities housed the aristocracy and their dependents, whereas the countryside was at their service and most of the productive work was done by slaves. In short, the city looked like a village but combined its own resources with the contributions from hundreds of villages. The contributions were consumed by a class of residents and their servants. The enslavement of the producers ensured their own subsistence and that of the nobles living in the two main centers, Mbanza-Kongo, in the center of the country, and Mbanza-Soyo, on the Atlantic coast. At São Salvador's height, the approximately 60,000 inhabitants surrounding the city allowed 9,000 to 12,000 privileged residents to enjoy a lifestyle that was relatively luxurious compared with that in the villages. Surpluses from the provinces also enabled them to engage in international trade for goods that were completely unknown in Kongo. Salt and *nzimbu* shells from coastal areas were traded for slaves and cloth from the east, which were in turn used in trading with the Europeans. The latter supplied weapons, alcohol, fabric, and the services of missionaries. The first sign of superiority was demographic. The population density of the two cities was probably ten times higher than that of the rest of the country.[54] Transportation problems limited the subsistence area of each city to a radius of 20 to 35 miles, but this also limited the size of the urban areas to be supplied. The capital was no exception. Small *mbanza* covered much less area. They had 1,000 to 2,000 inhabitants at the most and were not much different from surrounding villages except that some of the families living there owned slaves.[55] The function of the nobles living in the small *mbanza* was mainly to ensure that taxes were sent safely to the political rulers of the country in the capital. These chiefs (such as the Marquis of Pemba in 1652) got by with small armed bands of 20 to 30 individuals who practiced brutal repression by burning uncooperative villages and selling as slaves any peasants who did not escape in time. In short, Thornton's description suggests that the destructive Atlantic trade in black slaves, which at last pushed the system to a crisis by causing a cornered aristocracy to export its own people and thus to sign its own short-term death sentence, found this socioeconomic organization to be rather fertile ground.

## In the Kuba Kingdom

Despite his claims to the contrary, Jan Vansina suggests a fairly similar system for the Kuba, a small but tight-knit group located nearby, to the north of the Lunda and to the east of the Kongo. Vansina saw the Kuba state as relatively strong, based on sound links between the town and the countryside, to the former's profit. Discussion of Vansina's study belongs in this chapter rather than in the one on areas under Atlantic influence because he resolutely asserts that, even in the nineteenth century, the Kuba capitals were relatively sheltered from European influence. This assertion is partly questionable: The black slave trade had long prevailed, and established economic ties necessarily influenced the internal organization of the kingdom. The kingdom itself seems to have emerged toward the end of the seventeenth century from a relatively mobile group of chiefdoms, which were quickly dominated by the Bushdoong people. However, the social structures of the Kuba evolved less thoroughly than those of the Kongo kingdom or in the hinterland of the Gold Coast. What Vansina described of the nineteenth century might not have been fundamentally different from what is suspected by historians about preceding centuries. This might also have been due to the political myths transmitted by informers in the twentieth century, who wished to pass on to posterity a positive image of their state, although the image was somewhat altered by their desire, unconscious or not, to enhance their political centralization. Indeed, with respect to the Kongo, John Thornton showed how much one has to beware of subtle reconstruction by royal and local oral traditions gathered in the nineteenth century. In Kongo, storytellers of the nineteenth century performed the opposite operation and retranslated history, which, in the seventeenth century, was that of a rather strong, centralized, expansionist territorial state, into more scattered and competing chiefdoms. Congolese oral traditions interpret the events in terms of kinship, clientele, seniority, and slavery, as well as referring to fantastic migrations, because storytellers use history to justify the present dissolution of political power into a fine dust of scattered rural chiefdoms. This said, Vansina was conscious of the risks and did not claim that the mechanisms he described went back earlier than the nineteenth century. Indeed, in the nineteenth century, the Kongo were only the shadow of what they had been in the past, but the Kuba kingdom had climbed to its apogee from mere marginal status two centuries earlier.

In 1892, the capital of the little state was a settlement surrounded by a 40-inch-high fence. Inside, there was a walled royal palace, streets, squares, and urban buildings; all in all, it definitely looked like a city.[56] At the time, the capital was home to about 10 percent of the population of the heart of the kingdom, which totaled 120,000 to 160,000 inhabitants spread over a territory about two-thirds the size of Belgium. The city layout was similar to that elsewhere in the region, with a rectangular palace in the center and many constructions with more or less temporary fences and homes, similar to those of a village. The maintenance of each quarter was the responsibility of its chief. Prisoners cleaned roads and squares. In the royal city, one of the king's wives was in charge of all the maintenance assigned to women.

The exact location of the city changed at least once a reign but always remained in the same region, which was not very large: about 20 miles long by 6 miles wide. It seems that there was only one capital per reign, although King Mbakam Mbomancyell is said to have had three at the same time around 1680. The palace layout had ancient origins. The later expansion, particularly of the quarters peopled by royal slaves (*pokibaan*), was linked to the size of the provinces and the slave trade.

The city was both different from and dependent on the surrounding countryside that it dominated even while being provided with supplies. The deciding economic development was the introduction of South American corn at the end of the sixteenth century. It was far more nutritious than sorghum and replaced cassava in the region. In the 1620s, the Kuba, unlike their neighbors, began to increase production, achieving two and sometimes even three harvests a year, along with cash crops and beans. Tradition traces the idea of creating a capital city around the palace back to King Shyaam at the beginning of the seventeenth century. This idea was borrowed from northern Mongo; the Lunda and Kongo influence was crucial.

The capital city was the seat of power. Unfortunately, the earliest descriptions of the king's councils are rather late, dating from the late nineteenth century and early twentieth century, and only three of the councils seem ancient: the council of the crown, charged with the king's investiture and sometimes his condemnation; the chiefs' council, which met without the king and represented the territories' official counterbalancing power; and the tribute council, which was presided over by the king and open to all chiefs of clans, or *kolm*. The city was also a controlling military center. The residences of the leading chiefs corresponded to their rank in the army, which is an urban feature frequently seen in ancient cities. Under the direction of one of the king's sons, royal slaves formed a police force responsible for punishing disobedient villages. When a whole chiefdom rebelled, city dwellers and men from nearby villages were immediately recruited.

Vansina essentially describes a city with the typical parasitical economic relationship in which farming was explicitly excluded, which meant that city dwellers, who were generally, in other words, the wealthy, were exempt from paying tribute. Only servant women and slaves worked in the fields, drew water, or carried wood. The rest of urban society was made up of the king's direct dependents, dignitaries, and artisans and merchants and their families, as well as the various groups of royal slaves (messengers, soldiers, servants). The king owned approximately 500 slaves, but the rest of the free men owned few slaves. The relatively elegant and affluent lifestyle of patricians and holders of office made it possible to distinguish them from countryfolk, whom they called beggars (*bakou*). Later, in about 1920, the number of patricians and officeholders was estimated at around 2,000. The richest lived on large fenced concessions; there are many descriptions from about 1920 of houses with several rooms and often a separate kitchen, and slaves acting as servants, sometimes including a snake charmer or another talented man responsible for after-dinner entertainment. Men spent their time on court intrigues, while women wove raffia and managed the home. Nobles acquired their income from their share of tribute and their supplies from one of the city's daily markets, and especially from the villages they governed.

Many dignitaries were kolm, or chiefs of clans, who were forced to live in the royal capital with most of their entourage. Their presence guaranteed the docility of the villages, which was essential to the city's survival. The *bubaang* villages on the periphery of the city provided rou-

tine supplies, such as fresh food, firewood, and palm wine. Many villages
were under the king's direct control: some were slave villages peopled by
prisoners of war or residents of punished villages, others were owned by
the king, his mother, or the crown prince. This category of village was
subject to more severe obligations than free villages, the chief of which
was required to come into the city to pay tribute only once a year, toward
the end of the dry season. Tribute was the foundation of the city; it was
composed essentially of corn grown in a field reserved for that purpose
and of long-lasting dried food, such as yams, cassava, plantains, dried
meat, and smoked fish. These goods were supplemented by items that
were gathered or manufactured, such as salt, iron, hoes, knives, raffia
clothing, pottery, and baskets.

Village production was strictly regulated. Village inhabitants who
were not free did not have the right to leave their homes without authorization. Anyone who killed or found a noble animal (such as a civet
or pangolin) had to give part of it to the king (the skin of a leopard, a
horn of a buffalo, a tusk of an elephant). Taxation regulated the whole
organization: territorial chiefs all had to pay tribute to the king, and re-
fusing to pay taxes was considered open rebellion. In the villages, special
dignitaries controlled rare resources such as salt, iron, and clay for pottery. If the regional market was held in the village, a kolm was appointed
to maintain order and collect taxes from merchants; these were more or
less equivalent to rent.

On top of tribute, forced labor was required to build and maintain
the city. The construction and maintenance of each of the palace buildings except for the harem was the responsibility of a designated village.
Workers were recruited by the governors of the provinces in liaison with
two palace officers who, depending on the tasks, sent orders to bubaang
villages every day. Once they were in the capital, the workers were under
the authority of the royal architect. Likewise, men could be requisi-
tioned to maintain dirt roads and the bridge (luckily, there was only
one bridge in the entire kingdom), or perform as dancers, musicians, or
tam-tam players at official celebrations.

Even though Vansina's informers may have presented their history
as more systematic than it really was, the traditions, which were more
carefully collected and interpreted for that period than for preceding

periods, confirm the important fact that urban environments were not foreign to ancient African societies. This is true of every feature of urban society, and particularly the economic and political aspects. The rise of the slave trade probably affected life in the capital more strongly in the nineteenth century than the traditionists are willing to admit. Nonetheless, among the Kuba, regional life seems to have taken precedence over international activities. Headquartered in the capital city, the king naturally controlled long-distance trade, which was based on ivory and slaves. The small Kuba group was very inward-looking, as evidenced by the exceptional creativity of its wood sculptures and iron work devoted exclusively to the king, and internal organization was essential. It was based on tight links between the city and the countryside; its foundations lay in the control and exploitation of the latter by the former.

What we can draw from all this is the portrait of an area in which the dominant subsistence economy was familiar with urban life but clearly not conducive to it. Relatively exceptional circumstances were required, most often owing to the presence and marketing of a rare and valuable mineral (mainly copper and gold), to result in the primacy of urban centers in what were essentially farming societies. In such circumstances, sufficient power accumulated to set up a coherent whole around the royalty and aristocracy, based on both regional subsistence production and long-distance trade. The result was unquestionably, and for a long time, a city.

There was not really enough urban mercantilism to overwhelm the agricultural foundation, however. The city's supplies indeed came from and at least partly depended on the countryside. Yet most urban consumption took a route that had little to do with trade, properly speaking. Kinship relations and tribute were primary. The market economy was embryonic and "confined to the cracks" of the domestic circuit. It developed essentially when the city's rulers took control of "rare products circulating in a broad geographical region that could be called *international.*" Finally, the economic activity of the city remained "imprisoned in its political function" as a capital.[57]

Thus, everything depended on the degree of control that the city was able to exercise and maintain over the area. When the economy was purely regional, the hold was precarious. In some cases involving more far-reaching ties, the city's authority depended largely on the combination, lasting or not, of long-distance trade (even moderately long, such as that of Zimbabwe and Musumba) and the regional economy. This economy was mainly pastoral for Zimbabwe, and based on farming for Musumba. However, the interdependence between urban and rural growth was not obvious. There was a disjunction between the urban and rural economies. Downturns in the countryside did not necessarily result from the decline of the city. Indeed, in Zimbabwe's case, the opposite occurred, for reduced urban parasitism could maintain without change, or even reinforce, the domestic, lineage-based rural organization. Indeed, the latter worked very well elsewhere without any cities at all.

Guy Bois concludes that the city revealed itself in such cases to be "exclusively parasitical." This means that feeding the city was closely linked to its domination of the countryside. It commanded products and workers in the form of tribute and slaves but sent nothing back in exchange, aside from agents responsible for carrying out orders and collecting taxes. The subsistence economy (as opposed to market economy) of the whole region therefore depended very little on the city. In short, the rural environment maintained precedence. This is clear in the case of Zimbabwe, which was unable to overcome this contradiction and died because of it. This ancient example is the most revealing one. Elsewhere and later, while the growth of the capitals of Ganda, Kuba, and Kongo was real, the development of cities clearly deviated from its initial trajectory owing to additional factors—the slave trade and colonization.

# Islam and African Cities

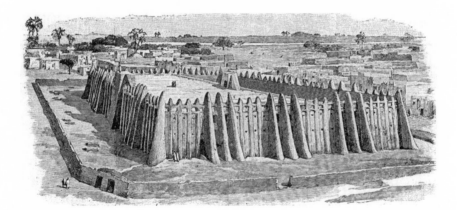

The old mosque at Jenne (reconstruction)

Félix Dubois, *Timbuctoo the mysterious*, trans. Diana White
(New York: Longmans, Green and Co., 1896)

## Chapter 4

# Islam and African Cities

One might think at first that since the city and related trade appear to have been the driving forces, the results of Arab-Muslim influence would be the exact opposite of what is described in the preceding chapters, when the subsistence economy rested more on the countryside than on cities. In reality, the dysfunction was reversed: the city and countryside were even less united than in Bantu cities. Except in the borderline case of the Hausa city-states, Islamized cities seemed to want to turn their backs on their hinterlands. This was probably their great weakness.

For centuries, the dreams of Europeans were inspired by the supposed wealth of cities such as Timbuktu, Jenne, Gao, and Kanem, followed a little later by Hausa cities such as Kano and Katsina and at last by the past of the Swahili cities on the eastern coast seen through the prism of Zanzibar. The mythical opulence of these centers was attributed essentially to Islam. When the first explorers reached the legendary cities, the poverty of the apparently rural agglomerations of earthen dwellings scattered over the arid steppe destroyed many illusions, but not the myth of Muslim power. This was because the grandeur of the medieval empires of Ghana, Mali, Songhai, and Kanem-Bornu was very real, as was that of the Hausa city-states. Arab travelers' marvelous descriptions of the empires' wealth were not really exaggerated for the time, nor were the reputations of their scholars or the skill of their architects. Western Sudan's impact on the rest of the world stems largely from the excitement created when some of the most famous kings of the western Sahel passed through Cairo when crossing the Sahara on pilgrimages to Mecca: the *mansa* Musa of Mali in the early fourteenth century, and the *askiya* Muhammad at the end of the fifteenth century. Al-Umari reported that Musa and his escort brought so much gold to Cairo that the price of the metal crashed. This is not surprising, since in medieval times western Sudan was the major supplier of gold to the Mediterranean and therefore to all of the West. This makes it all the more difficult to understand how political structures with such wide influence could have disappeared so quickly and left so little. Of course, the construction materials used were not lasting and the acidity of the soil is unfavorable to archaeological preservation, but another factor also played an important role. The medieval Sahelian economy was based on international trade, which was monopolized by an aristocracy based exclusively in cities. This is why trade was so slow to spread Islamic culture in the countryside. The fact that rural inhabitants largely remained outside the dominant current, except when the agricultural season was over and they worked as porters or laborers for the king, is probably why they remained unfamiliar with the powerful achievements of Mediterranean agriculture, such as use of the wheel and draught power in irrigation.[1] This also explains the extraordinary fragility of these empires, which could be destroyed in a single battle if the main city and trade routes were affected. This occurred in the Moroccan conquest of 1591, in which the invaders' dreams of riches were dashed by Timbuktu's poverty, but they were able to get by with a minimal force once they had pillaged the city. It was sufficient to spell the end of the Songhai Empire.

Muslim culture was then an aristocratic, urban privilege from which the rural masses were excluded since the production of wealth did not really depend on them; wealth lay in controlling trade in salt and gold, which was located beyond the state's borders. While the countryside did not change, new social structures and cultural practices developed in the cities. In parallel with the merchant class, the division of labor fostered the emergence of a flourishing community of artisans to serve the princes. Over the years, famous *medersas* maintained the Muslim heritage transmitted by the Arab world. Next to an urban habitat of Maghrebian- and Andalusian-influenced houses with interlocking terrace roofs and decorated doors, celebrated mosques were built as architectural translations of the faith and concrete expressions of the surrounding culture.

It was only a small step from this to seeing Islam as the conduit by which urbanization came to sub-Saharan Africa, and it was a step that historians used to be quick to take. As we have seen in the preceding chapters, this preconception was discarded only recently, not more than twenty-five years ago, thanks to discoveries such as Jenne-Jeno.

## From Ancient to Islamized Cities

### The Muslim City: A Concept in Need of Revision?

Not only could urbanization appear in Africa before Islam, but the latter's influence was subject to very specific conditions. First, especially in West Africa, the country was non-Arab. The major factor, however, was probably the fact that power was in the hands of local sovereigns who were often independent of the Arab-Muslim empires. Initially, they were often not converted; later, they were poorly converted. In the western Sudan, digs reveal Muslim quarters, not Muslim cities.

We still have to obtain consensus on the notion of a "Muslim city." This concept is found in the rather repetitive literature published after a specialist asserted in 1928, based on the specific example of North African cities, that Islam was essentially an urban civilization even though it was spread by nomads from the seventh century onwards.[2] From this point of view, Islam invented the two foci of the city: the mosque (the place of worship required for communal prayers on Friday and the intellectual center for a shared language) and the permanent market. These were generally complemented by a third feature, the *hammam*, or public bath. According to this theory, Islam imposed these elements on cities that were created out of, rather than modeled on, previous cities, since every new dynasty had to found a new city, either at the center of its empire or as a fortress on the border. In short, Muslim cities were the only places where believers could completely fulfill their religious and social duties. Thirty years later, Jacques Berque asserted the same thing by defining a Muslim city as a place of meeting and exchange.[3] It is difficult to see how this would make it different from a city in the Christian West, unless meeting is seen only at the level of exchange, in other words, in the mercantile sense of the term. The rest of urban sociability developed to a limited extent at the private level because the Muslim habitat is closed in upon itself, unlike Western habitats and, to a certain extent, African habitats south of the Sahara. The façades of the houses play a minor role in this since they are fairly high, closed, impenetrable walls—the antithesis of the western urban house open to the outside with windows, a decorative balcony, even a terrace and or- namentation designed to show the social rank of the inhabitants. There is nothing like this in a Maghrebian house of the medina, where recep- tion areas are hidden inside, making it possible to filter visitors by social rank and, naturally, gender. In Arab cities, private urban sociability was hardly ever displayed in the street, except in Moorish cafés for men and baths for women. In contrast, in sub-Saharan African cities, there was an open esplanade separate from the almost permanently busy market. The esplanade was available for public justice (executions and also pub- lic judgments made by the king), celebrations, and processions, and as a crucial meeting place between the people and the rulers (the chief, king, or, if the country was Islamized, sultan). It was a quasi-ritual feature, generally located in front of the palace, forming a no-man's-land that simultaneously guaranteed protection and access. The division of the city between the prince's domain and the popular quarters was willingly maintained in colonial times but reinterpreted as a space with military and sanitary and social segregation purposes.

Still based on the example of the Maghreb and particularly Fez, Orientalists assigned the market layout a quasi-ritual morphology, with shops laid out by specialization. Beside the mosque, there were incense and prayer book merchants; a little farther away, there were leather workers and slipper manufacturers; then there was the heart of urban manufacturing, with artisans, textile traders, and the covered market; finally came the jewelry makers, metalsmiths, and, near the city gates, harness makers and tanners linked with livestock trading.[4] These characteristics, attributed to the now controversial existence of guilds,[5] were found in many African markets, whether or not they were Islamized; if they were not, charms were sold instead of copies of the Koran. There was strict differentiation between business and residential quarters, perhaps out of a desire to keep women out of public life.

Another feature commonly attributed to the Arab-Muslim city by former Orientalists was that, unlike the Greek city (*polis*), it was not an autonomous association of citizens but only an administrative entity without its own identity. According to this point of view, the Arab-Muslim city was not a self-conscious whole governed by its own laws because it had no institutionalized civil or political authority. It was instead governed through a top-down system as part of an empire with a strong military and administrative structure built on a strict authoritarian hierarchy, an army of slaves, and a bureaucratic system of taxation. This is why classical descriptions of cities by Arab geographers often note that Arab-Muslim cities lacked an establishment that was obligatory elsewhere: the government's palace. Consequently, there was also no meeting esplanade, despite its great importance in sub-Saharan Africa.

From this perspective, in the medina, unlike in European cities, there were virtually no municipal institutions able to act as intermediaries with respect to the state. This assertion can be challenged in so far as it seeks primarily to contrast Muslim cities with their Western counterparts and tends to deny the ability of Muslim cities to establish themselves as independent powers, and therefore to minimize the dynamic power of the city.[6] Nonetheless, the argument is useful in that it highlights the importance of the origin of urban groups, which were based on ancient village communities in which the extended family was the essential social unit and which continued to govern themselves on the local level. This explains the predominantly ethnic division of the districts, in which the customary laws of each group seem to have compensated for the lack of a "municipality."[7]

However, urbanization is a process, not a result. Muslim cities, like other cities elsewhere, do not result from a preset plan. In his great work on the geography of the Muslim world, André Miquel takes a more complex, subtle approach. More an empiricist than a theoretician, he finally adopts a classical definition of the urban that is more universal than specifically Muslim. He sees the city first as the quintessential feature and most visible sign of the civilization. As elsewhere, it combines the elements that are the foundations of the civilization: a food-producing territory greater than simple fields around a village; power over that area and sometimes beyond or even over a whole province; and facilities that are related less to the monumentality of certain buildings (for mosques have been found in places other than cities) than to the socioeconomic situation at the time, as shown by the grouping of certain trades. What is special about the Muslim city seems to lie mainly in its constraints: the availability of arable land, variations on the theme of water, the need for a fortified wall, control over markets, the prestige of great mosques, and the need for special facilities, such as baths, promenades, libraries, and sometimes esplanades for celebrations.[8] These monuments, unlike in sub-Saharan cities, were often set outside the center or even outside the walls.

How can the Muslim aspect of the quarters be described more fully? Arab-Muslim cities shared the common feature of reflecting three socio-cultural requirements. The first rested on the basic distinction between believers and infidels, which resulted in more or less visible segregation based on neighborhood communities that were separate in both law and space. The second was imposed by segregation of the sexes, which gave rise to a typical organization of living space: absence of free, open public spaces, homes closed in on themselves, curved alleyways to hide women from the curiosity of neighbors. The third resulted from the first two and gave rise to land and real estate law that was not centralized but was instead left to the discretion of the individual communities.

## The Urban Layout of Islamized Cities

In a way, these elements, or at least the division between Muslim and non-Muslim districts, are found in the Islamized cities of the western Sudan but in inverse form: there is every reason to think that the quarter where Arab traders, that is, foreigners, lived was always separate. The abandonment of Jenne-Jeno in favor of Jenne in the twelfth century has been attributed to the concern with partition. The Muslim quarter is still the only one for which archaeological evidence has been found at Kumbi-Saleh, which was said to be the capital of the Ghana Empire.[9] Indeed, the local authorities, especially when they were not Muslim, also imposed segregation and control on foreign merchants. Even today in Asante cities and on the coast, such as in Lome, the *zongo* is the quarter reserved for the Hausa community of livestock dealers.[10]

Even though women were not often secluded, except in Swahili cities and in Hausaland, the inherited Sahelian urbanism reflects the ideal of closing the home to the eyes of strangers by using a series of blind walls and rooms that open only onto interior courtyards. The contrast is striking when architecture with Muslim heritage is seen next to buildings in the local tradition. In the latter, a relatively open enclosure contains as many buildings as there are families, and most of daily life, particularly cooking, which is done by women, takes place in the open air.

The seclusion of women is an urban phenomenon, since in the countryside women rarely have the leisure to practice it. We do not know whether it was practiced by Muslims south of the Sahara. Certainly it was not in medieval times, when the women offered to Arab travelers were slaves. In the western Sudan, only the Hausa have a relatively ancient practice of cloistering women, though the custom, which was confined until recently to a very small urban high bourgeoisie, has become more widespread only in recent years.[11] The practice is probably older and was certainly more widespread in Swahili cities where Arab influence on urban culture was more direct, even if not much is known about it. Archaeologists, who are the main source of information about Swahili culture, have hardly looked at gender relationship. In the past, according to tradition, the chador was not worn in Lamu, where high-ranking women were simply sheltered under large pieces of cloth held by slaves when they went out.[12] Seclusion, which has now become strict, seems not to have been introduced there until the relatively late domination by Zanzibar in the eighteenth century.

Having quarters governed by the rules of independent communities seems to be foreign to all traditions of Muslim origin. It is a form of organization much more widespread in societies strongly based on kinship ties and where city dwellers have gravitated into groups with shared ethnic and linguistic backgrounds. This occurred, for example, in the Yoruba cities of the nineteenth century even though the Muslim minority occasionally had real impact.

Indeed, Islam's influence on the evolution of African cities was sometimes strong. Present research is not facilitated by the gradual increase in Islamization of peoples and habits, which began asserting itself mainly in the eighteenth century and has become even faster in the twentieth century. L. Prussin's classic work on architecture, which is nonetheless superb and complete, goes so far as to assert that, no matter what artistic or architectural form is considered, everything in West Africa now shows traces of Muslim influence.[13] This position has been challenged,[14] in spite of the evidence of so many cross-cultural influences all over African history, source of so many cultural metissages. Nonetheless, many of the cities in the Sahel and even in the desert fringes flourished at the time of the "great empires," as they are called in Mali today, but there is no proof that some of them did not exist prior to that time. Indeed, the caravan routes and favorable local conditions were conducive to the establishment of agglomerations: for example, Agades was a crossroad favorable to traders, all the more so as the city was located at the foot of terraces facilitating irrigated cultures to feed the city. Some of these cities have survived; others developed later in Islamized areas under the complex influence and processes of introduction, merging, adoption, and change of intercultural currents. These sub-Saharan African cities were more or less Islamized throughout history, but they were certainly not historical "Muslim cities," except perhaps Timbuktu.

The layout of the cities where Islam was a force was nonetheless very different from earlier city plans. The corresponding political philosophy and lifestyle were completely disrupted. Unfortunately, there is not enough archaeology being done in this area to prove it. Our main sources, Arab geographers and later the first European explorers, generally had very little to say about the layout of the cities they visited, aside from whether there was a mosque, a few indications of what the market looked like, and very rare remarks about building materials. It does not really allow us to compare sites and city plans, or, more theoretically, urbanism and architectural rules. What is possible is to identify sub-Saharan cities that had a central public esplanade and those that did not. This feature is characteristic of African input south of the Sahara, and cities without such a space would be more likely to have an Arab-Muslim origin or dominant influence.

What is better known are the functions of the cities, which clearly met Muslim needs. There were commercial cities with wide-reaching markets, and they were often used as way stations on caravan routes. There were also intellectual cities, since a mosque went hand in hand with the teachings of reputed ulemas who promoted their own schools, and there were military cities that conducted campaigns (more or less proclaimed jihads) based on pillaging and slave raiding.

Luckily, some in-depth archaeological excavations have been rich in revelations. Those of Jenne-Jeno prove that cylindrical bricks, which are still characteristic of Jenne's architecture, probably date back to the twelfth or thirteenth centuries.[15] As in the cities of Bornu, this was a pre-Islamic technique that survived later, despite Muslim architecture's usual preference for stone. The most convincing evidence is, however, found at Awdaghust, where many specific details have been identified showing a single site's passage from pre-Islamic urbanism to urban forms imported by Islam and then gradually abandoned with the apparent decline of the Ghanaian empire.[16] The change could be felt as early as the very beginning of the Arab conquest of North Africa in the first half of the eighth century. A few objects from the north have been found, such as turned pottery and glass. Between 875 and 950, the urban landscape definitely changed. Neighborhoods became denser and were delimited by a network of quadrangular streets. Homes were more elaborate, through the use of adobe-covered stone, wallcoverings, and decoration. House plans, which included a courtyard, kitchen, and private well, were very similar to what is found in the Maghreb. More and more beautiful homes, rich in products imported from the north, continued to be built until at least the eleventh century. In short, a new spatial organization dominated for three centuries and was characterized not only by an architectural style but also by urban planning that showed economic and social differentiation. There was a residential quarter with the best exposure to wind, a crowded district where merchants had their boutiques, imposing public monuments, such as a market with a shaded entrance, a mosque that was rebuilt many times but seems to date from the tenth or eleventh century, and finally, toward the periphery, an apparently very busy quarter for artisans. Thus, the arrival of the Maghrebians "profoundly changed the perception and organization of urban space."[17] More or less the same observation has been made concerning other archaeological digs, such as those at Kumbi-Saleh, Niani and Yendi-Dabari,[18] and all the cities marked by Islam up to at least the sixteenth century: Jenne, Timbuktu, Gao, and Mopti, in so far as later reconstruction allows us to draw conclusions and hypotheses can be made in the absence of more detailed archaeological research. At any rate, at Awdaghust, the Maghrebian period occurred early and was highly individualized. When the Maghrebian influence waned after 1050, a looser conception of space returned, and "the street, the private home, collective monuments and the division of quarters according to urban and social norms" became blurred.[19] Urban space no longer tended to be determined by the social division of labor. Instead there arose a sub-Saharan structure more centered on the extended family in a vast enclosure.

Without traveling too far in this direction, since there is limited tangible evidence, we can reasonably posit that, depending on the period and region, Islam left its mark to some extent on most of the ancient cities that can be identified, sometimes elliptically, throughout the western Sahel.

## West Africa

### Ancient Cities in Niger and Chad, from North to South

The most ancient traces of Arabs can be found in present-day Niger, in the southern Sahara. The Arabs' arrival gave rise to or encouraged the development of the first caravan stops mentioned by travelers, some of which are corroborated by archaeological remains.[20]

#### The Kawar: Oases in the Desert

The Kawar was the oldest busy area. There were two reasons for this: the presence of alum mines (which were depleted in the fourteenth century) and the fact that it was on the central caravan route that left straight north from the loop of the Niger to Tripolitania. The Kawar was first mentioned by Abd el Hakkam (d. 871), in a report on an expedition that would have taken place in 666: Uqba Ibn Nafi apparently conquered all the *qsar* (small forts) before overcoming the capital, Kawar or Gasabat Kawar, "the fortified city," which may be related to the ruins of Guesebi three miles south-southwest of Aney.[21] Less controversially, in 891, Ya'qubi described the city of Kawar as "inhabited by Muslims of several tribes"; this is the first known mention of Islam in Africa south of the Sahara.[22] In the tenth century, Al-Muhallabi (d. 990) mentions the city of Al-Bilma and the capital Al-Qasaba (Kawar). In 1220, Ya'qut also refers to information from the tenth and eleventh centuries and describes the Kawar as containing "many cities," the largest of which was Abu 'l-Bilma,[23] which supplanted Al-Qasaba around that time before in turn being replaced by Ankalas (perhaps present-day Kalala, 1.5 miles northeast of Bilma) in the first half of the twelfth century.[24] Al-Idrisi describes the latter as "the largest and most commercial city in the Kawar, with mines of superior alum," which was traded eastward all the way into Egypt and westward to the Maghreb. He also speaks of Al-Qasaba, which was a "well-constructed city with very wealthy inhabitants who ... traveled and moved a lot between the other cities." The inhabitants wore wool clothing and their chief was native to the country; he was "independent [but] behaved in an appropriate manner," since he applied the *shariah*.

It should also be noted that most of the cities are described in terms similar to those used to portray Abzar: "small ... a knoll surrounded by palm trees and freshwater" (Al-Idrisi). In sum, they were oases. Nonetheless, thanks to the caravan stops, the Kawar served as a primary avenue for the penetration of Islam toward the south, and even a return toward the north, since a local chronology from the eleventh century says that the king of Kanem (1023–67) used the route to "settle 300 slaves" in Dirkou, Segueding, and Fezzan.[25] After the expansion of Kanem into the area in the thirteenth century, there was a decline in the fourteenth century. The last mention dates back to Al-Harrani (1332), who describes "large cities ... in the Kawar ..., such as Niklas ..., the city that was the largest and most important in terms of trade in the Kawar; Tatru ... , a city that used to be large but of which nothing is left, except for traces, vestiges and the remains of palm groves." Why did the decline occur? Arab texts are simply silent, but it was perhaps because the alum was depleted, Kanem had retreated, and the great caravan route that crossed Hausaland bypassed the Kawar for two centuries. The Kawar became a major route again only with the growth of Bornu, which took over the Kawar and Kanem at the beginning of the sixteenth century.

## Aïr

Not far to the west, Islamization spread quickly through the Aïr Mountains, where Muslim burial sites dating from the seventh or ninth centuries have been found near the present-day mining town of Arlit.[26] No descriptions of specific cities are known prior to Ibn Battuta's 1353 portrait of Takedda (Teguidda n'Tesemt, of salt), which should not be confused with the city of Tadmakka (es-Sûk).

Es-Sûk ("the market") was located in the mountainous area of Adrar of the Iforas, "in the middle of gorges and mountains" on the southern edge of the desert and western edge of the highlands of what is today northern Mali, around 40 miles northwest of Gao. It was a large, ancient Berber market that had been used as a way station for caravans since antiquity; rock paintings of chariots have been found there. The earliest written record of it is by Ibn Hawqal, dating from 973–75. It was also described by Al-Bakri in the eleventh century and by Ibn Said in the thirteenth century.[27] "Well-known to travelers and mentioned in books," "better built than Gana and Kaw-Kaw [Gao]," it was the city that "most closely resembled Mecca." It seems to have converted to Islam a few years after Ghana, at the very beginning of the twelfth century,[28] but according to Ibn Said, it was already Islamized at the time of Al-Bakri. The ruins that remain today seem to be highly structured and include the traces of two mosques, but nothing has yet been dated. The city linked Gao with Wargla by way of a 50-day walk, and from Wargla the road led to Kairouan. Plausible local tradition, recorded in an Arab manuscript, reports that the city was founded by blacks but occupied and developed by Sanhadja Berbers from the south. Did they cohabit with Arab traders? It seems that there were at most caravans passing through.[29]

Takedda was very different. Vertical aerial photographs show that the city was linked with an agricultural countryside.[30] The houses were built of red stone.[31] Takedda had a *qadi* (preacher and schoolmaster). In other words, living off caravan traffic and the leather industry and trade, it played an important intellectual and religious role. The mosques may have been built before 1515 and seem to have been the "most ancient mosques with adobe minarets in the southern Sahara."[32] Since it was at the crossroads between the north and south, Takedda seems to have been the path such architecture followed as it spread through the Sahel. At the end of the fifteenth century, the city became home to a reformer, or rather a vigilant defender of the orthodoxy, of Algerian origin: he was Abu Abdullah Muhamed, known as Al-Maghidi, who was a great traveler in the tradition of educated Muslims. He was born in the Tlemcen region around 1425 and, after having traveled through the Tuat and Aïr, where he visited Agades and Teguidda, went to Katsina and Kano in Hausaland. In Kano, he fought against the remnants of paganism and wrote a treatise on government. It is clear that he influenced the architecture of the mosque in Agades and perhaps also of those in Jenne and Gao, since he ended his career in Gao, where he wrote an epistle to the Askiya Muhammad.[33]

Teguidda was still notable in the sixteenth century for its famous local jurists. It has been associated with the ruins of Azelik, ten miles northeast of Teguidam-Tessoum. However, because it came into conflict with Agades when the sultan moved there in the mid-fifteenth century, it lost its economic dominance. It was finally destroyed by the sultan in 1561 and part of its intelligentsia moved to Agades, while the rest scattered across the Aïr.

### Agades, Capital of the Aïr and First Muslim Metropolis

Agades was undoubtedly the most famous city in the Aïr. It seems to have been founded in the eleventh century[34] and had a mixed population of Sudanese blacks, people from Gobir and Zarma, and the ancient Tuareg core. Until the fifteenth century, it remained modest and off the major caravan routes, although it was already developing its dye works. Its role changed in mid-century, when it became the seat of the sultanate that had been instituted in the Aïr in 1405 by the Sandal tribes, who had established themselves as a "privileged group bound by a pact" and acted as the guardians of a kind of federation. The sultan, who had been elected under their control, reorganized the ancient village around his fortified palace. The city's position was more advantageous for relations with the south, and more easily supplied than the previous centers, Maranda and Takkeda, because it was located in a plain, two and a half miles from the mountains. The sultan had taxation rights over caravans but paid part of the taxes back to the Tuareg guardians of the routes. Agades thus became a major caravan center south of the Sahara; according to H. Barth, the purely Berber word *agadez* would mean "stop-over" in Tamasheq. It became an economic, cultural, and religious center as well, although it did not find its way into written records until 1526, when Leo Africanus referred to it.[35]

Non-Muslims left the city. It is said that at the time of their departure (fifteenth or sixteenth century), the Aïr Mountains contained 150 mosques and places of worship, of which the most famous were built in the sixteenth century by renowned evangelists and scholars. Agades alone had 70. Each of its quarters had a mosque, and the famous mosque with the Friday minaret, considered "the key to Islam's establishment in the city's daily life," is supposed to have been built in 1515–17.[36] The impetus for building the mosques came from renowned "saints" or religious guides, the most famous of whom was the great builder Zakarya, who is believed to have been born in Ghadames, Sudan, around 1480. It is also possible that he came from Songhai with the askiya Muhammad, whose capital was Gao, which would explain the architectural kinship of the Agades and Gao mosques. The origin of most of the mosques standing today—all in the style later called "Sudanese," despite the Maghrebian influence—would therefore date from this period. There were also many tombs of saints, and a large cemetery.[37] At the beginning of the six-teenth century, Leo Africanus described the city as "the black city that resembles a white city more closely than any other, aside from Walata, and that has houses that are . . . finely constructed in the style of Berber houses because the inhabitants are almost all foreign merchants."[38] The city was surrounded by a wall fifteen feet high and seventeen feet thick. Each of the four doors through the wall was carefully controlled. Inside the walls, there were twenty-four districts, a large marketplace, and sub-urbs. In all, there was space for around 50,000 people, including many artisans who were renowned for leatherwork (tanning and dyeing) and metalwork (copper, silver, and gold), and a very large number of slaves, as well as an army of Tuareg warriors.

A long decline began at the end of the sixteenth century after Gao fell and the number of caravans from Songhai began to diminish. The seventeenth century was a time of incessant war against both the Tu-areg confederations and, in the south, the Gobir. Finally, there were natural catastrophes; the records of some of these have come down to us, including the severe epidemics in 1687–88 and the torrential rains in 1699 that destroyed 300 homes. There were also palace revolutions. At the end of the seventeenth century, the city seems to have been more or less supplanted by Assoderine, much farther to the north of Agades and southeast of Arlit, which begins appearing in texts in the sixteenth century and is mentioned increasingly frequently in the following cen-turies.[39] As soon as the Kel Away tribe came to the area, Assode became their capital and the focus of major commercial trade. Assode, on the fringe of the Aïr, was where the Kel Away stored supplies from the south that they sold to herders, and where their chief, the *Anastafidet*, had his political base and residence.

Over the centuries, however, like Timbuktu and Jenne to the east, Agades maintained a degree of intellectual and religious dominance around a few great masters who in turn trained the future conqueror, Usman dan Fodio, at the turn of the nineteenth century. Nonethe-less, when Heinrich Barth stayed there in October 1850, Agades truly seemed abandoned. The surrounding wall had disappeared in places and was threatening to collapse in others. The southern districts were completely deserted, and only 600 to 700 houses were still inhabited, suggesting that the population was only 7,000, including slaves. Only 200 to 300 children aged seven to ten were going to the fewer than ten schools still operating, and only ten mosques were still open, al-though Barth estimated that one house out of three had a second floor and that overall the city was not poor.[40] When the Foureau-Lamy mission arrived in 1899, only traces of the ancient surrounding wall could be found, three-quarters of the houses were in ruins, the palace and great mosque had been seriously damaged by rain, and only 5,000 inhabitants remained.[41]

The last disaster in the long decline occurred during World War I, at the time of the bloody repression that followed a threat of rebellion. The French column sent from Zinder hacked to death the marabouts of Agades, who had gathered in the two main mosques to request peace. This was the end of Agades' influence. The few residents who survived deserted the city, which, after the deadly epidemics of Spanish flu in 1918 and 1920, had a population of only 2,490. While the city retained its earlier prestige, its population had grown to only 5,000 in 1956.

### The Cities of Bornu

Today, it is hard to imagine that Bornu, a semidesert area, was home to cities. Yet from the beginning of the seventeenth century to the 1820s, it was the most direct terminus for the trans-Saharan route from Fezzan.[42]

The site of Garumele, fifteen miles southwest of N'Guigmi and less than half a mile from the main road today, may have been the capital of the Sefuwa kings of Kanem-Bornu before they moved to Birni N'Gazargamu at the end of the fifteenth century.[43] The city wall was nearly two miles in circumference. It finally disappeared in 1838, but its red bricks were still being used half a century later, in particular to build the home of the *commandant de cercle* (or French local colonial officer) of N'Guigmi. At its height, the capital city, Birni N'Gazargamu, founded in 1470, may have had up to 200,000 inhabitants. Of course, there is some debate over whether they were simple citizens or soldiers, for according to the chronicle of the reign of Idriss Alaoma (1564–76), holy war, actually based on systematic pillaging of neighbors who were put into slavery, had reached its peak.[44] Was it a city or a military camp? The chronicle's translator constantly uses the former term regarding the narratives of conquest, for example, "four Jarma cities" and other sieges of "cities." While some doubt may remain regarding other centers, the capital does seem to merit this appellation, especially in the centuries that followed.

Indeed, in order to counter the temptations of conspiracy, the *Mai* of Bornu required that all dignitaries (the only exception was the *galadima* of Nguru) and members of the court live in the capital city. Thus, the capital contained all of the ruling class, including the royal family, many free titled men, and royal slaves. The city was a formidable political and military center but also became a major market, since it was located at the terminus of the trans-Saharan route linking Bornu with Tripolitania via the Kawar and Fezzan. It seems to have had four Friday mosques, each of which could accommodate 12,000 worshippers. The city's famous ulemas also ensured that it played a significant role in spreading Islam in surrounding areas, particularly at the end of the seventeenth century and into the eighteenth century. The wall surrounding the city was 25 feet high and more than one mile in circumference, with five entrances. As elsewhere in Bornu, the preferred construction material prior to Islam was red brick. The main building was probably the royal palace, and the mosque was located next to it. These were both surrounded by the homes of dignitaries. Many large streets extended from the esplanade (here called *dendal*), typical of sub-Saharan cities, and these were linked by as many as 660 roads, if we are to believe one visitor.[45] As elsewhere, the rest of the buildings were made of straw and adobe. Unfortunately, we have no precise descriptions of the city because at the beginning of the nineteenth century, after the Fulani assault during Usman dan Fodio's jihad, the devastated capital was replaced by Kukawa.[46]

## The Great Desert Ports: Timbuktu, Jenne, and Gao

According to Ibn Battûta (reported in 1356) and Ibn Khaldûn (1375–82), the growth of the Arab-influenced Sudanese style was due to the Andalou architect Al-Sahili, also known as Tuwayjin, who was brought from Cairo when the mansa Musa of Mali returned from his pilgrimage, which took place in 1324–25. The architect moved to Timbuktu, where he died in 1346, but his descendents lived in Walata. Through his artistry and the wide-ranging cultural tastes that resulted from his travels throughout the Mediterranean, he popularized imported techniques in the cities of the Mali Empire. He was, however, certainly not the only proponent of an architectural style that would have been transferred nearly unchanged from North Africa, despite this representation, popularized by ancient Arab sources and uncritically repeated by Heinrich

Barth, Maurice Delafosse, and later European historians. This idea of an Arab architectural model having been imported does not fit with the cultural realities.[47] The only monument that is definitively attributed to Al-Sahili is the palace reception hall in the capital of Mali.[48]

Clearly, Arab influence over urban forms was more diffuse, more ancient and more varied. The progression and chronology of Islamized urbanism must be studied. For example, should we attribute, as Monteil plausibly does, Jenne's architecture and the decorated façades that are so characteristic of its doors (framed with pilasters and crowned with a canopy) to Moroccan influence in the seventeenth century, a relatively late period?[49] Or is there a distant heritage reflected in the long tradition of building with unbaked round bricks that was favored at the beginning of the Islamization of the Mali Empire? Moreover, did mosques with minarets really spread from the Aïr to the Niger? We do not know. In any case, archaeology suggests that Islamization, which remained an almost exclusively urban, political, and mercantile phenomenon throughout the whole period, did not follow a linear progression. The king of Ghana seems to have converted to Islam toward the end of the eleventh century. However, as Al-Bakri reminds us, this diplomatic and international influence extended to only one district of the capital. Later, between the twelfth and fourteenth centuries, the political and therefore urban decline of this corner of West Africa was, as in Awdaghust, apparently accompanied by a general decline of Maghrebian influence.

We have more information on the rapid, major impact of Muslim culture in the urban, political, commercial, and intellectual centers in the loop of the Niger. Muslim influence probably increased following Mansa Musa's glorious trip to Cairo and Mecca. Mansa Musa's extravagant wealth in gold was a revelation for the Mediterranean Arab world. Medieval Islam reached its height in Africa in the sixteenth century, before the fall of Gao. If we include the Moroccan period in the seventeenth century, its peak lasted at most two or three centuries, until the Tukolor marabout renaissance. In any case, this is the period best known to us, thanks to local chronicles written in Arabic by African scholars of Timbuktu, who began to transcribe former oral traditions at the end of the sixteenth century, although they are supposed to relate much more ancient events.[50]

Because there has been little archaeological research in these great cities, researchers have concentrated most of their attention on the cultural diffusion and conservatism of the three great metropolises traditionally considered, at least schematically, to be dominated respectively by trade (Jenne), politics (Gao), and intellectual life (Timbuktu).[51]

What cannot be challenged is the existence of a complex urban system based on the articulation of several complementary centers that tailored their activities according to which caravan routes were open; that in turn depended on the political and military balances of the day. Between the fourteenth and sixteenth centuries, the structure and focus seem to have moved from the Jenne-Timbuktu and Timbuktu-Walata pairs to Timbuktu and Gao.

### Timbuktu: A Colony of Islamized Scholars

Was Timbuktu as glorious as the Ta'rikhs suggest? Almost all of the ancient African writings in Arabic were by educated inhabitants of Timbuktu, and there probably was a temptation to write hagiography, particularly given competition from other cities and the decline in the seventeenth century, when it was good to remember past glories. Nonetheless, even though a very small number of texts from the educated inhabitants of Timbuktu have come down to us, the city was both more cosmopolitan and more receptive to northern influence than other cities. This was because it was located at the northernmost point of the Sudanese Sahel and the loop of the Niger, which was convenient for merchants from both the north and the south. It was also within range of Walata, which was isolated by sand, and Jenne, which was isolated by the river. According to tradition, Timbuktu was founded by a group of Berber nomads from the north and was then integrated into the great Manding empire in Mali in the fourteenth century. The Ta'rikhs give the mansa Musa credit for founding the great mosque and sending students to Fez when he returned from pilgrimage. Thus, under a strong northern influence, this was the beginning of the training of scholars: Berbers from the Sahel and the Sahara, Arabs from Maghreb and even the Orient, and Arabic-speaking scholars from Sudan. The Tuareg occupation in the fifteenth century encouraged this trend by enabling the city to get ahead of its rival, Walata, so that in 1469, when Sonni Ali made the city part of the Songhai empire, its Arab-influenced intellectual dominance could not be challenged.

However, this went hand in hand with intense commercial activity. Timbuktu was also described as a great trading center. It was the terminus for caravans, since camels could not cross the flooded river basin, where the only means of transportation was the pirogue. Arabs and Berbers brought thousands of camels to Timbuktu every year, from Marrakech, Meknès, Fez, and Tlemcen through the Tafilelt or the Dra, and from Tunis, Tripoli, and Egypt by Ghadames. They brought Mediterranean and Eastern goods, particularly salt from Teghaza and later from Taoudeni. Leo Africanus, who crossed the region between 1512 and 1514, described it as a busy city with about 70,000 inhabitants. Mody Cissoko[52] inferred a lively view of the local ruling class and bourgeoisie of major traders, often of Maghrebian origin, who had been living in the city for two or three generations and were linked with all the major centers in the Sahel. They belonged to the same social category, and even the same families, as the scholars whose prosperity they assured. Like the merchants, some ulemas willingly engaged in trade in slaves drained off the southern part of West Africa.

These notables, of whom there was probably only a handful, lived in different quarters, according to ethnic and religious affinity, neighboring the common people, many of whom were surely slaves. In the north, Sankoré was mainly Berber; the Sudanese had their homes largely in the south, and people from Tuat lived in the quarter near the great mosque, along with a few Arab theologians who had been invited from Egypt and Mecca. The city's elite became culturally mixed, resulting in the emergence of famous Manding and Soninke theologians from Jenne, Mali, Mosi, and elsewhere.

In addition to accidents of history, the preponderance of Arab-Berber and mixed ulemas who were resolutely turned toward Islamic values helps to explain why the city was more or less abandoned as soon as direct pressure from the Mediterranean ceased. Already, at the time of their conquest in 1591, the Moroccans were disappointed because they did not find the opulence they had expected, and they contented themselves with pillaging the city. However, in the end, they dealt it a death blow by deporting to Morocco those of its intellectuals who obstinately refused to submit to their rule. They left standing only a citadel, of which no traces now remain, and the fiction of a pasha, the last of whom was appointed by Morocco in 1604. Under the Moroccans' vague domination, Timbuktu never regained its celebrated luster.[53] Despite its mosques and quarters divided by ethnic, social, and occupational group, the Arab-style architecture was obscured by local traditions, since permanent, one-story houses were surrounded by "very low walls so that from outside one could see what was going on inside."[54] In the nineteenth century, when René Caillié discovered the city, he was also surprised to find so few traces of the legendary splendor described in Arab literature, although he noted that trade still reigned supreme and that there were many slaves and poor people living in straw huts.[55]

In fact, as a center of Muslim culture, Timbuktu had remained marginal in the sub-Saharan world. Its intellectuals were a product of the city, and their future remained linked to the city alone. Despite their work as Arabic-speaking missionaries, they were unable to establish many schools and exported little of the foreign written culture to the rest of the Sudan. Their action was limited in time and space and resembled a colonial settlement more than a merging of cultures. Indeed, the cultures merged only in the nineteenth century, when black Islam became popular. However, by then, Timbuktu had long lost its Maghrebian wealth. In 1928, Paul Morand described it in very sad terms:

> The city is no bigger than a big Negro village. Uniform in its geometry, flat, all that emerges from it are administrative buildings and the three mosques with gray nougat towers covered in wood studs, like fetishes pierced by nails. There are ruins, garbage and refuse everywhere. The walls are collapsing, sometimes the gaps have been filled by wickerwork of straw and reeds .... Where are the shining domes, the bags of gold and the ivory of the caravans that we read about in books?[56]

Toward the middle of the twentieth century, the city had about 40,000 inhabitants who spoke a mixture of Tamashek, Arabic, and Songhai (the latter strongly crossed with Arabic). It did not much resemble ancient Timbuktu, the ruins of which were twice as large as the twentieth-century city.[57] Even the architecture criticized by Morand was not original; Caillié spoke of round sun-dried bricks covered with kneaded clay, materials identical to those used in Jenne.

### Gao: The Political Center

Paradoxically, while there are some works on the Songhai Empire of Gao, we are reduced to conjecture when it comes to the history of its capital city, because it did not have a local chronicler, and little archaeological research has been done.[58] The lack of a chronicler suggests that historically Gao is more closely linked to the sub-Saharan world than is Timbuktu. Certainly, a number of Arab-Maghrebian sources claim that Gao was infused with Islam very early, by the second half of the eighth century, with renewed contact in the following centuries. By the end of the tenth century, Kaw-Kaw, as Gao was then known, had a Muslim ruler and was divided into two districts, one on each side of the River Niger. On the left bank, there were markets, and on the right bank were the fortified palace and mosques.[59] The city was already the capital of a kingdom at the beginning of the twelfth century.

Songhai traditions contradict this Muslim origin and describe Gao as a native creation. The little that we know suggests that it is an ancient city, which is not surprising since toward the end of the first millennium BCE, after all, the "chariot route" of the central Sahara went from Fezzan to a location somewhere near Gao.[60] Gao was probably maintaining peaceful relations with the north long before Islam arose and later welcomed Muslim merchants and permitted them to practice their religion.

Whatever previous contact there may have been, Sonni Ali, who created the Songhai Empire in the second half of the fifteenth century and conquered Timbuktu in 1468, was a black king from the area, and had been raised in an animist, rural culture. "A warrior who had just conquered the greatest Sudanese Empire at the expense of decadent Mali, he gave little consideration to white men, whom he had known only as marabouts, traders and herders."[61] The chroniclers portray him as not especially devout, and he did not fulfill the five duties of a faithful Muslim. Thus, there is every reason to presume not only a late, tolerant cohabitation of two cultures but also the predominance of animist populations and practices, which were described as "magic" by the purist detractors from Timbuktu.[62]

It was only with the coup in 1493, which led to the rise of the askiya Muhammad, that Gao resolved to "play the Muslim card" in a spirit of competition and domination with respect to Timbuktu. Unlike Timbuktu, however, Gao remained fundamentally a political capital of sub-Saharan Africa. Since it was located on the fringe of the flow from the north, it was able to consolidate its regional role by governing a largely uniform population of farmers, hunters, and fishers. It integrated cultural contributions from elsewhere only gradually, which meant a more balanced assimilation and a slower, sounder diffusion of new values. Between the sixteenth and eighteenth centuries, it was Gao, not Timbuktu, that at least partially spread the Muslim heritage to the Hausa cities that flourished to the east after its conquest by the Moroccans in 1591.

### Jenne: The Aboriginal Focus of Cultural Diffusion

To an even greater extent than Gao, Jenne was from the beginning an integral part of the pre-Islamic sub-Saharan world. The city was both isolated by and rooted in the River Niger, although Islamization changed its focus toward the end of the twelfth century or beginning of the thirteenth century. It was virtually unnoticed by the Arab world, since the caravans stopped at Timbuktu, yet it survived much longer and better than Timbuktu did because it was well integrated in the region that had given rise to it before the arrival of the Maghrebians:

There, in the middle of a vast desert, as if everything living had taken refuge on the island, there is a city like a sharply defined fortress of one- or two-story houses built in a style that immediately catches the eye . . . . The hundreds of multi-leveled terraces have an eastern air, and people can already be seen bustling about, calling to one another, from one home to the next. The focal point is the mosque, with three towers in the shape of truncated cones, attesting to the power that inspired the work of art . . . . In the interior of Africa, there is an extraordinary city that has survived intact since the Middle Ages, preserved in the homogeneity of its architecture. By what miracle was this city spared the destruction of time, conquests and modernization?[63]

In fact, Jenne was sheltered by a huge interior delta flooded with water six months a year, which protected it from almost all assailants. According to local traditions, it was able to resist 99 sieges, and its only conqueror, Sonni Ali, was able to maintain control of it for only seven years.

Timbuktu settled for being Jenne's port. Jenne was an exceptional market because it concentrated and distributed over most of West Africa all that arrived in Timbuktu, which was located on almost the same meridian. Through Timbuktu, it received salt in particular, which was extremely rare in the interior of the continent but was absolutely necessary for human health. It also received copper and blue and red fabric; red clothes were so rare that in a number of societies, such as in the Congo, they became the prerogative of chiefs. The goods were carried by hundreds of pirogues that navigated the river and offloaded onto camel caravans at Timbuktu. The *Ta'rikh al-Fattash* tells us that, when the Moroccans arrived, there were at least 2,000 pirogues in the vicinity of Gao.

When the Portuguese arrived on the coast in the fifteenth century, they gathered information about the Niger trade and cities to the north to help themselves gain access to the gold trade. Salt from the Sahara arrived in Timbuktu in large blocks at the rate of two per camel. In Timbuktu it was broken into pieces and taken down the Niger by pirogue (probably Songhai) to Jenne, where it was worth twice its weight in gold. In the port of Jenne, one can still see pirogues that look much as they did in the past. They are around sixty-five feet long, able to carry twenty tons, and built in two parts, front and back, that are sewn together in the middle. They have a semicircular roof made of mats, and the prow is decorated with multicolored geometric motifs.

## The Spread to the South: Begho and the Ghanian Hinterland

Unlike Timbuktu, Jenne was a major center for dissemination of Islamic culture because it was also a center for trade toward the Sahel and into the forested zone, and, from there, gradually toward the coast.

From the beginning of Mali's growth in the thirteenth century, Jenne supplied Timbuktu with gold, which was siphoned off from southern areas. To the south at the time were Mande-speaking groups, which grew strongly in the first half of the sixteenth century and spread toward the west, parallel to the coast, perhaps prevented from climbing toward the interior delta of the Niger by the expansion of the Songhai empire.[64] These groups included a specialized category of merchants: *Jula* ("merchants" in Mande and in Bambara today), who were originally associated with Soninke *wangara*, or gold traders, who spread their networks toward the south, into Manding and Yaarse country.[65]

Gold and kola nuts became of increasing interest to merchants. Gold was brought up from Lobi country along the valley of the Black Volta to some three hundred miles south-southeast of Jenne. With the depletion of the deposits in Bambuk and Bure, in upper Senegal, which had created the wealth of Ghana and Mali, gold probably also came from sediment deposits in the forests of the Ivory Coast and especially the Ofin and Ankobra river valleys, to the south of the future Asante empire, in what is now Ghana. Kola nuts grew naturally in the southern forests of what are now Liberia and Ghana and became increasingly sought after as the Sahel became Islamized, since they were the only stimulant authorized by the religion. Kola nuts came to play a growing role in hospitality rituals and social relations, a little like tea in Mauretania and coffee in Arab countries, because they were both refreshing and stimulating.

If we are to believe Valentim Fernandes,[66] who wrote in 1507, a Wangara merchant could have an annual working capital of $150,000.[67] Since it went hand in hand with their activities, these merchants converted to Islam very early. They were the key factor in the dissemination of Islamic culture from Jenne, which had good links with the south and southeast, as well as east-west contacts via the Niger, and relations with the Sahara via Timbuktu. Transportation dangers forced the merchants to institute a special form of communication, based on the establishment of small Jula colonies along trade routes. The members of the colonies were generally related to one another and set up way stations where they acted as hosts (*diatigi*) and retailers in local and regional markets. In the end, the way of life became so distinctive that the name gained an ethnic meaning.

These Jula are the people who made up the core of the first cities that flourished in the seventeenth and eighteenth centuries in the Akan hinterland, the savanna in immediate contact with the forest and the mineral deposits there. Pacheco Pereira and one of Timbuktu's Ta'rikhs mention some of these trading posts, including in "Toom country,"[68] where Valentim Fernandes reported that trade was the exclusive monopoly of the Wangara (local name for Jula). The Jula presence is also confirmed by archaeology. In the fifteenth century, the Jula were settled to the north of Paya Akan, at Begho (in Jula) or Bighu (in Hausa), today known as Banda, southeast of Kong, in an open area; it was one of the rare passages through the Banda hills and controlled access to the south. Begho became one of the larger market towns, if not the largest, in the basin of the Black Volta. It spread over almost 1.5 square miles and was also a center of Muslim learning. Tradition says that it had remarkable architectural monuments in the form of mosques. The bones of horses, which must have come from the north, have been found on the site. Apparently, the Moroccans already knew of Begho in the sixteenth century as a major center for trade in gold and kola nuts.[69] At that time, Begho was already divided, like the cities in the Sahel, into districts that were half a mile to one and a half miles apart. There were at least three: that of the local Akan and Brong populations, that of the Islamized merchants, and that of the Nume artisans, who seem to have had a caste-based society. The presence of the Nume, producing cloth, pottery, jewelry, and glass beads,[70] confirms the relationship between regional activity and long-distance trade: the Mande brought from the north to Begho objects made of copper and brass, beads, indigo and red blankets and silk cloth, spices, and slaves, which they traded for gold and kola nuts produced in the south.

At the crossroads of widely contrasting influences in the seventeenth century, Begho became a major interior storehouse of European manufactured goods. At the time, it had at least 5,000 inhabitants. It seems to have been ruined around 1640 by local wars that resulted in the emergence of the Asante military kingdom. Relatively recent archaeological dating (1989) indicates that there was again a large merchant population toward the end of the seventeenth century, when a revival occurred thanks to the rising Asante supremacy.[71]

About sixty miles to the south, the gold-producing city of Bono-Mansu, capital of the state of the same name, was founded around 1420, according to recently reexamined traditions. In the fifteenth century, it probably experienced similar growth with the expansion of Jula trade, before it was conquered by the Asante in 1722 or 1723. There seem to have been 500 households in the city, or about 5,000 inhabitants, and the city may have had more than 10,000 inhabitants from the end of the sixteenth century to the end of the seventeenth century.[72] The link with the north continued to the west through Bouna, Kong (about 350 miles from Jenne), Bobo Dioulasso (in Mosi country),[73] and Bonduku, which succeeded Begho as the main Jula center in the northwest of Akan country a century later. From there, routes also radiated out into the forest in the Ivory Coast and what is now eastern Liberia.

There were similar links to the northeast. The route from Gonja (sometimes spelled "Gwanja") to Bornu through the north of Yorubaland seems to have been open in 1433–54, when Beriberi (Hausa) traders came to settle in the city that controlled the kola nut–producing area south of the Volta.[74] A few of these cities survived long after the Saharan trade declined. Thus, Shingîti, not far from Ijîl salt sebkha in the Mauritanian Adrar, where the salt industry probably emerged in the tenth or eleventh century, was apparently not known by travelers before the sixteenth century. It only developed religiously and economically during the nineteenth century.[75]

## The Hausa City-States

*Origins*

Today, the Hausa population is one of the largest in Africa. The Hausa speak and write a language that was spread throughout the western savanna through dynamic long-distance trade and are among the most Islamized Africans, although the vitality of pre-Islamic customs and beliefs has remained strong. They share a specific historical-cultural feature, that of walled city-states. This means that each city had its own government and an autonomous ruling class, and the local community was composed of city dwellers and subjects living in a space over which the city claimed exclusive authority. Naturally, this did not exist without friction between neighboring cities of the same language and culture. The largest of the city areas, those of Kano and Zaria, could cover up to 24,000 square miles.[76] The smallest covered no more than a few hundred square miles. Tradition says there were at least five, and perhaps six or seven, "mother cities": Kano, Katsina, Daura, Gobir, and Zazzau (today Zaria), plus Gobir and Biram (in Bornu), along with a number of smaller ones, which seem to have constantly resisted the large neighboring empires, Songhai to the west and Bornu to the east.

When did this system originate? According to narratives of medieval travelers and texts written in Hausa in the last two or three centuries by Muslim scholars interested in the Arab world, not long ago this was seen as proof of the eastern or even Asian origin of Hausa populations. Tradition even refers to the departure of the son of a king of Baghdad.[77] More recently, an opposing argument has been made in favor of a settlement with ancient roots fostered by an ecological setting that was relatively conducive to a sedentary lifestyle in the heart of a relatively fertile area with sufficient rainfall, where grain crops of millet and sorghum could be combined with cotton and indigo manufacturing, livestock raising, and interregional trade.

In fact, the two approaches can be combined: the relative homogeneity of the language and culture indicates that the Hausa spread to the west from the Chad basin not much more than a thousand years ago. This would be consistent with the traditional description of migrations from the east.[78] The initial organization probably began toward the end of the first millennium CE. Archaeological research and oral traditions date to the twelfth century, but the gradually Islamized Hausa culture properly speaking did not flourish until the fifteenth century, when, in addition to interaction with Kanem and Bornu, regular contact was established with Mali through the intermediary of Mande-speaking travelers and merchants, who settled in peaceful colonies in the cities. Only the courts of the rulers received Muslim advisors, or even converted, whereas the rural populations were influenced very little.[79] The Songhai Empire's expansion to the east increased trade. Written sources describe advanced Islamization, at least in certain key groups of the population: the chiefs and the merchants.

### The Time of Prosperity

The cities flourished because they were relatively isolated; relations with the Saharan world were filtered to the west by Songhai and to the east by Bornu. The cities' location allowed them to benefit from the decline of their neighbors and take advantage of currents from the south, yet not suffer directly from European advances. It was mainly in the seventeenth and eighteenth centuries that the Hausa cities asserted their authority regarding their neighbors. Little archaeological research having been done, most of what we know comes from more recently collected traditions that anthropologists had to decipher and interpret.

This was when great markets, such as Kano, came into their own, and Hausa traders began to spread their language and culture toward the west and the south.[80] Classical historiography, which has an implicit preference for organized states and centralized cultures such as Muslim empires, has tended to see the growth of city-states as a sign of a long transition phase, or even as weakness and disorder as opposed to periods of more centralized power. Yet, during that period, local production and long-range trade both intensified. A very specific political system was linked to the scale of the whole. A city that wished to expand did so at the expense of its neighbor, which led to constant rebalancing. What is surprising is that the system lasted so long: almost three and a half centuries, from the sixteenth century to the nineteenth century.

Unlike the great empires that gathered most of their resources from tribute levied on long-distance trade, these tiny agricultural states set their roots in regional growth before linking with international trade. Most people lived in hamlets or very small towns near fields, which were grouped into *gandu*, socioeconomic units based on patrilineal kinship. At the same time, polygamy and frequent divorce reinforced matrilineal ties. These contradictory elements made the social milieu relatively open and especially conducive to the rise of city-states. The social organization integrated the countryside into the city because each Hausa defined himself or herself as belonging to his or her *birni*, in other words, his or her city.[81]

The chiefs also watched over the migrants that prosperity attracted into the city. The interconnection between ritual duties, kinship organization, and control of the land made it possible for the community to retain its identity while incorporating Islam when it appeared in the fourteenth and, especially, fifteenth centuries. The Kano Chronicle, which is probably a compilation of local legends and traditions transcribed around the mid-fourteenth century,[82] says that the first Muslims were the Wangara, Jula gold and kola nut merchants who came from Mali via the Niger River. They seem to have converted Kano's Sarkin around the mid-fourteenth century. The first Maghrebians apparently arrived at the very end of the century and imported *shariah* law. It is probably at Kano that Al-Maghidi, the famous jurist from Tlemcen, wrote a treatise on the duties of princes.

The cities' typical fortifications seem to have been an answer to the need for defense against Bornu, which wanted to impose tribute. Indeed, the cities combined commerce and war. Both offensive and defensive military apparatus became more sophisticated in the sixteenth century. The city walls were made thicker, cavalry was trained (thanks to horses obtained from the north in exchange for slaves), and the number of military chiefs in Kano went from eight in the sixteenth century to fifty-two in the mid-eighteenth century. Muskets and cannons were known in the early seventeenth century. Bornu even imported Turkish instructors to teach soldiers how to use the weapons. The cities not only had to defend themselves against their powerful neighbor but also fight each other and deal with civil wars.

This is why the cities have very different histories. From the fourteenth century to the mid-seventeenth century, Katsina and Kano com-

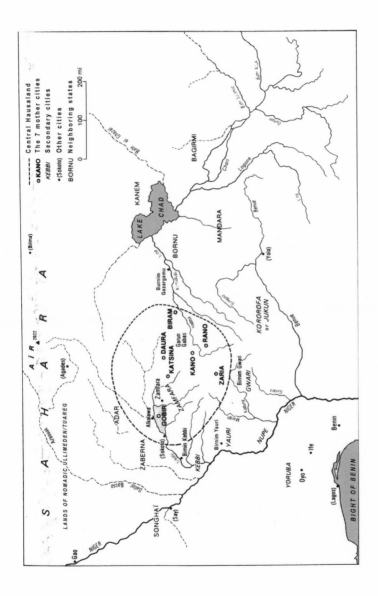

**Map 7. Hausa City-States and Their Neighbors**
Based on: "The Hausa City-States from 1450 to 1804" in R. Griffith et al., eds.,
*The City-State in Five Cultures*, Oxford: Clio Press Ltd., 1981, p. 147

peted with each other for international trade. Zaria, which was a way station for the north's major merchants, tried unsuccessfully to control its southern borders and resist the demands of its neighbor, Bornu. Gobir, undoubtedly the most cosmopolitan city, with colonies of Fulbe, Tuaregs, and other non-Hausa people, grew mainly in the eighteenth century, when it played a crucial role in the spread of Islam; one of its native sons was the Fulani scholar Usman dan Fodio, who came to power in 1807.

At the same time, the growth in productivity in the area, which had agricultural potential, enabled a class of artisans to expand and develop a high level of specialization, particularly among men: dyers, weavers, smiths, leatherworkers, butchers, herbalists, masons, musicians, griots, and so on. At the top of the hierarchy were merchants with highly profitable activities: commission agents, slave traders, lenders. Professions were not necessarily reserved for great families or a specific ethnic group. They were relatively open and constituted a kind of social class. Another special category was that of the highly educated Muslim teachers and their religious officers, the *mallanci* (from the Arabic *'ulema*). However, the noblest profession was that of the political, military, legal, and administrative leaders. It was reserved for aristocratic lineages, a network of protégés, and also slaves and free men who held positions bought with *sarantu* (cowry shells). These bureaucrats were later used by the Fulbe and the British. Finally, given the context, there were probably many slaves. We know that there were slaves in the palace and harem eunuchs; they accounted for perhaps 10 to 20 percent of the population. We have no information on the question prior to Heinrich Barth's explorations of the area in the mid-nineteenth century.

Two cities quickly took the lead: Kano, in strong competition with Katsina, and Zaria, which was more to the south and played a major role in the slave trade owing to its proximity to suppliers and purchasers.

### Kano

Kano, which has remained northern Nigeria's largest metropolis since this period, went through highs and lows at the beginning of its history. This is probably why it was the first to develop an effective army. At the end of the sixteenth century, according to the Kano Chronicle, the city had suffered eleven years of famine, but then it reestablished control over its hinterland and employed slavery to increase local output. At the time, it dominated a network of secondary marketplaces, such as Karmashe and Dirani to the east and Dabi and Birnin Gija to the south. In the sixteenth century, its inhabitants were described as "civilized artisans and wealthy merchants."[83] In the seventeenth century, it became the major market in the area, the terminus of trans-Saharan trade and a center for dissemination of Muslim culture. It continued to face strong competition from Katsina, which the traditions of the end of that century portray as the main commercial and intellectual focal point of northern Nigeria, and where "from all directions there came scholars seeking Arab knowledge.... In particular, if you were looking for Arab books from eastern countries, you found them mostly there."[84]

The Kano Chronicle, of which the first written version dates only to the mid-seventeenth century,[85] emphasizes the reforming and centralizing role played by the ruler Rumfa (c. 1560–c. 1620), who Leo Africanus claims modeled himself after his contemporary, Sonni Ali of Songhai. He not only introduced royal symbols (such as trumpets, ostrich feathers, a royal harem of secluded women) but also innovated by building a citadel to the east of the city that definitively established the location of the royal residence. He fortified the ramparts, using stone and brick to reinforce the ditch and wooden fence. Kano finally gained independence, and its leader took the title of sultan.

This prefigured a change that established the division into two distinct groups: on one hand, the scholars, who were men of prayer traditionally linked with the class of Wangara merchants, whose decline began with the fall of the Songhai empire; and on the other hand, the military chiefs, who gradually became the clear pillars of the regime. The poor economy was an obstacle to the city continuing in its traditional role as a marketplace in the eighteenth century, and the city was taken and pillaged twice at the beginning of the century. Military setbacks and the fall in trade revenue led the sultans to expand their control over the city and strengthen its relationship with the countryside. Thus, slave-based cotton, indigo, and textile production were increased. The city walls were expanded and reinforced. This economic policy made increasingly strong demands on the countryside in the form of greater labor and heavier taxes. Little is known about the details of this organization, but the Chronicle mentions a female dignitary with special responsibility over grain and the collection of sales tax. The luxury of Kano's court suggests the extent of the taxation required.[86] Kano supremacy developed at the same time and in the same way as Kumasi, in spite of their contrasted cultural backgrounds. The capital became the center of a ponderous bureaucracy that focused mainly on collecting taxes (which were levied on everyone, including the scholars in the city) and recruiting a large, cheap labor force for industry and public works.[87] The result of 50 years of this regime was to facilitate the jihad of Usman dan Fodio, who appeared as the liberator of both peasants and Muslim scholars.[88]

Nevertheless, from the sixteenth century to the beginning of the nineteenth century, the population grew from 20,000 to 40,000 inhabitants, who were accommodated comfortably within the walls; apparently only one-third of the space was built upon.[89]

## A Pluralistic Society

It seems that nowhere else was the urban lifestyle so pluralistic. This was because the Muslim rulers were very tolerant of unbelievers, who still made up, at least in the sixteenth and seventeenth centuries, the majority of the population.[90] Before the Fulani jihad, which finally destroyed their system, the Hausa had long been used to living alongside Fulbe (or Boroje) herders. Since the Hausa were farmers and the Fulbe herders, they engaged in complementary trade involving milk, meat, and manure. Until the nineteenth century, however, Fulbe animists continued to obey only their nomadic chiefs, the *ardo*, without really interfering in the urban lifestyle, politics, and culture of their Muslim neighbors.

A shared spoken language with few local variants guaranteed the unity of the whole, and the homogeneity of the language was fostered by its role as an instrument for trade, but tolerance was dependent on very strict social compartmentalization. The highly hierarchized society was conducive to two ethnic groups living together because it protected the *Hausawa*, or full citizens, from the strangers that it welcomed with open arms and who were needed for the society to prosper. In the cities, foreigners remained foreigners, even if they lived there for many years. Slave or caste artisans (such as smiths) passed their specializations and guilds on from generation to generation and had their own hierarchy. Their chiefs represented them in the market and to the political authorities; the head chief was the butchers' representative. The oldest local chiefs in the city stuck stubbornly to ancient patrimonial rules, and also governed the rural production as the *sarki noma* (kings of agriculture). Thus, all activities were oriented toward the capital, the *birni*.

The architecture of Kano had remarkable unity and was probably based on very old models. At the beginning of the twentieth century, an observer, with the help of the city's emir, suggested a chronology of construction techniques, some of which date back to pre-Islamic times, before the fourteenth century.[91] The use of sun-baked clay and the inherited habit of abandoning a home after the death of the head of the household resulted in constant rebuilding. The systematic reconstruction of the fortified walls apparently dates back to the eighteenth century.[92] Some building styles and techniques date from much earlier times, however. These probably include rounded clay bricks, domed roofs supported by columns and arches, and the city doors, which were made of carved wood and decorated with riveted plaques of steel and special locks; the locks have impressed travelers since the beginning of the sixteenth century.[93] The city was, and the heart of the old city has remained, surrounded by massive earthen walls that protected the palace and its mosque, the dignitaries' enclosures, the main marketplace, and a number of quarters, each centered around carefully maintained wells and at least one mosque; the mosque could be simply an arrangement of stones marking the prayer space on the ground or at the heart of a shaded area where the *mallams* taught Koranic school. Specialized districts, in which all the homes were built of earth, were inhabited by citizens, artisans (caste or slave), foreigners, who occasionally doubled the city's population at certain times of the year, and sometimes also by isolated groups such as lepers and blind people. Open spaces were used for agriculture or to house people from the countryside in case of siege. The layout was copied on a more modest scale in provincial towns, or *gari*, each of which was surrounded by defensive earthen walls and had a daily or other periodically held market.

The typical residential unit was also delimited by an earthen wall, which was more elaborate when the inhabitants' social status was higher. The enclosure was closed to outside eyes and the house was tall. The entrance was mazelike in order to ensure the seclusion of women, which was unusual elsewhere in sub-Saharan Africa. Inside, near the entrance, were the lodgings of the young unmarried members of the household; farther from the entrance were the slave quarters, near an enclosure where horses and donkeys were kept. From there, one could reach the large interior courtyard only via a passage with two entrances, which again cut the view. The chief's home was located in the middle of the courtyard, surrounded by the rooms, kitchens, and granaries of his wives. In a roughly concentric circle were located the homes of other heads of family, always surrounded by those of their wives. The bath and latrines were hidden behind mats at the back of the courtyard.

There is every reason to wonder about the links between the previous architecture and that which began developing in the nineteenth century, for, while the walls remained, the Hausa city-state civilization suddenly disappeared at that time. It was destroyed by Usman dan Fodio's jihad. The Hausa-Fulani caliphat, extending far beyond the borders of the former cities, weakened local autonomy, and the British conquest, favorable to centralized indirect rule, succeeded in completely eliminating it at the end of the nineteenth century.

## Swahili Cities

### From Shirazi to Swahili

Stone constructions seem to have appeared on the coast around 950. They may have been the result of Arab influence, although the settlements remained largely pagan until the twelfth century. The first wave of Islamization corresponded to the major flow of Shirazi immigration.[94] The Swahili culture, which covered a strip of the coast extending no more than seven miles into the interior, was then dominated by Islam, had a wealthy class of sea traders, and used stone for building. The introduction of cement revolutionized architecture in the mid-fourteenth century, underscoring the rise to power of the class of merchants whose homes symbolized their status.

Very few written sources exist. Little is known about the emergence of the Swahili language before the Portuguese period; the oldest transcribed poetry dates from 1652. The chronicles, of which the most famous traditional is the Kilwa Chronicle (known through its translations into Arabic and Portuguese), seem to have been composed in the sixteenth century and were initially transcribed into Arabic.[95] A few inscriptions, most of them difficult to read, have been found at Gedi, which means that the spread of literacy was minimal. Our knowledge is based essentially on archaeology. From the coast of Somalia (with the city of Maqdishu or Mogadishu) to the coast of Mozambique, there was remarkable unity in the design of homes, appearance of mosques, and decoration of tombs, especially from the fourteenth century on. The urban architecture reveals a degree of control over space that implies a central authority, a very dense population, and economic specialization of quarters. However, we find neither traces of large public buildings aside from the mosque nor evidence of a marketplace, whose role was probably filled by the port. We do not even find traces of large-scale urban planning. Such planning generally occurred only with colonization, initially by Zanzibar.

## A Coastal Urban Culture

The first Muslim cities were located on islands, forming the archipelago of Lamu, Pemba, Zanzibar, Mombasa, and Kilwa. These sites were obviously chosen to protect traders traveling by sea. The Islamization of the islands was apparently the result of the more or less political and diplomatic conversions of the families governing the city, who were eager to trade with the Arabs. Between the tenth and sixteenth centuries and possibly even for a few of them as early as the end of the eighth century, this Islamization fostered the gradual homogenization of the material culture that came to be known as Swahili.[96]

To the north, along the Somalian coast, is the only example of an extension of this Islamized urban culture into the backcountry. Here there are thirteen sites where the traces of 20 to 200 houses have been identified along the Ethiopian border, between Zeila and Harar. The cities were probably on the fringes of Ethiopian provinces linked to southern Egypt by the Red Sea and perhaps by routes through the interior as well. Chinese porcelain from the twelfth through fifteenth centuries has been found there, and the cities flourished most at the peak of the Swahili period, from the fourteenth to the sixteenth centuries. They were centers of trade in an area that was apparently peaceful at the time, for they are not walled. There is also no evidence of urban planning. To begin with the habitat was very plain; houses had one to four rooms, thick walls, dirt floors, and windows that were simple rectangles for ventilation. The homes were dark, but cool. The architecture shows the virtual impossibility of obtaining beams longer than eight feet locally.

In every location, there are traces of mosques, which were the only buildings for which cement was used; their builders sought a degree of monumentality, using arches and pillars. There are also cemeteries located on the edge of town. Many objects of international origin, such as glass beads, light green Song dynasty celadon ware from China, Egyptian pottery, fragments of glass, and a few pieces of Egyptian money, show that there was an active, open merchant community. The port of Zeila, which was laid siege and occupied by the Ethiopians in 1402, probably played a crucial role. The Island of Saad-Din, off the port and not far from Djibouti, also contains the ruins of many homes, although today it is uninhabited and waterless. In 1503, a traveler described the scope of trade in Zeila and the abundance of gold, iron, and black slaves sold at moderate prices. The Portuguese burned the city in 1516, and the Turks took it the following year. The rest of the country finally fell into the hands of Galla nomads who had come down from the interior. That was the end of this urban episode.[97]

A little farther south, Mogadishu, which the geographer Yaqut had described a century before as the largest city on the coast and as having a colony of foreign Muslims, impressed Ibn Battûta in 1331. When the Portuguese arrived at the beginning of the fifteenth century, the city was still flourishing. It had two-story houses, expansive palaces in the center, and four towers nearby. Here again, the decline was caused both by the

Portuguese occupation and by the fact that nomadic peoples from the interior gradually laid siege to the coast in the seventeenth century.[98]

Still farther south, Pate and Lamu cities were protected by solid walls of stone and mortar and were mostly inhabited by Swahili people who traded actively with the interior. The emergence of these fortified cities seems to have corresponded to upheavals on the continent caused by the intrusion of Somali herders between 900 and 1000 CE, which upset the previous balance.[99] Lamu, like Pate, is built on top of older remains. It seems to have been founded in the eighth century by fishers and sailors from Arabia, at a time when other small city-states were appearing in the archipelago of Lamu. Pate was a small port but had lively relations with southern Arabia and was a "big city" according to a visitor quoted by Nurse and Spear.[100] It was a center known for its silk goods, which the Portuguese exported at great profit to neighboring cities, which had no such industry. Malindi was known for its tall white houses and began exporting iron in the twelfth century. Around 1498, its "king" lived opulently, dressed in damask and satin, sat on a bronze throne with rich cushions, and was surrounded by musicians playing richly worked ivory trumpets.

Gedi, one of the oldest cities, was founded toward the end of the twelfth century. It flourished in the fifteenth century but was abandoned at the beginning of the next century in favor of Mombasa, which was leading the fight against the Portuguese who were allied with Malindi. Resettled by refugees toward the end of the sixteenth century, Gedi became a much smaller city. A few houses were restored, and the whole agglomeration was protected by a new, higher wall. However, the rebirth did not last much longer than a generation because the inhabitants fled, probably in the face of Galla advances.[101] The abandonment of the ruins is an advantage today because they provide a view of what a purely Swahili city was like. We can see the typical architecture of the houses, in which stairs led to the rooms from a courtyard on a lower level behind the façade. The oldest homes had two long rooms in the front with a corner for the toilet, to which were added two smaller rooms in the back, along with a storeroom or strong room, and sometimes a small additional courtyard for servants, most of whom were slaves. There were niches and notches for shelves on walls, and two-level washing benches in bathrooms. The ceilings, made of limestone cement, were generally heavy. The only architectural invention appears in tombs, the eastern façades of which were decorated with 15- to 16-foot-high solid masonry pillars with many different shapes (round, octagonal, square). Should they be given a phallic interpretation? The oldest date back to the thirteenth century and the most beautiful from the fifteenth century. The latter are found nearby, in Malindi. At Gedi, finds mainly include much Chinese pottery, which seems to have begun being imported through India in the ninth century, although no direct connection can be inferred. Thirteenth- and fourteenth-century glass objects with shapes typical of the Arab world, and locally made items, such as kitchen pottery, lamps, jars, turned bowls, and red, blue, yellow, green, and black glass beads, have also been found.

Mombasa, of which the oldest written record is in the work of the geographer Al-Idrisi, who visited it between 1066 and 1110, peaked in the fourteenth and fifteenth centuries. Ibn Battuta went there between 1329 and 1331; at the time, it was inhabited by Sunni Muslims who appeared rather poor to him, despite their beautiful wooden mosques and the relative luxury of their surroundings on the African coast.[102] Arab influence was visible in the houses and mosques also built of rough stone or brick masonry, and especially in the widespread use of porcelain and glazed pottery. However, around the mid-seventeenth century, most of the prominent Swahili families had either disappeared or been replaced by the Portuguese and city dwellers who had fled to Mombasa to escape the Galla invasions and resulting disorder in many areas to the north.[103]

Thanks to the persevering archaeological work by Neville Chittick[104] and to the Kilwa Chronicle, we know most about the chronology of the port of Kilwa in southern Zanzibar on the Tanzanian coast. According to tradition, it was founded at the end of the tenth century by a noble of the reigning Shiraz family.[105] Its growth was a result of its proximity to Sofala, which attracted Zimbabwean and then Mutapa gold to the coast at the rate of about ten tons a year for centuries.[106] The city's pre-Islamic origins probably date back to the eighth century, and Muslim pottery imported from Mesopotamia in the eleventh and twelfth centuries has been found. A new dynasty apparently took power around 1277. There is no archaeological evidence dating the Shirazi before the very end of the twelfth century; nevertheless, later analyses tend to discuss this point and push the chronology a bit further back.[107] The first buildings seem to date from pagan times and were of wood and earth. Stone, in the form of large rough blocks that were bound together using clay mortar, appeared more or less with Islam. Later, limestone-based mortar came to be used, and more stone mosques were built in the twelfth century. At the time, pearl imports from China increased, and commercial links were established with Zanzibar and Pemba. In the second half of the thirteenth century, construction began on the Great Mosque, including the minaret, which was begun in 1269. At the time, Kilwa was overflowing with wealth. The sultan's court in Kilwa was made up of immigrants from the Arab world who left their mark on the architecture, which has obvious similarities to Umayyadian and Abbasidian buildings.[108] The Great Mosque was made even larger, and excavations reveal more and more Chinese pottery and coins from this period. Ibn Battûta described Kilwa as "one of the world's most beautiful cities." It declined in the mid-fourteenth century, perhaps because of the growth of many competing cities, but it rebounded at the beginning of the next century. Two Chinese expeditions reached the eastern coast of Africa in the fifteenth century, and Chinese sources describe the city as having two- and three-story houses.[109] However, political and commercial competition between Arab and western Portuguese and Dutch traders and the prosperity of Mombasa were decisive factors in weakening the city. Finally, in 1505, the Portuguese landed 500 men, who burned the city, built the small fort of Santiago, and prohibited the inhabitants from trading with Sofala. In the nineteenth century, Burton describes Kilwa as abandoned. He says that when he visited, Kilwa had lost even the memory of its beautiful stone houses, mosques, forts, and towers made of coral and limestone cement. It was then simply a conglomerate of wooden huts.[110] All that remained were the blackened ruins of a single mosque and the remains of the tombs of the Shirazi Sheiks.

Toward the end of the fifteenth century, there were therefore about ten independent cities along the coast. The social organization seems to have been based on three main social classes: the ruling classes, made up of merchants of Arab or mixed African ancestry, all of whom were

Islamized; a middle class of landlords, skilled artisans, bureaucrats, and shopkeepers, who were also Islamized; and, finally, a lower class of Africans responsible for domestic and farm labor. The last group surely included many slaves, particularly among the women. There were probably also many foreigners and recent Arab immigrants who were gradually assimilated by the society.

Some of the cities, such as Gedi, Malindi, and Lamu, were prosperous and had some control over the surrounding hinterland. They both benefited and suffered from the confusion reigning in the countryside following the massive descent in the sixteenth and seventeenth centuries of new Oromo invaders from Somalia. The ports provided some protection to the refugees from the interior, who boosted the cities' populations. However, their reciprocal balance was the result of their alliances. Lamu tended to remain linked with its ancient patrons in Somalia and elsewhere, whereas Pate played the Oromo card, which enabled it to assert itself as the regional power. The cities that grew the most were Mombasa and Pate,[111] thanks to better farming conditions and, especially, a safer environment and the fact that they controlled trade between the Persian Gulf and the Indian Ocean, whereas Mogadishu controlled the northern market[112] and Kilwa trade to the south.

This was why the Portuguese vested these coastal cities with authority, thereby making it difficult today to separate the Swahili heritage from later additions. The city-states depended almost exclusively on international trade. The Portuguese conquered all of them between 1500 and 1700. The only one that tried to resist was Mombasa, which the Portuguese had to conquer several times, and where they built Fort Jésu in 1505; its remains can still be seen today.

Archaeology reveals that the cities were dense, with houses that were usually two stories high and built close to each other, often with shared walls and sometimes linked, which suggests that the occupants were related to one another. The alleys were narrow, although the houses often had gardens at the back. The roofs were flat and made of stones placed on square mangrove beams. They were thus heavy, which restricted the sizes of the rooms. The layout did not vary much. A door, which was especially impressive on the side facing the interior, opened onto a courtyard at the end of which there was a reception room, often with a veranda. The rooms were located in the back. There were no windows, aside from those opening onto the courtyard, and the interior was dark. However, the thick ceiling and walls kept the rooms cool, and there were latrines in every house—an exclusively urban innovation.

On the east coast, the undeniably urban but still fairly rough culture maintained the tradition of "colonial" cities: foreign settlers, in numbers large enough to constitute a lineage in the country, continued to produce a creolized culture that later defended itself against and enriched itself through Portuguese influences in the sixteenth century and Indian influences in the seventeenth and eighteenth centuries. This was the case in Lamu, among others, which, in the face of Pate's decline, experienced a kind of rebirth toward the beginning of the eighteenth century, when it had 15,000 to 20,000 inhabitants. This relatively late period was when many of the stone houses were built and architectural and artistic innovations occurred.[113]

We do not know how many people on the coast converted to Islam before 1500. The oldest permanent mosques built using coral cement date from the twelfth century but they are more often from the fourteenth or even sixteenth centuries. There may have been wooden or earthen mosques earlier, but it was definitely later, in response to foreign attacks, that Islam asserted itself as an integral part of Swahili culture. This happened when the insular cities, which served as major storehouses, received the greatest flow of new immigrants fleeing the insecurity inland caused by the expansion of the Galla nomads and the ambitions of newcomers from the Indian Ocean. Thus, a complex amalgam was established to enable Swahili culture to gain a foothold on the continent. The small coastal city-states lived in symbiosis with their immediate neighbors (*bara*), who ensured their subsistence through fishing and various activities such as raising produce, livestock, and crops on farms (*mahonde*) located a few miles from the city walls; the farms were tended by rural subjects and often supervised by a city dweller. More than ever, the population became a mixture of people with Arab ancestry and less cultivated Bantu-speakers (*shungwayana*), who nonetheless pledged their solidarity with the former in the name of a shared religion and claimed an identity based on a myth of shared exotic origin: the ancient Shirazi.

Arabs and free locals thus came to subscribe to a common culture called *uungwana*. The *waungwana*, the elite of real citizens who all ended up more or less related to each other, claimed ancient urbanity and were careful to ensure that their daughters did not lose their rank. In sum, they were a cultivated merchant bourgeoisie that had more or less become a caste. They lived in multilevel stone houses and secluded their wives; their political life, material culture, and scholarship, ruled by the common Friday great prayer and the attendance at Koranic schools, were based on Islam rather than ancient kinship ties and oral traditions. However, Arab-African fusion was characterized and promoted by the highly differentiated roles of men and women in urban society. Men often came from outside, were Islamized and literate; in other words, they were waungwana in the strict sense. Women were usually of local, often slave, origin and were African and illiterate—that is, *wanawake*. This gave rise to a mixed language within the framework of a society strictly controlled by men.[114] The very way that the language was made reveals its mixed origin: local Bantu adopted Persian words and, later, an Arabic vocabulary. For example, the words *koma*, *mizimu*, and *pepo*, used to designate ancestral, natural, and evil spirits, all derive from proto-Swahili or proto-Sabaki (Bantu) words, as do most terms referring to village life, farming, and fishing. In contrast, terms linked with Islamic concepts and institutions in religious, legal, and commercial fields derive from Arabic.[115]

The local culture reached its peak between the sixteenth and eighteenth centuries. Until the beginning of the nineteenth century, Lamu was a kind of republic, where power was based on wealth and number; a council of elders representing the main districts was presided over by an individual with executive power who was chosen more or less alternately from the two leading families.[116] This way of life was gradually eliminated as the waungwana were absorbed into the more resolutely Arabized culture (*ustaarabu*) imposed in the nineteenth century by both Zanzibar's domination of trade and the development of the Qadiriyya along the interior caravan routes.[117] This late change was part of the second "urban revolution" that occurred at that time.

# 5

# The Atlantic Period

Mina Castle in the Portuguese time

Collection of the publisher

*Chapter 5*

---

# The Atlantic Period: From the Sixteenth Century to the Eighteenth Century

Western influence on the architecture of coastal cities is obvious today, with respect not only to recent urbanism but also to what is usually described as colonial architecture. This chapter shows the extent to which this architecture is actually rooted in the period prior to colonization. Colonizers certainly used, adapted, and, in the nineteenth century, spread and codified "veranda houses," which had superior ventilation. Despite their dilapidation, many old colonial cities still have elegant streets with verandas and balconies, which only rarely date from before that period. These include St. Louis in Senegal, Grand Bassam in Ivory Coast, Porto Novo in Benin, Bathurst in Gambia, Mombasa and Dar es-Salaam on the Indian Ocean, and the ancient island of Mozambique (now linked with the mainland) not far from Nampula. Similar cities can be seen elsewhere, such as Port Haiti, where Christopher Columbus landed, and Jacmel, in Haiti, formerly Saint Domingue; Ormuz in the

Persian Gulf; Goa off the Indian subcontinent; and Salvador de Bahia in Brazil. The similarities put us on the track of a theme that has not yet received enough attention: the architecture's extraordinary spread around the time of great discovery, when the colonizing lords of the seas were neither the British nor the French but sailing people from the Iberian Peninsula, particularly the Portuguese, who explored the coasts of Africa.

This chapter will focus especially on the dissemination of cultural models, often in relation to urban domestic architecture. We will not focus too much on Europe's direct influence on the coasts of Africa since the fifteenth century. It is obvious and has been studied in relative detail. We know much less about how people in the hinterland, who were affected only indirectly by the West, were able to profit from the economic and cultural changes that resulted from the European exploration. For several centuries, particularly before the ravages of the slave trade began to dominate in the eighteenth century, mercantile societies and urban networks grew and flourished in a manner that was specifically African. Little known until recently, African urban development in the sixteenth and seventeenth centuries contains many surprises. The few examples available reveal a lifestyle that mixed its own roots with features from elsewhere, such as the Arab northern Mediterranean and the Atlantic world, to produce a veritable urban civilization.

## Before the Slave Trade

Our discussion will be guided by the fact that contact with Europeans has to be periodized. The stereotype that identifies European contact with the slave trade alone is simply mistaken. Certainly, slaves were traded from the beginning, but in a limited and, economically, secondary manner until the mid-seventeenth century, at least. The reason for this is well known: the demand for slave labor grew out of a specific economic project, namely the expansion of sugar cane plantations in the New World. This began in Brazil in the second half of the seventeenth century, spread to Jamaica and Barbados in the British West Indies toward the end of the century and to Guadeloupe, Martinique, and especially Saint Domingue in the French West Indies in the first half of the eighteenth century. From there it continued on to Cuba, the main sugar cane producer at the turn of the nineteenth century. Finally, when the slave trade was officially prohibited, demand came from cotton plantations in the southern United States. The slave trade almost exclusively dominated relations between Europe, Africa, and America from about 1680 to 1830, but especially in the eighteenth century, when it is estimated that half of all slaves were shipped across the Atlantic. Before then, economic relations with Africa were more complex and certainly more dynamic than destructive, unlike later developments. This break therefore has to be taken into account, since it had major repercussions on internal urban history.

## Coastal Forts

Coastal forts flourished with the slave trade, but they existed before that time, and the pioneer period will be our focus here.[1] It took the Portuguese more than half a century to explore the coast of Africa, from the time they rounded Cape Bojador off Morocco and came to Arguin Island on the southern edge of the Sahara in 1443, until they rounded the Cap des Tempêtes (Cape of Storms), rechristened Cape of Good Hope by Vasco de Gama in 1498. The slow progression was accompanied by the establishment of a series of small coastal settlements designed less to establish a foothold on land than to secure supplies and trade for later expeditions.

The extreme case was the Cape Verde Islands. When the Portuguese arrived between 1460 and 1462, they found only a scattered population that was too small to oppose their settlement. Portuguese settlers began arriving in force in 1466, when King Affonso V granted a charter to his brother, who had received the islands as a gift, and a few privileged Portuguese and Italians, provided they were Christian. The charter gave them control over all the "Moors, Blacks and Whites, free and slave" on the Guinean coast from the Senegal River to Sierra Leone, and the right in perpetuity to conduct commerce and trade in slaves. This promoted intense trade between the coast of Africa and Europe and the

West Indies; the Cape Verde archipelago acted as a way station. Ribeira Grande (today Cidade Velha), the major city in the archipelago, was chosen as the hub of transatlantic navigation, port of call, and supply and storage center because it was a sheltered port at the mouth of a wide river. A century later, it was a flourishing little *vila*, seat of the *capitania generale* and the bishop's palace, and had several churches, a treasury, a trading post, and many European homes and warehouses. The colonial settlement was built using stone imported from Portugal, a material that became typical of Portuguese forts on the coast. It had a square and a *pelurinho*, or exhibition column for public punishments, and was protected by a bastion and walls. It attracted settlers, traders, and adventurers, as well as nobles, knights, and "honest men" from Portugal, who came to seek their fortune.[2] It had approximately 500 inhabitants, who in turn had 5,700 slaves.[3] As the slave trade grew in the mid-seventeenth century, Praia, a port of call since 1515, took Ribeira Grande's place as the archipelago's leading city.

On the African coasts, properly speaking, Portuguese settlements were usually much smaller, but a distinction has to be made between the west coast, where forts were built using whatever materials were available, and the east coast, where the Portuguese conquered and then used settlements that were already heavily involved in trade on the Indian Ocean. In the sixteenth century, they gradually took over the posts that had until then been visited by Arabs, from the Island of Mozambique, over which they disputed bitterly with the Dutch in the following century, to Zanzibar, Pemba, and Mombasa in the north.

Despite the Portuguese monopoly proclaimed by the pope at the beginning of the sixteenth century, other European countries were eager to compete in trade, and soon became "interlopers," particularly in the west. In the next two centuries, when every European state competed avidly with its neighbors through a special national chartered company, at least nine western nations were involved at various periods and with different degrees of success.[4] The result was that the coasts bristled with settlements, which have rarely been studied as a whole.[5]

While forty-three major forts have been counted along the West African coast, from Arguin to Whydah (therefore excluding Nigeria[6]), the total number of settlements was actually much higher. The Mine Coast, renowned for gold, was the major point of interaction and competition among European traders. Thirty-two forts were built between 1482 and 1784 on a stretch of coast barely two hundred miles long, and if secondary posts are included, there were over a hundred. Many forts and posts changed hands several times, often as a result of European trade wars elsewhere. Thus, the fort of Elmina, founded by the Portuguese in 1482 as São Jorge da Mina, and that of Santo Antonio de Axim, first built between 1503 and 1506 and then moved in 1552 following a quarrel with the local people,[7] both experienced a Dutch period before Elmina was finally occupied by the British. Off Cape Verde, Gorée Island was taken and retaken about ten times, sometimes for only a few months, between the seventeenth and nineteenth centuries.[8] The question we are considering here is to what extent the forts influenced the real and theoretical development of the area's cities. The forts' role was economic, commercial, and cultural. They enabled merchants from the interior to come into contact with Europeans; for example, the Asante dealt with the coastal forts a hundred years before the first British mission reached their capital, Kumasi, in 1817.

It is clear that Western influence sometimes penetrated considerably beyond the settlements on the coast and nearby navigable rivers, despite Europeans' inability to acclimatize farther inland. From Axim, a major outlet for gold, the Dutch traveled up the Ankobra "in places where no one of our nation had ever put foot," and, in 1659, even rebuilt in stone the little fort that they had established there.[9] Every new wave of foreign competition (Brandenburgian in 1683, French in 1702, and English in 1756) led to a redefinition of Fort St. Antonio's jurisdiction. Likewise, in more or less every location, power tended to extend far beyond the settlement's walls. The cultures interacted for almost five hundred years. Should we conclude, like Lawrence, that "[I]n all history there is nothing comparable with the effects produced by the forts of West Africa; nowhere else have small and transitory communities of traders so changed the life of alien people who surrounded them, and indirectly of a vast region beyond"?[10] This tends to be confirmed by what we know about the Creole languages and cultures that developed there. But what were the chronology and crucial factors?

## Feudal Architecture

After Arguin, which simply stagnated, the first fort on the African coast of which there are still remains was Elmina in 1482. The last fort was built in 1784 and rebuilt in 1847, at a time when the very principle underlying such architecture had faded away. The purpose was to establish posts with economic and military goals that were so closely interwoven that it was impossible to tell which were most important. A post's *raison d'être* was lucrative export trade, which had to be protected from competitors. At that period of mercantile capitalism, competition came more from other Europeans (foreign charter companies and the growing ranks of interloping merchants, who were sometimes very rich and powerful) than from local inhabitants. Competition was so fierce that some places had three or four forts of different nationalities. Thus, the king of Abomey, who had come to rule over the coast through the conquest of 1727, recognized three main forts established at Whydah in the preceding century: the French fort, dating from 1671, apparently after Colbert sent a delegation to the king of Allada;[11] the Portuguese fort established in 1680; and the British fort, Fort William. Naturally, each fort kept a close watch on the others.

The word "fort" quickly lost its purely military connotations and became a leftover from the period of discovery. In most cases, the forts had been converted into private establishments and were run by merchants by the seventeenth century. The merchants had small teams of employees and sometimes a garrison for defense, but they depended on neighboring communities for labor and supplies. Generally, not only was the fort built with the agreement of the river chiefs, but the land on which it was situated remained the property of Africans to whom rent was paid. Pillaging may have occurred, but these conditions made it quite rare. It is true that slave stocks gradually grew, and sometimes had to be held for several months in coastal barracoons, which required strict security. The surrounding Africans thus became increasingly subservient to the European nation that dominated the coast. However, the transition to protectorate status was slow and occurred late. It did not take clear form until the end of the precolonial nineteenth century. Aside from Portuguese control over the Cape Verde Islands and the Luanda hinterland as of the sixteenth century, the English colonies on the Cape and in Natal in South Africa in the nineteenth century, and the special case of the British Crown Colony created in 1807 on the Sierra Leone peninsula to accommodate slaves freed from slave ships, the earliest example is that of the Fante on the Gold Coast, the future Gold Coast Colony, in the second quarter of the nineteenth century.[12]

Prior to that time, trading posts had to get along well with the surrounding people in order to survive. They supplied the posts with labor, slaves, and, of course, the food required for survival, despite reserves from Europe that, theoretically, were sufficient for as long as a year or more.[13] In exchange, the fort provided Western goods and protection in time of trouble. A large interior courtyard offered refuge to locals in case of need, for war harmed everyone, whether it occurred between tribes, European nations, or, as was often the case, involved both at once. The greatest fear of both the community in the fort and the Africans around it was an interruption in trade. Local wars were nonetheless numerous and accentuated by the fact that most local societies were highly interested in European weapons and ammunition, which they used to strengthen their control over their neighbors, provided the latter were not in turn supported by trade with another European nation.

This explains why the imported architecture, whose origin was contemporary with the late Middle Ages, long remained that of the castle. Three types soon emerged: the first two, the castle and the fort, differed only in size. Differences in design were limited to a few variations on the basic model, such as adaptations of defensive innovations perfected in the Mediterranean by Italian engineers. Overall, the structures were massive, generally rectangular, isolated on a promontory or elevated point, and protected by a surrounding ditch and wall. The drawbridge, originally a standard feature, was often reduced, as at the French fort at Whydah, to a wooden bridge that was simply removed in the evening.[14] The inside walls were thick and reinforced on the corners with towers that jutted out. The tallest tower was used as a lookout, to watch for incoming boats and perhaps attackers. In the front was a large courtyard normally used as a marketplace and in time of war as a refuge. At the back, there was a smaller space that was less well protected and used as a service area. There was also a prison for slaves. One inevitable addition was a tower with a clock that marked the time of day; sometimes there was an underground cistern to gather rainwater. The frequent lack of the latter, even in large forts, can only be explained by a lack of materials or skills, for cisterns were usually paved and vaulted in brick, although that rarely made them really watertight.[15]

The failure to build good cisterns was probably the reason that the architecture did not spread inland. Everything, or almost everything, was imported from the West: craftsmen, materials, and tools. In 1482, the Portuguese expedition responsible for building the fort at Elmina included six hundred men, of whom a hundred were masons and a hundred were carpenters, according to one account; another account speaks of only one hundred craftsmen and five hundred soldiers.[16] Once the castle was completed, the surviving craftsmen were sent back to Portugal, except for sixty men and three women. Later, the Portuguese trained teams of skilled slaves locally.

Boats delivered lumber, precut stone, large quantities of lime, tiles, bricks, and nails, and tools of all sorts. It seems that only the Portuguese went so far as to import stone, but bricks were widely used in construction and were carried as ballast in ships. Lime was the second largest import, but those responsible for the forts did not always know what to do with it. Most of the time, workers were not very knowledgeable, materials were lacking, and there were not enough skilled slaves. The Portuguese concentrated mainly on fortifications and invested little in storehouses and homes. The Brandenburgians and Dutch were the best builders. The English were chronically short of money, which was invested in India or elsewhere, and were known for mediocre buildings. The French built few permanent structures, and almost nothing remains of them, except for a few rare fortifications built or rebuilt in Vauban style at Gorée. The French fort of Whydah, or rather what remained of it in later centuries, was built of sandstone and originally had thatched roofs. It was later rebuilt out of red brick and then demolished in 1908. In 1933, a monument to the dead was erected on the site.

Technology and materials failed to spread partly because the little colonies were not numerous and European employees were most often limited to the governor, one or two assistants, and a few soldiers. The closed world of the fort, which was shut in on itself, did the rest. The monumental architecture did not resemble any of the traditional lo-cal buildings. A ruler had to be unusual and powerful, like King Henri Christophe of Haiti, to force the locals to adopt such fortresses, at the cost of incredible human effort given the lack of technology and finan-cial means.[17]

The third kind of building was called a lodge, which derives from the Portuguese *loja*, meaning "large store." It grew as the business itself grew and was only partially fortified, if at all. This kind of architecture endured over time, probably because it was more modest and therefore more flexible and was often built with local materials and techniques because of a lack of European resources.

In any case, the lodge, like the fort, fulfilled its purpose. It provided storage and shelter and sometimes had more than one story. Stone or lightweight partitions divided the interior into rectangular rooms. The wood-frame construction had a thatched roof and wooden lintels over the doors. There are no traces left of dozens or perhaps hundreds of lodges, such as the English lodge in Anashan, which was described in 1709 as "a thatched house garrisoned with two men."[18] Another lodge, this one on the Gambia River, was built of adobe and straw by Francis Moore in 1733. He described it as having several rooms, including a common room, which was the largest and used for communal activities: meals were eaten there, and it was used as an office and meeting room. It was in the middle, and opened to the outside through the only two doors in the building, one in the front and the other in the back. It also controlled access to three storerooms on the right and two lodgings on the left. The most remarkable feature is that the house had a veranda (*alpendre* in Portuguese). This was probably inspired by classical Por-tuguese architecture and seems to be one of the first known examples of what would become the standard house for traders from the end of the century on. Perhaps it can be linked with an analogous but much larger building: Cape Coast Castle, described by Barbot in 1682. It had a balcony all along the second floor, with gracious outside stairways on each side to link the garrison's lodgings. Under the balcony there were trading halls.[19] Could this be the link between the Portuguese fort, Afro-Brazilian veranda house, and English bungalow that we will men-tion again later? In some areas, such as in Yorubaland, Togo, and Benin, these three models were the architectural inspiration for most homes, particularly of those of slave traders.

It is surprising that the first attempts to adapt European architecture to a tropical climate date only from the eighteenth century. The purely military design of the forts shows no concern for ventilation. Indeed, for security reasons, the living quarters were pushed up against the surrounding wall and so were oppressively hot. Even on the second floor, the widow's walk was protected by a parapet that impeded ventilation, evidence that this was a period of transition. Since it represented a mercantile economy, the fort became obsolete with the liberalism of the eighteenth century. On the Gold Coast, the Dutch eliminated their forts by the end of the century. Thirty years later, in 1822, once the slave trade was definitively over for them, the English did likewise. Danish and Dutch forts were transformed into factories and sold to the English in 1850 and 1872, respectively, when African trade was over for these two nations.[20] Most of them had not been used for a long time, even though the upheavals of colonial conquest had made their military role relevant again to some extent. Thus, Fort Keta was besieged by Africans twice, in 1847 and 1878. The English themselves soon transferred their fort at Whydah to the Hamburgian merchant house of Goedelt.[21] The Portuguese fort at Whydah was maintained as a symbol of their authority during French colonization; a Portuguese resident was still in charge of it in 1946, but the independent government eliminated that symbol when it took control of the fort in 1961.

## The Beginnings of Urban Life? The Gold Coast

Naturally, since the Gold Coast has been the subject of the most intensive research, we have the best information about it.[22] There is every reason to believe that the arrival of the Portuguese on the coast was a strong stimulus to the local economy, but local urban life generally developed more freely and brightly in the back country than near European forts. Marion Johnson suspected this more than thirty years ago, although she did not have the data available today. In the sixteenth century, the rapid transformation into a society that was one of the world's leading gold exporters could not have resulted from the efforts of a handful of European merchants. The major cultural change was the passage from a rural civilization to an urban culture; it was not based on movements of "traditional" peoples but on a major inflow of foreigners attracted by opportunities. Merchants, artisans, and migrants of many origins came to offer their labor and skills.[23]

Throughout the whole period, Elmina was the port with by far the largest population. In the mid-sixteenth century, the city was almost 2.5 miles in circumference, and its population went from between three and four thousand inhabitants to between fifteen and twenty thousand between 1621 and 1628. Around 1709, after a slowdown at the end of the century (1682–1702) owing to both a smallpox epidemic and growing military conflicts between neighboring cities, the city was once again the most populous on the coast. It seems to have been exceptional, however: Until the end of the seventeenth century, no other port seems to have reached more than four to five thousand inhabitants, and none covered an area of more than one square mile. The only other really busy port was Axim, to the west, at the mouth of the Ankobra River and Volta basin. It was held by the Portuguese in the sixteenth century and then by the Dutch in the seventeenth century. It was far behind Elmina, however. In 1631, Axim was a small town with barely five hundred inhabitants, but grew to 150 homes and perhaps two thousand inhabitants by 1638. In 1690, there were two to three thousand residents, including three hundred soldiers. Aside from Axim and Elmina, none of the ports were autonomous. They depended on capitals inland, which were usually more populous and located a day or a day and a half away by foot. Even Cape Coast Castle, Britain's jewel, was not very big: twenty houses in 1555, two hundred around 1607, and more than five hundred in 1680—in other words, probably a maximum of around five thousand inhabitants when the slave trade was in full swing. In short, between 1550 and 1650, old ports continued growing while new harbors also developed, and there are indications that a nonfarming, urban population was flourishing.

The smallness of the ports is all the more surprising because shipping had increased considerably. Tonnage went from three thousand tons a year at the beginning of the sixteenth century to more than ten thousand in the mid-seventeenth century just before the boom in the slave trade. Most of the trade was of course a result of the opening of transatlantic trade, but it was combined with intense coastal cabotage from port to port and from fort to fort. Inland areas also affected the economy through internal distribution networks that were linked to the north with Muslim Sudanese trade related to the Jula expansion, the final upheavals of which reached the coast. Coastal trade was characterized mainly by variety and versatility. At first, the Portuguese were looking for gold. At the time of Eustache de la Fosse (1479–80), only ports that traded the precious metal had periodic markets. However, Europeans abandoned the illusion that Africa was a high-yield investment as soon as the sea route was truly open to Asia, for it was infinitely more profitable.

A century later, economic activity remained modest but highly diversified. Around 1660, all the ports had almost daily markets. They had become focal and meeting points for people and goods of all origins landing and going to sea, to and from all destinations. Some ports gradually became specialized in specific crafts and agricultural products. Takoradi was known for metalwork, pirogue building (also done at the Cape of Three Points), salt production (also done at Sega), and agricultural products for export, including small livestock. Winneba specialized in poultry, and later in slaves. However, the slave trade began as local cabotage to more active regional centers and became transatlantic only later. Elmina was known for gold, of course, but also for bead manufacturing. With some exceptions, secondary ports initially engaged only in small-scale, low-value commerce, such as trade in fish, salt, and handicrafts, and their range was limited with respect to cabotage and inland trade, which did not extend much further than twenty miles from the coast. Around 1680, however, there were at least twenty-five to thirty ports exporting gold. Some acquired judicial and administrative duties, became homes to tax collectors, and had dependent villages and hamlets. The frequency of the ports along the coast increased. At the beginning of the seventeenth century, they were on average fifteen to twenty miles apart. By the end of the century, the distance was only about seven miles.

At the time, agricultural trade was intense and lucrative, for travelers, merchants, artisans, and storekeepers all had to be fed. Food (dried fish, salt, and perhaps yams) cabotage across the lagoon and pirogue manufacturing were probably more important to the economy than Atlantic trade, which involved gold, a little ivory, and slaves for coastal warehouses and experimental sugar cane plantations in the islands. Unfortunately, we have no numbers except pertaining to the end of the seventeenth century (around 1660). Around 1700, according to Bosman,[24] particularly in the dry season, the Mouri market had to fill a hundred eight-ton canoes of food a day, for a total of eight hundred tons daily, destined for Axim and Accra. At the beginning of the seventeenth century, a secondary port would have had to import three hundred or more tons of agricultural products from its hinterland; around 1610, there were at least a dozen such ports, and twice as many at the end of the century. Cape Coast Castle developed similarly, since perhaps 80 percent of its three to five thousand inhabitants depended on the regional market for food. In 1709, the belt of urban gardens around the city was probably three to five miles in circumference. By around 1720, it had doubled. This means that all urban centers depended on local food production. The ports were able to survive only thanks to organized networks in the hinterland. This was obviously also the case for gold, since it always required far-reaching networks extending north up to Begho and beyond. By the end of the fifteenth century, Muslim weights were used to measure gold, which is indeed proof of the extent of inland networks.[25]

The development of a small port like Mouri to the east of Cape Coast is a good example. The Dutch built a fort there in 1612, and by 1618 there were three hundred soldiers and fifteen hundred slaves living on the site. In the surrounding area there was a nonagricultural labor force of around fifteen hundred people, such as fishers, canoemen, artisans, and traders. In 1667, there were one to two hundred sailors, and, in 1690, three to four hundred fishing pirogues able to carry at least three or four times this number, but only one hundred soldiers. At the end of the seventeenth century, Mouri was one of the most dynamic towns, with perhaps five to six thousand inhabitants in all. It was typical of the small centers that grew up around European businessmen, who were merchants in the sixteenth and seventeenth centuries but willingly became slave traders at the turn of the eighteenth century. Unfortunately, however, we have few clues to the social life in such places. Clearly, non-agricultural workers gathered there to seek employment as servants and artisans. They must have faced stiff competition from the slaves who made up most of the workforce.

Kea estimated that in the second half of the seventeenth century several million *dambas* of gold probably changed hands, and certainly not all of it ended up in the transatlantic market.[26] Caravan routes and networks to the coast increased and became more diverse, which is why African trade and urban life developed most not on the coast but along an inland line in the surrounding countryside, which had access to opportunities from both the south and the north. In the interior, flourishing supply networks grew, and capital cities emerged as leading trade centers that controlled ports and knew how to profit from them, at least until the international slave trade took its toll.

## Urban Centers and the Ghanaian Hinterland

### Densely Populated Micro-Areas

What makes this period interesting are the lively internal networks of small- and medium-sized towns that were more or less city-states or parts of medium-sized political systems. All things being equal, the situation was comparable to the emergence of the urban mercantile economy in France at the end of the High Middle Ages, as can be seen in Guy Blois' insightful analysis.[27] Taking into account the chronological differences and spread of Portuguese business practices through creolized African slave traders, we can even attempt a few analogies with Fernand Braudel's descriptions of mercantile Europe in the pre-modern age, though we must be careful not to exaggerate their scope. In both cases, a new economic framework was dominated by a basic division between the city and the countryside.

The new cabotage opportunities on the coast triggered the changes, but those opportunities were grafted onto much older networks. The northern factor was essential.[28] Originally, the Jula of Jenne spread their networks to the south. They were at the origin of the market city of Begho and therefore maintained contact between southern areas and the Niger basin.

Archeological findings in the south confirm claims in Portuguese, Dutch, and English travel narratives of the time. The political center was clearly made up of the largest, most politically organized inland cities, in particular, those that could benefit most from the northern and coastal currents. Their number and size increased significantly from the beginning of the fifteenth century to the end of the seventeenth century. In the first half of the seventeenth century, there were at least thirty capitals of small states separated by ten to thirty miles at the most, which was a reasonable spacing since all transportation was by foot. Have we looked closely enough at "the revolution in trade caused by the seeding of small towns and trading villages more or less everywhere in the area"?[29] Guy Blois estimates that in tenth-century medieval France, the twenty miles separating the towns of Lournand and Mâcon, along with the difficult terrain, were an insurmountable obstacle to intensive, regular relations between the two towns. Certainly, African peasants did have to deal with less rugged landforms, but they had no pack animals, aside from donkeys, which were used only later and mainly in the northern inland area. Male slaves, and women, whether or not they were slaves, walked quickly and carried everything on their heads. As soon as producers were within eight miles of the closest market, everything changed. They could go to market and come home in the same day. The city's domination of its hinterland finally became a reality.

There were probably up to two hundred different small administrative centers, but we should not think of them as dense villages. Some travelers speak of dozens or more quarters or wards, yet generally each was peopled by one or several large families (lineages or parts of lineages), and there could be large distances between them. The urban space was covered with large expanses of fallow and cultivated land, similar to the garden-cities of the Congo. These scattered settlements were also what made these cities seem so spread out.

Great Komenda, Akessim, and Great Accra each covered more than one square mile. Mankessim, Agoua, and Great Accra probably

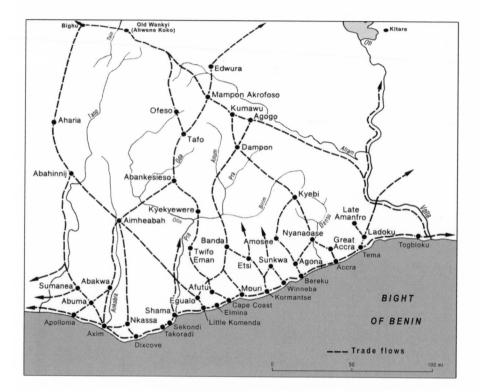

Map 8. The Hinterland of the Gold Coast
to the West of the Volta in the Seventeenth Century
Based on: After Ray A. Kea, *Settlements, Trade, and Polities in the Seventeenth Century Gold Coast*, Baltimore: The Johns Hopkins University Press, 1982, p. 31

had between ten and twenty thousand inhabitants each. One tradition even attributes forty to fifty thousand inhabitants to Great Accra. It was probably the largest of the cities; at the very end of the seventeenth century its ruins still had a circumference of several miles. The Fante city of Abora, which was established a little later and benefited between 1680 and 1700 from the decline of Kwaman and Mankessim, seems to have had ten thousand inhabitants at the beginning of the eighteenth century. Most of the other centers had three hundred to five thousand inhabitants. In the mid-seventeenth century, there were at least fifteen inland political centers between Apollonia Cape and the Volta, between present-day Ivory Coast and Benin, each with an average of four to five thousand inhabitants, for a total of at least sixty to seventy-five thousand city dwellers. The 1602 Texeira map shows approximately thirty inland cities, which could have been home to a total of 120,000 to 150,000 people. That is a lot, perhaps even too many, when we consider Guy Blois' population estimates for urban areas in the Mâcon area, which did not exceed 1,000 to 1,500 for the largest center, Mâcon, "including people from the countryside living in small courtyards within the walls."[30]

Unfortunately, nothing is known about the surrounding rural population, which must have accounted for about 70 percent of the total. Using the state of Accra before its conquest and depopulation at the end of the seventeenth century (1677–81) as an example, it is possible to imagine a capital surrounded by fourteen secondary cities of about five thousand inhabitants each, totaling an urban population of nearly one hundred thousand, which would have been almost half of the area's total population. In the seventeenth century and even at the beginning of the eighteenth century, the state of Akyem was highly urbanized, with a total population of around 120,000 to 200,000 before the series of demographic disasters that struck the region after 1740, and at least seventeen centers with about four thousand inhabitants each, thus totaling at least a quarter of the population.

We know less about the situation further north, on the fringes of the forest, around a day to a day and a half by foot north of the political centers. There, market towns provided links with Begho. The cities in the area, which were nonetheless essential production centers of gold and probably slaves, were rather small. Aside from a few exceptions, they probably had no more than five to ten thousand inhabitants each and averaged two to five thousand each. The city of Adumangya is said to have had seventy-seven "densely populated" *abron* (quarters). An oral tradition says that the city of Abotakyi had seventy to seventy-five thousand inhabitants ready to bear arms, but this is probably an exaggeration.

Obviously, this raises a series of questions, not only about the heterogeneity of socio-economic functions and activities within the city, but also about the city-country relationships required between urban entrepreneurs and rural food producers. It also raises the question of what the situation was in areas about which little if any information exists. Were societies always so unorganized, "traditional," and almost exclusively subsistence-based as has been supposed? There are indications that the territorialization of ancient Sahelian empires such as Mali and Songhai was much less loose than initially thought.[31]

## Urban Social Heterogeneity

As in the cities of central Africa, many notables lived in the regional centers of the Ghanaian area. A prosperous household, including protégés, dependents, slaves, and servants of all kinds, could contain up to 150 people. For example, when he died in 1675, Jantie Snees left behind forty wives, fourteen daughters, twelve sons, and at least a hundred slaves, including cooks; tam-tam players; sword, other weapon, and shield carriers; trumpeters; guards; and, of course, farmers responsible for supplying all the others. The big difference between these centers and the political centers in central Africa at the same period was that socio-occupational activities were much more diversified. In addition to people who could be considered large-scale farmers, there were those involved in administration, economic activities, and religious functions: civil servants, soldiers, militiamen; and especially merchants, innkeepers, slave traders, artisans, canoemen, fishers, salt producers, and laborers and workers of all sorts. For example, a fair amount is known about the canoemen, who were well aware of their rights and the labor market.

The canoemen, most of whom were Fante until the eighteenth century, specialized in the dangerous but lucrative unloading of Atlantic ships. One of their first attempts to have their claims heard dates back to 1664 in Sekondi, and their first strike was in 1753 at Cape Coast Castle.[32] All of those people worked much more for interregional trade than for the subsistence of the local group.

Most city dwellers were therefore not directly involved in farming. Prominent families, who lived on revenue generated by business, their tenants, and tribute, accounted for about 60 percent of the urban population. The rest of the inhabitants included many free men, such as artisans (organized into regulated guilds), peddlers, and laborers. They were paid in gold, not in kind. In inland cities, 40 to 70 percent of the inhabitants bought their food in the market.

## Integration of the City and Countryside

According to Kea, during this period city-countryside relations transformed into direct exploitation of the peasantry. Of course, notables got their supplies first from their own land, where a system of slavery, or at least serfdom, was widespread. However, mercantile production became more economically powerful than slave-based production in the sixteenth and seventeenth centuries. Kea made relatively simple calculations, based on the average amount of millet required per city dweller in the relatively large agglomerations: fifteen to twenty stalks of millet per inhabitant, per day. With production of around forty bushels per acre (one bushel accounted for two hundred stalks), a port like Mouri, which had about fifteen hundred inhabitants supplied by approximately two hundred peasants in the seventeenth century, consumed nearly four thousand bushels annually, which was how much could be produced on one to two thousand acres. Since each rural family already used about two to three acres for its own subsistence, the city required 1,200 acres more, and therefore rural families had to farm six acres instead of just two.

We have no information on the scope of rural operations, but reports consistently say that between Mouri and Asebu, which were about seven miles apart, local agriculture was as intensive as possible, given the technology at the time. Thus, it was spread out and required a great deal of labor. The same applied to inland cities. Of course, near the cities there were highly dependent villages that specialized in specific types of production, such as crafts (pottery, metalwork, tanning, pirogue building, ivory carving), salt production, and livestock raising. For example, Nkyenefo, located about four miles north of Cape Coast, produced up to five thousand cases of salt a year, each worth thirty-six dambas of gold, for a total of 181,000 dambas.[33] Even though half the residents of a capital city obtained food supplies from their own farms and forced peasant labor, the other city dwellers had to purchase theirs. Salt producers used about half of their profits to buy supplies for themselves and at least a quarter of their profits to pay taxes; this left them poor and exploited, but still able to participate in the circulation of money.

Gold became the means par excellence of exploiting peasant families. The most typical and convincing example from the seventeenth century is the city of Accra; its very size required it to import a considerable quantity of rural goods throughout the year for its large urban population. The goods therefore had to come from relatively far away. Gold sales in Accra were not greater than a million dambas in 1640–70, but Accra's twenty-five thousand inhabitants would have had to import between three and five million dambas of millet over the same period. Thus, a whole system of regional markets sprang up, in which supplies were traded for gold and a large class of intermediaries became rich. Peasants from the interior traded their goods for salt produced on the coast, a few handicrafts, imported items, and a little gold. They too needed money to pay their taxes, for, by the end of the sixteenth century and in the seventeenth century, urban political authorities required them to pay property taxes, which had to be paid in gold and could be considerable. A significant amount of the gold accumulated in the hands of the tax collector, a civil servant appointed by the capital city. For example, in 1601, the person responsible for a district town collected ten to twelve ounces of gold each time. This was equivalent to 3,800 to 4,600 dambas or three to four thousand bushels of millie,[34] enough to feed three to five thousand people for a year. The taxes in question were for eighty to ninety acres of land and accounted for between a quarter and half of the revenue from the annual rural production. This was clearly a regime of direct rural exploitation through property taxes and the circulation of money. Most peasants were miserable and in debt. Some paupers became bandits, in a similar evolution as when, in medieval and modern Europe, the emergence of mercantile capitalism impoverished the poorest rural producers. However, as it did elsewhere, the system mainly distorted the society. In the mid-sixteenth century, every village had a periodic market, where transactions also required gold, and there were no longer any rural areas where peasants were separate from the surrounding system, which was a hierarchical economic and political network dominated by its capital city. Growing mobility favored a relatively homogeneous material culture over a relatively wide area.

Trade between the city and countryside had become bilateral. As rural production became more commercialized, peasants produced more, sold the surplus, and came into the city to buy things that could not be found where they lived. From then on, urban growth involved the gradual penetration of rural areas, an expansion of the surrounding market.[35] Some of the luckier or more skillful peasants even made enough profit on the local markets to invest in businesses that were profitable at the time. They came to the ports and established themselves in turn as merchants and slave traders.

The net transfer of capital from the countryside to the cities put gold in the hands of the governing class, which was by definition concentrated in the cities. It was, *mutatis mutandis*, a mercantile capitalist system, on a micro scale to some extent, but indisputable.

### Ancient Urbanization in the Hinterland? The Case of the Yoruba

A key issue is whether what is known about the Gold Coast can be extended to other areas. In other words, did regional networks of mercantile capitalism surround economic and political centers? In contrast with the Kongo kingdom, which seems to have been based on a slave economy from the beginning, the case of the Yoruba strongly suggests that a diversified, hierarchical network of cities was established very early, before the Europeans arrived. Unfortunately, our knowledge of the situation prior to the nineteenth century is hypothetical. The best-known case, namely the southern metropolis, Benin City,[36] was undeniably already a city when the Portuguese visited it at the end of the fifteenth century, which supports the assumption that ancient Yoruba urbanism is not a myth.

### Ancient Urbanism:  Oral Traditions and Founding Myths

The general term *yoruba* is a colonial invention, covering a set of social structures the members of which claim a common culture. In other words, they share the same language and the same myths of origin, and surround their instruments of political and mystical authority with similar symbols. However, they speak a dozen similar but distinct dialects and, before colonial times, identified themselves as separate political entities. Thus, the Ije, Ijebu, Oyo, and Ondo had different states and city-states, or at least languages. The Yoruba region, which had nearly five million inhabitants in 1960 and now has ten million, covers southwestern Nigeria and used to extend into part of present-day eastern Benin, from the southern marshy and forested coast up to the northern plains of the treed savanna. The ancient history of Yoruba cities has been almost exclusively reconstituted in relation to more familiar nineteenth-century urban changes. Before that time, the oral traditions, which are very rich in religion, politics, and genealogy, hardly ever discussed the theme of urbanism and cannot be cross-checked or fleshed out with direct observations, such as those concerning the Gold and Slave Coasts. There are reports from neighboring areas where Europeans penetrated, but at most they allude to Yoruba cities, or rather states, and note their power, since the states were regularly described as having controlled neighboring lands for two to five hundred years.

The Portuguese had been visiting Benin City since 1486 and had heard of two powerful kings in the interior, who could have been the Alafin of Oyo and the Oni of Ife. João Affonso d'Aveiro reported that the Oba of Benin had to be ritually enthroned by a powerful monarch called Obane, who was the spiritual leader of a people located not far away and had authority comparable to that of the Pope in Europe.[37] Nonetheless, the Yoruba territory of Oyo remained terra incognita for Europeans until the Clapperton-Lander expedition around 1825–30. By then, Benin City had been known for three hundred years and Abomey for a century. In 1505–1508, Pacheco Pereira was the first to mention a Yoruba city, Geebu, which has since been associated with Ijebu-Ode, around thirty miles inside the Lagos lagoon. It can be seen on maps and in documents from the early sixteenth century.[38] The name Jabu can be found on a Portuguese map from 1501 and on Dapper's maps of 1668. An anonymous author described it as being thirteen leagues east of Kuramo in Lagos, and surrounded by a wooden fence. In 1647, another author mentioned the "big city" surrounded by a ditch, and John Adams' travelogues from 1786–1800 are remarkably consistent with this.[39]

The scanty documents mention peoples and states, rarely cities. Bosman, who visited Whydah around 1698, noted that "further inland" there was a warlike people who had horses. They may have been from Oyo. In 1793, Dalzelle spoke of the Eyeos (Oyo), and in 1727 Snelgrave again mentioned the formidable J-OE horsemen. From that date on, reference was often made to a powerful king who forced the king of Abomey to pay tribute. However, while Oyo is indeed on Anville's 1743 map, it was only at the turn of the nineteenth century that Adams mentioned the capital of the Hios, which seems to have been visited by a French officer who was part of a slave driver's crew. We learn that, at that late date, "the population of the city of Lagos [may have been] 5,000 souls."[40] Ondo was also mentioned, under different names, between 1668 and 1729. This is about all that is known before the first third of the nineteenth century.

In contrast, local oral traditions mention many cities.[41] These traditions are useful, although we cannot ignore the possibility of reworking or even reconstructing them for justification purposes at the time of the nineteenth-century urban recovery. By acknowledging the obviousness of the correlation between the existence of "large" cities and sacred authority, historians have tended to stick to the traditions without questioning them. Rather than suggesting that the cities resulted from the royal palace's attractiveness to migrants, would it not be more reasonable to advance the idea that it was the process of urbanization and the need to manage heterogeneous entities that resulted in the religious myth? To begin with, the argument corroborates the age of Yoruba urbanism, since verifiable references to the sites where the myth was founded date from long before the nineteenth century. Finally, despite our limited knowledge, there are too many traditions throughout the country that refer to Ife's ancient religious preeminence for it not to be rooted in history in some way.

Using the cities of Oyo and Ilesha as examples, Smith and Peel have shown that, with a good dose of speculation, it is possible to infer a reasonably plausible chronology from royal genealogies.[42] Old Oyo, located northeast of the Yoruba plateau on a treed savanna favorable to the horses that were the strength of its cavalry, was nonetheless constantly threatened by warlike neighbors: to the north and northwest by the Borgu and to the east by the Nupe. In the sixteenth century, the inhabitants abandoned the site for almost seventy-five years (Smith suggests between 1555 and 1610) and moved about forty miles to the southwest, where they founded a temporary capital, Igboho. The city reached its peak only after they returned. Peel proposes that Ilesha, which was probably not the first capital of the eponymous chiefdom, was founded in the fifteenth or sixteenth century. At the time, the city's interests seem to have been oriented more toward the north, but at the turn of the seventeenth century, it seems to have established relations with the market in Benin City, which was well supplied with the iron needed for agriculture and war. It also extended its influence considerably, south to Akure and east to Ekiti country. Like Oyo, Ilesha's urban peak was between the end of the seventeenth century and the middle of the eighteenth century. At the time, the city built walls and established well-defined quarters. At the end of the century, between 1770 and 1790, Oyo entered a period of decline; it was once again dealing with the Nupe expansion, and the northwest of the country was devastated by war. At the turn of the nineteenth century, the city probably swelled as new quarters were established to house refugees, which heralded changes to come.

However, oral tradition, in agreement on this point with the famous archeological find of tenth- to twelfth-century bronze heads and pottery at Ife,[43] dates the foundation of the first city, Ile-Ife, much earlier. Its establishment is attributed to the mythical founding ancestor Oduduwa; variations on the myth portray him as a colonizing hero who fell from the sky or a conqueror who came from the east. The sophistication of

Ife's art is, of course, no proof of urbanization, but it at least suggests that the ancient society was stable and well organized enough to give rise to artistic creation of such high quality. Ife, unlike most Yoruba cities, did not change sites over the years, maintained its role as a religious center for all Yoruba, and continued to acknowledge the ritual authority of its Oni, even though the power of Oyo's Alafin soon grew stronger. Indeed, the real power, which was also the sacred power since it was confirmed by the Oni, was transferred early on to Old Oyo in the northwest and to Benin City in the southeast. These two cities eventually became the two political foci in the area.[44] The Awujale of Ijebu-Ode also claimed the same kind of prerogative. Finally, in the nineteenth century, the new city of Abeokuta tried to gain similar power through its Alake.

In sum, strong oral traditions, particularly from Oyo (Katunga), allow us to reconstitute the interrelation between Yoruba urbanism and a kind of ideal political system, although we are unable to say with certainty whether it really existed or was essentially a later re-creation modeled on Old Oyo. Power, freed from exclusive dependency on the kinship system, would have been divided and balanced between three main authorities. First, there was the sovereign (Alafin), guarantor of the group's religion and survival, which was generally a hereditary position within the founding lineage since he incarnated the sovereign legitimacy, thereby confirming the power of the lineage. The Alafin was surrounded by princely dignitaries and slaves. However, his power was counterbalanced by two other authorities. The Oyo-mesi, a kind of state council, acted as an aristocratic opposition and control, and was made up of dignitary-councilors elected by their kin and responsible for electing the new Alafin and ensuring that he behaved in accordance with his dual spirit. Their power was therefore religious, but not exclusively, since their chief (*basorun*) was also the head of the army. The third authority was the Ogboni, which was a council recruited more widely from the pool of free men, on the basis of age, trustworthiness, and status. Its purpose was to act as an intermediary with the rest of the population; in its case also, the power had religious aspects, since the Ogboni had the power to impose ritual sanctions on both the Alafin and his council.[45]

The city's raison d'être was to serve as the residence of its religious and political chief, the Oba. Around the city there were satellite centers, but we do not know whether they were old villages that had gradually been incorporated into a hierarchy, or agglomerations that had been created by princes and other dignitaries sent out to "colonize" the countryside. In the satellites, a subordinate chief had, proportionately, more or less the same duties as the Oba. This explains why there is a clear distinction in Yoruba urbanism between the sacred enclosure of the *afin* (the Oba's palace) and the secular city. The afin was located at the heart of the system.[46] It was the visible symbol of the city-state's power and prosperity. This is probably why it was built whenever possible on a hill, where it could look over the other homes facing the palace and the major roads fanning out to the rest of the realm. At this level of generality, Yoruba cities were the same as other capital cities in ancient Africa, according to the information available from archaeology and in the old travelers' descriptions. What was more unusual was the imposing size of the walls separating the afin from the rest of the city and carefully isolating the Oba from his subjects. The custom was ancient, judging from the tradition that was the basis for Oyo's recreation at Ago (New Oyo). The traditions emphasize the magnificence of afin architecture in the past but, so far, no corroborating evidence has been found at Ife or Old Oyo. Some afins were probably quite large. Clapperton said that Old Oyo was about fifteen miles in circumference; the king's houses and those of his women occupied about a square mile. Clapperton appreciated that the posts supporting the verandas and the doors of the king's and caboceers' houses[47] were generally carved in bas relief, with figures representing a boa killing an antelope or a hog, or with processions of warriors attended by drummers: "[T]he latter are by no means meanly executed, conveying the expression and attitude of the principal man in the group with a lofty air."[48] But neither Clapperton nor the Landers were impressed by Yoruba urbanism.[49] The Landers describe enclosures fenced by irregular walls made of rough clay, with thatched roofs and earth floors polished using cow dung. Most walls and houses were decaying. The Landers again noted that the only difference between the chief's residence and those of his subjects was the number of courtyards and enclosures. The lack of written testimony, the fragility of the construction materials (earth and wood were used exclusively), and the poverty of archeological research prevent us from knowing more.[50]

## Weak Archeological Presumptions

In any case, urbanism appears to have existed at that time. We can suppose that it began around Ile-Ife, at the edge of the forest, which was an area favorable to trade, and then spread westward in the forested area and toward the wide expanses of open savanna to the north. This was the origin of the separate development of the areas of influence of Benin City and Old Oyo in the following centuries. The latter reached the peak of its power in the second half of the eighteenth century. What should we think of the Oyo "empire"? We should be careful not to give the word a European-style autocratic connotation. Essentially, it controlled the trade routes, forcing people in the hinterland to pay tribute and, especially, preventing them from pillaging the main roads. Many small leaderless groups existed without any other form of control. Whatever the case, Oyo's control extended over a series of city-states that had been more or less independent until then. This created an urban network that covered all of Yorubaland in the west, including parts of present-day Benin, and stretched toward the coast up to Whydah. The very scope of Oyo's ambitions made the capital fragile and unbalanced in the north, where it was increasingly threatened by the Fulani expansion in the nineteenth century. Chased from the savanna, the people of Oyo retreated to the edges of the forest in 1837.

Unfortunately, archeology currently provides only weak support for this hypothesis. A gap of almost a thousand years separates the first Yoruba datings from the last Nok datings (207 CE ±50), when people probably used proto-agriculture involving very long fallow periods. What happened between these dates? There were probably a gradual sociocultural integration of the inhabitants of the area and waves of immigrants starting in the tenth or eleventh century.

For the Yoruba period properly speaking, there are only a few sites, such as Ife (also known as Ile-Ife) and Owu, that provide evidence of an ancient, apparently large settlement.[51] Archeological digs at Ile-Ife have revealed three successive phases of growth. Originally, around the twelfth century (960–1060 CE, ±130), the city was only a set of hamlets; tradition lists thirteen. They were certainly already significant, because they were well situated in the center of a basin into which water from the surroundings gathered, thereby making it possible to farm year-round despite the long dry season. The fact that the agglomeration was encircled by a medieval earthen wall about 16 feet high and more than six feet wide—not combined with a moat and having a dozen doors—is not yet proof of the existence of a city. A more convincing piece of evidence would be the fact, reported in oral traditions but not yet discovered in the field, that the wall was soon reinforced with a second line of defenses. This would at least show that the city was able to offer refuge to surrounding farmers in case of danger.

There is more support for the second phase of relatively ancient urbanism. The discovery of paving tiles decorated with ears of corn (a plant known to have been introduced by the Portuguese) and cross-checking between genealogies corroborate the theory that this phase began in the sixteenth century or early seventeenth century. The ten-mile-long wall was preceded by a steep opposing slope and rose 20 to 25 feet over a moat partially carved out of the rock that formed the escarpment on which it was built. There were doors in the wall, four of which have been found, each protected by two towers. The whole construction is quite impressive and apparently influenced to some extent by the fortifications at Oyo, where the wall was fifteen miles long; indeed, oral tradition tells us that refugees arrived from Oyo between 1790 and 1815. Oral history attributes little importance to Ife in the first years of the eighteenth century, but its later rapid growth, demonstrated by the size of the wars against Ilesha, makes it possible to date the second, and better-preserved, outer wall from that period. Finally, the third phase seems to have been marked by the construction of the most recent wall, from 1845 to 1854. This suggests that the city was not completely abandoned then, although it seems it was at the time of the colonial intervention, from 1881 to 1894 and, again and especially, between 1909 and 1920.[52]

Given such meager vestiges, we can wonder whether the sites really were urban in earlier times. Were they really cities, or simply villages that were later idealized by oral traditions ready to embellish on past exploits? This question, which has been asked seriously by British researchers about later periods, is all the more pertinent with respect to times.[53] Robert Law, in particular, contrasts the obvious urbanism of the nineteenth century with the scarcity of clues to earlier times since, for example, there is no way to say how many inhabitants could have found shelter in the two best-known fortified sites. The urbanism was in any case less dense than that which took shape in the nineteenth century. For example, we know that the Ijebu, who suffered less than the other Yoruba from the wars in the nineteenth century, also had much less dense cities. The capital city was relatively small, and much of the population lived in surrounding villages that were subordinate, yet autonomous.[54] As early as the 1850s, a missionary already hypothesized that this arrangement reflected the ancient Yoruba urbanism that had been destroyed elsewhere.[55]

The formation of Yoruba "urban culture" dates back to that distant time, possibly to the sixteenth century, however. The culture was unique, and was no doubt reinforced by the merchant elite (immigrant or not) who deliberately tried to occupy, dominate, and even exploit the local populations, which were still largely unorganized. Oral traditions report many cases of hamlets and small villages that were forced to merge into "cities."[56] The authoritarian trend toward founding cities increased in the nineteenth century, in the troubled time of the Yoruba Wars. It was based in the nature of Yoruba urbanism, which considered the city more as the lifestyle of a living community than as a space with physical structures. The latter, eminently Western concept is linked to architecture using lasting materials. In Africa, however, buildings were less significant. since the earth and straw building materials could easily be used elsewhere. Since the city was the heart of both cultural and military conquest, it could move from place to place as circumstances such as wars and ecological disasters required, and that did not really affect its social unity. In sum, it was natural that the name of the former community be given to a new city, either because the inhabitants had decided to move or, more frequently, because part of the population had left the mother-city to settle elsewhere. In the latter case, an additional qualifier could be used to distinguish the new city from the old one. Thus, there are a whole series of cities named Ife, from the name Ile-Ife, the traditional cradle of Yoruba culture.

## The Process of Urbanization:  A Diffusionist Hypothesis?

Should we adopt the hypothesis of the English historian, John Fage, or the Nigerian geographer, Akin Mabogunje, according to which there was a kind of Yoruba colonial period, when the Yoruba migrated from elsewhere, conquered the area, and imposed a new system of government on the local people?[57] Without setting aside the probable spread of trends and people from the north and northeast, which would not be surprising given the scope of the Niger–Chad route at the time, the process of urban colonization could have arisen locally, with the growth of a governing elite that gradually came to dominate earlier tribal solidarity, with perhaps a little favorable foreshadowing from the ancient Nok civilization and certainly a gestation period prior to the famous bronze heads. The beginning of urban development in the strict sense does not seem to date much further back than the fifteenth or sixteenth centuries. As elsewhere, it would have been spurred on by a series of factors, such as contact with foreign merchants who came to trade with the local populations under the pressure of expanding east–west trade currents, and local improvements in production that expanded and diversified resources. For example, better iron tools increased farm productivity, as did the introduction of new plants, such as corn.

In fact, it is hard to see how the earlier economic networks would not have given birth to an urban civilization as they did elsewhere, such as in the inland areas of present-day Ghana, but in a different form. The Yoruba had a combination of relatively effective subsistence activities, since they were in contact with both the savanna (where Old Oyo and Ile-Ife were located) and forests (the Benin City area), which were crossed by major inter-regional trade routes. The northern influence was certainly present, through Nupe and, further north, from Bornu and Hausa cities that were at their period of greatest growth at the time. However, in a number of ways, the east–west axis was perhaps even more important than the north–south caravan routes.[58] At least from the mid-fifteenth century on, the northernmost route from Timbuktu and Gao extended into Hausa country up to Kano before going on to Bornu. All along the route there were secondary routes that branched off to the north and south. They connected with a more southern route that went from Jenne, through the Mande area in the south, across Begho and Bonduku, and then north around the Asante forest, through Salaga and Yendi, to arrive at Old Oyo, located at more or less the same latitude. From there, the route split again to the north to cross the Niger at Bussa. One of its branches went up to Kano, perhaps curving through Zaria, and the other went more to the south to Benue through the Nupe.

The circuit bypassed the forest and linked the east–west networks with the north–south networks, for example, to provide Yoruba country with salt from natron obtained in the northeast. There are some indications that an ancient route ran even farther to the south, perhaps from Ketu, linking the western savanna to the forest principalities of Ife and Benin City, and perhaps going from there eastward to the lower Niger, and perhaps even to copper- and salt-producing areas.

In the fifteenth century, activity increased along the central route under pressure from the Mande expansion, which was itself accelerated by rapid growth in European demand for gold.[59] The Mande lived along the Niger all the way to Jega and Bussa, where the rapids marked the final point of their eastward advance.[60] As at Kano, they brought kola nuts and helped to spread the slave trade. In exchange, they probably acquired iron and beads made of clay and glass.[61] There is no doubt that the route from Oyo to Bussa, which was preferred by caravans from the west because it was safer, although less direct, played a leading role in the city's history. The southern route was indisputably developed when the Portuguese arrived. Oyo controlled it to Whydah until the slave-trading Abomey kingdom expanded and began to compete with it in the eighteenth century. The slave trade, practiced at the expense of neighbors, contributed significantly to Oyo's expansion in the eighteenth century, and to its later fall.[62]

Thus we come to the question of the expansion of the Yoruba from Oyo between the sixteenth and eighteenth centuries. A little like the Gold Coast hinterland, it was a well-protected inland area with complementary local agriculture because it was located within the savanna–Sahel area. This probably encouraged regional micro-trade in food. Inter-regional trade was originally oriented toward the routes from the Sahel. In the beginning, contact with Europeans was only indirect and could not have a major effect. For example, until the seventeenth century, Ijebu, near the Lagos lagoon, was involved in Portuguese trade through links that were not necessarily direct and that were later monopolized by Benin City. Ijebu's diversified production included slaves and cloth that the Portuguese and Dutch sold on the Gold Coast.[63]

Benin City was too far to the south and was instead linked more closely to other analogous subcoastal or coastal networks that relatively quickly dealt exclusively in slaves. The site is famous for remarkable lost-wax bas-reliefs produced there between the fourteenth and eighteenth centuries and related to the art of Ife. Yet, despite this, the history of the city itself has attracted fewer researchers than has the state by the same name.[64] It seems likely that there would be a close correlation between Benin's art and the history of the capital. Indeed, we can read the Portuguese's surprise in their descriptions of their arrival in the city in the midst of the forest, several dozen miles from the coast. According to Pacheco Pereira, it was "a very large city."[65] At the end of the seventeenth century, when the slave trade had already caused many changes, a visitor described it as "larger than Lisbon; all the streets run straight and as far as the eye can see. The houses are large, especially that of the king, which is richly decorated and has fine columns. The city is wealthy and industrious. It is so well governed that theft is unknown, and the people live in such security that they have no doors to their houses."[66]

Benin City was quick to take advantage of the surrounding countryside. The city itself seems to have resulted from an earlier agglomeration of a number of large villages. Archeological findings indicate that about 2,500 square miles were farmed, and that the land had been cleared for farming since at least the thirteenth century, as in East Africa. According to oral tradition, Ife dominated the area from the twelfth century on. Its copper casters seem to have conveyed their knowledge to the area in the fourteenth century, and the territorial expansion appears to date from the fifteenth and sixteenth centuries, as indicated by the system of protection that was apparently upgraded shortly before the Europeans arrived in the mid-fifteenth century. Benin City had the most impressive wall yet discovered in southern Nigeria, measuring about eight miles long and nearly sixty feet high, from the bottom of the moat to the top of the earthen wall. It is estimated that five thousand men working full time for a whole dry season, about nine months,[67] were required to build it. Everything else is left to conjecture. There is no proof that the perfect match between urban planning and the social and political system, as described in nineteenth-century traditions, was reached before the time of the slave trade. At the time, there was a centralized administrative hierarchy made up of seven representatives of major hereditary families, the *uzama*, and two other groups of chiefs appointed by the Oba. The Oba was assisted by "palace chiefs" and "city chiefs" who were chosen from among the wealthy nobles.[68] Each dignitary controlled part of the territory, where he raised tribute. The city reflected this organization, with a large artery dividing it into two unequal parts. On one side were the king's palace and the residences of the palace chiefs; on the other side were forty or fifty quarters where the city chiefs lived, along with most of the artisans, who were grouped into corporations according to their crafts. The artisans included jewelers, copperworkers, woodworkers, ivory sculptors, tanners, dyers, and weavers, most of whom were women.

Prior to the sixteenth century, Benin City was the southernmost point of trade from the Niger. It probably exported ivory, salt, and cloth in return for leather and copper required by its artisans. The very growth of the state, and therefore of Benin's political influence, led it into direct contact with the Portuguese at the peak of its power. Their greed and the boom in the region's slave trade led to an initial phase of growth and prosperity followed by a decline in the local urban civilization that was all the steeper because the slaves sold by the people of Benin were rare and valuable. This was not because they had no slaves, but rather because internal consumption was lavish and high. In short, Benin City declined for reasons analogous to those that caused the better-known urban decadence in Congo. It also experienced the destructive drama of the Atlantic slave trade at its height.

## The Slave Trade Period

Our goal is not to focus on the history of the ravages caused by the slave trade. As we know, the effects on demographics, the economy, politics, and culture were fearsome in Africa.[69] Today, the history is relatively well known thanks to the publication in the last twenty years of a growing number of works. While the contributions may not be contradictory, they are not in complete agreement. The controversy will only increase our knowledge of the topic. I therefore refer the reader to the rich, constantly growing body of work.[70] In this book, the focus will be on how the growing slave trade changed the urban networks that had until then been more or less grafted onto the Atlantic, Maghrebian, and Swahili economies.

The changes were brutal and came in many forms. There was a fundamental break between the raiders and the raided. Thanks to the expansion of the slave trades, the raiders were armed by the Europeans. The new relations of forces between internal political neighboring chiefdoms and kingdoms, and especially the increased import of firearms, changed the power relations. The beneficiaries were mainly the sovereigns in charge of supplying the slave trade, political and economic authorities responsible for the raids, and magnates generally based on the coast. They aligned their interests with those of Western businessmen, and, at least initially, made huge fortunes from the expansion of the slave trade. They turned their states into war machines, and profits from the international slave trade went to a growing warrior class. However, war and trade went hand in hand. The warriors were joined by and often mixed with an extended class of "bourgeois" wheelers and dealers, local dignitaries and brokers, who began to adopt aspects of the Western culture and lifestyle. We should not forget that, especially in the eighteenth century, port authorities and slave traders made up a large proportion of the economic elite in the major Western powers, particularly in England and France. At the end of the eighteenth century, this social category also held an important position in African societies. Claude Meillassoux says that during the nineteenth century, a form of domestic slave trade economy became dominant,[71] and the Malian novelist Abdoulaye Ly describes that indigenous class of predators in a work that is lucid, painful, and cruel.[72]

In contrast, the people who were raided suffered terribly. They were oppressed and terrorized, and often fled and regressed, both economically and culturally. The phenomenon appeared in various forms and spread at different times in West and East Africa. West Africa suffered mainly in the eighteenth century, since that is when the Atlantic trade peaked. It is estimated that half of the slaves sold on the Atlantic coast were shipped in that century, after a meteoric start in the second half of the seventeenth century. The illegal slave trade was intense in the early nineteenth century and did not begin to ebb until the early 1830s. East Africa suffered most later, when the great slaving empires flourished there, partially because of the end of the Atlantic slave trade in the second half of the nineteenth century. Prohibited in the west, the slave trade became the monopoly of merchants linked to the Indian Ocean. The hubs of the international slave trade financed by the West—Khartoum in Sudan, the borders of Abyssinia, and the Ethiopian mountains—became havens for international traffickers linked with slave-trading kings in the Sahel hinterland. In the second half of the nineteenth century, Arab, Swahili, and more or less Islamized African slave traders dominated the eastern and southern coasts of Africa. Their slaving states, based on war, pillage, and terror, extended far into the interior.[73]

On the urban front, the effects were considerable. The ancient networks became disorganized and were eventually destroyed.

### The Revenge of the Farming States: The Asante

It is in these terms that Kea sees the decline of urban culture on the Gold Coast and the ascent of the Asante empire. It was not that the slave economy had played a negative role from the beginning. Slavery was both a growing source of outside profit and a social system of production, for the merchant elite used slave labor in trade for carrying goods, for example, and in gold or salt production and farming. As more urban centers active in the gold trade sprang up in the interior, the chiefs of those small wealthy states redistributed part of their fortune. Around 1660, Aduafo, chief of the state of Afufu, gave his dependents and the leading local families more than 2,000 dambas. Land rights, which became offices and privileges, led to more land being cleared by slaves. In the seventeenth century, rich families who had accumulated their wealth through urban trade began to migrate toward the relatively uninhabited north. Their southwest to northeast movements can be seen through changes in toponymy, the linguistic history of the place names that gave birth to family names. Oral traditions note the importance of blacksmiths and hunters in the new settlements. A few of them made profit enough to invest in land. Such investors in trade and craft acquired land by both conquest and, more frequently, purchase from local chiefs in exchange for gold dambas. The site where the city of Kumasi was later built had been bought for 25,000 dambas.[74]

Could it be that in the sixteenth and seventeenth centuries, land was beginning to be valued in terms of money, but the process broke down when the slave trade began to dominate? Ivor Wilks has suggested that the extensive clearing of the forest by settlers in the first half of the sixteenth century employed over ten thousand slaves bought from Jula and Portuguese traders, which would have meant an investment of 120,000 to 600,000 dambas a year.[75] The *abusua-kese* system, that is, the exogamous matrilineal clan system dominant among the Asante, seems to have taken shape in this period, based on the system of agricultural production. Farming was originally based not on kinship but on slavery, on control and ownership of the land, and on the expansion of agriculture historically linked with commercial capitalism and urban networks. The matrilineal clans, or *mmusua-kese*, set up a new form of socioeconomic organization. A landed aristocracy emerged, based on control of the land and farm labor. Gradually, the aristocracy came into conflict, which was sometimes open, with the families that used to govern. The mercantile economic organization had also created a hierarchy of leading families but was based on central markets, small intense output, divisions between crafts and agricultural labor, and a corporate professional structure involving brotherhoods of nobles and guilds of slave traders and artisans.

As direct slavery became dominant in the mid-seventeenth century, urban centers shrank. In the countryside, the disintegration of mercantile states resulted in increased banditry, which made earlier trade routes more fragile. The clearing of land placed the accent on farming. Territorial expansion became linked to military strength and family estates. The growth of the Asante military state, which consolidated the federation through incessant war at the end of the seventeenth century, seems to have sprung from this profound change, which was both economic and social. The establishment of a political center at the imperial city of

Kumasi led to the bureaucratization of an administrative hierarchy that was no longer linked with trade but instead with positions controlled by major farming families. The process also accelerated the decline and even disappearance of periodic markets and fairs, which had been earlier centers of trade. In short, under pressure from the Atlantic, a veritable political and social regression occurred. Western-style evolution was blocked.

## The Growth of Slave-Trading Ports
## and Cultural Creolization on the West Coast

Here, we will not review the history of the slave-trading kingdoms on the coast and in the interior such as Asante,[76] Abomey,[77] Porto Novo,[78] Wolof kingdoms in western Senegal,[79] Gabou,[80] and Calabar.[81] It is relatively well known and very well documented. We know that the emergence, growth, peak, and decline of these kingdoms occurred in remarkable synchrony with the rise, in the second half of the seventeenth century, expansion ("legitimate" in the eighteenth century and "shameful" in the first third of the nineteenth century), and drop in the mid-nineteenth century in the use of slave labor on Brazilian and Caribbean sugarcane plantations.[82] The point is simply to show the degree to which settlements on the Slave Coast were involved in the trade, and what forms of urbanism and urban culture resulted from it. At the same time that slave raids were hindering urban growth inland and ensuring the primacy of the military over merchants, the residences of the heads of the coastal states and city-states, formerly fishing villages and mediocre harbors, gradually became sizable political capitals. Unlike the urban networks of the Benin kingdom or the Asante empire, which involved fairly clearly differentiated societies, economic activity in the capitals was tightly controlled by an authoritarian, centralized state system, which was also small, in the case of the city-states. The economy focused on the import and export of slaves and became inseparable from war with neighboring peoples. Naturally, those with the closest ties to the coast, owing to proximity or skill, had the monopoly of the Atlantic market. They supplied it by preying on people in the hinterland and through the wars of commercial rivalry they fought with one another (Abomey against Ketou, Abeokuta, Benin City, and even the Asante).

The primitive forts on the coast grew. Many small centers were added. At Keta, Aneho, Great Popo, Whydah (populated by Fon people), and Offra-Jakin (populated by Ewe people) in present-day Togo, and on the islands at the mouth of the Niger, the establishment of a lodge or the presence of a slave trader's fort attracted an army of petty traders and workers hoping to profit from activities that were secondary to slaving. These newcomers included canoemen, longshoremen, brokers, merchants, town criers, and porters, who came to the European settlements and then did not leave. This gave rise to Danish, Dutch, English, Portuguese, and French quarters, depending on the number and nationality of the companies established in the city.[83] This can be seen in the well-known example of the layout and history of the French trading post, Whydah, which was the Atlantic port for the kingdom of Abomey and was annexed by King Agadja in 1727.[84]

These centers peaked between the mid-eighteenth and the mid-nineteenth centuries. All of them gave birth to an in-between civilization, known as a Creole culture. First, this meant the use of a working language, a pidgin tongue, that varied locally, depending on which European nation was dominant. In the Cape Verde Islands and the Rivières du Sud area, from Guinea-Bissau to present-day Sierre Leone, the pidgin was originally full of Portuguese words. English was common on the Gold Coast, and French around St. Louis du Sénégal. These linguistic variants, of which traces remain, have been studied mainly by Americans linguists. A privileged class of locals quickly began to master the language, business techniques, and material culture of the dominant Atlantic partner.

### Creole Society in St. Louis

The urban civilization in St. Louis has been the subject of much research. Mixing occurred early there. The post of St. Louis was created in 1659 out of a settlement founded by a merchant from Dieppe, who had arrived twenty years earlier. It was thus a French colony from the mid-seventeenth century on. Another twenty years later, the French took the island of Gorée back from the Dutch, who had built two forts and several warehouses on it in 1617. On the eve of the French Revolution, St. Louis had 7,000 inhabitants, of whom 660 were Europeans. The population of Gorée was 2,500, not including slaves in transit. St. Louis swelled with temporary inhabitants especially during the dry season, which was also the time for slave trading on the river.[85] Company agents with exclusive charters took turns spending time in these stations, which were both commercial warehouses and strongholds staffed by company employees and soldiers. The surrounding black population was initially made up of slaves, but eventually local lineages became established through the usual practice of temporary local "marriages," which were terminated by the Europeans when they returned home.[86] The famous *signares*, renowned for their elegance and acculturation, gave rise to a lively population of "mulatto"[87] traders, who mastered both cultures. They profited from business based on trade in slaves and Mauritanian gum in the ports or "stopovers" along the Senegal River. The Christianized local bourgeoisie was certainly few in number, with perhaps a dozen major traders at the peak in the nineteenth century. Nonetheless, its members accumulated a remarkable amount of wealth. Creole society peaked on the island of Gorée in the first half of the eighteenth century, when it was the center of trade, and in St. Louis in the following century, lasting until just before colonial imperialism. This creole domination continued until the second half of the nineteenth century, when white colonizers monopolized the import/export business. As of 1778, St. Louis's mayor had to be chosen from among the men of color and was in charge of relations between the governor and the people. The "habitants" (the name officially given to the Senegalese urbanites of the city) became French citizens, like all the *originaires* of what were called the "four communes" of Senegal.[88] The typical colonial architecture still bears witness to this. It was largely inspired by Portuguese buildings and can be found almost everywhere along the coast in the old posts. However, the oldest vestiges, which are very run-down today, date back only to the nineteenth century. Generally, the houses have two floors, with a warehouse and storeroom on the main floor, conveniently opening onto the street through a wide gateway on the same level. The servants' and slaves' lodgings were located at the back, around the courtyard. The living spaces were on the second floor and opened onto an elegant wrought-iron or stone balcony, which was suspended from the top or sometimes supported with columns. From the balcony, one could enjoy the breeze in the evening when the day's work was done.[89]

### The Fante on the Gold Coast: Early Acculturation

A case of creolization that has been studied in remarkable depth is that of the Gold Coast, where the English played an active role in the eighteenth century. The coastal Fante society was broken up into tiny chiefdoms but nonetheless won the monopoly of the slave trade with the interior. The English probably encouraged its independence from the Asante empire, which periodically tried to reclaim its very theoretical sovereignty over the Low Country. This objective political alliance went hand in hand with remarkable cultural interpenetration. It was remarkable because it began, as elsewhere, when European slave traders moved into the area. They settled, had children, and left their names and businesses to their local descendants, who were first of mixed blood but, after a few generations, became completely African.

The Brew dynasty is a significant example. It began with an energetic Irishman, Richard Brew, who lived on the coast from 1745 to 1776 in Brew Castle, a large home in Anomabu. The first Fante Anglican pastor, Philip Quaque, served at Brew's castle from 1767 to 1770. Brew's children were raised in England but returned to Africa in 1768. Brew's son Richard, who died in 1776, was a major slave trader. The first Richard Brew's grandson, Harry Brew, succeeded Cujoe Caboceer as the main local interpreter of Cape Coast Castle and local interpreter. He was the "best interpreter"[90] in the country, a position that involved much more than language, for he was also an influential merchant. His son, Sam Kanto (Samuel) Brew—the double given name indicates integrated Christianity—lived through the troubled period when the slave trade was being abolished. He remained a slave trader and was a major adversary of the British until the 1820s. However, in the following generation, one of Sam Kanto's sons, Samuel Collins Brew, became a leader of licit business. His marriage brought him into the "traditional" family of Chief Abura Dunkwa, and he participated actively in public affairs. The Brew family was involved in establishing the Fante confederation (in 1866), which

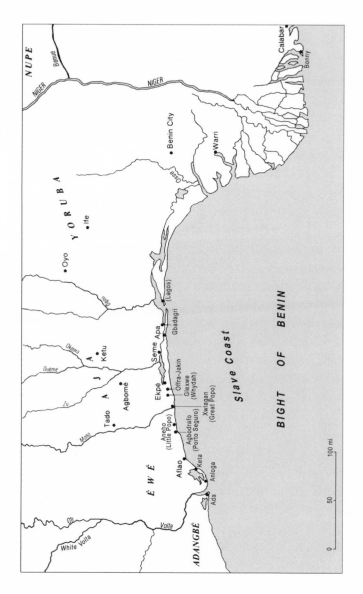

**Map 9.** Slave-Trading Cities on the Slave Coast East of the Volta in the Eighteenth Century
After N. Gayibor, "Les villes négrières de la côte des Esclaves," in C. Coquery-Vidrovitch, ed.,
*Processus d'urbanisation en Afrique*, vol. 1, p. 51, L'Harmattan, 1988

planned to hold a national assembly of chiefs once a year. There was also a plan to establish an executive parliament to unite all of the kings, each one of whom was supposed to be paired with an educated man. They were to determine the laws and collect taxes. The whole system showed an awareness of modern politics under British influence, though the government in London took the whole thing very badly. One of Samuel Collins's sons was hired by an expatriate firm, which marked the end of the economic independence of the African business world. His other son, James Hutton (b. 1844), was a political activist and journalist in the first twenty years of the colonial era. Educated in England, he began working as an attorney in 1854. In 1872, he met with the British governor as part of the Fante delegation charged with defending the confederation. In the 1890s, his relative, Samuel Henry Brew, educated at Wesleyan High School in Cape Coast, began his career in government but then began doing linguistic research. In the end, culture and the liberal professions became the refuge of the African intellectual bourgeois elite when triumphant imperialism evicted it from colonial operations.[91]

I have described this lineage in detail because it shows the development of a long-urbanized Creole class through the years of economic and political trials and tribulations between the colonizers and the inhabitants of the African coast. The way of thinking and the material and intellectual culture (homes, furniture, clothing, education, religion, and knowledge) of what the colonizers later called the elite did not always copy European models. Instead, African entrepreneurs and their families adapted European approaches from the inside, sometimes over a number of centuries.

### The Opulence of Afro-Brazilian Culture: An Unexpected Corollary of the Slave Trade

The Creole lifestyle is relatively well known in the case of the Afro-Brazilians on the Slave Coast (from present-day Benin to Nigeria) and, farther south, in Luanda (in present-day Angola). Afro-Brazilians were originally former slaves who had gained freedom, particularly in the eighteenth century, because they had been freed or had purchased their freedom and managed to return to more or less their own country; they were often of Yoruba or Mahi origin. The freed Africans and descendants of Africans, most of whom had been in Bahia, returned to Africa with a culture acquired in a foreign land. Their lifestyles and customs had been colored by those of Brazilians, Bahians, and the Portuguese. Their role is better known now, thanks to a number of works on the Black diaspora's South Atlantic culture. Although they had felt uprooted in Brazil, when they returned to Africa they asserted their Brazilian heritage. From America they brought their taste for cassava flour, the sweetness of guava, a Brazilian form of voodoo worship, and a style of architecture.[92] The term "Brazilian" quickly became a generic description of a group that was culturally homogeneous despite its members' many different origins. In the nineteenth century, the Afro-Brazilian community had become complex and included Portuguese merchants, Brazilians, mixed-race people of Fon, Yoruba, and Ewe origin, and local dignitaries protected by slave-trading kings. They shared the Portuguese language, Catholic religion, an aristocratic lifestyle, and needs and modes of consumption inspired by the West. Of course, they were all city dwellers. Very skilled in both Brazilian and African cultures, they made a fortune in what they knew best on both sides of the Atlantic: the slave trade.

The opulence of many Afro-Brazilians became famous along the coast. It is not clear whether the celebrated Francisco Félix da Souza (d. 1849) was actually an Afro-Brazilian. He became a powerful slave trader at the turn of the nineteenth century and then a favorite minister of the king of Abomey Ghezo under the name of Cha-Cha. It may be that he was a former Portuguese soldier from the fort of Whydah, or one of such a soldier's descendants. The descriptions and drawing we have of him do not even reveal whether he was white or of mixed blood. However, he remains a typical example of the local business community, members of which led an opulent lifestyle in the city of Whydah, the neighboring ports, and Lagos and were equally at ease both in the Christian culture and with ancestral beliefs and practices. Christian or not, Francisco da Souza had many children. He lived in a large home, surrounded by dependents, slaves, and luxury. Visitors were dazzled by his gold and silver dishes and extravagant lifestyle.

Leading merchants adopted an aristocratic style and employed artisans, masons, and carpenters from Bahia, where they frequently sent new apprentices for training.[93] In the nineteenth century, their economic power remained considerable as long as the illegal slave trade continued. Domingo Martinez became both more notorious and more prosperous than da Souza. He settled in Lagos in the early 1840s, when the port was still the most active center for the slave trade with the West. It is said he made a fortune of over a million dollars there before moving back to Porto Novo. At that point, he had a house in Whydah and another in Porto Novo, had invested part of his fortune in palm groves, and owned a herd of two hundred livestock. His hospitality was legendary. He imported his furniture from Europe, had a superb collection of precious stones and rare chinaware, bought huge amounts of European clothing that he barely ever wore, and claimed to live like the big plantation owners on the other side of the Atlantic, although his activities after the 1860s declined greatly and were more or less confined to trade in palm oil.[94]

Later, when they too were eliminated from political life by the colonial conquest, the Afro-Brazilians nonetheless remained a wealthy social class. As soon as missionaries arrived, their children went to Christian schools and became the foundation of the country's educated elite. In addition to their commercial activities and land titles, which allowed them to dominate palm oil production until the beginning of the twentieth century, they were quick to take advantage of every opportunity to enter liberal professions and journalism and later, in Ghana, to challenge colonialism.[95]

### The Portuguese-Brazilian Architectural Heritage

The key characteristic of members of this acculturated community was not that they knew how to read and write a European language, as the colonizers later thought condescendingly. It was that they had implicitly made a choice. They were all raised in an urban culture and hoped to speed up the evolution toward a Western civilization with more advanced technology than that of their own cultural heritage, going along with a Christian, Muslim, or, later, humanist spirit that would allow them to build a Western civilization that might also respect their views and lifestyle.[96] The group was relatively important but scattered all over the coastal areas of West Africa. G. Brooks estimates that Luso-

Africans, most of them quite Africanized, might have numbered two million in the seventeenth century (including residents of the Cape Verde Islands).[97] Afro-Brazilians coming back since the eighteenth century possibly added a few thousand. These people were usually urbanites and were remarkably well integrated into the larger society, which is probably why they had a strong influence on urban African architecture. Indeed, this group seems to have spread the Portuguese (and later Brazilian) style far into the interior.

The Brazilian-style home (*sobrado*) spread rapidly. It was introduced on the Slave Coast, moved into the Fon hinterland, and then even into Yorubaland.[98] How and why did local families find it so easy to adopt a style of house that seems so different from the traditional arrangement of ground-level huts with single openings scattered inside a large communal enclosure? A Brazilian urban home is, in contrast to the traditional style, a single, massive residence, usually with more than one floor and many windows, and more or less isolated on its land. This shows the receptiveness of the local people and architecture to innovation. They were open-minded because both the Afro-Brazilians and, more generally, the Yoruba already had urban habits.

There was more to it, however: Brazilian buildings did not contradict the earlier architecture, which, for example, already included verandas. Building the veranda around the outside of the house was an addition, rather than an innovation. Households were even more inclined to adopt technological improvements (new materials, such as the production of lime from ground shells, more openings, relative specialization of the rooms) that accompanied a habitat that did not contradict their principles of social organization, so long as a central space around the staircase remained open for group activities. The transition was facilitated by the availability of workers, such as brick makers, masons, and carpenters. The first of these workers were former slaves trained in Brazil who conveyed their knowledge to many apprentices, who in turn spread the skills throughout the country. Yoruba family and residential organization corresponded to the spatial organization. In Brazil, the slaves were crammed into the ground floor, whereas the masters lived above. The same organization was employed in Africa but based on a different presupposition: seniority, which was determined by age, wealth, and political authority. In order to assert their superiority, the "Brazilians" preferred to live upstairs, in the area that used to be reserved for their masters.

The Sagbo concession in Porto Novo, built in 1874 by the grandfather of the present owner, was still inhabited in the mid-1990s by the chief of the same line, his wife, some of their children, the children of his deceased brother, and two of his sisters, who are "paternal aunts" and who married elsewhere but came back to live with their children in the family enclosure. The return of the fathers' sisters is classical in matrilineal traditions. Paternal aunts are often responsible for voodoo worship and rituals at the family altars. The sisters and brother each have their own separate rooms and living rooms. The whole house is built out of clay, opens onto the market street, and has a courtyard in the back surrounded by smaller houses. The large central ground-floor living room, which has a pillar in the middle, was formerly used as a meeting place and for family ceremonies. Women now gather there to chat with visitors. Around the room and on the upper floor, there is a series of small rooms used for storage or religious purposes, as well as some larger rooms. Thus, there are the three components required for any residence: religious, political and private spaces.[99] It should be noted that "residence" (in town) and "enclosure" (in the countryside) are better words than "compound," a word of Indonesian origin, or the French-based "concession," since both of the latter have colonial connotations.

Houses reflected the social stratification even more clearly in that, particularly in Dahomey, where access to land was reserved for pure Dahomeans, the Brazilians used their urban homes not only as residences but as investments and for speculation. This became a private business that escaped the omnipotence of the state and control of the king. It was the sign of social status and prestige, namely, that of the city's influential merchant bourgeoisie. The same phenomenon is reflected in the brick houses of Merina people, which had verandas supported by stone pillars and were designed by the local Christianized bourgeoisie in Madagascar in the nineteenth century.[100]

On the domestic level, the changes in the material culture also reveal the passage from a subsistence economy to merchant capitalism.[101] The spread of the "Brazilian style" was clearly a result of the Atlantic culture, and a corollary of the triangular mercantile system that brought people, technology, and financial means into contact in a complex play of favorable international and interregional relations. The Afro-Brazilian style, coming back from Brazil, completed, a few centuries later, a process that began with the Luso-African style born from the direct exchanges between Portugal and Africa in the sixteenth century.[102] Throughout the nineteenth century, it spread rapidly well beyond Afro-Brazilian circles. In Yorubaland, this occurred just before colonization; today about 90 percent of the domestic architecture bears its traces.[103]

## The Political Capitals

The local slave-trading capitals were more sheltered from the West and had greater autonomy when they were located inland, which they often were. This enabled their sovereigns to maintain authority and avoid direct political and cultural interference from Europeans. This was the case of Abomey, Benin City, and, especially, Kumasi.

The question again arises of to what extent "traditions" and even indigenous urban ideas were at least partially reconstructed and manipulated in reaction to real social and cultural changes caused by the economic encounter and shock between African and Western ways of life. This can be felt clearly in the various interpretations given to the size of the royal, thus sacred, city of Abomey.

### Abomey and Porto Novo: Slave-Trading Cities

The interpretation also concerns the capitals of the kingdom of Dahomey (Abomey) and Porto Novo. According to oral traditions, there was a close relationship between the historical development of the agglomeration and the ethnic origin and religious beliefs of the groups living there.

The interpretation is certainly justified overall. Oral traditions tell us that the Agassouvi clan from Tado, the original cultural homeland of the Adja and Ewe, created the capital city of Abomey as part of its political plan to dominate all of the peoples on the plateau. In order to control the area, the king gave his dependents land (*E toun kpatin*). That made it possible for the king to infiltrate local communities and solve security problems by gathering trustworthy people around him. It also prevented his descendants from being tempted to try to seize power as soon as the princes became of age (a custom known as *E ton hon*). If we believe traditions, the site was chosen during the reign of Uegbadja (1650–79). However, in the early eighteenth century his successor, Agadja, was mostly responsible for consolidating the dynasty. Each king and each royal lineage around him were in turn magnets for social and residential power, which translated into the expansion of the city. Each lineage was associated with a different area because the crown prince always selected a new site for his palace.

The royal city covered more than ten acres and was surrounded by a moat.[104] It expanded as each new king built his palace, settled his court and many family members, and set up barracks for the royal troops. It was a city within a city, with homes, public squares, and streets. However, various quarters were grafted on all around the royal city. The quarters were organized around the homes of families who were kin to royalty, and most of the common lines linked with them. The result was a spiral that began at the center founded by Agadja, and then spread in a more or less counterclockwise direction. The various parts of the spiral determined a series of quarters that were the keys to the links with specific royal lines. Naturally, various practical considerations— water supply, defense of the city's doors, control of village communities around the central core—came into play in the choice of the sites, but there was clearly an overall structural design with a consistent symbolic representation of the kingdom as a whole.[105] The parallel growth of many markets simply reinforces this vision because, like all crucial actions in community life, the initiative to create the markets fell under the kings' authority, which they did not hesitate to use for economic and political purposes. The oldest market in the city, Adjahi, seems to have been created by the first king, Uegbadja. Others were transferred from conquered countries. Because there was little specialization in economic activities, most of the people who went to the markets were producers themselves. The king kept a monopoly over outside trade, which was controlled by the bureaucracy, and a class of regional merchants did not develop.

The main quarters are named after the "strong name" (a kind of sacred nickname) of each successive sovereign. The Adandokpodji quarter in the northwest is composed largely of members of the royal line of Kpengla (end of the eighteenth century) and of descendants of Kpengla's prisoners of war. Agblome, to the south of Adandokpodji, is dominated by the lines of religious servants responsible for gods imported during Tegbesu's reign. The Gbecon-Huegbo quarter, where everyone claims to be royal, mainly contains the real or adoptive descendants of King Agonglo, some of whom seem to be descendants of his successor, Adandozan. The Gbecon-Hunli quarter is largely the home of descendants of foreign servants rewarded by King Guezo (1818–58) for supporting him in the difficult period following the coup d'état that overthrew his predecessor, Adandozan. Farther to the east, the lineages linked with King Glele dominate the Djegbe quarter, which spreads out widely, forming almost all of the eastern half of the city. This is because during the slave trade wars, thousands of captives were transferred, many gods were introduced, and land was bestowed on the servants of those gods. The population of the city seems to have doubled from the end of the eighteenth century to that time, growing from 24,000 inhabitants[106] to about 50,000. In contrast, at Djimé in the northeast, on the road to Bohicon, the construction of Behanzin's palace did not really create a new quarter because the process was blocked by the French. In the south are the descendants of Agoli-Agbo, the last king chosen by the French.[107] The end of the dynasty stopped the development of the city because "no more king, no more crown prince, therefore no new quarter." This explains Abomey's unusual urban landscape, in which palaces, temples, public squares, and markets dominate, making the city look somewhat like a city sanctuary somewhat frozen in time.

The layout of the quarters was reinforced and to some extent determined by the location of many different religious sites. Some of the most typical features were small rectangular temples dedicated to *tohosu* and located beside homes. The tohosu was not really an ancestor but a "monster child" of an ancestor. It was worshipped by its kin and in turn protected them and ensured their well-being. Since any birth considered abnormal, including a miscarriage, could create a tohosu, in theory every family could have one. The fact that this was not so suggests that the possession of a tohosu was more a social and political mark than a biological or even religious phenomenon. Nonetheless, every king had a tohosu near his palace. Every family tohosu was linked with a royal tohosu, and common lineages without tohosus were linked indirectly with royalty through those that had one. Known since King Agadja, but generalized by King Glele (1858–89), the system was also one of the symbolic means of justifying the social and spatial organization of the city and consequently the national unity of Dahomey.[108]

This interpretation, exclusively based on traditions, may sound attractive. However, when the details are examined, the detailed perfection of the system is suspicious. It has been asserted much more strongly by a team of anthropologists and urbanists than by the historians whose work initially inspired them.[109] That the Dahomeian urban model requires justification is easy to understand with respect to politics; Dahomey was a well-organized, centralized small kingdom where the king's house and dependents played a major part. The more important their position, the closer to him they had to settle. However, this makes the virtually automatic match between home location and ethnic origin seem even more questionable. One reason the ethnic homogeneity of every district is doubtful is the complexity of common lineages. People do not explain the fact that they live in a specific quarter by membership in a clan (*ako*)—that is, a set of people claiming the same mythical ancestor. When examined more closely, membership in the twenty-five non-noble clans scattered throughout the city has only a weak relation to where people live. Residence fits with kinship ties on a smaller scale, that of line or *hennu*. Yet even this seems composite and even confused. Its integrity appears to be based on the mutual recognition by its members of a relation of proximity expressed in the language of kinship. The founding ancestors are presumed to have come from the same village. However, kinship ties refer much more often to geographical and spatial considerations: hennu members are the descendants of individuals who moved to live near princes for very different reasons, such as because they were forced to as slaves or for military, political or social interests. Acknowledgment of kinship seems instead an a posteriori explanation of an urban migration that did not necessarily differ from that experienced elsewhere.

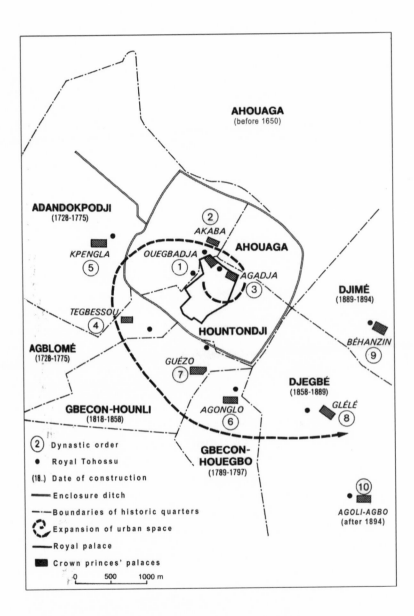

**Map 10.** Formation of Abomey's Historical Quarters (1625–1889)
Based on: Sylvain Anignikin, *Cahiers d'Études Africaines*,
EHESS, vol. 104, no. 4, 1986, p. 539

Porto Novo is as old as Abomey: it was founded in the late seventeenth century or early eighteenth century. It is interesting because it is neither a sanctuary nor, despite competition from the nearby economic center of Cotonou, a dying city. Its longevity and coastal location have enabled it to blend a strong local tradition with influences from the other side of the Atlantic. Unlike Whydah, which was a major port conquered by the Dahomeans in 1727 and described the same year by Snelgrave,[110] Porto Novo was a royal city. Its development was intimately linked with the slave trade, but it never had a fort. Its layout centered around the royal palace and the market.

Tê Agbanlin, prince of Allada, is supposed to have settled near the chief of Akron, whom he finally eliminated toward the end of the seventeenth century. He built a large house, Hogbonou, which later became the Adja name of the village, and he created a market, Takpimede. In fact, travelers' narratives first mention the location only around 1730. They speak of it as a new port (*porto novo*) where slaves were sent: more than 1,200 were exported from Porto Novo in 1765 alone.[111] The earliest description is that of J. Adams, who visited the city around 1800.[112] The first known map of the city, which dates from 1884, closely resembles his description. Adams estimated the population to be between 7,000 and 10,000, which would have made it one of the most populous cities that he visited, along with Benin City. The demographics were fluid, however, because they were very dependent on the prosperity of trade. It is possible that in the mid-nineteenth century the city had several tens of thousands of inhabitants. The local Gun or coastal Adja population was joined by Yoruba merchants attracted by the slave trade and a fairly large number of slaves, who were also Yoruba but were owned by rich local families. Yoruba women were at the origin of major cultural mixing. A tiny minority (today 1 percent of the population) of Afro-Brazilian brokers, often also of Yoruba origin, enjoyed a special status. When Europeans settled in Porto Novo on the eve of colonization in the mid-nineteenth century, and the slave trade declined and was replaced by palm groves, power relations changed.

Adams said that there were many artisans and that products from Brazil and England could be found in the market. The city was built in the form of a steep semicircular amphitheater on the plateau leading down to the lagoon. It was fortified, surrounded by a deep moat and a wall a little over three feet high. In the center there was the palace (*hommé*, "inside the door"). The Yoruba-inspired central part of the building was constructed around courtyards bordered by walkways. In the nineteenth century, it was made of adobe and had a thatched roof; it probably replaced other similar buildings. The size of the rooms was limited by the building techniques, but the number of rooms indicated the status of the home, as did special architectural details such as open galleries, columns, sculpted doors, and pieces of furniture used for religious purposes. According to traditions, some sovereigns had other palaces in other quarters, but nothing remains of them except for the one built by the last king, Toffa, on the outskirts of the capital in the Gbecon Quarter.[113] The city's adobe houses were separated by high walls that were also fortified and had gun slits. This made the city look even more like a trading center that had to protect itself against raiders. Artisans, including potters, smiths, tanners, and dyers, lived in the heart of the city. Their quarters contrasted with the quarters to the north and west, which were sparsely populated and included the residences of princes and relatively large farms, as well as the governor's residence, the *migan*, which was located outside the city. Fishers had their homes to the south. The market, which was the center of economic activity, was held in front of the royal palace. This was also where the "market of men" and "market of children," in other words, the slave markets, were located.

Origin myths emphasize the importance of the period attributed to Tê Agbanlin, but this insistence may be incorrect, since the population had to have been very small in his time. It does, however, show the concern with asserting the city's identity as a community, athough the community seems to have been made up of immigrants of various origins. This said, the socio-religious references based on kinship are analogous to those in Abomey. Each group is defined by a founding ancestor and the deified *vodun* associated with him. He is always in his temple and considered to be the origin of the mythical-historical migration from Allada. The founding ancestor received his land from the king. This form of ancestor worship was the responsibility of the chief of the dominant line or *hennugan*, "head of the house" (*xweta*) of the quarter that is home to most of the ancestor's descendants or those who claim to be and believe they are his descendants.[114] What is different from Abomey, because of the cosmopolitan nature of the city, is the origin that the tradition attributes to the quarters. Those most closely linked with the royal power are those said to be founded by princes or vodun priests called upon by kings to protect the realm. In contrast, others are somewhat independent of the authorities because they were created by the original but deposed dynasty, or by those not belonging to the royal family, or even former slaves. This does not include more recent quarters founded by a Brazilian merchant (the *Fiekone*) or, after the Europeans arrived, Yoruba traders whose religions were not specifically linked with royalty.[115]

Reality or reconstruction? As at Abomey, there is a collective memory of a relation between the urban space and authority, since the city was built in the image of the palace, as a very large enclosure, or concession. The whole thing was designed to reproduce the Aja-Tado kingdom and the migration that resulted in the creation of the kingdom of Allada, from which it seems the kingdoms of Abomey and Porto Novo both sprang. The urban space was structured as a political capital designed to reinforce, by its very existence, the power of the leader.

### Kumasi:  The Political Center in the Interior

Kumasi was special because it was located in the interior. The Asante were in contact with the forested south and the Europeans on the coast, but they developed their relations with the countryside to a much greater extent, based on large-scale trade in kola nuts. They were major producers, but the market for kola nuts was in the north, throughout the Sudanese-Sahelian area of Islamized West Africa.[116] Kumasi was the only place where the earlier urban culture survived, though it had not been maintained without change. Despite the origin of the Asante empire in military campaigns and the conquest of rural land, the city became the symbol of the strength of the regional economy, which was able to develop partly in connection with and partly independently from or only on the borders of the slave-trading economy in the West African back country.

Kumasi thus became the capital of a large empire. The conquered provinces were administered, in other words, taxed, by the city's prominent families, who thereby concentrated the wealth in their own hands.

It was only at the end of the eighteenth century, after 20 years of incessant fighting and disorder, that a great king, Osei Kwadio, succeeded in breaking the power of the military and landowning oligarchies and creating an administration of imperial civil servants. The civil servants were not high born, and their authority and fortune depended on him alone, which guaranteed their loyalty. The state's central secretariat was set up with the help of educated Muslims. Treasury accounts were kept in gold, empirically but efficiently.[117] The city's authorities were organized very similarly to those of Abomey. In both cases, the links between the monarchy and the regional lords and their allegiances to one another were renewed each year through major celebrations (*odwira* in Kumasi, *coutumes* in Abomey) that brought together in the capital all those with authority in the empire and all of the military forces. War and trade were the foundations for power, but both activities remained under the strict control of the central power. As in Dahomey, in the nineteenth century there was less war because war became less profitable with the decline in the slave trade; there was more trade, based on regional agricultural production of palm oil in Dahomey and kola nuts in Asante. This led to what may be defined as a "precolonial state capitalism," with a tradition of investing in gold, cowry shells, and slave labor to increase profits while participating in complex, wide-ranging trade in West Africa. Kumasi became the most powerful trade center in the area.

However, the Kumasi mode of organization, which was probably quite typical of the socioeconomic organization of West Africa from the seventeenth to the nineteenth centuries, was initially not very different from the large secondary satellite markets. These markets included Salaga and, farther away, Buna, capital of a small independent kingdom on the Mopti-Jenne-Bobo-Buna-Bonduku-Kumasi caravan route, about a twelve-day walk north from Bobo Dioulasso toward the Sahel; Kong, the largest Jula city to the west; and Bonduku, to the south, toward the slave-trading ports. The structure of precolonial Buna, which was both a political capital and market city, was analogous to that of Kumasi. It was characterized by the presence in the city of all of the aristocracy, with three branches of the royal family corresponding to three of the city's main quarters. Each of the city's approximately twenty different quarters corresponded in principle to a specific social status, social role or occupation, origin, and sometimes language or religion. This differentiation was only as an initial approximation, however. In reality, the original clans assimilated other individuals and groups throughout Buna's history. New family groups came and left, living beside or assimilating with the groups already settled. Each quarter thus has its own unique history and reflects both the links that existed among its various components and the social development that kept people there.[118]

Kumasi's advantage was that it was located in the middle of interconnected concentric circles of trade routes designed to channel longdistance resources away from competing routes, particularly that of the Volta. The need to control the area justified maintaining a military culture. Kumasi also kept its monopoly by blocking the growth of a class of local merchants who could have come into dangerous competition with the authority of the king and his aristocratic bureaucracy. Trade was reserved for carefully controlled foreign communities of Islamized Jula and Hausa merchants, for whom special districts were reserved. Kumasi's market was initially a compulsory terminus. Traders from the savanna could not go farther south, and the people from the forest were prohibited from going farther north. In 1840, control became even stricter. Merchants could no longer enter the capital but were required to live in satellite towns, the largest of which was Salaga, in the middle of Gonja country. Salaga was about two hundred miles north of Kumasi and became a major market and terminus for Hausa caravans in the eighteenth century. In the nineteenth century, it was a transit center for kola nuts, and in 1870, it had between twelve and fifteen thousand inhabitants and was visited by about ten thousand merchants per season.[119] Situated next to these lively transit market towns, Kumasi thus became a luxurious residential capital able to live off the fruits of its control of the area.[120]

There are many nineteenth-century descriptions of Kumasi, and we can assume that at least the layout resembled that of the city at the end of the eighteenth century. The most detailed map is by Bowdich and dates from 1817.[121] The old city, destroyed under British colonization, was located on the eastern flank of the hill, where today we find the heart of the business district. At the time, it would have been around four miles in circumference, but the city center covered a little more than half a square mile. In an empire that Bowdich estimated had a total population of a million inhabitants, the heart of the capital had perhaps twelve to fifteen thousand, a density five time less than that of London at the same period, which is considerable when we remember that the houses had only one floor.[122] The population may even have doubled by mid-century. Since it was not enclosed by a fence, the same number of people may have lived outside the city proper, which had seventy-seven quarters. Presumably, the layout was similar to that of the other African capitals, and the political center and palace were surrounded by an urban and rural nebula where families of lower birth, artisans, and slaves lived in scattered hamlets and plantations.[123] Aside from the jewelers who were located in the city because of the value of gold, artisans were grouped into specialized villages three hours at most from the palace. A real technological revolution accompanied the Asante rise to power around the end of the seventeenth century. It involved, not radical changes to tools and techniques, but rather a merging of the original know-how of many different peoples, which was the result of bringing artisans from conquered lands together to serve the central power exclusively.[124] The first artisans came from the former state of Denkyira, which used to produce gold and was conquered by the Asante. Next came artisans from other conquered areas, mainly slaves taken as war booty and kept in the service of the king; these artisans included smiths, weavers, dyers, potters, royal parasol manufacturers, tam-tam makers, and wood carvers.[125] Lodging the artisans, their families, and apprentices probably created logistical problems, such as that of obtaining enough porters to deliver the quantities of food required. Since artisanal work was very compartmentalized, it was more efficient to locate artisans in specialized villages near one another, where they could take care of their own subsistence and produce what the court needed.[126] For similar reasons, this arrangement was also frequent in precolonial capitals of some importance.

The city center was therefore reserved for notables. There was nothing original in this; all the other political capitals were the same. In Kumasi, all the streets were named and each was under the responsibility of a senior dignitary linked with the palace by highly visible public servants who had to travel constantly and convey orders; heralds and sword carriers brandished the golden insignia of their offices. The only people who had the right to live there were the king's dependents, in accordance with a complicated hierarchy of responsibilities. Their essential function was to ensure that the palace operated smoothly and was properly provisioned.

The palace was located in the eastern part of the city, not far from the marshy area, where the main market and train station are today. It covered more than five acres. Most of the buildings of the royal city were constructed out of traditional materials, except for the *aban* made of stone. Like the rest of the buildings in the city, buildings of the royal city were topped with bamboo-framed roofs covered in palm leaves. Administrative offices along the entrance wall separated the rest of the city from the various royal rooms, which opened onto a huge courtyard approximately forty yards long by seventeen yards wide. The courtyard was edged by an open gallery built after 1820 but based on earlier sketches; it had square columns resting on bases decorated with bas-reliefs in red clay that were "polished and brilliant, utterly magnificent."[127]

The *zongo* of the Hausa merchants was situated to the northeast, while the sacred quarter, containing the mausoleums of the kings, was to the northwest.[128] The whole area was essentially devoted to the capital's government, however. Large urban spaces and buildings contrasted with the density, disorder, and filth of coastal cities. The streets were wide and shaded by banana trees. Sanitation was remarkable: houses had latrines on every floor (washed regularly with boiling water) and, as one observer noted, "every household burns its garbage every morning at the end of the street and the homes and people are both equally clean and well groomed."[129]

The four main avenues were half a mile long and fifty to one hundred feet wide. They were edged by two-story houses of a very distinctive architecture. Most were raised nearly more than six feet above the ground, and that space was decorated with bas-reliefs made of red ocher polished stone. On a small number of homes, white clay decoration extended all the way up to the roof, making the house look as if it had been whitened with chalk.[130] Maintenance of the façades was under the king's control because architecture was an aristocratic privilege. Only the leading dignitaries had the right to have a loggia or *adampan* (literally, "open room"); the space was a kind of hall used for offices attached to the home and opening onto the street.[131] The actual living quarters were in the back, invisible from the street. There could be up to thirty or forty rooms scattered around a large open space. A single household could contain 50 to 250 inhabitants, depending on its head's rank.

This gives us a picture of a very special kind of urban design. It combined the urban features of a city, divided into quarters and controlled by a very visible authority, with traditional African residences similar to those found everywhere else and made up of large enclosures ("concessions" in colonial language) containing relatively open residential units.

Kumasi is especially fascinating because of its remarkable local urban continuity. It was once the capital of a brilliant empire, then a major hub of the cocoa economy, and is now Ghana's second city. It has always been a regional capital, and it played a leading role in the local economy. It was born of the accumulation of land titles that fostered the clearing of virgin land at the end of the seventeenth century but became a veritable war machine in the eighteenth century, living from conquest and slave trading. In the nineteenth century, it was transformed into a center for agricultural-commercial capitalism combining slave labor with trade in kola nuts. Natural rubber and food products became the focus at the very beginning of the colonial period. Know-how, capital, and labor (officially freed) were then vigorously reinvested in cocoa plantations. This was the beginning of the modern city's prosperity until the economy declined under the Nkrumah regime (1957–66).

The city's exceptional location, at the crossroads of complementary areas, helps to explain its flexible vitality, as does the continuity of links between neighboring peoples, from the ancient paths to the modern railway. However, the Asante's dynamic strength and social cohesion have also enabled them to ensure their capital's fortune in a very wide range of contexts.


## The East Coast: From Swahili Cities to Slave-Trading Ports

We have much less information on urban developments on the east coast of Africa in this period. This is not because it was not flourishing: the Indian presence increased in the eighteenth century, but it remains

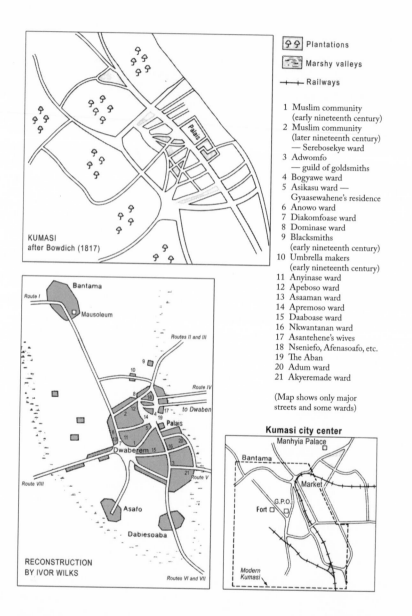

Plantations
Marshy valleys
Railways

1  Muslim community
   (early nineteenth century)
2  Muslim community
   (later nineteenth century)
   — Serebosekye ward
3  Adwomfo
   — guild of goldsmiths
4  Bogyawe ward
5  Asikasu ward —
   Gyaasewahene's residence
6  Anowo ward
7  Diakomfoase ward
8  Dominase ward
9  Blacksmiths
   (early nineteenth century)
10 Umbrella makers
   (early nineteenth century)
11 Anyinase ward
12 Apeboso ward
13 Asaaman ward
14 Apremoso ward
15 Daaboase ward
16 Nkwantanan ward
17 Asantehene's wives
18 Nseniefo, Afenasoafo, etc.
19 The Aban
20 Adum ward
21 Akyeremade ward

(Map shows only major
streets and some wards)

KUMASI
after Bowdich (1817)

Bantama
Route I
Mausoleum
Routes II and III
Route IV
to Dwaben
Palais
Dwaberem
Route VIII
Asafo
Dabiesoaba
Routes VI and VII
Route V

RECONSTRUCTION
BY IVOR WILKS

Kumasi city center
Manhyia Palace
Bantama
Market
G.P.O.
Fort
Modern
Kumasi

**Map 11.** Kumasi: The Old City (Main Roads and Quarters)
Based on: Ivor Wilks, *Asante in the XIXth Century*, Cambridge University Press, 1975, p. 380

little studied.[132] This coast had many advantages. It was favorable to navigation, and the ports were relatively welcoming in comparison with the inland areas, which included desert in the north, high grassy savanna suitable only for nomadic populations to the south, and marshy lowland forests. Given this, it is hard to understand why the Indian Ocean coast experienced such a decline. It has been argued that it became more difficult to get water, that the soil was fragile and became too poor for farming, that tropical illnesses such as sleeping sickness spread, and that there was an increasing imbalance between population and resources. However, when we consider the extreme environmental variations of a coast thousands of miles long, these arguments are not persuasive.[133] Political and socioeconomic factors were probably decisive factors.

### Urban Decline and the Ambiguous Role of the Portuguese: Mombasa and Mozambique

What we do know is that the arrival of the Portuguese increased commercial competition. This translated into general instability maintained by unending wars sparked by the international interests that passed the ports from hand to hand. The frequency of invasions and sieges of cities, the resulting alternation of domination and independent governments, and the occupation of the hinterland by advancing peoples new to the area (and who were often hostile, such as the Galla) made the period uncertain and not very conducive to the development of urban culture. The Portuguese dominated from the end of the sixteenth century and throughout all of the seventeenth century. In the north, after pillaging the city three times (1505, 1529, and 1586), they controlled Mombasa from 1589 to 1593. In 1632, they stopped pretending to govern in collaboration with the Sheik of Malindi, their main ally. However, the Imam of Muscat (later the Sultan of Oman) replaced them from 1698 to 1735 and installed an Arab governor before the Portuguese returned briefly from 1728 to 1729.[134] When the Portuguese first arrived, they admired the city's beautiful gardens, high towers, and spacious, busy port full of ships loaded with wax, grain, ambergris, ivory, precious metals, spices (pepper, ginger, and cloves) from Calicut, and women dressed in silk and covered in gold jewelry.[135] In 1735, the Mazrui dynasty, who had originally arrived as the imam's governors, established themselves as the ruling family before falling under the domination of the Zanzibar sultans a century later.

Paradoxically, it was with the decline of their culture that the Swahili identity took clear form. For example, at the time, there were twelve "tribes" (*mataifa*) in Mombasa. Another word was also used to refere to them: *maji* (plural *miji*), the primary meaning of which is "settlement" or "city." These tribes were in some sense miniature "nations," supposedly descended from prominent families that were then in decline. However, they actually resulted from an amalgamation that gradually formed around certain clans out of various more recent influxes of migrants.[136] They were broken into ethnic and political factions, each of which was led by a chief (*sheikh* or *shehe*), and formed two rival groups. Nine of the factions (*tisa taifa*) claimed to come from the Shirazi "founding fathers" of the city; they were known collectively as "the people of the old city" and forged a local identity. The other three clans (*latha taifa*) reacted against the trend to assimilation. Aware that their large number gave them weight, they formed a separate group. The Arabs of Oman molded the system into a kind of loose government, but many quarrels arose, thereby weakening the city.

In the south, the Portuguese landed at Kilwa for the first time in 1500. With a force of five hundred men, they burned the city down in 1505 and prohibited the inhabitants from trading with Sofala, the source of gold from "Mutapa." A long series of quarrels between local sultans and the city's Portuguese "captains" followed, leading to the decline of the port, which was more or less deserted by the inhabitants.[137]

The Portuguese continued to assert their power over the coast of Sofala, which controlled the legendary flow of gold from southern Africa; it is unlikely that there was ever a city there properly speaking, but rather a series of ports of call.[138] The Portuguese left the mark of their urbanism on the island of Mozambique, located two and a half miles from the mainland. It became the primary transit port for the slave trade, in which the Portuguese were victorious over the Dutch. The city was completely destroyed by the latter, who occupied the island at the beginning of the seventeenth century (1607–1608). It lost its ancient Arab and Swahili ties (when the Portuguese arrived, the city boasted the sheikh's white house, with its veranda, and a mosque), though the

Arab influence was felt again with the rise of the Oman sultanate at the beginning of the eighteenth century. In the end, the city was gradually rebuilt in an admirable architectural style that made it a jewel of Indian-Portuguese art. It was protected by the fact that the whole island was the property of the Portuguese state, which made generous donations to religious orders to facilitate the construction of churches and monasteries. The "city of stone" (*cidade de pedra e cal*), in contrast with the city of earth (*cidade de macuti*), has a remarkably consistent style because the inhabitants used the same materials—limestone and termite-resistant hardwood beams—and the same masonry techniques for centuries. The façades were whitewashed with lime and had rectangular windows tucked in along straight bands of walls. White cornices, windows and doorframes, and pilasters indicated a similar attention to detail. The same system of terrace roofs was used to gather water, and the pavement was of black and white stones typical of classical Lisbon. Algarve, the southernmost area of Portugal, was the major architectural model, but there were also Arab and Indian influences. For example, the gable of the Church of Misericordia, which dates back to the sixteenth century but was rebuilt in 1702, has arabesque ornamentation in the center, a border decorated with slender Indian-style ledges, but an overall baroque style that is typically Portuguese.

The city stretched north–south on the narrow island, which is two miles long and less than half a mile wide. Its layout included a series of warehouses and businesses along the coast and more luxurious residences on the facing hillside. It was considered preferable for the latter to be some distance from the complex center, which was a mixture of administrative offices, boutiques, and housing. While many changes were made in the nineteenth century, when the city expanded into the southern part of the island, it was still possible to see the eighteenth-century urban system composed of a tight network of winding alleys. In turn, the alleys surround the seventeenth-century center. Between 1940 and 1960, the city had eight thousand inhabitants, but we do not know its earlier population.

At the north of the island, construction on the present Fortaleza began in 1558, fourteen years after the first inroads into the interior. The vestiges of two stone walls and an entrance gate redesigned in 1712 can still be seen. The Campo de St. Gabriel, the garrison's parade grounds, which separated the Fortaleza from the rest of the city, was on the site of an old Portuguese cemetery of which a few traces remain. The Jesuit St François-Xavier College was rebuilt between 1618 and 1620 on the ruins of the Old Tower, which was erected in 1507, soon after the Portuguese arrived and left a small garrison of 15 men. More than a century later, in 1760, it was expropriated for use as the governors' residence (*capitães generães*) and transformed into St. Paul's Palace. Its elegant pink façade is similar to that of the eighteenth-century palace near Belem in Lisbon that now houses the overseas agricultural museum. It opens onto a broad flagstone esplanade lined with trees: the Largo de S. Paulo, which was built in the nineteenth century to give the palace a view of the sea but required the destruction of a whole series of old houses. Today's hospital dates back to the end of the nineteenth century and was built over that of S. João de Deus, which had been built in the seventeenth century in the southern area, which was uninhabited at the time.[139]

Mozambique's architecture gives the impression of much contact with many different powers, including opposing forces, which achieved the intense cultural mixing seen in its cities: Swahili influences mixed with Indian, Portuguese, and, naturally, local cultures.

Trade on the Indian Ocean remained highly diversified. It included traditional local products, such as tortoise shells and coconuts, as well as copper and gold, which probably were traded as they were at the time of the Zimbabwean and Mutapa empires (tenth to sixteenth centuries), although we know very little about the organization of this trade. Ivory, highly valued by Indians, became dominant in the eighteenth century, which increased and complicated relations with the interior, where elephants were hunted.[140] Trade in slaves, who were used systematically by local Arabized planters and probably by city dwellers as well, became dominant toward the end of the eighteenth century, later than on the west coast. Among other things, the slave trade was the foundation of the Sultan of Zanzibar's fortune in land. In 1818, the sultan imported the first clove plants from the islands of Mauritius and Bourbon (the latter became La Reunion).[141] Cloves replaced the traditional coconuts and subsistence rice crops, and clove exports quickly became the basis of his international wealth.

## The City of Zanzibar and the Transition to Capitalism

Before 1818, the only major urban growth was in the city of Zanzibar. At the time, it was unique. It illustrated true colonization based on slave trading by a minority that was at least partially from the coast but claimed its roots in the religious and political culture of Arabia. As a colonial power, Zanzibar encouraged but controlled some of the way stations on the African coast, such as Kaole, a military and administrative post located about twenty miles to the west of Zanzibar; Kaole's port became choked by mangrove at the end of the eighteenth century.[142]

Bantu occupation of the Island of Zanzibar, with an area of 637 square miles, dates to the fourth or fifth century. Later the Bantu mingled with Shirazi from the coast, who initially settled at Pemba Island, which soon became the breadbasket of the Swahili world because its climate was more humid and therefore a good place to raise rice. The remains of an ancient capital city, approximately twenty miles from the final site of Zanzibar, appear to date from the ninth century, before the Swahili period. An inscription from Hijra year 500 (1107 CE) is the oldest record known of written Arabic in East Africa. When the Portuguese arrived in the sixteenth century, they found the land already very much in use for raising rice, millet, and sugarcane. A small number of Portuguese settled in the fishing village that was to become the city of Zanzibar. They built a church and a few houses before 1591, developed trade with the mainland, and exchanged cloth, beads, and iron objects for ivory and ambergris; however, many of their actions were belligerent.

In the early seventeenth century, Arabs from Oman began to claim control over the Indian Ocean. After conquering Ormuz, they took Fort Jesus at Mombasa in 1698. They sent a garrison to Pemba, and in Zanzibar they exiled the queen, who had remained loyal to the Portuguese, to Muscat in Arabia and set up an Omani governor in the fort. The latter was built around 1700 and still remains facing the harbor, which is one of the best in eastern Africa and used for centuries by dhows brought from Arabia by the northeast monsoon between November and March. According to tradition, around 1725, Sultan Hussan decided to clear the peninsula on which the city is built today. It seems that only one of its mosques dates back to the seventeenth century, and the others were not built until the eighteenth century or later.[143] Zanzibar became the major storehouse for Arab merchants and Swahili planters from the African continent who had begun to settle there during a new wave of Shirazi immigration. In season, about 100 large dhows came from India and Arabia for slaves, ivory, tortoise shells (from the mainland), coconuts, and rice (from Pemba).

The turning point for the emergence of the Sultanate of Zanzibar was when Sultan Seyyid Said, who had ascended to the throne of Oman in 1806, decided to make Zanzibar his principal residence around 1840. He asserted his power against the Portuguese and, naturally, the local peoples along the coast, from Somalia to Mozambique; until his death in 1856, he made Zanzibar the focal point of trade in East Africa. He also encouraged Arab planters: Zanzibar produced mainly copra (dried coconut meat) but also, thanks especially to Pemba, acquired a virtual monopoly on clove production. From then on, the enterprising governing bourgeoisie was divided into those who were largely of Omani origin and owned slave plantations, and a dynamic group of merchants who were often of Indian origin and had settled in Zanzibar. The two groups ended up merging to stand up to the caravan drivers, who were also of Omani origin. Various social strategies, particularly with respect to marriage, widened the divide between the groups because the caravan drivers were gradually led into debt, which increased their tendency to retreat back into the interior of the continent.[144] They went deeper and deeper and were the first to reach the Congo basin. Toward the end of the nineteenth century, they traveled from the stopover town of Ujiji on the edge of Lake Tanganyika to Burundi and Rwanda, which had until then been closed to foreigners. The oldest permanent Omani settlement was Bujumbura, which only dates from 1905.[145]

While its architecture remained traditional, Zanzibar also gained stone buildings in the mid-nineteenth century, which is why the old city is still called Stone Town. This part of the city is located between the sultan's palace and an arm of the sea (today the commercial artery of Creek Road). This historical quarter covers a space that was at the time a small island of at most five hundred acres. The quarter is full of mosques (there were forty-eight in the 1990s) lost in a maze of dark alleys and hemmed in by two-, three-, and even four-story homes that used to belong to Swahilis and Indians and are built around a patio that was open to the sky, with living spaces on the upper floors and terrace. The facades, which are now very damaged, were decorated with stucco friezes, and the wooden doors had carved arabesques that married Arabian and Indian styles by combining geometrical figures with lotus flowers. The town was dominated by the House of Wonders, which was the sultan's former palace. The palace was rebuilt under the British protectorate, after the British destroyed it in 1896 to impose their own sultan candidate. The new palace, supposed to be reminiscent of the previous one, had three tiers of wrought iron pillars and balconies imported from Glasgow in the late 1890s. Visitors found the house itself just as amazing as its new elevator. In clear weather, the mainland was visible from the top of its hundred-foot tower.[146] The last independent sultan, Said Bargash (1870–88), modernized Zanzibar by having water brought into the city via canals and linking his summer palace with the city via a railway more than five miles long.

The city's population was twenty-five thousand but swelled to forty thousand in the business season. The total population of Zanzibar and Pemba may have reached two hundred thousand around 1870; of this number, eighty percent were slaves. This was both Zanzibar's peak and the beginning of its decline. As the slave trade grew, mainland cities took the lead. Zanzibar, which had been able to adapt the slave trade to a veritable slave-based economy targeting the Western market, had been moving toward colonial capitalism for nearly two centuries. In a way, and at virtually the same period, it was a system based on slave labor and plantations strangely similar to that of the southern United States, aside from the difference in scale. Was it pure chance that the first Westerners to establish official ties with the sultan in 1828 were the Americans?[147] They signed a treaty of friendship and trade in 1833 and set up the first foreign consulate four years later. However, toward the end of the nineteenth century, the island of Zanzibar became the main target of the British antislavery crusade in the Indian Ocean, as the sultan was very slow to accept the idea of suppressing such a profitable activity, which was the basis of his empire's prosperity. In order to alert the Western world to the scope of slavery in Zanzibar, Stanley used it as a base to prepare his expedition to find Livingstone in 1871, nearly a decade after the abolition of slavery in the United States.[148]

Muslim Arabs and the Portuguese had one thing in common: their disdain for the local people, who were robbed and exploited to death. This partially explains the crisis of the urban coastal civilization before the emergence of the Omani power. At about the same period, after the maelstrom of war resulting from Shaka's revolution and the *Nguni* migrations that ravaged and partly emptied the hinterland, life in the ports mainly resumed in the second half of the nineteenth century, and then in a new military and local form that was possibly similar to the Asante style when it emerged as a military power in western Africa.

Along the Indian Ocean, compared to the research done on the coastal cities in the nineteenth century, until recently little work was done on the urban history of the continental ports during the seventeenth and eighteenth centuries. It was a chaotic time between the apogee of the Swahili cities proper and the emergence of new precolonial and colonial slaveholding stations.[149] Basil Davidson's theory is that the predatory style of Portuguese exploitation, which focused mainly on procuring tribute and plundering slaves, was efficient in destroying earlier civilizations. Regional history does not contain many records of the Portuguese as builders of cities there. However, there are remains of military architecture at Mombasa (Fort Jesus), and monumental dwellings are suggested by the governor's palace and the remains of former homes on Mozambique Island. The architecture can be compared with that at São Salvador in Brazil and Goa in the Indian Ocean. Thus, we should also test the hypothesis that merchant capitalism might have affected earlier urban features that have since been lost. It is probable that the slave-based economy in Zanzibar on one side, and the Nguni's raids on the other side, were at least as harmful as the Portuguese and Dutch enterprises.

What is certain is that in both East and West Africa, the nineteenth-century upheaval in international economic relations, which was related to every stage of the Western world's Industrial Revolution, contributed to formidable political and cultural changes in Africa. It is not surprising that a new wave of African urbanization was both a corollary and a catalyst.

# The Nineteenth-Century Urban Revolution

Sea view of Beit al-Ajaib (House of Wonders), Zanzibar

Collection of the publisher

*Chapter 6*

# The Nineteenth-Century Urban Revolution

The nineteenth century was a time of dramatic upheavals in the economy, politics, and religions of sub-Saharan Africa. We will not review this history, which is relatively well known.[1] What should be noted, however, is that while the primary reason for the upheavals was the same (changes in the world market following the Industrial Revolution in the West), the forms of and therefore the effects on urban development in Africa were very different on the Atlantic and Indian Ocean coasts.

On the Atlantic, or west, coast, the major factor was the relatively early prohibition of the slave trade, by the Danish in 1803 and, most importantly, by the English in 1807. The end of the Napoleonic Wars imposed restraint on all of Europe from 1815 on, though, of course, contraband trade continued to flourish on the coasts of Africa at least until the 1830s. The slave-trading states were not ready to give up the source of their wealth. However, one thing was certain: that form of international commerce, onto which were grafted many activities, networks, and powers in the interior of the continent, was doomed. Moreover, the new demands of world markets provided other lucrative trade opportunities. The West, particularly Great Britain, became a major importer of raw materials needed by industry but unavailable in temperate zones. West Africa was a rich, untapped area that could be exploited, initially for unprocessed vegetable oils, such as palm and peanut oil, and later, in the colonial period, for natural rubber and cotton.

Palm oil was first exported between 1800 and 1810 on the Slave Coast by the microstates on the Niger Delta. Local chiefs began farming the palm groves of Porto Novo and the Kingdom of Abome in the 1840s. At the same time, in rural Senegal, peanuts began to be produced for export. The economic and social changes were huge. Slaves' status gradually shifted from that of merchandise to that of tools of agrarian production.

A largely slave-based form of production emerged in the former slave-trading kingdoms. It branched into the interior all the more easily since the back country, which traditionally produced slaves, was finding fewer and fewer markets for its wares on the Atlantic coast. The slaves on site were enrolled in professional armies, which grew rapidly and facilitated expansionist empires. The accompanying political instability and social unease also led to mass conversions to Islam. Religious ideology was used as the basis and justification for fearsome military theocracies, the very ones that, toward the end of the century, would oppose the colonial conquest. In 1804, Uthman dan Fodio created the Sokoto Sultanate in what is now northern Nigeria; Al-Hajj Umar and his son Ahmadu spread the jihad throughout the western Sudan; in 1865, Samori established a warlike commercial empire that extended from the Niger River to the Ivory Coast. Other slaves went directly into production, in particular, into the urban textile industry that was booming in the Sahel-Sudan (for example, at Kano in the north of present-day Nigeria) and was based on a naturally abundant raw material: cotton.

In the east, in contrast, the opening of the economy was initially disconcerting. Paradoxically, the closure of the western slave market caused a boom in the slave market on the Indian Ocean. The Muslim world was used as both a screen and a relay by the European market. The engine of growth was trade in weapons, which was again a corollary

of the Industrial Revolution. The upswing began at the end of the Napoleonic Wars, which resulted in an enormous stockpile of useless military scrap in Europe.[2] The Belgian city of Liège became the center of a
profitable industry that recycled weapons into "slave guns" that could be
sold on the African market. Throughout the nineteenth century, every
technological advance was accompanied by new weaponry, which was
immediately adopted by all European armies. Each time, this resulted in
obsolete weapons that could be sold cheaply in Africa. Tripoli in North
Africa and Khartoum in Sudan, in addition to long remaining tolerant
of slave trading by the Portuguese, became hubs of the international
arms trade, which increased in the second half of the century. Restric-
tions on weapons sales, such as those that were emerging in Europe,
were unknown on the Indian Ocean. European adventurers (including
the French former poet Arthur Rimbaud), Arab traders, Zanzibarians,
and Swahili and more or less Islamized Africans immersed themselves
in the arms trade, which exacerbated intra-African power struggles.
Aside from ivory, the preferred currency was slaves, around a third of
whom were used to produce goods in Africa itself. They provided labor
on Swahili cotton, sugarcane, and clove plantations, which thrived on
the east coast and at Zanzibar.[3] This was the route to the world market;
it is a mistake to present the area's economy as exclusively predatory, as
did—for good reason—European missionaries and conquerors at the
end of the century. All along the coast, long-distance trade was thus
grafted onto flourishing regional and local agricultural production,
which was again based on slave labor: coconut oil and cloves for export,
cotton for local textile production, and food to feed everyone.

In the interior of the continent, where elephant hunting and slave
raiding advanced ever farther inland thanks to more effective weapons,
the system gave rise to expansionist slave-trading warlords. In the last
third of the century, they carved out empires that reflected their power
in Sudan and around Lake Chad (Rabih), in Nyamwezi country (Mirambo in modern Tanzania), in the Upper Congo (Tippu-Tip), in Katanga (Msiri), in Mozambique (the Yao), and elsewhere. They certainly
upset the equilibrium among inland settlements. In order to escape the
raids and pillaging, groups tended to divide up into small temporary
camps in the bush. Communities were also decimated by epidemics and

epizootic diseases that spread as people moved more frequently and came into contact with foreigners. Sleeping sickness and cattle plague caused major damage in the last 20 years of the century.[4]

Despite the obstacles to an urban lifestyle, the new chiefs rallied and drew people to them. They put up the strongest opposition to the colonial conquest between 1880 and 1900. Many people sought protection by gathering around the capital cities. The slave workforce also increased the size of the new centers. What should we think of the camps of warriors and traders? We have only rare, brief descriptions by the first travelers and missionaries who visited them. Paradoxically, aside from the Ethiopian cities and Zanzibar, we almost know more about the first generation of abandoned stone cities in southern Africa and medieval Swahili ports than we do about the process by which the military and commercial centers were formed in the nineteenth century. At least the archeologists studying prehistory have asked whether the ancient ruins were the remains of an agricultural and pastoral civilization or proto-urban vestiges. Indeed, why should we deny that there was anything urban about the capitals of Mirambo, Msiri, and Tippu-Tip, or even the "tata" of Rabih to the north? Thus, the hypothesis is that there were not only places where goods were stored and people gathered, such as ports and a few large markets, but many smaller centers that we still know little about. The smaller centers may have moved from place to place and served as caravan stops, portage resting points, military posts, and slave markets on a more or less temporary basis. Together they made up a complete, structured trade network. Why should we suppose that East Africa had only camps when we hardly hesitate to speak of towns in the cases of the Akan and Yoruba markets that developed between the sixteenth and eighteenth centuries in West Africa? Anyway, in both cases, it is clear that the centers had become dependent on more than just agriculture.

This set the stage for an urban revolution that coincided with the emergence of Western capitalism. It opened the African economy to market economics. The new phase began at the turn of the century in West Africa, where there was direct contact through the export of tropical oil seeds and import of manufactured goods. In the interior, the adverse political and religious repercussions of geographical and economic change spread the wave of popular Islamization throughout the countryside. The great religious reformers galvanized the movement, and the jihad destroyed the previous social order, particularly in the cities. There was also contact between the Western world and East Africa, but by more complicated paths and later, mainly in the last third of the century, through Arab merchants who supplied slave traders with weapons. Europeans were far from absent, however; in addition to the heirs of the former slave traders (Portuguese and French on the Indian Ocean), merchants and (especially English) missionaries began to criss-cross the country. In 1848, the energetic missionary Livingstone, who was as passionately interested in geography and trade as in religion, was appointed by the British government to the unusual office of "Consul of the East Coast and Unexplored Interior of Africa."[5] The White Fathers and Holy Ghost Fathers also began establishing missions in the 1870s.

Thus, the precolonial period saw profound changes to the networks and mechanisms of a long-distance, interregional, and international economy rooted in slave-based domestic production. The changes were accompanied by more mixing of groups with increasingly different ethnic origins, economic activities, and religions. This created a new form of urbanism that reflected both the intensity of internal migrations and the growing complementarity of rural and urban areas.

The contrasts between urban development in West and East Africa could have come from differences in the impact of the slave trade. In West Africa, the establishment of states and centralization of power developed, authorized, and accelerated the growth of the slave trade in the seventeenth century. This occurred in the Yoruba states and even to a certain extent in the slave-trading kingdoms of Abomey and Porto Novo, and in the Asante Empire. It also happened in the small interlacustrine groups, such as in the Buganda kingdom in central Africa. In East Africa, in contrast, the states that arose in the nineteenth century were based only on slave trading, and the caravan trails that they used were not generally controlled by a single political authority. They remained vulnerable and were always subject to competition among rival powers whose expansion depended exclusively on the supply of weapons. This helped spread the Swahili culture and language, which was used as a common denominator along the trails, regardless of the history of the small slave-trading groups that succeeded one another here and there. In West Africa, urban development took an openly mercantile and pro-tocapitalist form. On the east coast, in contrast, the reigning violence affected local urban centers—military camps and ports—in ways that were sometimes adverse, but always very specific.

## Ports and Markets in East Africa

### The Decline of the Ancient Cities

When Burton visited in 1857–59, the ports on the Indian Ocean were mere shadows of their former selves. Even Mombasa, considered the jewel of the coast, looked shabby. It should be noted that the city, al-though dominated by Zanzibar, had a small European presence, proof that the sultanate could no longer do without that presence. There was also a Protestant mission nearby.[6] At the time, Mombasa traded copal, ivory, rhinoceros horn, food (corn, rice, and livestock), and slaves from Zanzibar; the most coveted slaves came from the Kilwa area. The city imported cotton (since local production was limited), glass beads, and stoneware and was the only city on the coast that had its own currency, which was initially cast from an old bronze cannon. At the time, Mom-basa was still huddled on its island and separated from the mainland by a narrow channel. During their brief period there in the 1820s, the British had created a basin called "English Point" and built a wharf. The city had an Arab, or rather Swahili, quarter connected to a "native" suburb and an old Portuguese quarter. The homes were rudimentary: little four-sided limestone and coral rag houses with thatched roofs. In the suburbs, all of the buildings were made of sun-dried clay, and all that remained of Mombasa's "twenty churches" were a few ruins. The ramparts were also half abandoned.[7]

The city of Kilwa, formerly so prosperous, now had only a few Arab merchants; it was suffering from a serious cholera epidemic when Bur-ton visited. Economic activities were concentrated in the hands of Indi-ans: 53 Hindus and about 100 Muslims.[8] The city, which was located on the mainland by then, was especially wretched and nauseating because of poor drainage. Its main trade was in slaves raided from the Lake Nyasa area. When Burton was there, a French ship was in port seeking slaves, under the pretext of hiring indentured workers, supposedly hired under contract, for Bourbon Island, later known as Réunion. The city's former site on the island was invaded by vegetation, from which emerged a few rare Swahili and Portuguese ruins. Almost nothing remained of the famous mosque with 360 columns.

## The Urban Renaissance at the End of the Century

There was a veritable renaissance in the nineteenth century, both on the coast and in the interior. Long-distance trade based on weapons and slaves, as well as ivory, copal, and coconut oil, took on unprecedented proportions. More and more people, both free and slave, flowed from west to east. Thousands of people became accustomed to an urban lifestyle, and foreigners introduced new habits and ways of thinking that spread far into the interior. Merchants and artisans originally from the coast spread not only their language, Swahili, and religion, Islam, but also their way of dress and other customs. Their homes were built of sun-dried bricks and had terraces on the roofs, or of adobe with verandas and thatched roofs. The culture's great strength was undoubtedly its tolerance toward ethnic differences, economic interests, and social traditions. Throughout East Africa, urban centers became places where people met, mixed, and traded goods and ideas.

Not only did former fishing villages on the coast become urban, but small settlements in the interior also became major warehouses and caravan stops that brought together a mosaic of people of every origin. From the coast to the heart of central Africa, centers with very different histories were linked together in a community of interest and clear interdependence, because they had stakes in the same products, employed the same people, and had the same business practices. These activities gave rise to quasi-urban conditions in which slavery paradoxically guaranteed a degree of "openness" in the society. Large numbers of people without roots were fed and housed by their masters and formed heterogeneous multiethnic communities, where a good dose of individual initiative was required to reconstitute kinship ties that could legitimize new social relationships.

### The Capital Cities of the Slave-Owning Potentates

The inland capital cities that grew up around the gradually Islamized slave-trading potentates were the least "modern," that is, westernized, of the capital cities. Thus, at the peak of his career, the Nyamwezi trader Msiri made the capital city of Bunkeya the hub of his business in the center of Garenganze country, where he established his empire. The city was in fact made up of a number of areas: 42 villages with a total population of 25,000, according to the first Belgian estimates.[9] Msiri's first wives were women from the local aristocracy, and he made them powerful civil servants if they were loyal and effective. He gave them control over large communities made up mainly of female slaves, who provided most of the farm labor. Like the port cities, Bunkeya's essential function was to supply caravans through its own farms, which dotted the area surrounding the city. A striking feature was that, since men went to war and were employed in caravans, the city's stable population was mainly female. This was probably far from exceptional, but it has almost never been studied elsewhere.[10] Trade relations and subsistence production were combined across the capital city, leading to a social hierarchy among women, who were no longer simply the objects of matrimonial exchange and kinship strategies. By superimposing the patrilineal law adopted by Swahili and most Nyamwezis on the matrilineal system of the Garenganze, Msiri accorded leadership roles to a small minority of royal wives. The large numbers of slave women were used as the principal tools of subsistence production and for a wide range of other purposes because they had no customary protection. The principles by which the city was organized were not much different from those of the provinces, where noblewomen were also married to subordinate local chiefs to reinforce central control. However, at Bunkeya, the frequent flow of caravans and military expeditions and the presence of a busy slave market in the way station were conducive to sexual freedom, polygamy, and frequent divorce.[11] This had little to do with ancient customs and helped to blend peoples and customs.

The great Yao chiefs of the nineteenth century, who built their power on trade in ivory and slaves between Lake Nyasa (now in Malawi) and the outlets at Kilwa and the Island of Mozambique, employed an analogous structure. Unfortunately, Livingstone did not visit their country until 1866. Before that time, they were known only through their caravans, which traveled to the coast once a year. When the Portuguese Gaspar Bocarro went down the Zambezi from Tete to Kilwa in 1616, they were already well established in the area. They traded tobacco, hoes, and skins for salt, cloth, and beads from the coast and then traded the goods from the coast for livestock from their neighbors in the southwest.

The powerful chiefdoms of the nineteenth century probably had their roots in the eighteenth. One of the best known chiefs was Mataka I (1800?–1876/79), whose capital city, Mwembe, was home to two hundred of his wives. As at Bunkeya, female slavery was reinforced by the matrilineal system and the settlement's growing demand for supplies. More and more people also sought refuge from raids by fleeing to the city. Livingstone estimated that there were at least a thousand homes in Mwembe. Twenty years later, W. P. Johnson described it as a city with more than five thousand "tenements." In 1877, J. F. Elton found that it was already a large settlement; ten years later, Bishop Smities saw it as a very large city, by far the largest in the area.[12] Was it really a city? The necessities of supply made it a kind of "garden city," where even the smallest open spaces were carefully tilled.[13] Government in the area seems to have been reduced to a minimum; tribute was not even collected, although at Mwembe the Mataka delegated some of his powers to four judges.[14] The Swahili influence was indisputable, however, and relatively early. Livingstone noted the marks of coastal architecture in the square buildings that were replacing the older round huts. He also noted that all of the inhabitants imitated the "Arab" style of dress and habit of chewing tobacco mixed with lime made from the ashes of freshwater shellfish, instead of betel nuts. In 1890, a Portuguese report described the Mataka, who had converted to Islam a few years earlier, as "a Moor rather than a Yao."[15]

Arab influence was even more marked in the capital city of Chief Makanjila, who converted to Islam in 1870. Elton, who visited it in 1877, said that the inhabitants built *dhows* as on the coast, the chief spoke

Swahili, and a *mwalimu* had a Koranic school there.[16] In 1885, the local British consul lived in a house with carved doors as in Zanzibar, and when the city was stormed in 1891, Harry Johnston found six boxes of letters written in Arabic and Swahili in the chief's home.[17] At Mwembe, the Mataka was buried under the mosque's veranda. The Arab influence clearly preceded the wave of Yao Islamization, which began after 1890. Today, 80 percent of the inhabitants consider themselves Muslim.

## The Ujiji–Tabora–Bagamoyo Caravan Route and Branches

The growth of the cities along this central caravan route is a good example of the changes. The path linked the port of Bagamoyo on the Tanzanian coast to the Tabora way station in Nyamwezi country, and from there to the port of Ujiji on the north shore of Lake Tanganyika. In 1811, Zanzibar sources described the Nyamwezi territory as rich in elephants. Indeed, a few caravans from the coast probably reached and even crossed Lake Tanganyika before 1830.[18] Not until the last third of the century did the Ujiji–Tabora–Bagamoyo route, which crossed an area with remarkable political stability, become the major route for ivory traffickers. The Nyamwezi were the most highly valued hunters and porters in the region.[19]

Undoubtedly, even if only indirectly, the heavy trade also extended beyond the central African formations discussed in chapter 3. The capital cities of the small Bantu states in the interior, such as Rwanda and Buganda, flourished and changed in a local environment that was less welcoming to foreigners, although it is unlikely that it was closed to the major economic currents of the time. Before then, the heart of central Africa had been affected only indirectly by the spread of Indonesian plants, in particular, the banana tree, which had been introduced long before, and American plants, since manioc, corn, and sweet potatoes do not seem to have been grown regularly before the beginning of the nineteenth century. In Ankole, on the site of the ancient capital city Bweyorere, three glass beads have been found. Carbon-14 dating says they are from the mid-seventeenth century (1640±95), but it is not known whether they came from the Atlantic coast or from the Indian Ocean coast. However, Arab merchants from Tabora, preceded in the

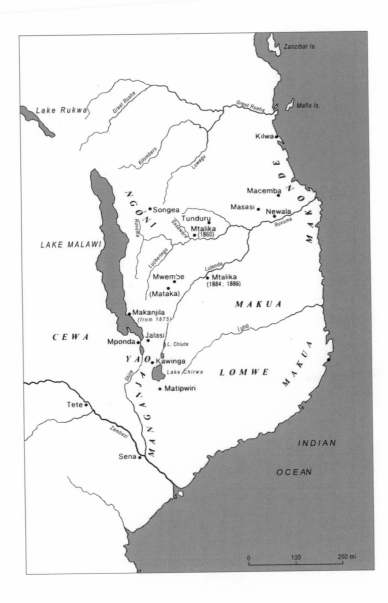

**Map 12.** Cities in Yao Country, Central East Africa
(End of the Nineteenth Century)
Based on: F. A. Alpers, "Trade, State and Society among the Yao in the 19th Century,"
*Journal of African History*, X, 3, 1969, p. 408

eighteenth century by a few Swahili, do not seem to have traveled north in the Koki area, south of Buganda, until a little before 1832. They reached the court of the *kabaka* (Ganda king) in 1844, and also seem to have arrived in Busogaland from the east around 1853.

Their penetration into the rest of the interior was even slower. In Ankole, the first known contact dates from a few years before 1852, and in Rwanda the first "Arabs" (the term covered all Islamized merchants from the coast) did not appear much before 1876, although their goods arrived earlier. Tradition has it that Kabaka Kyabagu used plates and drinking glasses at the end of the eighteenth century. During the same period, cowry shells appeared in the area. Initially, two were enough to purchase a wife, whereas a century later it cost twenty-five hundred to buy a cow: the shells were less rare than they had been a century earlier. Kyabagu's successors also claimed a monopoly of trade in blue beads (*nsinda*) and the use of blue cotton. For those goods, they traded mainly ivory and the slaves who carried it. While nothing is known about the scope of the trade, Ganda pirogues from the south of Lake Victoria were certainly drawn to Tabora. In any case, even in the sheltered areas between the lakes, it is impossible to imagine that there could have been a trend toward autarchy in the nineteenth century.[20]

*Ujiji: The Lake Fishers' Harbor.* Ujiji was originally a fishing village. Because of its exceptional location at the entrance to one of the rare passes through the walls of hills overlooking the lake near the fertile Luiche River valley, it became a reloading center. As at Tabora, a few adventurous Arab and Swahili merchants settled there around the middle of the century. The Jiji were not only skillful canoemen, with flotillas of six to twenty pirogues crisscrossing the lake for several weeks at a time, but their knowledge of the terrain, familiarity with traditional trading practices in the region, and access to areas that produced supplies made them the best agents of the new settlers. As everywhere else, the center's growth resulted from the combination and specialization of regional trade (dried fish, salt, palm oil, and iron) and long-distance trade, which required good supplies for caravans. Even though we know little about the market town, it is estimated that its population grew from around three thousand in 1875 to five thousand in 1883, and to fourteen thousand in 1910.[21] While there were not many foreigners, Ujiji was so strongly influenced by colonization that its residents and the peasants in the surrounding areas considered it to be a Swahili city. The turning point occurred toward the second half of the century, when the barter economy was replaced by the use of monetary equivalents. *Sofi* beads began to be used for small transactions around the time Burton visited (1858). The cost of expensive items, such as slaves and ivory, were estimated in pieces of fabric, piastres, or even guns.

The small Swahili colony, which was very independent of the faraway Sultan of Zanzibar, formed a united group administered by a leader (*liwali*) who acted as a judge, spokesperson, and main dealer with the Jiji authorities. Relations with the royal village, to which tribute was paid, were generally good, but a few major crises broke out concerning market and land title issues. They were usually settled informally through agreements between the Liwali, local authorities, and other prominent people. However, in 1880, all foreign business people were almost expelled following a brawl in the market. The following year, a serious conflict pitted porters against farmers. This was because during caravan season, the number of slaves increased dangerously. When they arrived in the city after traversing a long, harsh route, the hundreds of migrants freed of customary rules saw the opportunity to engage in all sorts of excesses: dances and tam-tam playing, gun shooting, womanizing, and drinking. In 1881, bands raided the harvests and burned the homes of peasants near the city, and it took days to reestablish calm. Social instability was undoubtedly the greatest problem facing city authorities.

*Tabora: Way Station for Ivory Hunters.* A way station for caravans at the midpoint of the route, Tabora experienced even sharper growth. It went from five thousand inhabitants in the early 1870s to twenty-thousand in 1891 and thirty-seven thousand in 1910. It was located in the center of a wide, dry plateau where the ecological conditions were not particularly favorable, yet nineteenth-century travelers were struck by the apparent agricultural wealth of the areas surrounding the city, which were full of livestock, and rice, manioc, corn, millet, and sorghum farms.[22] The Nyamwezi had long been traveling by foot to obtain copper, iron, salt, and dried fish from distant sources. They were able to adapt their traditional know-how to new demands and modern trade practices. The ease in recruiting porters facilitated contact with and transportation to both the east and the west.

The first Nyamwezi merchants appear to have arrived on the coast at the turn of the nineteenth century. This led their communities in the interior to expand their hunting operations and set up more caravans. Throughout the century, they developed their own ivory and livestock production, as well as portage services for Islamized merchants. Arabs and Swahili moved to Kazeh and Tabora, the little Nyamwezi village in the Unyanyembe chiefdom not far from the royal village of Fundikira.[23] Along this route, slave trading and ivory hunting were less destructive than elsewhere because of the association between local and foreign stakeholders and because the new activities were grafted onto a strong prior structure. Instead of leading to war, the international trade in weapons and slaves became part of the interregional trade of copper from Katanga for cloth and ivory, beads for salt and palm oil, and salt for ivory and slaves. There is a record of only one serious confrontation, when the powerful Chief Mirambo attacked the city in the 1870s.

This promoted the growth of interior markets, which was also stimulated by the flow of goods and people. Increased long-distance trade also fostered the formation of small Nyamwezi diasporas more or less everywhere, from Katanga and the Upper Congo to Zanzibar. The city of Tabora, however, experienced more political conflict and greater income disparity. In time of crisis, such as drought or famine, the Nyamwezi died of hunger while the Arab settlers drew grain and livestock from their farms.[24] The foreign merchants, who were powerful because of their wealth, weapons, and numerous protégés, sought alliances with the Nyamwezi chiefs but tended to refuse their demands for payment of duties for right of way, which they considered too high. The political balance was always precarious.

*Bagamoyo and Pangani: Major Precolonial Ports.* Bagamoyo, which overlooked a wide, shallow, welcoming bay, was only around twenty miles from Zanzibar. Before 1880, it had only four to six thousand inhabitants, but in the next ten years its population grew to twenty thousand, although its decline began as soon as the Germans arrived in 1888. The Germans came into conflict with Bushiri, who was supported by the *diwans* (chiefs) of Bagamoyo (1889–90). This led the Germans to move from Bagamoyo to a station that they created in 1891: Dar es Salaam. By 1910, Bagamoyo's population had fallen back down to five thousand. However, in the last third of the nineteenth century, it was indisputably the best-armed port in the region, and in 1866, the Holy Ghost Fathers chose it as the obvious best location for their future permanent mission, which was established two years later.[25]

The site had been occupied by fishers and farmers before the eighteenth century, but the turning point was the arrival of Muslim (perhaps Swahili) nobles or diwans known as the Shomvi, the tombs of whom can be seen in the city's cemeteries. The oldest legible date on the graves is 1793–94 (Hegira 1208). Ming dynasty porcelain corresponds to that period. Every diwan asserted his authority, and that of his household and slaves, over an area of land. The first known political crisis broke out at the turn of the nineteenth century, when the city was invaded by the Wakamba from the interior. The warlike local Wadoe and Waxaramo tribes allied to defeat the attackers. At that time, some of the Wadoe, who were very useful as protectors of the city, settled there as fishers, which seems to indicate that they had received compensation in land. The Wazaramo chiefs forced the diwans to pay tribute for use of their land. There seems to have been a kind of division of power: the Wazaramo, whose chief received the title of *Pazi haoni maji* ("he who does not see the sea"), controlled the hinterland, while the diwans, whose chief was called *Shomvi haoni jua* ("he who does not see the sun") controlled maritime trade.[26] The alliance between the locals and the diwans seems to have worked relatively well until around 1875, guaranteeing both parties a communal government that was relatively independent of Sultan Bargash. The latter nonetheless asserted his authority over the city by visiting it in 1872.[27] The report of his visit shows clearly the complexity of political relations at the time. The Sultan was received somewhat coolly by the *jemadar*, or military commander of the area (who was also responsible for collecting customs duty on behalf of the Sultan), even though the Jemadar was normally chosen by the Sultan from among the Baluchi mercenaries working for him. However, the Sultan had a better rapport with the White Fathers' mission, to which he made a donation.

The Sultan of Zanzibar's tolerant approach can be explained by the need to handle the economic activities of the city with care, for it had become a major warehouse at the turn of the century. The region provided salt, dried fish, and copal gum, and was soon to produce copra oil for soap. Thus, once again, trade in arms and slaves was grafted onto productive and commercial activities that were already well established. In the mid-nineteenth century, "Arabs," essentially Swahili, arrived in the area. Some settled as fishers, but most began businesses. Said bin Awadh Magram, for example, arrived at the end of the 1850s, began a coconut plantation, invested the profits in caravans, and established solid relations with both the Diwans and the Holy Ghost Fathers. Around 1885, he was one of the richest men in the city and owned many slaves, although this did not prevent him from adapting to colonial law and being appointed as city *kadhi* (judge) by the German authorities. Other foreign communities gained remarkable economic power: the Baluchi, who were former Muslim mercenaries from Mombasa and Zanzibar, also often took up trade, as did Indian settlers. There were enough Hindus to build a temple toward the end of the 1880s. The Muslims were mainly Ismailis and also descendants of migrants from Lamu, Mombasa, and Zanzibar who had arrived around 1840. In 1870, their population had reached 137, and that won them a visit by the Aga Khan in 1899. One of them, Sewa Haji (d. 1897), made many donations to the city for wells, a school and other public buildings.

Despite its reputation as an "Arab" city, Bagamoyo was peopled first and foremost by Africans, whose numbers continued to grow in the nineteenth century. The city seems to have been remarkably resistant to ecological crises and precolonial politics, and to have become increasingly attractive as a refuge for victims of famines and civil wars. This was despite the recurring cholera and smallpox epidemics (in 1869–70, the mission recorded fifteen hundred deaths due to cholera) and the risk of typhoons (like the one that occurred in 1872). Many refugees settled permanently in the area as fishers, salt gatherers, and farmers. Porters tended to be temporary inhabitants and crowded into the miserable quarter of Kampi Mbaya six months a year. All the different people resulted in a high rate of racial and cultural mixing, with a tendency to adopt Islam, the lifestyle of which provided them with a common culture that guaranteed social advancement.[28] Bagamoyo's reputation as a cultural center remained after its decline, and it became one of the headquarters of the Qadiriyya, which had schools with influence from the eastern Congo to Nyasaland. Twenty-five years after the foundation of Dar es Salaam, Bagamoyo remained for the locals the most important center in German East Africa.[29]

To the north, the port of Pangani controlled the route to Masai country and western Kenya. From the conquest until 1867, Pangani was second only to Bagamoyo in terms of ivory exports, and far in front of all the others. In the 1840s, coastal trade to the north of Pangani was still in the hands of the Kambas from the northeast, who were pioneer ivory hunters and had strong trade relations with the Kikuyu and Masai. Around 1830, the Swahili began competing with the Kambas and gradually gained more and more control over the ivory trade until they completely cornered it in the 1860s. Like the Omani, the Swahili had an advantage over people from the interior because they had access to credit, which was available only from Zanzibar and took the form of six- to eight-month advances on merchandise. In Pangani after 1860, Arab settlers dominated the city thanks to their huge slave plantations, where they produced sugarcane and coconut, as well as thanks to their alliance with Indian businessmen, who financed caravan expeditions into the interior. At the end of the 1870s, exports doubled. Sesame, which was introduced from the northern archipelago of Lamu only around mid-century by French and German merchants, was one of Pangani's major exports by 1880. Women brewed beer, dyed cotton, and sold mats made from raw materials they grew in their fields or bought from Indian merchants. The use of imported raw materials spread. Smiths used iron from Europe, and more and more people began eating rice from India, especially on festive occasions. At the peak of the slave trade, even the most humble citizen produced a surplus. After 1870, cash payment in Maria Theresa Thalers became the norm on the coast and in the nearby hinterland. Merchants lived in two-story stone houses; there were two hundred such homes at Pangani when the

Germans arrived, whereas in the other ports on the coast, there were at most one or two near the mosque. Most of the other homes were built of cob and thatch (*makuti*), and sheltered the masses of people of many different origins. Thus, the Shirazi felt it was important to distinguish themselves from the invading urban crowd, namely the people from the caravans, who streamed toward the coast and became the majority in the last third of the century. In September, when the caravans arrived, Bagamoyo had as many as ten thousand Nyamwezi porters, who lived in a lower quarter and were completely indebted to Indian merchants, who charged exorbitant interest rates that left the porters at the mercy of their employers.

Thus, the configuration of very ancient Swahili cities changed with the ascendancy of Zanzibar's colonization and the growth of trade in ivory and slaves. Mombasa (the former Swahili center ruled exclusively by the aristocratic family of the Mazrui), Bagamoyo, and Pangani are interesting examples of major terminuses for caravans from the interior that were located across from Zanzibar. Saadani, located between Bagamoyo and Pangani, also flourished briefly: the Omani never managed to impose a governor because they could not overcome the combined interests of the Swahili and the people from the interior. While Saadani was still only a village of a few hundred inhabitants when Burton passed through in 1857, in the 1870s it became the primary gateway for Europeans into the interior. In 1889, it was competing so strongly with Bagamoyo that the Germans tried to destroy it when they settled at Dar es Salaam.

In the nineteenth century, these ports did not become strong centers of Swahili conservatism, but rather large, highly diverse cities in which there was an ancient aristocracy and a thriving bourgeoisie of merchants and plantation owners, along with slaves, laborers, porters, and others from the interior of the country, who formed the bulk of the population. At the time, plantation and caravan slaves also made up much of the city's population. In the port of Pangani, they were the Swahili aristocracy's labor force before they submerged their masters. They rose together in the explosion of anger in 1888, but they were infuriated more by Zanzibar's authoritarianism than by the actions of the Europeans, which they also, inadvertently, facilitated.[30]

## Dar es Salaam: Urban Planning Before Its Time

Dar es Salaam is a classic example of a city created out of nothing. It was established in the late 1860s some forty miles south of Bagamoyo by Sultan Seyyid Majid, who named it *Dari Salama* ("the haven of peace" in Swahili). The city was truly created out of nothing, established at the port itself and not at the nearby village of Mzimima, which it later absorbed. The Zanzibar ruling classes had a great plan to open a port for large ships, particularly steamships, on the eastern coast. The idea was also to create a center more directly under the Sultan's control than Bagamoyo, where established local and regional interests thwarted his authority. Foreign diplomats, particularly French missionaries wishing to increase their influence in the region, also had a hand in the affair. The Sultan was in favor, and probably considered transferring his capital city there to avoid control by the British, who were against slave trading.[31] From the beginning, the Sultan therefore planned to make the new settlement the main terminus for caravans from the interior, which were taking ever more southern routes and arriving at the coast near the site. For example, Tippu-Tib, who had a sumptuous house at Zanzibar, between the port and the Sultan's palace, said that his caravans from Katanga initially reached the coast at Mboamaji, a little to the south, and claimed that he was the first to bring caravans to Dar es Salaam.[32]

The Sultan made the decision to build the city in 1862, but construction began only in 1865–66. It seems that the agreement of the local Zaramo population was acquired in exchange for wharfage fees; they were apparently well aware of the potential commercial advantages. There was a veritable urban plan: streets were marked and stone wells were dug in the north of the port. The work required many skilled masons and other craftsmen, and the labor force was provided by slaves imported from Zanzibar and recruited from surrounding areas. Coral from nearby islands was used in the masonry. A steam tugboat was ordered from Hamburg to land large ships, though this was in fact premature. Swahili settlers were encouraged to establish plantations, particularly of coconut trees, in the Gezerani area.

The Sultan's palace was to be built at the southwest end, facing the sea. An engraving based on an old plate from 1869 shows a two-story building adorned by a parapet with embrasures. Adjacent stone buildings included a domed mosque. Buildings with sloped roofs, probably thatched, were located along the shore and used as warehouses. In September 1867, work on the site was far enough along for the Sultan to invite the British, French, German, and American consuls to a "European-style" dinner, probably to celebrate the inauguration of the new port. At that time, there were around 900 inhabitants.

Alas! The Sultan died in 1870. Bargash, who succeeded him, lost interest in the great plan; part of the site became overgrown by vegetation, and most of the buildings rapidly fell into disrepair. However, in the two decades that followed, until the arrival of the Germans from the East Africa Company in 1887, Dar es Salaam became rooted in Africa. Neither the Swahili nor the Europeans were quite willing to give it up. Indeed, the latter were favorably impressed by the site's potential. In 1877, the English even began building a road to link the port with Lake Nyasa, and in 1881, before the project was abandoned, the road cut eighty miles toward the southeast, across Uzaramo country. By 1885, the Germans had forced the Sultan to grant them a concession to operate the port of Dar es Salaam so that better links with the interior could be established. Sultan Bargash asserted his prerogatives, appointed a governor assisted by Arab and Baluchi troops and an Indian agent responsible for collecting duties for the city, and maintained the coconut plantations.

Finally, and above all, the local Uzaramo people did not miss the opportunity. We have no exact statistics on activity in the port and trade in the area, but the numbers available show that trade in copal gum, rubber, coconut oil, rice, fish, and other supplies, particularly those used in the city, increased in the coastal settlements, along the waterways, and in the hinterland. Indian merchants in particular took charge of retail trade, which increasingly employed cloth, small iron bars, and beads as currency. Even though the slave caravans tended to avoid the city, which was too closely monitored, in favor of more discreet southern posts, a slave market also developed in Dar es Salaam; during the great famine in 1884–85, many Zaramos were sold. Despite the fact that it was officially abandoned, the port attracted an increasingly mixed population of Swahili and Zaramos, as well as Muslim soldiers, plantation and ship owners of various origins, and Arab and Indian merchants. In 1873 there were already about twenty merchant families, and the number grew in the following years. The number of permanent inhabitants was swollen by a floating population of travelers, slave traders, and porters, who came into closer and closer contact with urban Swahili life. Integration into city life did not clash with their former lifestyles, thanks to the solidarity of a customary institution, the *utani*, which provided support for migrants in new locations. The utani (from *kutania*, which can be translated literally as "treating someone with familiarity and good humor") was a "joking kinship" relation between adjacent social groups. It linked them together like beads on a necklace. Custom had always allowed people to travel freely in neighboring countries. If a traveler fell ill, the corresponding network automatically helped him. If he died, his host was responsible for the funeral, as if he were a member of the same group. Adapted to new needs, the utani became not only a means of protecting travelers on the caravan routes, but also a way of establishing personal contacts in the city, and of conveying information among members of the group living in the city and those remaining in the interior. It therefore played a major political and cultural role, in terms of both maintaining relations between the city and the countryside, and protecting new city dwellers. The solidarity explains why migrants tended to move to quarters open to the region from which they came. It was a form of solidarity that is much more than a simple "ethnic reflex," the usual essentialist reference to ethnicity not offering a convincing explaination.[33]

When it arrived in 1887, the German company found three to five thousand inhabitants. After twenty years of apparent stagnation, which nevertheless enabled the city to become part of local and regional life, Majid's great artificial project had just begun to develop in symbiosis with the surrounding people and establish the viable economic system that resulted in its spectacular growth in colonial times. Dar es Salaam is perhaps the best example of how the urban revolution preceded colonial intervention in both East and West Africa.[34]

### Urban Signs in Southern Africa

As early as the first half of the nineteenth century, South Africa was a special case about which unfortunately little is known, aside from quite recent information in post-apartheid regional studies. Southern Africa was already part of colonial history at least half a century before the rest of Africa for a combination of reasons: the English occupation around the Cape from the beginning of the century, officialized in 1815, with Natal made a British colony as early as 1844, and the Boer penetration into the interior, which accelerated in 1836 when these settlers of former Dutch descent decided to begin their great Trek (or travel northward) to flee the British authority and the British ban on slavery. Nevertheless, a transition phase began at the turn of the nineteenth century, with the destruction of ancient cities by the so-called Mfecane (or Nguni wars of expansion), and ended with the emergence of colonial cities. In Zululand, for example, the military camps inherited from Shaka were probably more or less similar to the Ethiopian imperial camps and included a large number of soldiers of both sexes, women, servants, and slaves responsible for maintenance and the subsistence of the whole group, and whose tasks were only partially agricultural. There was a large number of nonproducers to lodge, serve, and feed. This required not only a strong authority but also transportation networks and means of storing supplies, weapons, and goods of all kinds.

Another suggestive example is the city of Mafikeng, a refuge founded not far from the Boer border by Chief Molema and twelve families from Barolong that were already Christianized around the mid-nineteenth century, before the southern Tswana chiefdoms fell under colonial rule. Molema's knowledge and skill as an intermediary allowed him to prevent the direct establishment of a mission in the city and fostered the emergence of local political and religious elites. The *stadt* of Mafikeng, in other words, the original site of the city, remained the center of the African quarters after the British established their administrative post nearby and twisted the name into Mafeking.[35]

From the beginning, these gathering places were cultural melting pots with inhabitants who were all the more mixed because they came from nearby areas that had recently been ravaged by series of conquests. Can these agglomerations be reduced to simple camps or military posts? Once again, the question remains, for later history shows that they had much more continuity than traditional colonial history has supposed.

## The Urban Revolution in Sudanese Africa

Linked with the decline of the Atlantic slave trade and upheavals caused by entry into a market economy, the urban revolution was initially proto-capitalist, or at least mercantile. The settlements that were established or expanded became production centers and joined broad market networks in an economy that was more regional than international. At first, coastal villages were handicapped by their recent slave-trading past. Spurred on by the international campaign against the "shameful trade," Europeans thought they should take direct control immediately. There was a jump straight from the slave trade to colonial metropolises. In West Africa, this was of course the case with Freetown, since the city was created to settle imported colonists in 1792. However, it also occurred in the Fante cities of Elmina and Accra, which experienced a slump in the first half of the century. Lagos came under English control in 1851. The first French colonial cities in Senegal (Gorée and St. Louis) had some difficulty in substituting "legitimate" gum arabic and tincture wood businesses for the still highly profitable slave trade.

In the interior, in the Sudanese area, things were more diversified. In eastern Sudan, major caravan way stations flourished near Khartoum, a colonial capital created as a military camp in the 1840s by the Egyptian conquest. Some large Islamized metropolises in the Sahel were remarkably open to the opportunity presented by the huge stock of slaves made available by the closure of the Atlantic market. The best example of this is certainly the large Hausa city of Kano, which set up a resolutely slave-based production system to become a major producer and domestic exporter of cotton cloth sold throughout West Africa. This is the best example, but not the only one: Bouna, Zaria, Ouagadougou, Bundu in the Sahel, and many small settlements became thriving urban centers. They began to falter only through direct colonial intervention, at the very end of the century.

Finally, in Yorubaland, where the people are the most urbanized in tropical Africa, and perhaps have been so for the longest time, there was an extraordinary case of urban transition that has been the inspiration for much literature.

## Sahelian Urbanism in the Nineteenth Century: A New Beginning

### The Cities of Eastern Sudan: Islam and Mahdism

The cities of central Sudan were ancient. Some of them dated back to the post-Meroitic Nubian tradition, which was later influenced by the early Christianization of northern Sudan.[36] Before the Turkish-Egyptian invasion of 1821, the northern and central portions of present-day Sudan were dominated by two different political bodies: the Funj kingdom of Sennar in the east, including the Nile Valley, and the Darfur kingdom up to Kordofan, which was more or less linked with the Uadai kingdom to the west. We know almost nothing about ancient urbanization in the upper Nile, except that the remains of Soba, the southernmost Nubian capital, suggest a very large but loosely organized city. When the Muslim city was seized around the sixteenth century, the rupture with the past was not so clear because Arabs and Muslims had been gradually penetrating the city demographically, economically, and culturally for centuries. The information available becomes more detailed only with the emergence of three empires: the Funj (c. 1520–c. 1820), then especially the Turkiyya (c. 1820–c. 1884) and finally the Mahdiyya (1884–98) sultanates.[37] Parallel phases of urbanization can be identified with these three periods of unequal duration.

In ancient times, almost all people were either nomadic herders or peasants living in a few communities scattered across an immense area, except in the Nile Valley. Darfur's total population in the eighteenth century probably did not exceed two hundred thousand, and most of the city's inhabitants lived in camps of one to two hundred people.[38] A loose network of transit towns marked the caravan routes. The towns were both rest stops and commercial and administrative centers: in Nubia, Derr had 200 houses, Gerri 140, Damer 500, and Shendi, one of the largest, between 800 and 1,000.[39] Sennar, the capital, which was visited by a European in 1699,[40] was a crucial node linking the routes between Nubia, Darfur, Cairo, Fezzan, and Bornu toward the port of Suakin, held by the Egyptians, on the Red Sea and toward Ethiopia, from which the routes to the south and west departed along the Blue Nile. Sennar had two major markets where ivory, tamarind, civet, gold, and slaves, all of which more or less came from Ethiopia, were traded for spices, paper, copper, iron, arsenic, vermilion, and Venice glass beads, all of which came from the north.[41] It still had nine thousand inhabitants around 1820, at a time when many had fled the Turks,[42] but it had only four thousand in 1860, when Khartoum took over.[43] Along the river there were also other way stations that were used as local marketplaces and storage centers for caravans, such as Shendi, to the north of Halfaya, and Damer, which also produced cotton and was a sacred site. The largest city in Darfur was Cobbe, the capital, which controlled the famous 40-day route toward Upper Egypt and through which passed caravans of up to two thousand camels and one thousand slaves.[44]

Little is known about the layout of these ancient cities, aside from the fact that they had large marketplaces and urban architecture was virtually nonexistent. Sources of water were the keys to development of the agglomerations, which sometimes had several thousand inhabitants. Districts were scattered, often formed along ethnic lines, and sparsely populated. Their rural appearance was reinforced by the relatively large scope of agricultural and pastoral activities within the city. Generally, the houses were low and had flat roofs; in the south, where it was more humid, they were conical with thatched roofs. The only building material was earth. In Darfur, people of high rank covered the clay of their houses with plaster that was tinted white, red, or black. Homes were encircled by two walls: the interior one was made of clay and the exterior of thorny bushes to prevent livestock from escaping. Wells were essential components of the enclosures, since families worked the land close to their homes. The enclosures were very large; for example, Cobbe had only around a hundred compounds despite the fact that it was more than 1.5 miles long. Yet it was indeed a city, and most of its inhabitants were merchants of cosmopolitan origin, including people from West Africa and the Nile Valley, members of Sudanese Arab tribes, Egyptians, and even Tunisians.[45] Sennar's urban planning seems to have been different from that of the other cities, however. It had two architectural styles: the classical round huts with conical roofs found in the countryside, and Nubian- or Egyptian-style rectangular houses, some of which had a second story. It also had a four-story tower, which was probably the tallest building in the Sudan.[46] This shows that Islam was not yet widespread, since political power was stronger than the religious power

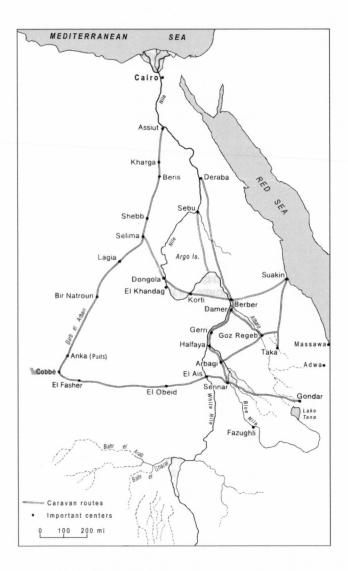

**Map 13.** Cities and Caravan Routes in the Sudan
(Nineteenth Century)
Based on: *Sudan Notes and Records*, LII, 1971, p. 64

of the mosque. It is therefore possible that the rise of popular Islam and the parallel growth of a class of merchants dependent on a market economy caused the decline of the Funj empire.[47]

At the time, Sudanese urbanism was unique owing to ancient religious traditions in that part of East Africa, which were not necessarily linked only with Islam. The most striking feature was the exceptional role played by intellectual leaders. There were always crowds of believers ready to be inspired by the teaching and charisma of individuals renowned for their wisdom and ability to lead the populace. The establishment of religious schools was facilitated in Sennar by the rulers' custom of giving land to holy men.[48] A sure architectural sign of this is that the tomb of a saint was often built in the center of the city that he had founded, and the tomb was often much more famous than the mosque, which is a classical monument elsewhere. The *qubabs* were traditionally the largest buildings in Sudanese villages. They were holy sites, places of prayer and pilgrimage, and miraculous powers were sometimes ascribed to them. It was only the Turks and, particularly at the time of colonization, the British who encouraged the construction of mosques, which were often designed by Greek, in other words foreign, architects.

This is why the cities were so large for the time but also transhumant and sometimes short-lived: for one reason or another, the holy man disappeared or moved, so the city and market also disappeared or moved. A good example is the city of Damer, founded by Hamad al-Majdhub al-Kabir (1693–1776), who moved to the site near the junction of the Nile and the Atbara Rivers to preach among nomads, many of whom settled around him to form a city. It was one of the rare agglomerations to survive the death of its founder; in 1814 a European traveler noted that many students came to Damer from Darfur, Sennar, Kordofan, and the rest of Sudan to follow the teachings of famous wise men who claimed to be descendants of the sheikh's family.[49] Such Islamization, which targeted the working classes more than the aristocracy, went hand in hand with technology that was little developed and closer to that of the sub-Sahara than to that of North Africa or the Middle East.[50]

At the beginning of the nineteenth century, the state fell under the nominal control of the Ottoman Empire, though in fact it was governed by Egypt. Initially, the Turkish intervention was destructive, but in the end, toward the mid-nineteenth century, the cities had not changed much. They were still crossroads for caravans, and some played an important role in the development of sects; one such was Al-Ubayyid, which the Turks chose in the 1820s as the capital of Kordofan, and which was also the center of the *tariqua* of Ismailyya founded by Ismail ibn Abdallah (1793–1863). In addition to their commercial functions, they were also assigned a military role in colonization, though the process did not really have time to bear fruit and they remained scattered outposts of the Empire.

Evidence of the changes was a garrison infrastructure: barracks for soldiers and a line of fortifications. The primary example is Khartoum (then known as al-Khartum), which, along with a few others such as Kasala, played both military and administrative roles.

At the very end of the nineteenth century, with the rise of fervent millenarian Mahdism, Umm-Durman (Omdurman), the capital of the new state, became the only real city, though a few remains of the ancient way stations survived. Unlike the ancient cities, but like Khartoum, Omdurman was an artificial political creation. Khartoum's purpose was military; Omdurman's was religious. It was the largest city that the Sudan had ever known, with 100,000 or perhaps even 150,000 inhabitants (believers and soldiers), and it functioned as both a political and military center, and an economic hub that grew rapidly for about ten years. Yet little remains of it today.

In some ways, Omdurman's growth breathed new life into the religious tradition of the Funj period. Prior to its foundation, the area was almost deserted. The name appears on a map in 1798,[51] but until the end of the nineteenth century it was only a name for a village on the left bank of the White Nile, across from its junction with the Blue Nile. The city was born in 1883, when the troops of an unfortunate English expedition set up a camp there, protected by earth walls. In 1884, Gordon reported that he had 240 men stationed at Fort Omdurman, but they nonetheless had to surrender to Mahdist forces in January 1885.[52] From then on, the city was built around the teaching of an exceptional man who disappeared shortly afterward: the *mahdi*. His disciples, who were peasants from all across Sudan, were probably not aware that they were founding a city.

The following year, Caliph Abdullahi made Omdurman the country's new capital. Unlike Khartoum, which was surrounded by two arms of the river, making it a defensive colonial site, Omdurman was open to the west and the desert in Kordofan, where most of the Caliph's supporters lived. Unlike the Egyptians who depended on it, the Mahdists distrusted the Nile. The city raised its defenses along the river, whereas Khartoum had done the opposite, protecting itself from the desert. In 1886, the city's simple thatched houses extended for four miles along the river; in 1888 they covered six and a half miles. From the beginning, the population included people from all of the Sudan's tribes, and they were soon joined by Egyptians, Indians, Arabs from Mecca, Syrians, Greeks, Italians, Turks, and Ethiopians.[53] Its market was immense, which is understandable given the number of mouths to feed. Its size required urban planning, if only to establish quarters, which seem to have been assigned to different groups in an authoritarian manner.[54] Western Arabs tended to live in the south, whereas people from the valley gathered in the north. However, the details of the layout remained largely temporary. The streets were narrow, twisting, full of holes, and nauseatingly filthy. The population density was relatively low given the spread of the city and because many people continued to farm along the Nile.[55] Only the mosque's land was initially marked off by an earthen wall. The Caliph was the first to build a brick home, though he was soon followed by his brother and other dignitaries. However, the dominant form of architecture remained the sub-Saharan clay enclosure protected on the outside by a wall; within the enclosure were separate homes for men and women in the courtyard.

Omdurman undoubtedly profited from the transfer of some state, administrative, and military services from Khartoum. It was primarily a religious center, however, theoretically forbidden to infidels and focused on Friday prayer and, in later years, pilgrimages to the imposing tomb of the founder, which was rebuilt by his son. Nearby, the only large building was the two-story palace of his successor, the Caliph. The city was soon converted into a military camp to resist General Gordon, who came from Khartoum on the other side of the river to lay siege. All that remains of that period are the tomb and the palace, the vestiges of the defensive wall along the Nile, and the names of a few quarters.

### The Capitals of Bornu:  From Birni to Tata

In the west, the urban changes in the nineteenth century were no less clear. Kukawa was founded in 1814 by Sheik Al-Kanemi, who, called to protect the Mai of Bornu against the Fulani Jihad, gradually came to dominate the Mai. When Denham visited it in the 1820s, he was impressed by the city's prosperous appearance and economic activity marked by trans-Saharan trade. In front of the Vizier's palace, he counted two hundred richly armored and well-dressed horsemen, and he noted that Manchester cloth was in fashion for women. The old city was surrounded by a wall of white clay that had four doors. The *dendal* in front of the palace was still used as a market. However, the city was partly destroyed twice in the first half of the nineteenth century, once by the jealous Mai allied with the Sultan of Bagirmi, and once in 1846 by the army of Uadai, which led to a change of dynasty. Heinrich Barth traveled there from 1850 to 1855 and described it as one of the biggest cities in Bornu. Apparently, it had reached the peak of its power. He left a sketch that shows the Arab-Muslim influence very clearly through the regularity of highly specialized quarters. The city had a grid pattern; at its center the palace faced a large esplanade (*dendal*) from which wide streets stretched out to a high, strong wall. Social differentiation was visible: the city was divided into two distinct parts separated by a space some 550 yards wide, which was a busy meeting place. The aristocratic city was located to the east around the ruler's palace and the Vizier's home, while the working-class quarters to the west were divided into separate areas inhabited by people of more modest means and of various ethnic origins. The city was a major center for trade and resolutely cosmopolitan, peopled by Kanem and Kanuri in the north, Kanembu in the southwest, and Shuwa in the southeast.

Outside of the city on the west, there was a vast "Monday market" (Kasuku Leteninbe), which was also used as a slave market. It attracted ten to fifteen thousand producers from surrounding areas, who came with cattle, camels, grain, butter, dried fish, cotton fabric, and hippopotamus meat. It was also used as a center for long-distance trade, which was facilitated by merchants from the Maghreb who had settled in the city. The colonies from Tripoli and Fezzan who still live there today date back to that time. All forms of currency were used: copper bars, bands of cotton fabic (*gawawa*), cowry shells, and Maria Theresa thalers.

The decline, which began in the middle of the century, was accelerated by the slave trade ambitions of Rabih, who conquered the city and the area in 1893. The ruined capital was replaced by Dikwa. Rabih, who came from the east, was a great builder of *zariba*s, or fortified camps and holding areas for slave traders. In Bahr el Ghazal in 1865, he built for his employer, Al-Zubayr, the most famous and magnificent camp, which was also the busiest and used by traders from farthest away. In accordance with custom, it was named after its owner.[56] After the 1880s, Rabih left the banks of the Nile, which were militarily dangerous and commercially exhausted, and moved to the shores of Lake Chad. There he again scattered zaribas. Cha was built in 1883, and Denze three years later. The sites have not yet been identified, but both were probably located within Dar-Kuti and in Saraland (present-day Central African Republic). The zaribas contained booty from campaigns: ivory, ostrich feathers, gold, and, of course, slaves, all of which were destined for sale. They were also the camps of thousands of soldiers, who were constantly training and were divided into family groups around their chiefs in areas where tribute collection verged on predatory violence.[57] In 1891, even farther west, where he was then operating independently, Rabih, whose army was the backbone of his power, established his main camp at Gaye, near Bagirmi on the left bank of the Chari. According to a pilgrim, it had a broad expanse of huts with a baked-brick powder magazine and was full of merchants and goods. In the spring of 1892, Rabih went to Bagirmi, where he visited Busso and laid siege to Manjaffa, the fortified capital, by surrounding it with a series of fortified palaces (*tata*) linked by trenches. In early 1893, Manjaffa was attacked, and then the Kotoko cities in northern Bagirmi were occupied. Finally, Bornu also fell after two decisive battles, and Rabih entered the capital, Kukawa, in May or October 1893 (tales vary according to the storytellers).

From then on, Rabih stopped roaming and concentrated on turning the new capital, Dikwa, into a well-ordered, large, elegant, and populous city. He ruled for seven years, until he was eliminated in 1900 by the French. Thus, the urban model was imported, although it was generally quite well suited to Bornu society and economics. Rabih built an imposing tata, which was said to have 1,000 rooms around a huge interior courtyard. It is now a tourist attraction. Dikwa remained a historical city in northern Nigeria, but in the end it was abandoned by the British government, which did not appreciate the floods that made it inaccessible for much of the year. In 1942, the British moved their administrators to Bama more to the south, and then to Maiduguri to the west.[58]

### In Hausa Country: Sokoto and Kano—A Political and Military Capital and an Industrious Modernizing Metropolis

Following the jihad led by Uthman dan Fodio, who arrived from Gobir between 1807 and the British conquest of 1903, the new capital of the empire was Sokoto (Sakkwato), which became the Caliph's home in 1817. Curiously, we know little about it.[59] The city was a military stronghold, controlled the junction of the Rima and Sokoto Rivers, and was at the crossroads of the Gobir routes to the north, the Kebbi routes to the south, and the Burmi-Zamfara routes to the east.[60] In 1823, Clapperton described it as the most populous city he had visited in the interior of Africa,[61] with streets laid out according to a regular pattern (unlike the streets in Hausa cities), and surrounded by a twenty- to thirty-foot wall with a dozen doors that were closed at sunset. So many refugees fled to the city to escape the war that its walls had to be extended in 1827 to encompass a new quarter called Sabon Birni ("new city"), which is still known by that name. At the time, the city had two mosques and, in the classical style, an esplanade in front of the palace and another large square used as a marketplace. The market was held daily and was well stocked with cotton and wool cloth, kola nuts, copperware, spices, silk, beads, salt, and, of course, slaves. The homes of Fulbe dignitaries included groups of clay buildings with terrace roofs in the Moorish style, and were also surrounded by high walls. Most artisans, such as masons, leatherworkers, and smiths, were slaves.

However, it was Kano in particular that became the economic metropolis of the north, and remained so for a century. Unlike its neighbors, Kano adapted remarkably well to Fulani domination. Local clans in favor of the jihad minimized the city's resistance, and it surrendered with little difficulty. Initially, it profited from the defeat of Katsina, which had always been its rival. The Katsina princes were expelled by the Fulbe, who considered that they did not believe strongly enough since they lived with non-Islamized Arna people from the north. Indeed, buoyed by its prosperity, Katsina had taken the lead of the resistance, and when it was conquered most of its inhabitants fled to the new city of Maradi in present-day southern Niger.[62]

The Fulbe leaders who moved to Kano at the beginning of the nineteenth century appeared rather like liberators, at least at first, when their government was still light-handed. They eliminated most of the heavy Hausa taxes and replaced them with undemanding ritual Muslim taxes, such as *kharaj*, *zakat*, and *jizya*, that the mainly Fulbe *mallam*s did not have to pay. They were also quick to adopt local Hausa terminology to refer to relations of authority. Thus, rather than the Hausa term *mai*, which implied membership, the local variation of the Arab term *amir* (emir), which was used at Sokoto to designate the sovereign as the *amir-al-muminin* (leader of the believers), was replaced in Kano by *sarki*, which in Hausa implied a role of authority, no matter what rank was in question. The head of the Kano Emirate became the Sarkin Kano; the leader of a secondary district such as Rano became the Sarkin Rano; the leader of a gang of children could be called the Sarkin Wasa.[63]

The concept of power was thus painlessly assimilated by the people of Kano for whom the Sarkin already had absolute power. The Fulbe structures adapted smoothly throughout the nineteenth century, with a small Fulani ruling class (*masu sarauta*) that theoretically acted for the good of its subjects (*talakawa*). The Hausa acknowledged three groups: Muslims (*musulmi*), people of the book (*ahalul kitabi*, specifically Christians— *nasara*—and Jews—*yahudawa*), and pagans (*arna* or *kafirai*). Since at least 98 percent of the city's inhabitants were and remained Muslim, the problem of religious identity did not really begin to arise until colonial times, when Nigerians from the south and Europeans moved to Kano. Hausa religious practices also did not cause any problems thanks to individuals who adapted smoothly from one period to the next: the *mallam*s, who mastered both the Arabic language and Islamic learning, were responsible for teaching and in some cases, particularly Fulbe mallams, held positions of authority. The only major difference was perhaps the feeling of identity, which for the Hausa was closely linked to language and home city. (At Kano they were initially the Kanawa.) In contrast, Fulbe citizens identified themselves first as Fulbe, even when they spoke Hausa and not Fulfulbe. Finally, the Fulbe shaped the city to match their clan structures, and grouped the districts around the five main mosques, three of which were built just after the conquest, and the last under the reign of Emir Bello, between 1882 and 1893.

Kano's prosperity continued to grow throughout the century. During that time, the population probably increased from 30,000 to 100,000, which explains why the habit of leaving fallow some of the land inside the city walls was abandoned. The Sokoto Emirate provided the countryside with some security. In 1824 and 1826, Clapperton, who was the first European to visit the city, admired the prosperity of its hinterland, where cotton, tobacco, indigo, and grain were grown. He noted that there was already a heavy flow of people and goods. He met rich Arab dignitaries in the city, along with many merchants from the west and North Africa. At the time, the city had around forty thousand inhabitants. When Barth visited the city in 1851 and then again in 1854, it had grown even larger. The permanent population was about the same but could swell to sixty thousand during the caravan season. It was an industrious city, with many skilled textile and leather workers. Natron, salt, and even European goods were sold. There were many slaves: at least four thousand in the city and perhaps twenty thousand in the region, which means there were as many free men, able to form an army of twenty-seven thousand. In 1885, the city was still flourishing and had a huge market that was the destination of many caravans. This sometimes increased the city's population to sixty or even eighty thousand, particularly during the slave-trading season between January and March.[64] In 1891, the Frenchman Monteil, who lived in the city for over three months, confirmed that its hinterland extended for about sixty-five miles in all directions. He estimated that in a single year about a million travelers came to the city, although actual trans-Saharan trade, which was monopolized by the North African markets even though Robinson counted several hundred Hausa speakers among the inhabitants of Tripoli in 1894,[65] accounted for only about a fifth of the city's international activities.[66] Trade in salt from Bilma and natron (some of which was used in Kano's dye industry) from Bornu was equally important. However, it was mainly toward the south that the Hausa conducted their own business, based on slaves, ivory, and kola nuts, of which the city was a large consumer. On the eve of the British conquest in 1894, Kano had reached the peak of its prosperity, with some 100,000 inhabitants, half of whom were slaves, crowding within its impressive walls.[67] There were still 60,000 people in the city at the time of the British conquest.

All observers were struck by the number of slaves. Especially under the second Fulani ruler, and then his successor Usman (1846–55), the princes' extravagant lifestyle led to new pillaging jihads designed to replenish the government's coffers. The consequence was that the Sokoto caliphs increased the trade in slaves, who were sold to the south to increase the production of palm oil for export, or kept on site to work in local industry. A major consumer, the city of Kano had to increase its labor force to produce more and more textiles for trade, particularly the famous cotton cloth that was woven in long, narrow bands and gradually conquered the whole West African market, from the Mediterranean to Gonja and Kong, and from Uadai to Timbuktu. The cloth's popularity waned only when faced with colonial competition from English cotton. According to Heinrich Barth, the market, which reached Arguim on the Atlantic coast, involved some two to three thousand tons a year and was limited only by "the nudity of pagan *sans-culottes.*"[68] At the end of the century, Kano probably clothed more than half the inhabitants of the western Sudan.[69] Kano's artisans also produced leather goods, particularly sandals, and Barth claims that at least fifty thousand pairs were exported to North Africa every year.[70] The regional market was no less busy. Kano was a net exporter of grain and agressively marketed cotton of lower quality in the populated areas nearby. The city was inexpensive: a family could live comfortably on an income of fifty to sixty thousand cowries a year($20 to $24).[71] Obviously, however, only large manufacturers who owned slaves enjoyed relative luxury. Later calculations show that at Sokoto in 1911, a textile producer could make a profit of 2,000 cowries on the sale of 4,000 cowries of fabric, while the owner of a dye-works could make a little more profit, earning 2,250 cowries on fabric purchased for 4,000 and sold for 7,000 cowries.[72]

In short, the city grew in two ways. Freemen involved in the jihad, particularly the mallams favored by the authorities, increased their business. For example, Mallam Hamza, who did not have to pay taxes, ran a dye-works and a large farm where his slaves and students were employed.[73] Displeased by Usman's decision to tax businessmen, whether or not they were mallams, Hamza gained so much control over the troops that he managed to defy the authorities. He was defeated and killed in the city of Duwa in 1855. The adversaries of the Fulani theocracy grew in number: dissident mallams, who were mainly Hausa, sought refuge in the Ningi Mountains and established their capital at Lungu where, supported by the surrounding pagan people, they defied the Kano, Bauchi, and Zaria emirates throughout the second half of the century.[74] The wars provided Kano with a large supply of slaves from pacification missions launched by the Fulbe in the area. Natural growth from urban prosperity did the rest.[75]

While Kano was the most promising and by far the largest industrial city in the Sahel, it was not the only one. Many small manufacturing towns sprang up, such as Bundu to the west, in present-day Mali.[76] Bundu was a small center, with around 5,200 inhabitants at the beginning of French colonization. Located on the edge of the Sahel, where sedentary and nomadic populations met, Bundu was able to support markets in both of its main quarters. Food (mostly millet, but also corn, peanuts, peppers, onions, shea butter, and fresh and dried meat) was sold by local women and heads of families, who entrusted their merchandise to their wives or professional intermediaries. However, the markets really focused on textiles produced by a large slave labor force. Grain, peanuts, and bands of cotton were traded to Moors for other goods. Slaves accounted for between a fifth and a quarter of the town's population; some families owned thirty to two hundred.[77] Thus, at the end of the nineteenth century, Bundu was going through economic and social change as a slave-based system of production became dominant. The process was broken only by the colonial conquest.

## Renewal of Yoruba Urbanism: Rupture and Transition

Like the Hausa but unlike the people living in the Ghanaian hinterland, the Yoruba did not wait for Western penetration or influence to begin urbanization. Although a few researchers disagree, and oral traditions of the nineteenth century may have embellished the past, there are indications that the Yoruba already had an urban culture that was several centuries old. This is what makes it so interesting to see how the first generation of cities changed and adapted to the upheavals of the nineteenth century.

### Destruction of the Ancient Cities

What is very clear from nineteenth century texts is a consensus on the end of a previous wave of urbanization followed by the emergence of a new generation of cities. Many of the cities visited by Clapperton and the Landers in the 1820s[78] had disappeared by the time T. J. Bowen passed through around mid-century.[79] About 1837, the old capital city Oyo-Ile or Katunga, called Old Oyo by the Europeans, was destroyed and abandoned in favor of a settlement eighty miles to the south: Oyo of today. The most striking example, and chronologically the first to disappear, is the city of Owu, one of the leading cities in ancient times, if we are to believe the tradition. It was the chief Yoruba city in the south,[80] and had around thirty thousand inhabitants, but it was so completely destroyed by Oyo in 1827 that researchers still have trouble identifying which of three possible sites was its location.[81] The controversy is quite legitimate since three village sites close to modern-day Oyo have archeological remains and contain the famous name: these are Orile-Owu, Ago-Owu (formerly called Owu-Ipole), and Owu-Ogbere. This corroborates the Yoruba custom of moving both the inhabitants and the name of the corresponding urban community.

Why did the cities disappear? At the same time but for only some of the same reasons, this part of West Africa experienced a phenomenon similar to what occurred in central-southern Africa. In the latter case, Shaka's military victories and his successors' Mfecane conquered the earlier cultures.[82] In West Africa, the civil wars, known to historians as the Yoruba wars, ravaged the country for more than 50 years. There is an almost direct correlation between the interregional circumstances and the world situation at the time.

The first event was the Yoruba cities' desertion of the north in response to the jihad-inspired Fulani expansion. This was all the stronger owing to Uthman dan Fodio's powerful sultanate, which was established in Hausaland around the capital, Sokoto, in 1804. In the extreme north of the country, there was an attempt at integration: the hinterland of Ilorin, a former Yoruba city that seems to date back to the beginning of the eighteenth century, was infiltrated early by Fulbe and Hausa herders, who mixed with the local Yoruba farmers. In 1817, a Yoruba chief in rebellion against Oyo took control of the city and, to secure power, enrolled many of the migrants in his army. So many were signed up that they ended up taking power in turn in 1823. The city, the majority of the population of which was by then Muslim, fell into the hands of a Fulani emir. The tomb-altars characteristic of Yoruba culture were gradually replaced by mosques, but even today there is a remarkable integration of Fulbe and Yoruba, which can be seen in the different building styles in the various quarters. The Fulani quarter is closed in on itself, with large compounds in which the mainly clay dwellings echo the various family groups. Yoruba housing is more densely populated and includes homes in larger buildings where rooms open onto common spaces.[83]

The classic Yoruba reaction to warfare was to move. The formerly Yoruba savanna experienced unprecedented population movements at the very beginning of the century. The most famous was obviously that of Old Oyo, but many other settlements were destroyed or abandoned by their inhabitants, who fled to the south to escape death or slavery.[84]

The great conversion movements and the rise of theocracies in the western Sudan were phenomena internal to Africa. However, they can be partly explained as ricochets of parallel upheavals in world politics and economics caused by the Western world. First, the expansion of the slave trade in the eighteenth century terrorized people in the interior and drove them to hide behind the new ideologies launched by their leaders. At the turn of the nineteenth century, the flight of non-Muslims to the south increased the demographic pressure there. The various southern city-states, which were all involved in the slave trade, were prevented from expanding to the north by their powerful neighbor and therefore began raiding one another to supply the market.

Competition increased at the worst time: right when the Atlantic market began to shrink in the first half of the century. From 1800 to 1900, the gradual disappearance of the slave trade disrupted interior networks and markets. African economies were powerless against the international imperative that eliminated what had been the source of wealth for nearly two centuries. Initially, the reaction was to increase prices, not of the individuals sold (which was impossible given the relative "overproduction"), but of transit duties on trade routes, which had to be controlled at any price in order to survive. As of the 1860s, English control over Lagos, which became a protectorate in 1851 and a colony in 1861, made the situation even more tense by making obvious the triumph of the market economy, which was, moreover, welcomed by some "modern" urban African businessmen. For reasons that changed over time, the situation remained constantly unstable and dangerous and set the scene for the Yoruba wars in the forested south.[85]

### The Energy of the New Cities

The result was an extraordinary urban transformation. A few more cities disappeared: the first "civil war" broke out in the south at the end of the 1820s and was marked by the disappearance of Owu in 1827; its inhabitants all migrated elsewhere. The Egba, who had been freed from Oyo's control in the 1780s, suffered from the fall of Owu on the border of their territory and experienced so much internal unrest that they in turn were expelled from their land.[86] The survivors needed to hide in a prosperous, safe center that was willing to receive and protect them. Depending on luck, they managed to do so individually, with their whole family, or as an urban community complete with Oba, leaders, ancestors, and gods; this was remarkably frequent in Yorubaland. The most famous case is that of New Oyo, but there were others, as can be seen from the many settlements in different locations that have the same name. Nevertheless, refugees most often brought with them one of the major characteristics of urban migrations: individual and collective heterogeneity. The result was that either they increased the size of existing cities, usually by establishing new quarters, or they created new cities virtually from scratch. This began at the end of the eighteenth century.

One of the first refugee cities was also the only one to last throughout all the events, and it was the most sacred: Ife, the cradle of Yoruba civilization. For this reason, it remained outside the divisive wars and was protected from the Fulbe incursions by its forested location, which could not be reached by cavalry. People continued to move across the country until the early 1840s.[87] Ibadan, which had been deserted by its Egba inhabitants, was restored by Oyo and Ijebu soldiers of various origins who had fled the army. Abeokuta was created at the very beginning of the 1830s by the influx of the Egba community, which was said to be made up of people from 154 different places.

Whatever the city's origin, it had to deal with the same urgent problems: a larger and denser population, related security problems, difficulties in adjusting to a new environment, social and political integration issues, and economic challenges. The number of inhabitants is not the least of the questions raised by historians. Given reports from the time, it can be estimated that out of thirty-six main cities, at least six (Ibadan, Ilorin, Iwo, Abeokuta, Oshogbo, and Ede) had more than forty thousand inhabitants; six had ten to twenty thousand; five had five to ten thousand; and another five had one to five thousand. Even though travelers may have exaggerated, the numbers are large for premodern times. They are at least comparable to those of medium-sized cities in Europe at about the same period.[88] Safety was certainly at the origin of the increase in population density, since people were frightened and refused to live in the countryside, where they were too exposed to raids by slave traders. This resulted in cities of peasants, where many residents remained farmers.

This explanation is probably not sufficient because the neighboring Igboland in the southwest of Nigeria was just as populous but, being smaller, had even higher population densities (perhaps double) at the time. Yet Igboland was and remained until the colonial era a resolutely rural zone with an extremely fragmented society. Family units, which were linked only by religious secret societies, lived scattered throughout the forest along winding footpaths even though the danger of raids was just as great.[89] The difference in defensive strategies can probably be explained by different ecological and cultural pasts. On one hand, there was the forest, where the Igbo had always lived; on the other, there were Yoruba memories of the open grasslands. Here again we have to reexamine the frequent assertion that the Igbo were ignorant of urban life. It is true that the people who lived in the backcountry were not familiar with the city, but this was not really true of the slave traders in direct contact with the Atlantic market via the ports. Of course, the ports of Calabar, Bonny, Brass, Gwato, and Warri scattered along tributaries in the Niger River delta were not large cities, but they were not little fishing villages either. As of the seventeenth century, their function as locations where slaves were gathered for export made them the economic and political centers of small city-states, each of which controlled one or more rivers in the huge delta. The largest was probably Calabar, the precolonial origins of which can still be glimpsed in the lattice of ancient narrow streets at the heart of the modern city.[90] As soon as the English forced them to sign a treaty abolishing the slave trade in 1841, the Efik were quick to focus on the profitable and booming market for palm oil. The city became not only a major market that relied on increased slave labor in the palm groves in the hinterland, but also an administrative post that was very valuable to the British, and a missionary center that sped the early and massive conversion of the region's inhabitants to Christianity. Thus, it was natural that in 1901, the English made it the capital of their protectorate in southern Nigeria.[91]

It may seem contradictory to explain Yoruba urbanization by the dictates of war but accuse the slave trade of having forced the Gold Coast's ancient urban centers to disperse into the bush because they were too vulnerable to raids. Yet the fact is that in the seventeenth century the slave trade was just beginning, and the urban societies at the time had no defenses against it, whereas Yoruba urbanization grew when the slave trade civilization was in full swing and among people who had long been hardened to the situation.

We always come back to the ancient "urban tradition" referred to by Yoruba city dwellers. The changes that occurred in the nineteenth century simply reinforced and codified rooted habits. Security required fortified walls, but there was a long-standing tradition of such walls in the area. Ife built a new surrounding wall. Ibadan was encircled by a wall that was nine miles in circumference and had four doors opening to the routes to Abeokuta, Ijebu, Oyo, and Iwo, along which the city's primary farms were found, outside the walls.

More surprising is the speed with which people from the savanna adapted to a forest lifestyle. Again, the Yoruba were probably assisted by the ancient permeability of the two areas, but it seems that the cities did not encounter supply problems even though the new arrivals had to adapt quickly to different cultures and other lifestyles. The fact that they were used to markets probably helped: it did not matter which products were carried as long as one was in an area that was part of the distribution network. Given the relatively long distances between the farms that supplied the large cities (up to thirty miles for Ibadan) and the security requirements, merchandise traveled along a complex route before coming to consumers. In the south as in the north, the network was structured, with a ring of periodic, more or less specialized markets around every major road leading to the city. In Yorubaland, such markets were generally held every four or every eight days. This system seems to have operated smoothly from the sixteenth to the twentieth centuries, from the north to the south of the country.

The major wholesale "interstate" markets were usually held every eight days because of the relatively large distances involved. Most were held in mid-sized towns located on the border between competing neighbors. The neutrality of those towns was in principle guaranteed by the fact that they were transit and meeting places. This was how the markets at Oyo, Ife, Owu, and Ijebu operated at the beginning of the nineteenth century. It is revealing that the spark that ignited the Yoruba wars was a dispute that arose in Ijebu's market. Toward the end of the century, trade had moved to the market at Eruwa, a small city protected by the Alafin of Oyo, the governor of Ibadan, and the chiefs of Abeokuta, cities from which it was more or less equidistant.[92] The regional semi-wholesale markets covered smaller distances and were held every four days. They attracted merchants from all nearby locations[93] that were generally less than a day's walk away. Such markets were very numerous and provided general redistribution and brought into circulation the products of local and regional artisans. Since each supplied its surrounding area, it was possible for urban markets, the history of which was often linked to the arrival of migrants, to be held daily, as they still are today.[94] Cloth (mainly indigo), iron goods (hoes, hunting equipment, and household tools), carved wood products (doors, tam-tams, pillars for verandas, statuettes), beads (mainly at Ede and Ife), especially the valuable *agra* beads sold on the Cape Coast market for their weight in gold, copper, and leather goods, and herbs were among the products available. Women spun and dyed cotton, and both men and women wove it. Women also handled pottery; a primary center of pottery making was Tokpo. Women were also in charge of producing and preparing food and household products: oil, yam flour, soap, and sea salt, particularly at Ajido on the coastal lagoon and to the east at Arugbo.[95]

### The Strength of the Urban Community: Ilu

At the level of the city, political integration was also remarkable. It was and still is based partly on the concept of *ilu* (see chapter 1 of this book). Ilu reveals not the inability of the Yoruba to become urbanized but rather the extraordinary reuse of patriarchical structures in local urban contexts. Indeed, the patriarchical structures endured there better than elsewhere and were able to resist the influence of European customs.[96] What is therefore striking among the Yoruba is their ability to use the kinship organization for political and economic purposes and to integrate a population divided on the basis of kinship into a centralized economy and political system within a specific territory.

The city was closely linked with its environment. It was seen by its inhabitants as their home, and they felt that it was an institution to which they owed allegiance. S. Goddard did an in-depth study on this in a district in Oyo: the Abu compound.[97] While the research was carried out in 1965, his analysis provides a detailed picture of an ancient lifestyle that has changed very little. Officially, the inhabitants of Abu have the same primary lineage and consider that they share a common ancestor: the first known inhabitant of the site. Not all members of the group are able to specify the exact nature of the relationship, however, and it seems that there are three main "families," the last three generations of which have direct kinship relations.

In 1965, most of the members still lived in the surrounding countryside, which could be divided into two concentric areas: the *oko etile*, the area four to six miles or less away, and the *oko egan*, farms in the bush, forest, or savanna. The etile could be reached on foot or by bicycle, but people did not work there full time. The etile's inhabitants generally worked in the city as artisans such as carpenters, tailors, or bicycle mechanics or as small merchants. However, in the egan, which extended in a thirty-mile circle out into the surrounding land, the inhabitants were full-time farmers who lived with their families. The extent of the belt was limited, particularly to the south, by the encroachment of neighboring cities that were smaller than Oyo but completely independent, with the exception of enclaves that expanded southward because the cocoa belt was still profitable at the time.

The farmers in the egan did not consider themselves rural: they lived in Oyo, and the fact that they belonged to Oyo was made concrete by having a home in the city. Three villages had special links with the Abu quarter, though each of them also included guests without such links since it remained the custom to grant access to free land without worrying about the origin of the person who would use it. Thus, Elesu, located thirteen miles from Oyo, had 99 inhabitants in 1965, of whom 70 belonged to Abu and the rest to Alapinni, another quarter in Oyo. In all, 204 people claimed to live in Abu, but only 85 had their principal residence there. The 119 others were farmers whose economic interests were located in the countryside, although many owned a home in the city and went there regularly because that was where they had social and political ties. The key was that the city was the focus of family life. Unlike most other areas in Africa, where people return to the village for major family ceremonies, it was in the city that births and marriages were celebrated and funerals held. This is why a survey of nineteen homes in the Abu quarter showed that only six were fully occupied all the time, five were empty for most of the year, and two had never been occupied since their construction two or three years earlier. The others were used only some of the time by one or two people, a tiny portion of the family.

In all, permanent residents accounted for only around forty percent of the urban population, and the percentage could vary considerably depending on the primary activities in the area. For example, it was larger in areas known for special crafts such as weaving. Handmade textiles were a very important product in the nineteenth century, and the industry probably dated back to ancient times, although the nondurable nature of the product means that there is little archeological evidence. We know that the great Yoruba chiefs used their wealth to attract numerous dependents, purchase horses from the north, and import silk and damask fabric from the south. We know virtually nothing about the mobilization of labor on a larger scale (for example, did the artisans work in the palace?), except with respect to the construction and maintenance of the *afins* (palaces), which was done communally by all those who acknowledged the *oba*'s power. The oba's lands also provided annual tribute, and the overall result was a structured network of main political and economic centers that controlled a diversified network of secondary regional centers administered by *bales* (uncrowned obas). The circulation of people between the city and the countryside remained strong, and utterly confusing to those trying to conduct Western-style censuses.

The political system of a Yoruba city was therefore neither accidental nor naïve. It reflected the way activities were structured in space as well as the fact that nonrural activities such as politics and artisanal production were centered in the city. Since in Africa, power derives from control over work rather than land ownership, it seems consistent to make full use of inherited structures to ensure the political and economic preeminence of cities. It is a form of urban organization that should be considered a systematic whole, with its own functions and processes of change.

### The Nineteenth-Century Yoruba Metropolises: Ibadan and Abeokuta

It was a time of major change, and the political solutions that Yoruba cities adopted in the nineteenth century were only partially based on their heritage. The latter was obviously very strong in New Oyo, which called itself the heir of the ancient empire, but it was much less so in the two most dynamic cities at the time, Ibadan and Abeokuta, which by mid-century had approximately 60,000 and 100,000 inhabitants, respectively. Ibadan, founded around 1829 by an influx of soldiers from more or less everywhere, was initially a military camp. Almost every Yoruba city had kin at Ibadan,[98] and the heterogeneity of the naturally undisciplined population made it impossible to reproduce the traditional political system, because no *oba* appeared to claim his rights.[99] The city made it a rule to be welcoming to strangers,[100] and the individual was provided with more support there than elsewhere, no matter what his or her degree of nobility or income. The arrival of a handful of people from Sierra Leone and especially some Afro-Brazilians toward the end of the century only accentuated this feature. In the early years, the city's leadership was somewhat disorganized because the primary activity was war and there was no acknowledged law of succession. Originally, there was a kind of loose federation of warlords and the leading slave-owing families who controlled large farms and therefore supplies. A somewhat democratic system emerged insofar as every individual of Oyo origin, no matter what his place of birth or social status, could rise to the highest position. Thus, the *balogun* who ruled the city from 1854 to 1864 came from Ogbomoso, his successor from 1865 to 1867 was from Fesu, and another, who ruled from 1871 to 1885, from Ilira. However, although it became the leading Yoruba military power in the 1870s and was a major mercantile town, the main center of the Oyo and the primary route for weapons from Lagos to the interior, Ibadan did not succeed in establishing a real internal civil authority until the British intervened in 1893.

Abeokuta's history is even more revealing of the nineteeth-century innovations. Despite the city's original cultural homogeneity, the diversity of the Egba groups made it difficult to establish a balance between competing powers, because every group claimed traditional rights on behalf of its ancestors and chiefs.[101] Immigrants quickly established 150 different quarters, each of which was reluctant to acknowledge a shared authority and developed its own government. Around 1852 there probably were more than four thousand people involved in governing.[102] A little later, when it became clear that they could not return to their country of origin, they decided to form four (later five) large quarters. Government continued to be essentially on the local level of the main lineages, despite the energetic but temporary assumption of power by Chief Sodeke, who was both a warrior and a politician; he died in 1844 or 1845 and was never really replaced. The situation was further complicated by the permanent rivalry between the military class of the *ologuns*, who were in favor of the slave trade and strengthened by the reigning insecurity, and the traditional civil government of the *ogbonis*, who formed a council responsible for appointing and monitoring leaders while maintaining customs.

The problem grew thornier with the arrival of a group of Saros, former slaves who had been liberated by the British at Freetown.[103] In the early 1840s, they succeeded in convincing members of the Church Missionary Society of Sierra Leone to send a representative to Abeokuta to spread the good word. The project pleased the British, who wished to use the opportunity to promote the three supposedly inseparable "Cs" (Christianity, Commerce, and Civilization) in the heart of Yorubaland. Henry Townsend and his companions arrived in the city in 1846. Townsend stayed there for twenty years and certainly played a role in the Saro attempt at westernization. It was a good opportunity: the recent death of Sodeke had weakened the traditionalists, and Ibadan's leading role in the slave trade gave the partisans of "legitimate trade" related to Western capitalism the hope of turning Abeokuta into the center of the movement.

Townsend established a missionary school, introduced a printing press so that a bilingual newspaper, the *Iwe Irohin*, could be published, and served as secretary to the leading chiefs, to whom he gave advice about their relations with the British government. He also encouraged the production of cotton as a "legitimate" substitute export, and created an industrial institute that introduced brick-making technology, among other things. It goes without saying that he used the Saros as conduits of dissemination of Christianity.[104] Soon, however, the Saros began profiting from what the West had to offer. Their proto-nationalism intensified the friction with the British, who did not appreciate their initiative when they took control of Lagos.

Buoyed by economic success, the Saros wanted to play a political role. Faced with the *parakoyi* (traditional merchants' guild), which had long been seeking to impose its control over all the city's commercial activities, the Saros created a commercial association, which was transformed into the Egba United Board of Management (EUBM) in 1865. The EUBM's secretary general was a Saro businessman named George William Johnson, a tailor who had lived in England. The chairmanship was entrusted to the Egba *Basorun* in order to win the support of at least some of the traditionalists. Johnson's goal was to make the

EUBM a governmental team that would help modernize the country by controlling the principal grants and eliminating Townsend's obstructive influence. The British refused to acknowledge EUBM as such, and most of the city's notables were committed to their own provincialisms and not really to the EUBM. At the time, more and more hostility was being displayed toward new converts to Christianity. Johnson would have liked to transform the Board into a political council made up of representatives of all the city's social, economic, and political bodies; but finally the required compromise with the traditional authorities paralyzed all serious attempts to overthrow precolonial forms of production, in which the slave trade network still played a big role. In the end, the decision made by the British at Lagos to give priority to commercial and political relations with Ibadan sank all hopes of bringing Abeokuta into the modern economy.

Abeokuta's history is even more illustrative than Ibadan's of the crisis experienced by the new cities, which were moving away from dependence on the slave trade but were unable to take the leap on their own because they were handicapped by the weight of their cultural heritage and thriving European imperialism. The colonizers thus took power.

## The Vigor of the Mercantile Towns

### Transit Markets in Akan Country

We know less about the development of the Asante hinterland in the second half of the nineteenth century than about the development of Yorubaland and its people, though it was somewhat similar. There was one major difference: the domestic economy was less dependent on the slave trade, and therefore less dependent on the West. In the 1830s, trade underwent an unprecedented boom thanks to the extraordinary expansion of a substitute product: kola nuts. Kola nut production had a long tradition, but it became big business, partly because of the decline of the slave trade but mainly because of the wave of popular Islamization, which made kola nuts the only stimulant permitted in the grassland countries. The Asante empire profited from this until 1874, when the sack of its capital Kumasi by the British put an end to its preeminence. The Gonja revolt forced the Asante to replace their main market, Salaga, with two new centers: Atebubu and Kintampo, which were joined by Bonduku, in the eastern part of present-day Ivory Coast.[105] All three cities were located on major west–east trade routes, which had been linking them for over three centuries with Jenne, Timbuktu, Segu, Bobo-Dioulasso, and from there with the Yoruba and Hausa lands (Nikki, Yuri, Zaria, and Kano). This resulted in the development of transit market towns, which gave rise to a remarkable domestic mercantilism that was, all things being equal, similar to what had taken form in the area under completely different circumstances before the time of the slave trade, during the heyday of gold.

Bonduku and Kintampo (the latter began in the eighteenth century as a modest kola nut storage center, and began to flourish at the end of the nineteenth century) were located between the forest and the savanna, where pack animals (mules, donkeys, and even horses) could be used. Jula, Mosi, and Hausa caravans took advantage of this. The convergence of so many merchants required a good supply of food and equipment, which was made possible by the relatively bountiful agriculture in the area. The market sites became permanent; every city had several daily markets of different sizes. Local products (food, wood, water), regional products (kola nuts in particular, but also livestock, pack animals, and, naturally, slaves), interregional manufactured products of Hausa and Mosi origin (cloth, pearls, and leather, copper, and iron goods), Mediterranean products (cotton and silk), and European products (various manufactured items) were sold. Monetization was quite well developed. Gold dust and cowry shells were used, but so were many other monetary forms, such as Maria Theresa thalers, United States and Mexican dollars, and English coins. They were used more as jewelry than as currency, however.

These market towns, while not very large, were quite highly populated until the conquest caused them to decline. Kintampo seems to have had forty thousand in 1884,[106] Salaga had ten to fifteen thousand in 1876 and 1888, and Bonduku had between seven and eight thousand in 1898.[107] Only L. Binger, who is more conservative than his colleagues, cuts the estimates for each city down to approximately three thousand inhabitants in 1892.[108] The population of each town fluctuated and was much larger during the slave-trading period between November and May.

Some centers were full of artisans such as basket makers, dyers, tailors, carpenters, smiths, and jewelry makers. There was a diversified labor force that included young people, women, slaves, prostitutes, and also marabouts who ran public and private schools. In short, social heterogeneity meant that these centers were cities with a specific urbanism. There was a clear distinction between the local Akan society, which balked at Islam and considered it a public danger, and the colonies of foreigners that it nonetheless welcomed, as long as they kept their distance. This resulted in urbanism based on origin. Landlords, who were sometimes Akan but usually from the same community as their tenants, played a fundamental role. They provided foreigners with lodging and information about the market, acted as intermediaries in transactions, and controlled the wells, particularly in Salaga, where water supply was a problem.

The Akan preferred walled or fenced compounds with ten to twenty round huts inside. The Hausa built large rectangular clay houses with more or less flat thatched roofs, and a few fairly rudimentary mosques. Binger noted only three outstanding buildings at Kintampo: the mosque, which was a kind of large rectangular hall entered through a series of doors and encircled by a veranda; the home of the *Sakin Zongo* (the head of the merchants' quarter), which was Portuguese in style and had a small wooden staircase leading to a narrow balcony; and his host's home, which had two parts—a large thatched house with apartments for his host's wives, and a large Arab-style hall that was ventilated by openings at the base of the roof. On the homes of the richest merchants, the façades were sometimes decorated with arabesques.

The city's government abided by the division between local and foreign urbanites isolated one from the other by diverse ethnic origins, which is why there was no official local power. This facilitated the task of the Asante tax collectors sent by the *Asantehene*. The local authorities asked their guests to provide them with an income in the form of fees, grants, and rent. Aside from that, they kept foreigners at arm's length by housing them in a reserved quarter: the *zongo*, a special enclave for Muslims and specialized merchants. Every group lived under the control of its own leader, and the cities apparently did not use a general council with powers that could have included the resolution of disputes among communities. Muslim practices tended to dominate, and Hausa was adopted as the language of communication at Salaga and Kintampo.

K. Arhin used the concept of "transit market" to describe this form of urbanization.[109] It was a specific type of mercantile organization that was very open to the rest of the country, and this was accentuated by the fact that the cities did not have fortified walls.

### Maintenance and Resurgence of Market Towns in Manding and Jula Country: From Trade to the Army

The notion of transit also seems to apply in Manding territory. The Ouagadougou chiefdom, led by the *Mogho-Naba* (chief of Mosi country), was a small but strong Mande formation that was probably founded in the twelfth century. In the fourteenth century, probably around 1333–34, the Mosi even took over Timbuktu for a short time.[110] Once again, however, traditions tell us very little about the capital city, although they do provide information about the various Mosi chiefdoms,[111] governments, and politics, particularly with respect to the way the central authorities dealt with the provinces. We also know that Ouagadougou had the advantage of being located at the crossroads of trade routes that led north and south, as well as a series of transversal routes; in this it was like Bobo Dioulasso (literally, "the city of the Jula") to the west, which controlled the routes between Bonduku and the Ivory Coast and toward the Ghanean hinterland. According to H. Barth, at least six major caravan routes crossed through the country from the Niger River toward the Ivory Coast, the Gold Coast, and Ewe country (Togo). The nineteenth century was a time of relative prosperity for the region. While for the western Sudan it was a generally chaotic and brutal time, these centers were located in transition zones on the fringes of the major political structures that were developing. Since they were on the periphery of the issues at the time, they suffered little violence. They were too far from the core to attract the interest of conquerors such as Al Hajj Umar and Samori Ture.[112]

Mosi country was certainly already more densely populated than its neighbors, which made possible a relative concentration of power and greater production than elsewhere. Periodically, the Mogho-Naba received tribute in kind from the countryside, which the chiefs of outlying areas delivered with great ceremony during the celebration known as the *soretasho* (completion of the road) at the end of the harvest. The ceremony involved first cleaning the streets of the capital city in order to clear the way from the home of every chief to the palace. On the morning of the celebration, baskets containing tribute were lined up along the road, and then the procession began, accompanied by tam-tam players and a parade of workers armed with their tools, such as hoes and hatchets. The tribute was then stored in the palace's stockrooms and warehouses. There was also the *basgha* festival (celebration of the royal ancestors) at which only money and livestock were given; it too brought the chiefs and dignitaries from outlying areas together in the capital city. The Mogho-Naba and his ministers also received considerable resources from taxes on artisanal products sold in the markets. Tailors, dyers, metalworkers, and jewelers were taxed in cowries or, more often, required to deliver part of their production to the palace.

Finally, taxes and gifts came from the many donkey caravans that visited the capital city loaded with merchandise of all kinds (food, such as millet, rice, manioc, peanuts, and kola nuts, and other items, such as cotton, salt, mirrors, beads, amber, and perfume). At the end of the nineteenth century, the Mogho-Naba seems to have required horse merchants from Katanga and Hausa country to sell him their products at one-hundredth of their worth.[113] The leading merchants were the Yarse (assimilated Manding Muslims), who were joined over the years by Islamized Jula and Soninke refugees. They crisscrossed the country, from the Niger River to the coast. Ouagadougou was the key stop for travelers heading south to forested areas. Throughout the whole century, the cities were thus able to develop their commercial activities, either in a centralized manner in the case of the Mosi at Ouagadougou or in the open tradition of the Jula at Bobo.

We still know next to nothing about these two cities, aside from some elliptical descriptions expressing the disappointment of a few rare travelers who visited them at the end of the nineteenth century, at the time of exploration and conquest. The first European, a German named Krause, entered the Mogho-Naba's capital city where he stayed in

1886–87.[114] He was followed by L. Binger the next year. Binger was not very impressed; like Crozat, he saw only a big village.[115] He had heard so many tales in surrounding areas about the chief's wealth and the number of his wives and eunuchs that he was very disappointed by the palace. It looked to him like a collection of miserable huts surrounded by pavilions that were used as shelters for captives and griots, along with a courtyard jammed with sheep, other livestock, and monkeys.[116] We know even less about the city, or rather the large market, of Bobo Dioulasso, the exact history of which remains to be told. In colonial times, it was the major commercial hub that competed with the capital city that the French decided for political reasons to establish in the center of Mosi lands.

Further north, Sikasso is a good example of an urban settlement that was established just before colonization and juggled two partly contradictory functions: commercial and military. It was rooted in Jula trade, and not until around 1870 was it chosen as the capital of the Kenedugu chiefdom, which had been founded in the 1820s by the Traores, a family of Jula origin living in Senufuland. The choice made good economic sense because the city was on the Segu, Jenne, and Mopti routes to the north, with branches leading to Bamako, Kong to the south, the Mosi states to the west, and, also to the west, Kankan through Bobo Dioulasso.[117] The chief's income came from tribute in kind (rice, millet, sorghum, cotton, and livestock), largely produced by slaves and sent by subject villages, as well as war booty (slaves, agricultural products, and, more rarely, weapons and horses). There was so much merchandise stored in state warehouses that the inhabitants of the city were able to hold out for two years during the siege by Samori.

Indeed, at that late date, the city controlled commerce in the form of two main weekly markets, one for major trade and the other for local products, thanks only to its supremacy as a military stronghold. In the mid-1880s, King Tieba surrounded all of Sikasso's quarters, including the ancient village, the warriors' homes, and his own palace, which was already fortified, with a single wall made of earth, stone, and clay. When Samori laid siege to the city in May 1887, the wall helped it to resist him successfully. In 1891, thus convinced of the wall's usefulness in protecting the city from artillery fire, the chief began building a new wall ten or fifteen feet from the first and then filled in the empty space so obtained. The new wall was fifteen to twenty feet high, seventeen feet wide at the base and nearly fifteen feet wide at the top.[118] The simple fence (*diasa*) that had preceded it was replaced by clay fortifications (tata). The city was in turn divided into three parts, each with its own system of defenses. Every group of houses, and every military commander's home (there were over 20 at Sikasso), was also encircled by a wall, thereby creating small fortresses. Tieba's palace was located on a rise in the southeastern part of the city and was also surrounded by a strong wall twenty feet high. Not far from there, a two-story (forty-foot-high) fort was built. The French called it the dungeon after they conquered the city. The more time that went by and the more resistance there was to the French conquest, the more the city protected itself. Balemba, Tieba's successor, increased the city's area by a third in 1896–97 by including within the wall a new quarter that had been created a few years earlier. The wall was then five to six miles in circumference but was increased to seven in 1898. In case of siege, the city, which was the home of the king, his court, and his most important chiefs, was thus able to shelter within its walls most of the surrounding population. Given the lack of security outside the walls, the city continued to grow, going from four thousand inhabitants in 1887 to nine thousand (half of whom were warriors) in 1892, ten thousand in 1897, and probably up to thirty-five thousand the following year, when Kenedugu fell. Aside from the king's family (eighty to one thousand people in Balemba's case) and the warriors, most of the inhabitants were slaves, whose jobs included building the fortifications. Not much is known about the artisans (weavers, potters, carpenters, construction workers) because most of them were slaves or worked in cottage industries. However, we do know that there were enough merchants for them to have their own quarter in the north, known as the business quarter.

Although the city was not ancient and was pillaged and destroyed by the French in 1898, it is interesting to note that what had been established in only three decades proved sustainable; when it was rebuilt, Sikasso became the leading city in the French Sudan and remains a medium-sized city in Mali today.

## From Ancient Recoveries to the "Colonial" Transition

At the end of the nineteenth century, there were a number of signs of transitional forms of urban planning. Cities were still in the hands of independent local authorities who were tied to the past but willing, and perhaps perfectly able, to modernize. However, such interesting local initiatives were in most cases aborted or taken over by the new conquerors. The cities where this occurred include Foumbam, capital city of the small Bamum kingdom, which was slow to come into its own because German colonization was beginning at the same time in Cameroon. The city nonetheless modernized because of the international context and surrounding economic and cultural changes.

The best example of the inevitable westernization is undoubtedly the creation of the new capital of Ethiopia, Addis Ababa. Ethiopia was the only ancient formation remaining at the beginning of the twentieth century, and it is precisely for this reason that the history of Addis Ababa reveals the inevitability of the changes, which were more a result of the world situation than of the virtually complete colonization of Africa.

### Foumbam, Capital of Bamum:  A Late Local Creation

The Bamum kingdom was a fairly extraordinary political structure that developed independently, even though it was already at least partially under German control. Snug on a sheltered plateau more than three thousand feet high in Cameroon, the kingdom began to take form in the early nineteenth century. At that time, in the face of Fulbe advances northward toward Njola, the Bamum dug a large trench around their capital, Foumbam, in order to protect it from cavalry. Resistance against the Fulbe and the wars that followed enabled the Bamum to extend their control over an area of about three thousand square miles and to increase their population accordingly, although it was still only sixty thousand at the end of the century. Certain captives were chosen to serve the king, which considerably increased the number of royal servants. The king awarded conquered lands to princes and nobles who were the descendants of important servants. Captives were housed on farmland, while their owners (merchants, artisans, and, especially, royal dignitaries) lived in the urban perimeter of the capital. Most information on the city's layout comes from the time of its peak, at the end of the nineteenth century and beginning of the twentieth century.

The last king, Njoya, ascended to the throne around 1890, when the Germans were gaining a foothold in Cameroon. He was a great politician and maintained his prerogatives until 1924, under the French occupation, which began in 1916; he died in 1933. His achievements covered the period of transition and included the invention of a form of writing based on Arabic and European languages and used in his time for the kingdom's records.[119] The territory's small size and isolation made it possible for Njoya to maintain the intangibility of ancient values for an exceptionally long time. The values incorporated kinship-based military and proslavery structures and symbols. The capital city was built in the image of Njoya's palace and power and seems to have come out of the ancient past while expressing an inevitable passage to modernity, paradoxically promoted by a "traditional" king.

Foumbam long remained a simple collection of villages, as many mountain chiefdoms still are, where the king lives in the head village, established on the ruins of the home of the former local chief. Digging a trench to circumscribe a protected area was not an isolated phenomenon. Most of the homes of chiefs conquered by the Bamum were protected in the same way. It was the concentration of population behind the trenches that created a city of twenty thousand out of what was originally the king's home surrounded by a group of homes of heads of lineages.[120] Part of the population stopped farming and got its supplies from what had become, in contrast to the city, the countryside. From then on, the king's entourage, including his servants, guards, artisans, and heads of leading families, was maintained through the work of slaves and wives. The city's structure soon extended beyond individual households and shaped all the king's politics.

The historian and anthropologist Claude Tardits argues that a city's urbanism reflects its society. In Foumbam, the key central point was naturally the palace, which was always rebuilt on the same site, in contrast with royal customs elsewhere, and according to a traditional design based on the remains of ancient buildings. Surveyors were responsible for identifying exactly where to build and the dimensions of the building required. The last traditional palace was the one Njoya began building in 1913, the year in which a fire sparked by lightning destroyed an older home. In 1917, he had a modern home built of brick; it was rectangular, had three stories, and was inspired by the home of the German governor at Buea, which Njoya had admired when he traveled in the south in 1907. The new home showed the skill of King Njoya and his entourage. Unlike the previous palace, it was not the product of a long history. Its design, in the form of a single building, had no precedent in ancient customs. In contrast, the 1913 home was built in a large rectangle more than three hundred yards long by one hundred yards wide and surrounded by a bamboo fence. It had a huge interior courtyard that was as wide as the façade, a massive central complex made of about a hundred interlocking square houses, square spaces, and courtyards, and finally the wives' houses arranged in three lines all along the large courtyard and central complex. In addition, there was a large area in the valley behind the residence, where the storehouses were kept and to which the king could withdraw in case of danger.[121] It was a city within a city, where a considerable number of people lived, carrying out many different administrative, economic, and social functions.

The rest of the city was made up of a series of enclosures that were more or less miniatures of the royal home. It is striking to see how closely the city reflected the social hierarchy. With a few exceptions, the quarters closest to the palace were also the most densely populated, while those nearest the outside were almost empty. Each district belonged to a high-ranking royal servant; ninety percent of such servants lived in the city. More than two-thirds of the acting dignitaries and almost the same proportion of princes lived in the areas closest to the palace. In each reign or series of reigns, the oldest lineages located near the palace tended to decrease in favor of new ones. The most senior lived outside the capital city in the secondary settlements of Njimom and Mayap, either because they dated back to the time when the royal residence had been located there or for military or personal reasons.

What was remarkable about the city of Foumbam was not so much its layout, which was faithful to the ancient design of Bantu political capital cities, but its stability and success in the twentieth century. It was apparently able to incorporate at least some aspects of modernity, thanks to the king's intelligence and desire for independence, and also, it must be said, the self-interested tolerance of the German authorities. The king welcomed European merchants to Foumbam, and the first travelers spoke of thousands of people in the market. The king introduced his artisans to a few technological innovations, such as the saw and plane, and northern-style weaving. In 1906, he allowed the Basel Mission to open a station in the capital city. Sixty children were housed there. In 1910, he opened a school in the palace to teach Bamum writing. The initiative spread, and a report from 1918 shows that more than three hundred students were attending approximately twenty royal schools. At the time of his fall, the king was preparing to inaugurate a lost-wax printing press designed by his own officials for the local language. He made major changes to customs, for example by creating a civil status office for recording births, marriages, censuses, judgments handed down by the royal court, and sales of land and persons at Foumbam and in surrounding areas. Some 2,440 administrative documents were compiled by 1922.[122]

As soon as the French began direct government, however, they began dismantling the system in Foumbam because it contradicted the principle of centralization of power by the colonial administration.

### Ethiopian Cities:  From Transhumance to Capital City

The differences between contemporary cities and ancient African cities include the fact that, for various reasons, the latter were often mobile or even nomadic. The stability of the royal palace at Foumbam was probably related to its late establishment. Previously, it was often an explicit or implicit rule that capital cities had to be transhumant. The new king was required to build his palace, and even his complete residence including dependencies, at a certain distance from the home of his predecessor, as at Abomey in West Africa. This practice resulted in a series of new quarters, or even, as in central Africa in Buganda and Ankole, new capital cities. Indeed, it is fairly common for modern African heads of state to turn their place of birth, often a previously obscure village, into a presidential capital, and one might wonder whether this is not in some way related to such ancient practices.

Nowhere can the history of such nomadic cities be studied better than in Ethiopia, thanks to the great age and continuity of sources of information, particularly since the arrival of the Portuguese.[123] At the end of the nineteenth century, before colonial intervention or, in Ethiopia's case, outside of direct colonial influence, the overall change in the economic and cultural equilibrium between societies inevitably put an end to the transhumance of urban settlements.

*Factors Pertaining to Mobility.* The geographical stability of cities was determined by factors that were obvious, but generally new. They included the goal of "pacification," in other words, control and policing of the populations; the administrative need to identify, count, and tax people, as well as to recruit economic partners; and business people's desire to ensure that their new, heavier material investments paid off, which required greater stability. In short, it is easy to see why the colonizers and, more generally, Western economic interests worked together to expand capitalism and fix the location of cities, which were centers of power and action, state capitals, ports, and stations along rivers, railroads, and routes.

In earlier times such requirements were rare. Regional and international trade required good storehouses, but their location could vary. Of course, river junctions, oases, and high ground from which lower-lying areas could be dominated were attractive, and therefore stable centers were established in such locations so long as the food supply was also good. However, in other locations, political, economic, and ecological factors tended to combine to result in short-lived transhumant cities, particularly in the case of capital cities. The reasons for this were similar to those that applied in most ancient preindustrial cities, whether they were in Persia or in lands ruled by the last Merovingian kings or Charlemagne, or even in the legend of King Arthur. The first was military: the capital city was also an army camp, and mobility increased effectiveness. This argument is particularly strong in the case of Ethiopia, which was a vast empire divided into highly centripetal regions. Pacifying them required that the emperor be present and able to intervene quickly and in many ways. Thus, the imperial home was transformed into a movable camp that was always ready for action. In addition to the military argument, there were more general political reasons. At a time when communication links and means of conveying information were slow and unreliable, it was in the emperor's interest to assert his authority by his physical presence, and that of his court, in every province, which he had to visit one by one to consolidate administrative power and, in particular, reinforce taxation from time to time. However, the most widespread reason for urban mobility in Africa was ecological. In subsistence farming and herding societies, that is, societies with few food surpluses, a large dense population that included people who were not directly productive, such as dignitaries, artisans, warriors, and court slaves, was very demanding on the environment. The slightest imbalance could result in serious subsistence problems for the whole group. If there were several years of drought in a row or an invasion of locusts, or military setbacks caused by devastating raids, the city's supply lines could be permanently broken. Another possible calamity was an epidemic, which was always more deadly in densely populated areas and left city dwellers with flight as their only hope for survival. Even if there were no natural disasters, urban demography itself could be a reason for mobility. If too many people were grouped together in the same area for too many decades or even centuries, the land might not be left fallow long enough, and the earth might become barren. As we have seen, this is what happened at Great Zimbabwe, and that was certainly not the only case, especially since in areas with long dry seasons, a lack of wood for building, cooking, and heating could create the same result in the surrounding area.

*Phases and Constants in Urban Mobility: From Gondar to Wandering Camps.*
Islam's expansion led to the gradual relative isolation of the Christian center Axum, which in the seventeenth century still played the role of asylum and had 150 to 200 homes, and probably more than a thousand inhabitants. Nevertheless, the political heart of Ethiopia slid farther south where, from the end of the thirteenth century on, the instability of the dynasties and constant wars resulted in highly mobile imperial residences. It was truly the time of wandering cities, whose history is best known from the fifteenth century to the beginning of the seventeenth century (1412–1636).

At the latter date, the empire's centrality was vigorously reestablished and the emperors sheltered themselves in the inaccessible heart of the realm. After having tried many different sites around Lake Tana, they settled the capital in the north, at Gondar. What was new was not that the emperor lived at Gondar all the time (he did not), but that his successors chose to imitate him by also acknowledging Gondar as their principal home. This was a significant change because the emperor no longer sought a new site, but at most built a new palace in the same city not far from that of his predecessor. Gondar remained the nominal capital for two centuries, until 1855, although in fact it was truly the capital for only one century, until around 1755, while imperial power remained strong. After that time, central authority fell apart again, which led to the rise of provincial capital cities, each of which controlled a virtually independent area, testifying to the power of the local dynasties and the strength of regional factors. In 1855, Emperor Theodore reunited the country and settled at Magdella for about ten years. Instability returned with a vengeance until Menelik II, who became emperor in 1889, made Addis Ababa, which he founded in 1890, the capital. That was the end of the cycle of the wandering city.

Even in the days of Gondar, however, Ethiopia's capital could not be considered the emperor's permanent home. At most, it was where he preferred to spend the three-month rainy period in the summer, when travel and military expeditions became impossible. The emperor's custom was to build a permanent residence for that period of calm. Construction techniques improved after the Portuguese arrived in 1541, since some of the newcomers remained in the emperor's service, and Jesuit missionaries became architects and builders of churches and palaces to ingratiate themselves with the rulers until they were evicted in 1632. The first residences were simply low buildings with thatched roofs, but it became increasingly frequent for castles to be built in stone. Gondar's stability made it possible to turn it into a city that was truly a symbol and reflection of imperial power.[124] In the center there was the imperial city, which was large and spacious, and included palaces, churches, and various buildings inside an oblong cut-stone wall that was more than one mile long and twenty-seven feet high, and had twelve fortified doors. The enclosure contained the homes of the emperor and queens (the emperor's wife, the queen mother, and princesses), four churches,

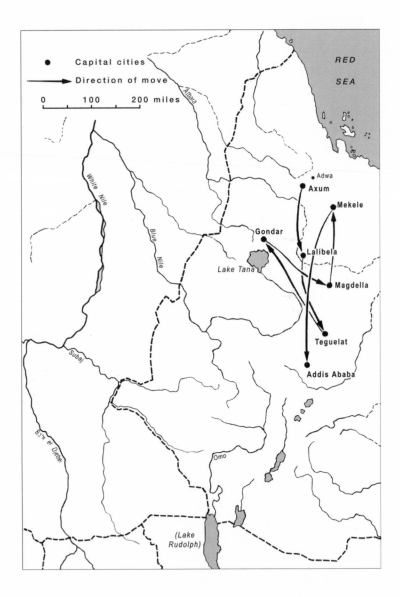

**Map 14.** Ethiopia's Main Capital Cities from
the Fourth to the Twentieth Century
Based on: Ronald J. Horwath, "The Wandering Capitals of
Ethiopia," *Journal of African History*, X, 2, 1969, p. 208

palace services, an imperial guard of several thousand men, and related dependencies. There was also room for the thousands of heads of livestock that could be brought back as spoils from military expeditions. In the eighteenth century, the imperial palace was a large square building flanked by towers. Originally, it had four stories, but it had been partly destroyed by fire. It still had impressively large rooms, including a reception room that was thirty-six yards long. Outside the walls, the city looked like a huge garden, with churches nestled here and there in groves of slender green trees across a bare, hilly countryside sprinkled with many neighborhoods, each generally specializing in a specific economic activity and housing a specific portion of the population. At the center of each neighborhood was the house or palace of a dignitary or rich landowner. Such homes were generally built out of permanent materials. The dignitaries included the two rival leaders of the Ethiopian church: the Metropolitan and the Abbot, and the particularly restless clerics who followed them. Gondar had 44 churches, an eminently significant symbolic number. It was crawling with priests, monks, clerics, and poor people, for all the needy from the surrounding countryside came to the city and monasteries for help.[125] The other houses belonged to protégés and servants, and were round, with bister-colored cob walls and thatched roofs, similar to the homes in the villages throughout the central plateau.

On the other side of the large, irregularly shaped marketplace, which was the center of trade, there was the merchants' quarter, which was isolated on the river bank at the foot of the hills. It was inhabited by Muslims who sometimes came from abroad, particularly from Yemen. There was also a quarter for Christian traders and a large colony of Greeks that was linked with other Greek communities abroad, such as at Cairo. The Greek colony was made up mainly of artisans and merchants and remained socially diverse, for it also included servants and agents of the emperor, who were sometimes rich landlords. Finally, farmers lived in the shady suburbs around the city.

The city and suburbs formed a significant agglomeration, which the Scottish traveler J. Bruce estimated to include ten thousand households (of which seven thousand were Christian and three thousand Muslim) at the end of the eighteenth century. The total population would therefore have been fifty to sixty thousand in peacetime,[126] and perhaps twice that when campaigns were being prepared. However, at the dawn of the twentieth century, it was a ghost town with fewer than a thousand inhabitants. This was because Gondar's purpose long remained, at least in part, the same as that of other Ethiopian cities; it was a military staging ground. During his thirty-one-year reign, Gondar's founder, the Emperor Fasiladas, spent only five years without conducting a campaign.

Other cities were temporary residences of the emperors, or strategic strongholds with castles. Market towns were more rare. The best-known capital cities became the residences of princes in the eighteenth and nineteenth centuries and were used as bridgeheads by local dynasties. Examples of this are Debarwa and Digsa, which took turns as the capitals of the Baher Nägash, and Adowa, the Tigre's principal city and a major manufacturing center of white cotton in the eighteenth century, with a population of a few thousand.[127] Like Gondar, it was located on the trade route that linked the southwestern countries that produced raw materials, such as gold, skins, ivory, and civet, with the Port of Massawa (Massaouah) on the Red Sea. The earliest nineteenth-century estimates place the latter's population at 1,500 to 2,000, with about a hundred stone houses, two hundred shops, and two hundred wooden houses. In the southeast of the country was another merchant town, which was one of the most continuously inhabited: Old Harar, which had a fortified stone wall. In the mid-nineteenth century, Richard Burton, the first European to enter it, estimated that it had about 8,000 inhabitants, at least 2,500 of whom were Somali. The population seems to have grown quickly with the increase in international trade, reaching some eight thousand houses and two thousand huts (perhaps 35,000 inhabitants) at the time of the Egyptian occupation in the 1870s.[128]

From the sixteenth century to at least the end of the nineteenth century, the capitals were surprisingly similar.[129] They were simultaneously military camps, royal cities, market towns, and capitals of the empire, but the number of inhabitants continued to fluctuate hugely throughout the year. In the rainy season, the sovereign retired to his residence of choice, and most of the soldiers returned to their provinces and fields. A few thousand inhabitants of Gondar remained with the ruler, and sometimes the number declined to only a few hundred servants, slaves, and members of the personal guard. When the dry season returned, the capital again became the country's political and military center. The Amhara and Tigre elites and their men converged on the city, whose population could grow to twenty or forty thousand, not including the innumerable work and pack animals, which included fifty to a hundred thousand horses, mules, donkeys, and heads of livestock. If it had no castle, the capital came to look like an immense camp of white cotton tents, the privilege of the feudal elite, and huts of earth and straw, the lot of the lower-class masses; extending across the plateau as far as the eye could see,[130] it could look anarchic to the untrained eye, and in fact it took several centuries for researchers to understand the city's organization. In the center was the imperial compound, preferably located on a hill; it was surrounded by a fence that was one and a half to three miles in circumference and had twelve doors, as at Gondar. The compound contained tents for all purposes: imperial residences, the treasury, quarters for priests, guards, and slaves, storehouses, and kitchens. A wide esplanade directly in front of the main entrance was used as a meeting place. On the other side was a tent used as a courthouse, and there were also prison tents and church tents, among others. Outside, the thousands of tents and huts in the rest of the camp were laid out around the leading dignitaries' residences, which were modest copies of the imperial compound. If one of the chiefs left the city for some reason, a whole quarter made up of his warriors, dependents, and servants also disappeared, thereby amputating from the city a large section of its population. There was a marketplace, with a Christian section used mainly for local and subsistence products, and a Muslim area reserved for major international trade and used by a certain number of foreigners. Finally, many people were lodged in the homes of the inhabitants of surrounding villages because custom required peasants to provide board and lodging to all those in the emperor's service. The problem was obviously to feed such an incredibly large number of people. Thus, one of the capital's major functions was redistribution of all that was due and paid to the emperor, including individual and property taxes, market and land fees, tribute, spoils of war, and slave and feudal labor. This form of operation required a rotation of royal residences in order to avoid exhausting the resources.

The way that cities moved could not have been simpler. All the emperor had to do was get on his horse or mule and leave. Traditionally, he left in the greatest secrecy: the news came in the middle of the night while the camp was sleeping, and there was no choice but to follow him early in the morning. The commoners bundled up their meager possessions, including pots, mats, and the posts used to hold up their homes. The nobles put their slaves and porters to work: at least five to six thousand were required to carry only some of the emperor's provisions, religious objects, and weapons. The goods could be moved at a maximum speed of ten to thirteen miles a day,[131] but F. Alvarez reports that it once took over a month for the emperor's bags to make it across a gorge.[132]

Naturally, the frequency of such moves varied greatly. When campaigns were being carried out and secrecy and mobility were required, the emperor could move very often, sometimes once or twice a week. However, emperors increasingly tended to settle down during the rainy season, and mobility was in inverse proportion to their power. They tended to move more at the beginning of their reigns, even though moving a capital city seems like the privilege of a sovereign who has reached the peak of his power. In any case, this is what Menelik II planned to do, although he was forced by circumstances to stay at Addis Ababa.

*The Foundation of Addis Ababa and the End of an Era.* The birth of Addis Ababa marked a turning point in the history of an urban culture that until then focused on its past. It was the incarnation of an independent African ruler's ambition to graft aspects of a new modern urbanism onto ancient roots. The price was the surrender of mobility.[133]

The tradition, as reported by the chronicler Guebre Sellassie,[134] must be handled with some prudence; it clearly shows the transition, which took around fifteen years. Menelik, who was at the time only the King of Shoa, dreamed of restoring the empire to the power it held during the great age of Gondar. He planned to reestablish links with history by founding a capital on one of his ancestors' chosen sites before the disastrous Gran invasion in the seventeenth century. In 1843, Menelik's grandfather Sahle Sellassie had uncovered the remains of a church only ten minutes by foot from the Filwoha market, the site of present-day Addis Ababa, and had thought of establishing a capital city there.

Around 1878–79, Menelik made a commitment to the renaissance of the former capital of Lebna Dengel, which, according to tradition, had been located at Entoto, about five miles north of Filwoha. Since the exact location could not be identified, Menelik initially contented himself with setting up his camp close by, until in 1881 ruins were discovered of an ancient city that seemed to have been built by Emperor Dawit at the end of the fourteenth century. Menelik visited the site, asserted that it was the location of ancient Entoto, and decided to rebuild it. Other less poetical considerations probably also came into play, such as threats to his camp, which was at the time very exposed to attacks by the Galla, and the defensive advantages of Entoto's location, which was at six thousand feet in altitude, at the watershed of the Blue Nile and the Awash. It thus opened onto all of central Ethiopia. Entoto was designed in accordance with the classical model of an Ethiopian royal camp. Few buildings were built to last, aside from the palace and two churches. The explicit reference to the past meant that architects and masons had to be brought from Gondar. At the same time, modern innovations were employed for the first time to carry materials, with half a dozen ox carts built according to a design by a German missionary and the use of sleds instead of porters to carry building stones.

The site was soon found to be very inconvenient. Because of its altitude, it was very cold and windy, and wood and water supplies were insufficient. The steep mountainside also made access difficult. Menelik and his wife, Taistu, were soon attracted to a lower site with a climate made milder by the Filwoha hot springs. Taistu called the place "new flower" (Addis Ababa), perhaps because of the local abundance of mimosas, and had a home built there in 1887. Construction on the camp seems to have begun even before the emperor was crowned on November 3, 1889. Reports by foreign witnesses suggest, however, that the city began more slowly; the location was used as a residence only occasionally in the following years. The decisive moment occurred at the very beginning of the 1890s, when the exhaustion of Entoto's wood supply forced the ruler to once again move his residence, which reports say may have been home to fifty thousand people. This seems to have been when the first lasting building was built. The primary distribution of land to the leading feudal lords, which traditionally accompanied the establishment of a new camp, occurred early in 1891, with the grant of hereditary land rights.

For the first time, Menelik made major use of European technology, with the help of three Swiss engineers who had arrived in 1878. One of them, Alfred Ilg, remained in his service for a long time and played an important role in modernizing the country. In 1894, the major innovation was running water in the palace. This was achieved using a series of canals carrying water down the mountain from Entoto to watertight reservoirs. This was followed by the introduction of electricity, which lit the great reception hall (*aderash*) with sixteen chandeliers; however, a hydroelectric power plant was not built until 1911–12. The construction boom occurred mainly after Adowa's victory in 1896: nearly two thousand Italian convicts were forced to build roads. Foreigners, specifically Arabs, Greeks, Armenians, French nationals, Italians, and Indians under British protection, took over the marketplace.

Despite the innovations, there was no sign that Menelik had given up the custom of moving the capital city. The reasons for this remained the same: the emperor's desire for prestige, which led him to devote huge amounts of money to major undertakings, and, more prosaically, the poverty quickly resulting from the exhaustion of nearby natural resources, notably food and construction materials, particularly wood. At the time, Europeans made many predictions, calculating that the departure would take place as it had at Entoto a few years earlier. The cost of living soared at Addis Ababa because of the supply crisis, and no wood could be found within at least fifteen miles of the city. Naturally, the emperor was tempted to suggest the same ancestral imperial remedy to the problem: a move. He explored the surrounding area and seemed to settle on the site of Mietta, twenty-five miles to the west of the city and much closer to the wooded area. The empress gave it the significant name of "New World" (Addis Alem), and in 1900–1901, the emperor had a palace built there. The Italians were so convinced of the immediacy of the move that they immediately established their legation in Addis Alem.

The change had already occurred at that point, although the outward signs were certainly not obvious. At the turn of the century, all foreign travelers were struck by how unwesternized Addis Ababa appeared, aside from the palace. Between 1900 and 1910, however, it probably grew from fifty to a hundred thousand inhabitants. Most of the city's buildings were made of temporary building materials. Corrugated iron was initially imported by rail from Djibouti in 1905–1906, but the quarters still looked like villages full of horned animals (cows, sheep, and goats) and mules. Ravines and rivers made walking difficult. In short, there was almost no urban planning, and virtually no road network. Until the Russians built the first stone bridge in 1902, there were only two wooden bridges, both built by the French. Nonetheless, the essential features of the city's layout were in place: the emperor's palace was located at the east, not far from the bishop's palace, and leading dignitaries had been assigned large tracts of land nearby. The business district, which was run by Europeans and Indians, was downtown, where land prices continued to climb, thus encouraging businessmen to invest in real estate. In 1910, there were still only around a hundred Western-style houses, compared with twelve to fifteen thousand Ethiopian *tukuls* and perhaps two thousand tents. The major market spread out toward the west, facing St. George's Church, which was consecrated in 1897 and stood on the site now occupied by the cathedral, built in 1906 by an Italian entrepreneur using plans by a Greek architect.

What caused the emperor's about-face? According to reports by westerners, European businessmen, merchants, and bankers persuaded Menelik to abandon his plan to move. Their influence is clear. However, more generally, Addis Ababa had become too deeply rooted. The headquarters of an empire that was beginning to open up to technological progress had begun to require an unprecedented and wide-ranging system of political, diplomatic, economic, and technical services. The palace was increasingly operating like an agricultural and manufactured goods business that was at once the government, a farm, and an industrial complex. Since 1897, major expansion and beautification projects had been undertaken in the imperial compound, of which the jewel, St. Gabriel Church, had been carved by Indian artisans. Around 50 buildings were built there within a few months. The same year, the first permanent barracks for the emperor's soldiers were built. They no longer had to raid the surrounding area to meet their needs because in 1892 the emperor had standardized a tax (tithe) on all production in Shoa in order to supply them with provisions. A revealing sign was that the day after the Adowa battle, the city lost its traditional function as a military camp: the emperor ordered that most of his men were to be reassigned to the various garrisons in the regions.[135] The population quickly took on the cosmopolitan appearance of a multifunctional city and labor market and attracted nearby Galla peasants, who specialized in the transportation of fresh food, and people from the south, who did not have the same prejudices against manual labor as did those from the north. Around 1910, the city's population included people from all parts of the country. Around a third were from greater Amhara, including Goam, Shoa, and Tigre provinces; most of these were nobles, courtiers, and soldiers. A third were from Galla and formed a more or less floating local population, and a third were migrant workers, including Falasha Jews and some twenty-five thousand slaves.[136]

Therefore, Menelik was gradually led away from the traditional move and toward a series of measures designed to solve the problems created by the maintenance of a large agglomeration. Thus, in 1903–1904, according to his order, much of the land that had been confiscated during the repressions was restored to the Galla peasants. Trade between the countryside and the city was encouraged, and in 1900, the Greeks introduced two or three mechanized grain mills. Menelik had one set up in his palace in order to prepare the enormous quantity of grain needed for huge customary banquets, to which two to six thousand people could be invited. A little later, in order to secure the water supply, he had wells dug and the number of reservoirs increased.[137] In 1905, an engineer left a fascinating report on the palace's industrial activities. Since he had run out of electrical supplies needed to improve local facilities, he took it upon himself to find the lacking three hundred meters of wire in the imperial storehouses. He found what he needed because the stocks of imported goods were as enormous as they were varied.[138] This also gave him an opportunity to explore a veritable manufacturing universe, which included bakeries and sewing, weaving, carpet-making, and masonry workshops. Menelik imported sewing machines and hired foreign specialists to train artisans, including an Albanian who was an expert in gold and silver embroidery on silk and leather. This was also when a telephone and telegraph were installed in the palace. In short, the turning point had been reached. In 1902, the emperor made it official by ordering that the palace at Addis Alem be turned into a church. It was the beginning of a new urban vision.

At the same time he decided to improve the road used to supply Addis Ababa with wood. The inevitable problem of wood, which would soon have to be brought from more than twelve miles away, was finally solved in a modern manner through the introduction of eucalyptus trees. The first experiments were carried out between 1894 and 1899; in the years 1904 and 1905, the emperor imported four or five different species from Australia. He encouraged plantations by distributing seeds and granting exemptions from land fees.[139] By 1906, there was visible progress and within ten years complete success. Reforestation was victorious and, looking down from Entoto, the city and its surroundings were transformed into a mass of green. It was the end of a heavy handicap. Addis Ababa became the focus of Menelik's modernizing initiatives. He introduced a hippodrome in 1903, the Bank of Abyssinia and a first-class hotel in 1907, a school named after himself in 1908, a hospital in 1910, and a state printer in 1911. In 1905, a British banker wrote that given the buildings, roads, bridges, and other projects currently under construction, it was obvious that the choice of Addis Ababa as the capital city had become irrevocable.[140]

## From North to South: The Colonial Transition

The Yoruba were the most urbanized people in West Africa. In the nineteenth century they were unique in that their urban revolution had occurred without any direct European influence. This was not the case elsewhere, such as in Ethiopia, as we have just seen, and, for even stronger reasons, on the coast, where Western colonial influence is clear in many places. Even though the slave trade continued to dominate everywhere except in Sierra Leone until the 1830s, colonizers were already at work.

In several parts of Africa, colonization lasted at least two or three centuries in almost every location. The colonizers were first Portuguese at Loanda (the spelling "Luanda" was not adopted before the end of the nineteenth century) and Mozambique Island, then Dutch, and soon British on the Cape and in Freetown, French in Gorée and St. Louis (and Libreville beginning in 1848), and even, in a special form, American in Monrovia. It would be wrong to think that colonization occurred only in the classical form. In sub-Saharan Africa, there were other forms of colonialism that do not fit the description of colonial imperialism: for instance, the Oman-Zanzibar occupation of the ports on the Indian Ocean, particularly Mombasa, and, in the following century, the Egyptian and even Ottoman expansion into Sudan. Indeed, Khartoum was initially an Egyptian creation and was taken over by the British only at the end of the century.

The oldest European colony was in the city of Loanda, which was occupied by the Portuguese almost continuously from the sixteenth century on, aside from a brief Dutch interlude from 1641 to 1648. Only a few forts, such as Elmina (previously São Jorge da Mina) on the Gold Coast and St. Louis in Senegal, were occupied by Europeans for a similarly long time. Early examples of colonization in the nineteenth century are Freetown in Sierra Leone, which was supported by English missionaries, Monrovia in Liberia, established by American missionaries, and cities in Lagos and Senegal (Gorée and St. Louis) that were similar in some ways to the South African cities of Durban and especially Cape Town. Indeed, like the future "communes" in Senegal, Cape Town was created in the seventeenth century. This is where we see the real junction between precolonial and colonial cities: the authoritarian end to centuries of cultural mediation.

## Khartoum: From an Egyptian Military Creation to British Control

From domination by the Egyptians to colonization by the British, the rocky history of Khartoum's modern renaissance is a good example of continuity. At the junction of two great rivers, the Blue Nile (the avenue of access from the plain of Gezira to the heart of the Ethiopian mountains) and the White Nile (which has its source in Lake Victoria in the center of Africa), the site was a natural crossroads for many routes linking various parts of the Sudan to the rest of the continent. It is therefore not surprising that it often became the focus of military undertakings.

From what is currently known, it seems that despite the advantages of its site, Khartoum was created by the military relatively late and virtually out of nothing. There is only one source, dating back only to the nineteenth century, that describes a faraway past, based on an old chronicle that seems to have been lost.[141] According to the narrative, the site was an important way station in the seventeenth century. In 1691, a famous scholar apparently established a *zawiya* there and attracted hunters and fishermen, who eventually formed an agglomeration of perhaps fifty thousand inhabitants. It would therefore have been a relatively large center for more than a century, until it was pillaged by Sheluk nomads around 1780. When Muhammad Ali's army of 5,500 soldiers led by his son Ismaïl arrived in 1821, all that remained were three huts and a large cemetery.[142]

At the time, the village was so poor that the troops could stay only three days because it was impossible to find supplies for the men. According to a Frenchman who was accompanying the expedition, the army camped across from the village, on the site of Omdurman.[143] It then continued on toward Sennar, which was the capital at the time.

Muhammad Ali had undertaken the conquest of the Sudan on behalf of the Ottoman emperor. After hesitating between a number of sites, and given the insalubrity of Sennar, he finally decided to set up his main military camp at Khartoum. In 1826, Khursid Pasha, the governor general of the Sudan, built a prefectural office (*Moudirie*) and a mosque there and introduced clay construction techniques to replace the reed and skin style. A census of the villages in the Gezira was conducted so that taxes could be collected. In 1829, the site had about 30 clay houses and barracks for 800 soldiers. The other houses were made of sorghum straw and looked like "little kilns or bee hives."[144] About 20 stalls sold food (grain, coffee, and sugar) and very expensive assorted goods from Cairo and sometimes even India. Slaves were also auctioned in the governor's house.[145] In 1829, a French explorer noted that there was a hospital and 400 to 500 houses, and in 1831 an Austrian said that it was the most important strategic position in East Africa.[146] In 1834,

Khartoum became the official capital of the four provinces of what was beginning to be called Sudan.[147] In fact, at the time, it was not yet big enough to qualify as a capital but was already the "first city" of Sudan.[148] The center grew in importance under its successive pashas, who built various monuments and buildings, including a warehouse for ship repairs and, after 1850, a palace, offices for the central government, and forts. The governor lived in a home that was a surprising mixture of very humble elements, such as earth floors, and extreme interior luxury, including many slaves, carpets, silk, and expensive china.[149]

Through Egypt, Western ideas began to appear. Indeed, there were four Sudanese among the Egyptians sent to Europe in 1929 to study and acquire technical knowledge.[150] One went to England to study silk weaving, and the three others went to France to learn about, respectively, cloth, arms, and sealing wax. Muhammad Ali himself visited Khartoum in 1838 and considered introducing a railway, a telegraph (which came into service in the 1860s), and works to make the rapids navigable.[151] Travelers and researchers, European and Egyptian doctors employed at the military hospital, and Egyptian, Greek, Maltese, Italian, and French merchants and adventurers also began to arrive in Khartoum, encouraged by the elimination of the state monopoly over trade in the 1840s and by the enormous profits to be made from trade in ivory and slaves. Various consular representatives lived in Khartoum throughout the century. There was a French representative in 1829, and there were Austrian, British, Italian, and German representatives as well. Curiously, two Coptic merchants represented Persia and the United States, respectively.[152]

In 1840, there were about twenty thousand inhabitants. The population dropped to only thirteen thousand in 1843, but it rose to between thirty and forty thousand ten years later. In 1856, a cholera epidemic led the government to move to Shendi, so by 1862 Khartoum's population had fallen to thirty thousand and by 1870 to only twenty thousand.[153] There was no urban planning, aside from that required for government buildings, gardens requiring proximity to water sources, and embarkation points. The rest of the city, which was poorly protected from floods by an unreliable earthen dike, was a mixture of homes and open spaces that gradually filled up and finally gave it the form of a parallelogram, which is the shape of old Khartoum today. At the time, when the slave trade was in full recovery, there were fifty to fifty-five thousand inhabitants, of whom two-thirds were slaves. The European colony had been growing since the beginning of the century, from only a dozen individuals in 1841 to about thirty persons or families in 1860.[154] The first Christian mission, a Belgian initiative, was established in 1842. Beginning in 1846, Jesuits and then Franciscans were responsible for evangelizing the country. They founded a school for European and black children bought on the slave market. In 1878, most of the two hundred employees on the Khartoum docks had been educated at the mission's school of commerce. It is remarkable that the only building that was at least partially built out of stone, aside from a tall mosque, which was the only building made of fired bricks, was an impressive Catholic mission begun in 1856. Its façade, to which two wings were soon added, was over a hundred yards long. One of the Italian masons who helped to build it founded a family in Khartoum, and we know that he was still living there in the time of the Mahdiyya because he helped to build the caliph's house.[155]

In the 1860s, the city was becoming relatively large. There were a number of docking points along the very busy river for consular boats, merchant ships armed with a cannon at the bow, and a fleet of fishing boats. In the 1870s, a few steamships appeared, including the governor general's vessel. Every hundred steps or so, there were points where water could be drawn for gardens, although a few pumps were beginning to be used, at least for the palace and mission gardens. Above the riverbank and strip of gardens, fruit and palm trees followed the line of a long earthen wall, which was first described in 1837 and replaced in 1855 by a stone parapet; beyond the wall the roofs of houses could be seen. A few large homes were built next to the traditional temporary constructions. They each had a large outside courtyard leading to a reception hall, and an interior courtyard reserved for the harem. A beautiful garden was connected to the interior courtyard. The palace faced the riverbank. Rebuilt in brick in 1851, it had two two-story buildings, one of which was for the harem, and a square tower above the entrance. It was rebuilt in stone at the time of Major Gordon, between 1871 and 1876, in the neo-Renaissance style of the mission. Again it had a second story with a stone staircase at the end of one wing and a wooden staircase at the end of the other. There were a few windows covered by green blinds, a long hallway that ran along each level, and a terrace roof. There is a photograph of it, probably dating from 1877.[156]

Upstream from the palace there were grain silos, the arsenal, and then a hospital that is said to have had 270 beds in 1873. The military quarter was behind the hospital; not far from there, was the sailors' district. Downstream, on the other side of the palace, there was a set of old buildings, most of which were made of brick, including the home of the city's governor and various official buildings. The Catholic mission was farther downstream, and beyond that there were a few gardens and the homes of the richest merchants. Toward the interior, most of Khartoum's quarters were called *hilla* (villages) because the city essentially resulted from a cluster of more or less scattered older settlements. A high stone wall surrounded the brick mosque, the minaret of which was rebuilt in 1860. Even though it was too big for Friday prayers, another mosque was built in 1873–76, and a third at the beginning of the 1880s. Nearby there were two long covered brick markets, one large and the other small. Much of the city's economic activity was concentrated there. In the surrounding area, Greek traders had stalls and large warehouses where the most valuable imported goods were stored: textiles, European clothing, shoes, porcelain, and various other items. The small market was run mainly by local people and essentially offered local and imported food and drink, including beer and wine. The surrounding streets were crowded, and the picture painted by all of the ordinary people going about their business, old Turks playing chess and backgammon, butchers with their stalls, water carriers, and sellers of pigeons and fowl strolling by, was not very different from what can be seen today. There was also a Coptic district, with a three-domed church and a cemetery that was noted in 1863. That "almost elegant" district faced the *teras*, in other words, the wide sandy plateau, covered with many small clay homes, that was located at the southwest of the city, just above the flood level of the White Nile.

Khartoum was a large cosmopolitan city that brought together a wide range of different peoples: rich established merchants, including many Muslim Egyptians; Copts, who were mainly clerks and employees; at least eighteen thousand Nubians from Upper Egypt, who sometimes worked in commerce but were mostly servants, sailors, and mercenaries; local people who often worked as peddlers; Abyssinian, Nilotic, and Darfurian blacks, of whom at least thirty thousand were domestic slaves or porters; Turks and other subjects of the Ottoman Empire (including Circassians, Albanians, and Armenians), most of whom were soldiers; a small European colony; a few Jews; Syrians linked with the houses of Cairo; a few Algerians who had arrived with the conquering army; and a few women from Abyssinia, especially Galla, who were wives, concubines, or prostitutes. Wealth rubbed shoulders with misery, luxurious homes rose next to wretched hovels, and slavery, prostitution, filth, and illness flourished.

The decline began with the climb of Mahdist power.[157] Soon after General Gordon arrived in 1884, a decision was made to strengthen the city's defenses. The trench was deepened and the ramparts inside raised by an equivalent amount. An additional fort was built at the junction of the two rivers. This did not, however, prevent the city from falling to the siege by the Mahdists, who took control in January 1885. The Mahdi maintained Khartoum but chose Omdurman, on the other side of the White Nile, as the capital city. He frequently crossed over to Khartoum, where one of his wives had her home and some of the chiefs in his entourage had decided to live. Caliph Abdullah, who came to power in June of the year the Mahdi died, took a different approach. He ordered that the capital be evacuated and destroyed. Most of the materials were reused to build Omdurman, and even though Khartoum's docks and arsenal continued to be employed (for obvious reasons), the city was forgotten for twelve years.

When the British-Egyptian army conquered the Sudan in 1898, General Kitchener destroyed Omdurman and made Khartoum the capital once more. This not only created a break with the preceding period but also made it possible to use an infrastructure that had sound colonialist foundations, despite the Mahdist pillaging. The city was therefore revived and redesigned on a much larger scale, according to a geometrical pattern based on the Union Jack. In 1900, the arrival of the railway from Halfa marked the beginning of the city's renaissance.

## An Ancient Portuguese City: Luanda

Thanks to the weakening of the Kingdom of Kongo, the Portuguese were the first to adopt a system of direct domination in Africa. In 1574, they conceded a charter for Angola to Paulo Dias de Novais, its conqueror. He became the governor for life of the royal colony between the Dande and Kwanza Rivers. The gift included a *capitania* (estate) to the south of the Kwanza estuary, extending thirty-five leagues along the coast of Angola and as far inland as he could control.[158] Everything was at his expense, and it was up to him to recover his costs by imposing taxes. In the area granted, the Crown reserved a monopoly over the slave trade, although Novais had the right to export forty-eight per year tax-free. The armed intervention that saved King Alvaro I from the Jaga invasion in 1575 enabled the Portuguese to gain a permanent foothold at Luanda, which they had been visiting regularly for slave trade purposes ever since their first contact with the King of Kongo in 1482. In 1597, the Diocese of Angola and Congo, the seat of which was originally to be São Salvador (Mwanza-Kongo), was almost immediately transferred to Luanda. By 1700, the colony had a structure that remained much the same until 1900.[159] In principle, the governor, who changed about every three years, assisted by the *Camara* of Luanda, controlled a relatively large hinterland, which at the end of the eighteenth century extended to the Benguela Plateau. It was divided into *presidios*, each controlled by a military officer assisted by a judge and a chaplain. Each presidio included a series of chiefdoms that remained in the control of local leaders. Of the three cities occupied by the Portuguese, namely Luanda, Benguela, and Massangano, Luanda was clearly the most important. Massangano was located in the interior near the Kwanza River and was more difficult to control, and Benguela had begun exporting slaves directly to Brazil before 1727. Despite an attempt to build a fort to the north in Cabinda in 1783 in order to combat Dutch, English, and French competition, the Portuguese never really managed to maintain a position there. However, at Luanda they built the São José de Nkoje Fort in 1759 and encouraged settlement in the surrounding area. At the same time, they maintained cordial relations with what remained of the Kongo Kingdom. Proof is that in 1804, two princes were invited to study at the Saint Anthony of Luanda monastery in Luanda for several years at the Portuguese government's expense.[160]

There is an exceptional wealth of sources concerning the history of Luanda. Unfortunately, most have not been studied in depth.[161] Luanda was built on a long island in the bay of the same name, but it also had a business district on the mainland. The upper town was built on the rocky spur that rose above the huge storehouses along the water and the sandy shore. The city's main fort, the governor's palace, the bishop's home, the Jesuit college (until 1759), and the Portuguese-African quarter ran along the crest.

In Luanda, it was not always easy to find a balance between the governor's rapaciousness and the Portuguese colony's demands for independence. For example, in 1666, Governor Tristão da Cunha, who had recently arrived from Brazil, had to face a settler's revolt that forced him to get back on the same ship that had brought him there.[162] At the time, the Church was naturally just as much in favor of the slave trade as the rest of the population, since it was part of the socioeconomic structure on which the Church depended. Thus, in 1693, the Crown created an assembly of missions at Luanda and provided it with resources in the form of the right to seven hundred slaves at the market price. Thus, bishops, too, had slaves, who worked in the fields or gardens and carried their masters' litters through the city and countryside. The Portuguese government's official suppression of the slave trade in 1836 was probably very poorly received by Luanda's inhabitants and long remained insufficient to end local slavery.

Until the beginning of the eighteenth century, the expatriate population was maintained by an inflow of rather miserable migrants, most of whom were unlucky slave traders who landed there after having failed elsewhere, such as in America or Portugal. Most of them were small merchants who would have been junior civil servants or penniless nobles in Portugal, but who lived like petty kings in Luanda, trading slaves for profit and making lavish use of black slaves in their homes. According to a colonist report in 1694, slaves were brutes without intelligent understanding: one could almost say, irrational beings,[163] so their masters could treat them as they pleased. Yet the Portuguese, whose racism stemmed from their belief in the superiority of their Christian mission, were themselves often illiterate and had low status. Many were *degrega-dos*, in other words, condemned criminals sent to the colonies, a practice that continued into the twentieth century. Usually they found tempo-rary shelter in the commercial district of the lower town before leaving for Brazil or, more often, succumbing to the perils of the climate.

A tiny minority founded families and decided to stay. One famous example is that of Francesco Honorario da Costa, who arrived in Angola in 1777 as a young employee of the Companha Geral de Per-nambuco e Paraiba. He took responsibility for the company's failures in Luanda and then set up a local company with an Angolan named Antonio José da Costa, who was one of the leading slave traders in the country. Francesco Honorario da Costa moved to Kasanje in 1794 but faced repeated failures in the interior and finally had to leave in 1815. He became famous by sending two of his *pombiero* slaves from Luanda to Mozambique; they became the first people known to have traveled all the way across the continent on slave routes.

Around 1720, Portuguese-African slave traders predominated, and the city's atmosphere was largely African.[164] Colonization by settlement had encouraged mixed marriages and relationships, especially since the Portuguese population had originally been almost exclusively male. In 1846 in the kingdoms of Angola and Benguela, there were still only 1,832 whites, of whom only 156 were women.[165] However, the slave pop-ulation was mainly female because young adult males were more highly prized on the Atlantic market. The 1777–78 census in Luanda found that there were forty-three male for every hundred female slaves.[166] According to the same author, in total in the nineteenth century there were approximately 5,800 mulattos in the colony (half were women), of whom only 28 were slaves. However, there were 86,000 black slaves (including 40,000 men), most of whom belonged to the hundred or so white heads of families, and a few to mulattos. Finally, there were 300,000 free blacks. In other words, when the slave trade was at its peak, Luanda was a small leading city with a white and Creole minority that had virtually absolute power. It was a hub of colonization and dif-fusion of westernized culture.

De facto segregation increased in the eighteenth century. The two communities lived together in both symbiosis and distrust. On one hand, there were the pure Portuguese traders who had been born in Europe, and on the other hand there were the Luso-Africans, or Creoles, who had been born in Angola, often outside of Luanda, and were generally of mixed race since there were virtually no Portuguese women in the country until the end of the nineteenth century. Portuguese men therefore had to marry local women, which increased the degree of Africanization in each generation while improving business relations with chiefs in the interior, who were quite willing to arrange such marriages for their daughters.

Throughout the eighteenth century, the city gradually became more heterogeneous. The small influential core of immigrant merchants began to control the flow of European capital that fed the trade in arms and slaves with the hinterland. The immigrants represented a wide range of occasionally contradictory interests. For example, there were British capitalists, tax collectors with royal charters, and free merchants linked with Asian interests. Generally, they arrived as agents for houses in Lisbon and sold, at huge profit, textiles, Portuguese food and handicrafts, and manufactured goods from northern Europe to Luso-Africans, who provided supplies for the slave trade in the interior. The Luso-Africans preferred to accumulate their capital in money (in Brazilian gold *cruzados*, Spanish silver *patacas*, or Portuguese *reis*, the local currency, which was convertible into either metal) rather than in slaves, which they simply shipped since they had little personal use for them aside from as domestic servants. Thus, they proudly dissociated themselves from the slave traders, even though they were dependent on them. The merchants incarnated European market capitalism based on commodities and credit, which contrasted with the traditional slave trade between Brazilian plantation owners and Luso-African slave traders. In 1760, more than one-third of them were living in the bourgeois merchant quarter of the lower town, near the port, in the parish of Our Lady of Mercy (*Nossa Senhora dos Remédios*). It was the district where the major trading companies and related service suppliers were located.[167]

As the economy changed, an increasingly wide social rift developed between the Luso-Africans and the Portuguese. The latter became more numerous and gradually drove the Creoles out of the lower town. At the same time, the Creoles lost more and more of their power over international trade and were hired by the Portuguese as clerks in the city or retailers in the interior, which thereby reduced their presence in the city. In 1740, the Luso-Africans lost control of international trade. However, some of them still lived in luxury in the city, with homes in the upper town, in the parish of Sé at the foot of the main fort. In that quiet quarter, there were also a few retired Portuguese as well as most of the people employed in European liberal professions, such as doctors, writers, and the only lawyer in town. Since business marriages were still arranged between European merchants and daughters or sisters of Luso-African traders, the frequent early death of the husband resulted in Creole households run by wealthy widows, many of whom lived in the most beautiful homes. The 1777 census found that in the Sé parish, there were sixteen "white" and five "mulatto" women (the classification was certainly more related to a woman's social prestige than to her color), each of whom had more than seventeen slaves. In other words, these women alone (although they accounted for less than a third of the wealthy local "white" or "mixed" population) owned more than two-thirds of the slaves in the quarter. However, most such wives lived in the lower town, where the census found there were forty-eight, half of whom were counted as white. They lived as semi-recluses in their beautiful two-story homes, coming out only to go to church, in which case they arrayed themselves in expensive dresses, rode in palanquins, and surrounded themselves with slaves in livery. Their aristocratic lifestyle required the import of luxury goods, such as fine fabrics and silverware, and luxurious materials were used to decorate the interiors of their homes and churches and adorn their family tombs. The role of these women seems to have grown in the eighteenth century, probably because the number of such marriages increased and because their husbands were forced to spend more time conducting business away from the capital. At least one of the women, Dona Ana Joaquima dos Santos e Silva, became a veritable commercial power in the hinterland in the mid-nineteenth century.[168]

In Luanda, the large two-story houses known as *sobrados* became the symbol of success. In the upper town, windows and balconies looked out over the sea, making the rooms more comfortable and, it was believed, healthier. In the lower town, the ground floors of the huge homes were used as warehouses and stores that opened at the front onto the sandy street and at the back onto the servants' quarters. Even though the city is now tragically decrepit, few other centers were able to maintain for so long the cachet and charm of Portuguese colonial architecture, which marked so many cities in the world, such as in Mozambique and Goa islands, Macao, or Salvador de Bahia.

## Black-White Capitals

Two neighboring experiments that look similar on the surface were in fact very different: Freetown and Monrovia. Both were undertaken in the wake of abolitionist movements, but they were based on very different premises. Originally, Freetown was based on a premonitory universalist aspiration, while Monrovia resulted from a complex movement colored by racial, if not racist, undertones, from which the black community in Liberia has not really been able to free itself.

### Freetown:  From Humanitarian Utopia to Creolization

Originally, Freetown, the name of which describes its goal, was an initiative of the English abolitionist movement led by Granville Sharp, who created the Province of Freedom in 1787–91 to provide a home for poor blacks left without resources by the suppression of slavery in London. In 1787, the first 411 settlers left from London. Most were former slaves who had been "repatriated" by the movement, and they were accompanied by around a hundred whites. They bought about twenty square miles on the peninsula from a local Temne chief, and their first village was christened Granville Town. That initial undertaking failed, but it led to a more elaborate plan: British donors founded a chartered company, the Sierra Leone Company. The need to strengthen the colony led it to welcome free blacks who had fled to Nova Scotia, Canada, following their participation in the American War of Independence. The second wave of settlers was decisive. About twelve hundred blacks arrived in 1792 and founded Freetown, which had some two hundred houses in 1794,[169] and about twice that number by 1796. At the time, the houses were still all made out of wood, although shingles were beginning to replace thatch for the roofs.[170] The city plan followed the classical grid pattern, and covered eighty-five acres. The streets met at right angles, and were all five hundred yards long and around eight feet wide, except for the one that ran along the river, which was twice as wide.

However, relations between the governor and those who came to be called the colonists deteriorated with the war between France and England: the company planned to levy a tax on the land but the colonists refused to pay. Originally, the colony was infused with the humanist Christian message of its founder, who had inherited the ideas of the century of the Enlightenment. The ideal was to achieve a utopia in Africa based on the reason that all human beings shared. Naturally, slavery was abolished, and the colony's economy was based on free labor. The colonists were supposed to elect representatives, first one for every ten families (*tithingmen*) and then one for every hundred families (*hundredors*), who were responsible for the colony's self-government. However, given the problems (every settler had received only five acres instead of the twenty promised), a new charter was drawn up to strengthen the power of the governor and board, both of which were appointed by the company, while guaranteeing the colonists a jury-based civil and criminal justice system. In 1800, the colonists' rebellion was put down promptly by the arrival of 550 new blacks, who were ex-Maroons[171] from Jamaica, and 45 British soldiers. These three groups formed the core of the capital city's original population. A merchant bourgeoisie began to grow, particularly among the Nova Scotians, who set up their first wholesale company around the end of the 1810s.[172] A press appeared, and although it was initially official (the *Royal Gazette* and the *Sierra Leone Advertiser*), it was rapidly joined by relatively free letters to the editor and other popular publications (particularly the *Sierra Leone Weekly News*, which was a private paper published by a colonist). New ideas, including freemasonry, soon appeared.

In 1807, England abolished slavery. While the first colonists had been joined by new arrivals from the United States before Liberia was established (refugees of the War of 1812, people fleeing the Fugitive Slave Laws between 1793 and 1850, and blacks from California fleeing the same law in 1852), they gradually became a minority, except in the city. Slave cargos found by the British fleet that was responsible for fighting

**Map 15.** Location of Freetown in the Nineteenth Century
Based on: *Geographical Review*, vol. 46, 1956, p. 335

contraband along the coast were disembarked in Freetown. In all, sixty to seventy thousand were freed between 1808 and the 1860s; they were called the liberated slaves. Governing the area through a private company without any resources became impossible, and the territory was proclaimed a Crown Colony. Soon it contained an extraordinary mosaic of languages and cultures: Igbo, Ijebu, Popo, Egba, and more. The most closely united groups were the Yoruba and the Kru. The Yoruba had arrived in large numbers and were often referred to by the generic term *Aku*, especially if they were Muslim. The Kru, who originally came from the Liberian coast, were skillful canoemen and had been working for whites for salary since the sixteenth century, although the number of such migrant workers, not including families, was rarely more than a thousand at Freetown in the nineteenth century.[173] The colony then covered nearly 270 square miles, but the protectorate established in 1896 was a hundred times bigger.

The peninsula's organization and success were in no way chance results. While the original chartered company had not really known how to take advantage of it, Freetown was in a choice location in the internal and external structure of the West African economy. As we have seen elsewhere, the growth in the nineteenth century resulted from wise exploitation of favorable economic factors. There was a very strong international network controlled by British and American interests, along with ancient regional and interregional links, which had been revived by the vitality of *krio*-native interactions. Four complementary ecological regions were located in the Sierra Leone–Guinea system.[174] The forested coast, which had long been in contact with Atlantic trade thanks to an exceptionally welcoming bay protected by the Freetown peninsula, produced fish, salt, rice, and mangrove wood. Stretching up toward the Sahel, there was a long corridor of grassy savanna, where kola nuts were the major crop. To the west, there was the southern Futa-Jalon, which was irrigated and crossed by many valleys and produced bananas, palm oil, and rice. It complemented the dry interior plateau, which extended toward Timbo and was used exclusively for livestock. Active interregional trade circulated salt, fish, oil, kola nuts, livestock, and other local agricultural and artisanal products, such as calabashes, pottery, cloth, and raffia mats. Toward the end of the nineteenth century, the system covered at least 350 miles west–east, from Kankan and Siguiri to the coast, and 150 miles north–south, from Futa-Jalon to beyond the southern shore of the Rokel River, which led to the bay of Freetown. The city and port became one of the main destinations of the network, which sometimes stretched to Segu, five hundred miles away. Freetown linked the interior network with the Atlantic system by increasing cabotage along the coast, and especially by importing massive amounts of European manufactured goods. Thus, Freetown became the starting point of a series of trade routes that involved not only the Creoles in the city but also the inhabitants of the whole hinterland. More and more links were created. Throughout the century, they gave rise to many diplomatic contacts and treaties that finally resulted in a relatively smooth transition, at least at first, to the protectorate of 1896. This is one of the reasons for the major migration toward the capital city, and the establishment of a multicultural urban society, which was a major breakthrough at the time.

Establishing a political system was no simple task, however. Alliances were formed in accordance with status and class aspirations. In short, small merchants and intellectuals, who were mainly liberated slaves, tended to cooperate with the locals, while the wealthier bourgeoisie and members of the liberal professions tended to side with the colonial authorities. The authorities tried to maintain the physical isolation of the Creoles by controlling where colonists lived, not only on the peninsula but also in the city—they were forbidden to purchase individual lots directly from local rulers. Throughout the nineteenth century, the result was that that they were led to believe in a myth, which sometimes became reality, of a permanent native threat hanging over the land that had cost them so dearly.

In the Caribbean, the Maroons had long experience with an original and very "modernist" form of organization based on self-sufficiency and self-defense. After various settlement attempts, they were finally allocated 103 urban lots near Fort Thornton, near the governor's fortified home at the top of the hill. The difficulties they encountered as they tried to integrate into the community were such that some left the colony. The others were assimilated by the liberated slaves. The most innovative and independent group was the Nova Scotians, who formed a close-knit, predominantly Methodist community. They quickly became familiar with the interior, where their merchants acted as scouts. They sought the assistance of fellow Wesleyans in Britain and used their representatives (*tithingmen* and *hundredors*) to great advantage in their relations with the authorities. The arrival of liberated Africans destroyed the apparent balance of pioneer life: supposedly indentured in the city, local Africans were in fact used as slaves by their black employers. The flow of newcomers had to be managed while avoiding the abuses that the colony had been established to fight against. In addition to the indenture option, which was maintained, two other avenues were gradually developed: a black military force, which was set up in 1814, and settlement in pioneer villages around Freetown under the guidance of the Church Missionary Society, which had been asked for help by the British Crown. Missionaries were officially responsible not only for educating but also for governing the new communities according to the MacCarthy Parish Plan elaborated in 1816.[175]

Freetown was becoming a real capital city. Governor MacCarthy (1814–24) was a builder. Around the same time (1816), Bathurst, the current capital of Gambia, was founded as a settlement for liberated Africans, and it was for a time under Sierra Leone's control, beginning in 1821.[176] Bathurst was "well built," despite the lamentable condition of its small hospital and rudimentary nature of the military station occupied by about three hundred men. It had a wooden wharf and a large marketplace and brought together a very diverse crowd, which included Fulbe, Manding, and Wolof Muslims, liberated Akan and Igbo slaves assisted by missionaries, and finally "wild, half-naked pagan Jolu" (Jola from Casamance).[177]

At Freetown, the governor managed to have the annual equipment grant doubled in order to improve the city, set up villages, and provide each with a church and school. In the city, he completed the St. George Cathedral, which was neo-Gothic on the outside but simply whitewashed inside; built homes for key administrators; and bought part of the land belonging to an old Nova Scotian settler to create a Kru district (in other words, an upper town) to lodge the main labor force for the construction boom. The district was covered in small thatched huts separated by the remains of uncleared brush. When Burton visited, the city was three to five miles in circumference.[178]

Land speculation began with the first settlers. At the same time, the construction of districts for "native" people fostered the arrival of liberated merchants and artisans from surrounding areas, for many continued to immigrate to the capital, where they grouped together according to language, affinity, and occupation. Little by little, a kind of parallel authority was established, which helped new arrivals deal with the lobbies that the colonists had already established. Every liberated person needed a lodging-house keeper who also provided work or helped find work for tenants. The leaders of the liberated slaves gained more and more importance and became known as headmen and community representatives. Support for these leaders was not along purely ethnic lines, and their administrative and political role was finally acknowledged by the colonial authorities in 1905, when they were made part of the government and paid for their services.[179]

The land title system was at the heart of relations between the African communities and the colonial power and merits a study of its own.[180] The land register was its stumbling block. From 1813 on, all land title operations were supposed to be performed before a judge and recorded in the registers, but there were only twenty in 1857, three years after the requirement that inheritances be declared. Indeed, the land title tribunal created in 1867 still had problems getting landowners to show written documents.

The city soon began to look cosmopolitan. At the end of the 1830s, there were four categories of buildings, each representative of the main social classes. Europeans, Nova Scotians, and Maroons lived in houses made of stone or square timber covered in planks and with shingled roofs. The stone houses were furnished entirely in European style and reflected the relative luxury in which their owners lived. Some of them were quite imposing, such as Wesleyan College on the sea front. Facing the bridge across a narrow waterway, there was a series of buildings more or less corroded by rain. The largest were the police station and courthouse, and a few brick warehouses along the beach. The wood houses sat on stone foundations and sometimes had two stories. Their walls were painted various colors (blue, gray, all shades of yellow, from pale yellow to deep ochre, red, and even black), and some of the interior furnishings and decorations were European. The wood houses were most often the homes of storekeepers and merchants.

In contrast, the most recent immigrants lived in adobe or bamboo shacks, some of which were improved by replacing the adobe with wood. The people who lived in the shacks were artisans, peddlers, and small retailers with stalls in the market or more or less informal street stands offering small inexpensive items, such as needles, thread, and small jars of pomade, or food, such as fruit and fish. The wealthy inhabitants began to complain about how the British city plan was deteriorating. In 1817, a journalist drew his readers' attention to how many building façades failed to meet city standards, and to the proliferation of alleys that reminded him of "the contortions of a wounded snake."[181] In 1869, the Reverend James Johnson left a description of the city that reveals all of its complexity.[182] At the time, it had three hundred thousand inhabitants, about half of whom were Krio and half considered native. The word "aboriginal" was also used; today "provincial" is used. The population was therefore quite large, especially considering that nearly a century later, in 1948, the city had just barely doubled in size.[183]

The social structure was clear from the beginning, but urban society was mixed and there was a great deal of mobility. There were many "housekeepers" whose status was similar to that of the *signares* in St. Louis, and the children born of those unions contributed greatly to creolizing the urban population. There were also many marriages between liberated slaves and "natives." The urban culture was shaped by a number of shared factors: first, a language, Krio, which was necessary because, unlike the first settlers, who were all more or less English-speakers, the newly liberated slaves came from many different places along the coast and spoke a wide range of languages. Krio developed gradually throughout the nineteenth century. Many different customs, styles of cooking, forms of dress, and celebrations also merged. Moreover, despite appearances, "Krio" does not come from "creole," but seems to derive from the Yoruba word *akiriyo*, meaning "he who goes from one place to the next after church"[184] or, less elegantly, "parasite."[185] Then again, curiously, it is possible that the Yoruba word itself may have been reimported from Brazil. By the end of the nineteenth century, Krio had become a real language that was written and published, in particular by the local press.

It was a mixture of English, Portuguese, French, and, of course, various Bantu languages, for thanks to the liberated slaves, Freetown became a linguistic hub of Africa. It is well known that the German missionary Koellë, who was a linguist, identified more than one hundred Bantu languages spoken in Freetown in 1851 and was able to compare them at his leisure, without having to travel out of the city.

The inhabitants of Freetown, who called themselves Sierra Leoneans, soon made Krio the basis of their whole culture.[186] They also identified themselves by certain traditional foods, such as *fufu* (cassava flour porridge), the name of which came from the Maroons. Urban celebrations were perhaps the high points of cultural syncretism, with a general inclination toward prayer-based ceremonies. There was also a penchant for European-style education, and the richest families had their children attending Fourah Bay College or, if possible, sent them to school in Great Britain. By the mid-century, a Muslim culture was also developing. Initially, its members were liberated slaves, but a Krio Muslim minority began to grow. In 1875, the Muslims even succeeded in having the authorities accept a petition concerning their marriage system, which included polygamy.[187] Paradoxically, study of the colonial city shows that cultural and ethnic mixing was much more active and effective in the nineteenth century than after the protectorate was established, when the white authorities tried to resegregate the British (who were moved to the white "sanitary" city of Hill Station) and their subjects.

However, in the nineteenth century, British officials were wonderfully skillful in facilitating cultural exchange. For example, they popularized a typical English pastime: the picnic. The governor and his escort left the downtown or even rented a train and went somewhere nearby to celebrate major religious and civil British events, such as Queen Victoria's Jubilee (1887) and the coronation of King Edward VII (1902). The local people enthusiastically adopted such innovations. For example, the party at the end of Ramadan in 1905 was organized by the Young Men of Fula Town, that is, the inhabitants of the Muslim quarter, who chartered a train to take seven to eight hundred people on a trip outside of the city.[188]

Publicly at least, the city's social life brought together people from all walks of life. At the governor's arrival or departure, the elite rubbed shoulders with the masses on the wharf built in 1867. In the first half of the century an especially popular annual celebration was the Freetown Fair, which lasted a week and blithely alternated official receptions and popular events. Toward the end of the century, another very popular celebration was Pope Henessy Day, which reveals the degree of political and social reconciliation in the city.[189] Pope Henessy Day commemorated August 22, 1872, the day on which a recently appointed governor acquiesced to the recommendation by the superintendent of the Wesleyan missions that a very unpopular tax—the road tax levied directly for road maintenance—be eliminated. Many European merchants took part in the celebrations, which involved various activities such as dancing and was organized by two volunteer Krio merchant associations: the Kissi Road Traders' Association and the Native Association. The holiday was maintained until 1900.

John Peterson claims that in 1870 three Krio urban cultural leaders were emblematic of the city's diversity. They were Amara, John Ezzidio, and Joseph Wright. Amara was a liberated Aku (Yoruba) who had arrived in the 1830s and had become the imam of the Muslim quarter, Fulah Town, and one of the principal leaders of the Muslim community. John Ezzidio was born at Nupe, indentured at Freetown, and became the first liberated slave to become a member of the legislative council, to which he was elected in 1863 by the Methodist merchant community. Joseph Wright was a Creole born in 1840 in the village of Hastings. He came to work in Freetown as a cobbler, got married there, and, after having gone into trade in Lagos for a few years, came back and settled in the city in 1870. He amassed a substantial fortune, and his son became mayor in 1908. This shows clearly that a new culture, acknowledged by all, was in the process of emerging. It took another form under colonization, because in 1893, three years after the protectorate was established, the city finally acquired a municipal government.[190]

### Monrovia: American-Liberians and "Natives"

Sierra Leone is by far the best-studied case of urban development. It would be nice to have such accurate information on the growth of the city of Monrovia in Liberia, which was founded in a similar manner.[191] A contradictory alliance between American abolitionist missionaries in the North and slave owners in the South resulted in the founding of the American Colonization Society (ACS) in 1816. It began to raise money to "repatriate" to Africa the liberated slaves that no one knew what to do with. In 1821, the first ship of colonists landed at Cape Mesurado, the future site of Monrovia. From the beginning, the rift between the American-Liberians (as they called themselves) and the Africans was total. The former stuck to the coast and maintained two governments: one for "citizens" and one for "natives." The hinterland began to be annexed officially only in 1904, but the notion of subscribing to a shared "negro nationality" was far from accepted.

The "colonial" society was itself divided. At the beginning, the ACS took some care to recruit relatively literate mulattos. However, Nat Turner's revolt in 1831 in the United States changed everything and triggered massive immigration. From then on, the goal was to get rid of as many liberated slaves (most of whom were freed for this purpose alone) as possible by sending them to Africa. Finally, there were the "recaptives" or "Congolese," as they were called, who were, like the Saros, slaves who had been liberated by the American fleet, and were of various origins. Some 5,500 disembarked between 1846 and 1860. Generally, there was little immigration after the American Civil War.

The original idea was to encourage profitable farming of tropical products and demonstrate to the "natives" how far behind they were. However, in 1843, the 912 colonists in Monrovia had cleared barely a hundred acres. Most of the colonists were former domestic slaves descended from white masters and black mistresses in Maryland, Virginia, and North Carolina. They preferred to engage in trade, and some were successful, particularly in trading dyewood and palm products for imported goods required by the colonists. They became merchant-princes. In 1841, one of them succeeded the white American governor. In 1847, for reasons related essentially to trade, the colonists freed themselves of the ACS's control and established the colony as a republic. At the time, the merchant elite was clearly concentrated in Monrovia. The Liberians did not assimilate or even associate with the local people, whom they kept in a situation of dependence by spreading the "indenture" system. They then found themselves faced with the beginnings of the colonial conquest, which nibbled away at the territory that the Liberians claimed, although they did not really exercise any control over it. This increasingly isolated them from the Western world to which they felt they belonged. The failure of farming and the decline in trade forced them to take refuge in the service sector. Around 1900, the descendants of the merchant-princes were lawyers, jurists, and journalists. It was said that Monrovia had one industry: government.[192] Since there were so few resources, salvation came from reviving the slave trade in the form of organized recruitment of contract or indentured workers, who were rounded up in the interior and shipped throughout the rest of Africa, to the Portuguese islands of Fernando-Po, to French Gabon, and elsewhere, to make money. This scandal (many others of a similar kind had occurred elsewhere in Africa) was stopped by the League of Nations only in 1930.

Monrovia was a "colonial" town from the beginning, with an urbanism and lifestyle that contrasted strongly with the rest of the country. Unfortunately, at the current stage of research (one has to wonder why American researchers have spent so little time on the topic) we can only suspect that around the middle of the nineteenth century Monrovia's urban and social development was largely similar to that of Freetown. The service-oriented "elite" depended at the beginning on the "Congoleses" (as imported workers from the outside were nicknamed) for all productive activities, then came to use paternalistic indenture practices to capitalize on the growing immigration of local inland people. The generalized practice of apprenticeship to train these usually young workers at low cost led to extensive cultural mixing on the coast. Nevertheless, the contrast grew between the hinterland, left in the hands of the natives, and the city, which had become, intentionally or not, the cradle of a new urban civilization.[193]

## Senegal's Leading Colonial Cities: Gorée and St. Louis

We will discuss this example briefly because there is a relatively recent high-quality bibliography on the topic.[194] The Senegalese coast brings us closer to colonialism, since St. Louis came into the French sphere in the mid-seventeenth century. It became the headquarters of the Compagnie française du Cap-Vert et du Sénégal in 1659 and remained so until 1791, when the rights granted to the companies that succeeded the former were abolished.

Gorée Island was occupied and named by the Dutch in 1617. It came under French control soon after St. Louis (1677).[195] Throughout the eighteenth century, the French were concerned with restoring Gorée's two forts in anticipation of war with the British. After it was occupied again by the French in 1763, the French governor left St. Francis Fort to live in the St. Jean Pavilion, which belonged to a mixed-race signare and was located near gardens. The house ended up being used as a government building. This was the beginning of residential integration, with whites and Africans living side by side in the same neighborhood. The city grew from fewer than 250 inhabitants at the beginning of the eighteenth century, with a dozen huts occupied by blacks or mulattos in 1698, to 1,840 in 1785 and 2,500 by the end of the century. At that point, there were, on average, a hundred men in the garrison, and three times more female than male slaves out of a total of 197 slaves in 1749 and 1,566 in 1785.[196] The signares, who were under the protection of their European masters or husbands, rose in society as businesswomen. Out of the forty-nine landowners with titles registered in 1776, forty were women, including thirty who were known as signares.[197] Gorée was the primary storehouse in the sea off the Cape Verde Peninsula, which was very unhealthy at the time owing to yellow fever, which killed most of the few survivors of the *Medusa* shipwreck in 1817; the future explorer Gaspard Théodore Mollien was among those who made it to shore. Free families lived in square houses, but slaves lived in round ones; all the homes had thatch roofs. Expansion began with the English occupation, which permitted building in the area known as the *cinquante pas du roi* along the seashore and on the old ramparts, where construction had been forbidden since the reign of Louis XIV. In 1763, there were still only seven "inferior" stone houses,[198] but there were fifteen in 1770 and eighty-five in 1786. From then on, masonry terraces and roofs began to replace straw.[199] European colonists began building better ventilated and sometimes very comfortable stone houses in the lower part of the island, where they mixed with free Africans.[200] Yet, the city remained a warehouse and fortified site for protection and defense. The island's

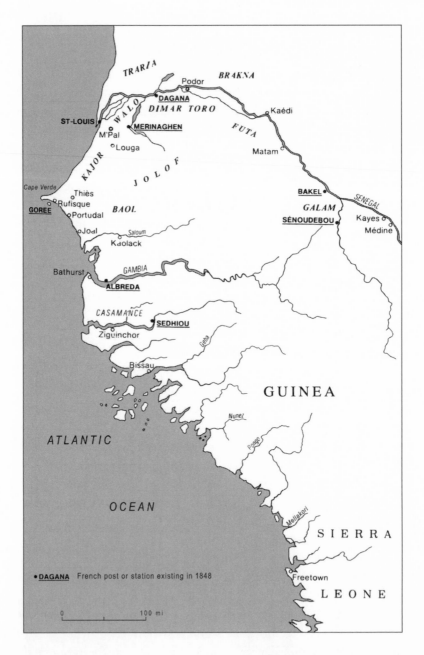

**Map 16.** Senegal and Southern Rivers in the Nineteenth Century
Based on: Jean Delcourt, *La Turbulente histoire de Gorée*, Dakar: Clairafrique, 1982, p. 17

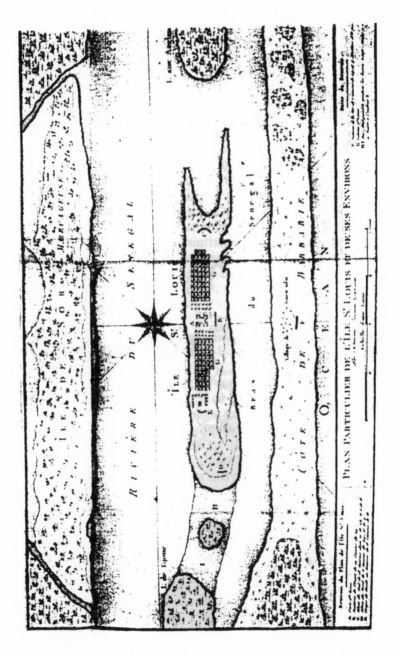

Map 17. St. Louis Island and Surroundings in 1789, by Pruneau de Pommegorge (*Description de la nigritie*)
Source: Camille Camara, *Saint-Louis-du-Sénégal*, Dakar: IFAN, 1968, p. 36.

main problem was obtaining supplies, particularly water (there was no spring on the island) but also firewood, construction materials, and food. Moreover, because Gorée was very small, the idea of moving to the mainland emerged at the end of the eighteenth century.

On the eve of the French Revolution, St. Louis had 7,000 inhabitants, not counting slaves in transit and including 660 Europeans. Permanent buildings were springing up. Although they were miserable little strongholds peopled by employees of trading companies and a few soldiers surrounded by a black populace most often made up of slaves, St. Louis and Gorée had still managed to make some progress. As on the Gold Coast and in Sierra Leone, a class of Christianized mulattos known as "locals" (*habitants*) took control of business. Initially, as elsewhere, a few adventurers and slave traders settled in the city and, thanks to the signares, fathered a merchant bourgeoisie whose French names sometimes still reveal their distant origins today.[201] Starting in 1778 at St. Louis and Gorée, in accordance with a "custom considered consistent with the system of merging Europeans and natives that is so important to maintain and even extend,"[202] a mixed-race mayor was traditionally chosen to handle relations between the governor and the people. The mayor's appointment became official only in the First Empire. Aside from one exception, when Faidherbe managed to impose a European mayor on St. Louis, the mayors of both cities were always of mixed race. They were responsible for publishing and enforcing the government's orders and for controlling the police. They were also responsible for roads and acted as officers of the court and conciliation magistrates. In 1848, the mayors also became civil registrars. They were sometimes even required to negotiate with local leaders. From 1823 on in St. Louis, and probably soon after in Gorée as well, the mayor had two assistants, to which a third was added at the end of the century. That innovation had a lasting effect on the "assimilation" policy. In 1872, a municipal and electoral system similar to that of Paris was introduced in Senegalese cities. It included an elected municipal council and a mayor who was appointed, and then elected as of 1884. This soon tempted people to become French citizens.[203] In short, as elsewhere, cultures were blending together.

The revolutionary period brought about the first major changes, beginning with the official suppression (which remained definitive in spite of contraband activities) of the slave trade by the British when they occupied Gorée during the Napoleonic period. While the city's future plan was adopted in 1828, it was delayed by the economic change resulting from the transition from trade in slaves to trade in goods; the plan did not actually start before the new trade in goods proved profitable. The main exports became gum arabic produced at way stations (called *escales*) along the Senegal River and the beginnings (still tentative in the 1840s) of the export of locally produced peanut oil.

With the appointment of Governor Faidherbe to Senegal in 1854 and the beginnings of his conquest of the interior, colonial urban growth became meaningful. From then on, St. Louis and Gorée had military and administrative functions. Gorée thought it would become a capital, when it was a short-lived colony between 1854 and 1859 with outposts scattered along the coast all the way to Gabon, including the "Comptoirs du Sud," that is, the factories along the southern coast that later became French Guinea. Merchants as far away as Sierra Leone continued to use its warehouses, and it had the advantage of a free port regime that was confirmed by decree in 1852. However, since the city was limited to the island, it remained small and never had many more than four thousand inhabitants, including the Lebu from Cape Verde and people from neighboring coastal areas.

St. Louis became the governor's home and the administrative and economic capital. Products from Waalo and Cayor (especially peanuts once the St. Louis–Dakar railroad was built in 1883–85) as well as from the "escales" along the river from Medine were shipped to the city.[204] Its wealth grew until the middle of the century thanks to the European market for gum arabic. Following a mid-century recession caused by the world economy, St. Louis's Creole merchants flourished again until the 1890s. It was only then that Dakar became preeminent.

Indeed, St. Louis too began to suffer from its protected location, which had been a requirement in the preceding centuries. Trapped on its island (1.5 miles by 300 yards) in the middle of the river, it was no longer big enough. The central part was crowded with official buildings, including the governor's residence, offices, barracks, the church, and the permanent homes of the leading merchants. Urban growth made a new city plan necessary in 1860. Houses were laid out in a grid, and sanitary measures were taken; for example, a dock and dyke were built to prevent floods when the river was high, and the main streets were paved. At the tips of the island, however, straw was still used as a building material in the poor quarters, which were often ravaged by fire. A mosque was built at the northern end of the island. In 1856, the city was linked to the narrow strip of land known as the "langue de Barbarie," where an old fishing village became a permanent working-class quarter called N'Dar Toute. The central market was moved there in 1863. At the other end, Europeans built homes that allowed the sea breeze in to chase away the unhealthy "vapors" of the rainy season. The classical home had two stories, with a peaked red-tile roof. On the first floor, a typical boutique had a rectangular room divided lengthwise into two by a counter more or less covered in display cases. Above the door there was a rectangular or arched vent bordered with iron spikes, which was a vestige of the air vents in slave cells. The vent opened onto the interior courtyard. On the second floor, a row of rooms opened onto an interior veranda that looked out over the courtyard where the cistern was located. On the street side, the rooms opened symmetrically onto a wooden balcony that was supported by strong pine posts and had a wrought-iron railing. Today, there is still one example of typical eighteenth-century architecture in St. Louis: a fortified house known as the "signares house," which is now used as a mosque.[205]

In the nineteenth century, the fresh-water problem had not yet been solved and would not be solved for a while. A tanker brought water from upstream and distributed four liters per person per day to officials and soldiers. Other inhabitants had no choice but to build their own cisterns, when they could afford to do so. Those who did not have the means, in other words, the majority, dug wells in the dunes, where they found only brackish water. Faidherbe Bridge, which was built in 1865, linked the city to the mainland and changed the economics of the whole area. By that time, Faidherbe was leaving Senegal, and the city had doubled in size in a hundred years, growing from seven thousand inhabitants in 1786 to around fifteen thousand. Five-sixths of St. Louis's inhabitants still lived on the island, but the composition of the city had changed. Europeans still accounted for only a few hundred at the most, but the mulatto "habitants" had begun to lose their commercial and political supremacy, and, as elsewhere, the "assimilated" aspect of the urban population was beginning to be seriously undermined by the colonial ostracism of the end of the nineteenth century. The great majority of the population was then made up of recent African immigrants, who were primarily Wolof but also included people from all areas along the river (Sarakolle, Fulbe, even Bambara from Segu, as well as former black slaves who had escaped from the Moors). Immigration was encouraged by the government because the labor force remained small.

In short, at the end of the Second Empire, St. Louis especially but also Gorée were real cities and prime crossroads for contact between different civilizations. It was in those two cities that Senegal's cultural mixture took root, before spreading to the "modern" colonial cities that were created later (Dakar in 1857 and Rufisque in 1859) and gained prominence during the time of colonial imperialism. However, that is another story.

## Lagos: From the Apogee of the Slave Trade to Colonialism's Lessons

Though Lagos has been much studied, its colonial ups and downs in the twentieth century are much better known than its beginnings on the eve of the protectorate (1851–61) and the first decades of colonization.[206] While it has often been described as simply a village before British rule, Robin Law is right to note that in the nineteenth century it was the largest slave-trading port on the Bight of Benin (which was both the official and real reason for English intervention), and already had a long history.

The surrounding islands had been attracting slave traders from Yorubaland from the time of the first contact with Europeans. The first to settle on the site seem to have been Awori from the west, who have been claiming their rights as the first occupants since that time. They were followed by the Egba from the northwest, the Ijebu from the north, and the Edo (Bini) from the kingdom of Benin City to the east. It seems that initially the Awori established a hunting and fishing station on the coast, but then moved to Iddo Island for greater safety. Since the island was just a little more than one square mile in area, it was too small to support a growing population. Gradually, the marshy area that is now the Island of Lagos was taken over. In the 1790s, the Portuguese were invited to engage in trade there. At the time, the Yoruba and Fulbe wars provided large numbers of slaves whom the site was well situated to receive since it was protected by many lagoons and creeks. A city-state thus came into being. Previously, the island had been called Oko ("lagoon"). The Edo called the growing city Eko ("camp"), and in 1854 it became known by its Portuguese name, Lagos ("lagoon"). In the first half of the nineteenth century, it welcomed "Brazilians," freed slaves sent back from Brazil after the 1826–33 revolts, and Saros of Yoruba origin who returned to the area. Many became rich slave traders. Thus, from the beginning in Lagos, power resided with business owners and those who had money, rather than with those who controlled the land. It was money from international trade that gradually enabled the chief of Lagos to turn what was originally the leadership of a council of elders (which was in principle subordinate to the Oba of Benin City, to whom tribute was paid until the nineteenth century) into a veritable local kingship, with the rituals and institutions of a Yoruba chiefdom.

British missionaries and merchants were quick to try to intervene in local politics to promote legitimate trade. The Oba at the time, Kosoko, was a slave trader. His uncle Akitoye promised to eliminate slave trading if the British got him the throne. The British therefore bombed Lagos in 1851, expelled the Portuguese, and exiled Kosoko. However, Akitoye and his successor did not really manage to impose their legitimacy. After Docemo was forced to sign the treaty making Lagos a Crown Colony in 1861, Kosoko made peace with the British and came back to the city. The descendants of the two rivals continued to vie for power well into the twentieth century. In works that cover periods outside of the chronological scope of this book, researchers have focused mainly on the strength of and changes in these elite groups and local institutions through the prism of colonialism. Despite their differences, those works often seem to share the presupposition that Lagos's history began only with the English intervention.[207]

Unfortunately, very little is known about the period prior to British occupation, although there are Portuguese archives that merit study. However, it does not seem as if commercial structures were greatly changed by the arrival of a colonial power that long remained in the background. Initially, Lagos had a British administrator (1848–53), then a council (1853–61). It was briefly under the control of a local governor (1861–66), then that of the governor of Sierra Leone (1866–74), and finally that of the governor of Gold Coast (1874–86). It was only in 1886 that an autonomous colonial organization was set up, for control had been won over a wider hinterland, thereby providing revenue to a colony that had no financial means at first.[208] Before then, the British authorities had simply fought against contraband trade. The fight had been making progress since the beginning of the century owing to growth in the market for palm oil, which maintained the profits of the local elites: in 1851, ten percent of the population was Saro. Their numbers continued to grow,[209] accounting for twenty percent of the population in 1865 out of a total of twenty-five thousand city dwellers, a city of considerable size for the period.

The cultural melting pot began working early on, and the creolization of an elite that was already cosmopolitan occurred largely before the British gained control. Records mention Koranic schools from 1816 on, and the first mosque was built mid-century. A Saro who belonged to the Church Missionary Society introduced European-style education in 1852. It was modeled on elementary schools that were already operating in Badagry, about twenty miles to the west, and Abeokuta. Baptist Americans and Catholics were quick to follow the example in 1853 and 1868, respectively. Education rapidly became widespread: in 1862, there were still only four schools, which served some 400 students, of whom thirty-eight percent were girls, but nearly twenty years later, in 1881, Lagos had twenty-nine schools with a total of 2,257 students, of whom forty-two percent were girls.[210] At that point, a local press was established. In the following years, the gradual emancipation of Brazilian slaves led to a new wave of immigrants: there were five thousand Afro-Brazilians in 1873.

Liberated Hausa slaves formed the core of the police and army. The rest of Lagos's inhabitants increasingly included fugitive slaves from the Yoruba hinterland. Such fugitives made up much of the city's common folk and were true city dwellers who were from the beginning cut off from the rural areas where they had no ties aside from slavery. They were used as municipal workers and as apprentices to Brazilian artisans. Most lived in the former barracks located in the south of the island (today's Marina district). The residential area was located in the west, but the marshy ground and small size of the island (only 1.5 by 3.5 miles), long remained obstacles to expansion.

From the beginning, the city therefore suffered from overpopulation in dense quarters with twisting streets and deplorable sanitation. This was aggravated by malaria and insufficient fresh water, which was provided by shallow wells of dubious quality. Despite a dynamic commander's short-lived effort to drain the marsh and relieve overpopulation in the center in 1870, the situation deteriorated until the first third of the twentieth century, culminating with the plague epidemic in 1924–25, ten years after the epidemic in Dakar. The governor then once again acknowledged that Lagos had the dubious distinction of being the most populous, crowded, and unhealthy city on the west coast of British Africa.[211]

## Cape Town: The Only White City in Black Africa

Because it was the only white city in sub-Saharan Africa, Cape Town was for a time the colonizers' ideal. In fact, when the post that became Cape Town was established in the mid-seventeenth century, there was no plan to build a city. Sailing between the United Provinces and India took six months, however, and Table Bay at the foot of Table Mountain was a good harbor halfway between the West and the East. The Dutch East India Company landed a small expedition there on April 6, 1652, and planned to set up a station where ships could take on fresh supplies, such as livestock, fresh water, and grain. A fort was built in 1666 to protect the site from incursions by the Khoikhoi; the Dutch, who found their click-based language incomprehensible, called them Bushmen and "Hottentots." They became quite early a highly "colored" population; most Hottentots were descended from Dutch men and Khoikhoi women. The company waited five years before allowing a few settlers to begin farming on the flanks of the mountain in order to supplement the goods obtained through barter from the natives, which were insufficient to meet the fresh-food needs of the Dutch ships and agents. The small Salt and Liesbeek Rivers served as temporary borders between the company's land and the local people. However, slave-owning white farmers armed with guns rapidly succeeded in ensuring that the Bushmen, who were armed with bows and arrows, kept their distance. Imported diseases, in particular a smallpox epidemic in 1713, helped to decimate the local population, thereby quickly pushing back the eastern frontier. At the beginning of the eighteenth century, it was some 150 miles away from the city, but at the end of the century it was 450 miles away.

The city grew slowly around the church (Groote Kerke), which was built in 1717. It served as a small administrative center and agricultural market for the hinterland.[212] Houses were built in tiers around the fort, along the river, and around the market gardens covering the side of Table Mountain. At the time, the city had the fort, the church, a hospital (in a bungalow), and about a hundred houses. There were only two main roads with drainage ditches. The city also had a building for the company's slaves and exiled convicts transferred from Batavia to Cape Town; in all, some seven hundred people crowded into the building, which has now been converted into a museum.[213] Not including those men and the garrison, De Kaap had few more than 1,450 inhabitants (free men, liberated slaves, and slaves) in the 1720s, 2,500 around 1750, and 4,500 twenty-five years later. It was only at the end of the century that the population really began to grow, since it tripled under English occupation after the economic boom of the 1780s. In 1795, at the end of the company's reign, there were 1,200 houses in the city, almost all of which had slave quarters, as did the surrounding farms. Indeed, in 1806, at the time of the first British census, there were almost twice as many slaves in the city as white settlers (9,307 slaves versus 6,435 free inhabitants, of whom a little over 800 were liberated slaves).[214] Everyday life was dangerous and hard, and law enforcement was a matter of expediency, since it was still partly the responsibility of former convicts used by the *fiscaal* (chief of police).

At that time, very few Africans, all Hottentots, lived in the city, accounting for only four percent of its inhabitants: 626 out of 16,500. To that number must be added 264 slaves that the British government had inherited from the Dutch company, 4,000 men in the garrison, and a

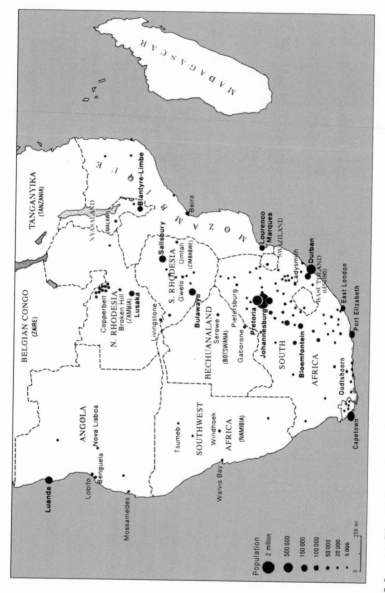

Map 18. The Urban Network in Southern Africa at the End of the Colonial Period: An Inheritance
Based on: N. C. Pollock, "The Development of Urbanization in Southern Africa," in R. P. Beckinsale
and J. M Houston, eds., *Urbanization and Its Problems*, New York: Barnes & Noble, 1968, p. 315.

floating population of sailors who in some seasons, such as the first four months of the year, significantly increased the population.

The city was almost entirely composed of immigrants and their descendants. Earlier, the Dutch company had imported slaves from more or less everywhere in the Indian Ocean, including the Mozambique coast, Madagascar, and especially the Philippines, Malaysia, India, and Ceylon; Asians were considered better artisans, merchants, and clerks than Africans, who were used mainly in the countryside or for manual labor such as carrying water and cutting wood.[215] In total, between 1652 and 1795, the Dutch company imported into South Africa not many more than four thousand African slaves from the coast of East Africa, and at most five hundred from the coast of West Africa. Many more Asian slaves were brought as ballast in ships coming back to the United Provinces from Batavia.[216] Cape Town's popular culture and cooking were therefore strongly influenced by Asia. The language of slavery, which was mixed with lower Malaysian and the lingua franca derived from Portuguese, played a role in creolizing the Dutch spoken in Cape Town, which eventually resulted in Afrikaans.[217] Islamization was also imported with the slaves from Asia throughout the century.[218]

Between 1840 and 1850, whites became the majority in the city. From the end of the slave trade in 1807 until emancipation in 1834, the slave population had continued to shrink. This was not because many slaves were freed, since that was very limited (rarely more than fifty a year), but because the sex ratio was so unbalanced that reproduction was infrequent. There were no more than 5,800 slaves in 1831. In contrast, the number of free men doubled, both because of natural growth and because the city continued to be used as a harbor by immigrant sailors, most of whom were Dutch or German. In 1840, after emancipation and at the time that the racial category "colored" appeared, there were 10,784 whites but only 9,304 "coloreds."

Former slaves lived in miserable suburbs at the city gates, and the government did not concern itself much with them.[219] The remains of fish and other garbage most often rotted where it was left, and water was rare because the city had only sixty-three pumps and fountains, most of which were concentrated in the residential area. Most blacks (78 percent) were fishers, dockhands, launderers, and artisans (mainly in construction); others (16 percent) became guards or servants or eked out a living as small retailers; the rest were laborers. There were also European, especially Irish, immigrants in the poor quarters of the port, the lower town, and the east (which later became District Six); until the first half of the twentieth century, Cape Town was one of the least segregated cities in Africa. Only a few lanes were reserved for the city homes of the richest white farmers. Elsewhere, free men, blacks, and especially people of mixed race mingled with one another, and more than one rich merchant had a "colored" wife.[220] In 1843, when the British reorganized the municipality on the basis of the census, forty percent (830 out of 2,000) of voting landowners were classed as "colored."[221] Initially, the distinction was mainly social, and included the language used: creolized Dutch by the poor (including whites) and English by the rich.

White South Africans have inherited a vague nostalgia for that period, along with a typical, graceful architecture known as Cape Dutch. Houses in Cape Town usually had two stories, terrace roofs, and gables with decorated eaves. They had large guillotine windows, often with shutters, that were placed symmetrically on either side of the front door. Arson by slaves eliminated the option of thatched roofs early in the city's history. The fronts of the houses had a slightly raised veranda (*stoep*), where the family could take the cool evening air while watching passersby. Later, smaller houses with verandas and gabled parapets were built on the slopes of Signal Hill for emancipated slaves. That quarter later became the "Malay Quarter" and is now the oldest district of the city.[222] Most of the houses have recently been restored.

By the mid-nineteenth century, Cape Town was losing steam, and in 1850 for the first time its exports were overshadowed by those of Port Elizabeth, which had become the largest exporter of wool in the Eastern Province.[223] In 1859, despite the position held by the English merchant community and relative strength of its chamber of commerce,[224] the region's industrial activities were still limited to fifty-six companies serving local markets (lime kilns, foundries, breweries, grain mills, soap and candle manufacturers, fish wholesalers, and printers).[225] The population remained more or less stable until the mining boom at the end of the century following the discovery of diamonds in the Rand in 1867 and then gold twenty years later. Since Cape Town was the primary

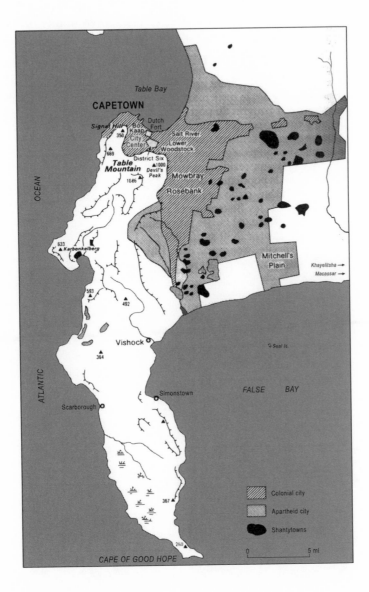

Table Bay

**CAPETOWN**

Signal Hill

OCEAN

Dutch Fort

Kaap City Center

Salt River
Lower Woodstock

District Six

Table Mountain

Devil's Peak

Mowbray

Rosebank

Karbonkelberg

Mitchell's Plain

Khayelitsha →

Macassar →

ATLANTIC

Vishock

Seal Is.

Simonstown

Scarborough

FALSE          BAY

Colonial city

Apartheid city

Shantytowns

CAPE OF GOOD HOPE

0          5 mi

**Map 19.** The "Colonial" City from the Cape to Today's City Center
Based on: J. Western, "Undoing the Colonial City,"
*Geographical Review*, vol. 75, no. 3, 1985, p. 349

market for British interests, it became the country's leading outlet for the precious metal. Construction began on a railway at the beginning of the 1860s, and on docks in the port in 1870. The number of inhabitants doubled between 1875 and 1904, climbing from 33,000 to 78,000, but the city did not remain white because African workers began to gravitate to it. This was the end of the ban on African settlement in Cape Colony. Cape Town was entering the era of imperial capitalism, and the policy of segregation, to give birth to apartheid, was becoming a defensive weapon.

# Conclusion

When you close this book, perhaps you will simply say that every city is unique. Is there any point in generalizing about African cities, and is it even appropriate to use a single concept—"the city"? This question was asked at the beginning of the book. The closer we get in history to the twentieth century, the more we are led, particularly by the greater abundance of sources, to treat the topic in a series of monographs on urban life, each different from the next. Yet there remain a number of facts that should be weighed. The first is the age and complexity of African urban history from the earliest times. According to archaeological evidence, the cities' heritages extend more than a thousand years into the past, and their histories—including strong indigenous dynamics—include the assimilation of Islamic, Mediterranean, and Asian influences and the convergence of contact from the Indian and Atlantic Oceans. This book represents an attempt to provide a detailed analysis of the succession, accumulation, and interpenetration of all these elements. The major disruption probably was not colonialism, but rather occurred before the period of imperial colonialism, which, except in South Africa, did not begin before the 1880s. The nineteenth-century urban revolution had already spread across most of the continent, over areas with very different histories, and prepared the way for the adoption of Western modernity in all African cities, no matter where they were located. The cities that were able to hold onto power were those that more or less adopted the change ahead of time, particularly more from a political point of view than in relation to economics alone. Finally, we have shown the incomparable leading role always played by cities with respect to both politics and culture. Urban culture is probably the variable that is the most difficult to define, but it is also the most crucial in this history.

Let us review these points in greater depth.

To begin with, the richness of the history of urban Africa has been, if not ignored, at least very neglected until recently. Yet, in Africa as elsewhere, the urban phenomenon was as historically widespread as it was diverse, except perhaps in the Congo forest basin and the southern edges of the Kalahari Desert. In both time and space, African cities were not physical constructions but spatial and social dynamics that were constantly changing. The relations between the urban population and its environment were always structured in accordance with a number of political and social pressures, as well as ecological, technological, and ideological constraints. The chronologies and events were extraordinarily diverse. For example, in southern Africa, a network of colonial cities already existed in the mid-nineteenth century, from the Cape to Transvaal and Natal. On the coasts, creolization began at the latest in the eighteenth century, much sooner than that in Portuguese cities, and still earlier in Swahili cities. The Islamization of the desert ports began in the Middle Ages, while the layout of Bantu capitals long reflected the structure of a military- and lineage-based society. Many of these elements have combined over the years, laying the foundations of a complex history full of contrasts. If this book succeeds only in pointing out that urbanization occurred over the long term in sub-Saharan Africa, that the processes were part of a continuum rather than the result of ruptures, and that even the ruptures were never sudden but grew out of apparently imperceptible adjustments that combined to revolutionize mentalities and societies, then my objective has been achieved, at least in part.

## The Importance of Economics

Another key point is the way the importance of economics has been neglected by most historical anthropologists interested in Africa's urban past. The major tendency was to differentiate if not to oppose social structure and economic incentive.[1] Nevertheless, as Paul Bairoch noted,[2] urbanization in Africa as elsewhere is related to the beginnings of agriculture because farming was required to concentrate the population and make it denser. This makes the city and the countryside inseparable. Of course, there can be countryside without a city, but there can be no city without a countryside. Food production is so necessary to the city that one can wonder whether cities, as the organizational centers of such production, very early and quickly became conditions perhaps not for farming but for agricultural progress. Clearly, the reason that the emergence of cities sometimes seems sporadic in Africa is because the "Neolithic revolution" was less clear-cut and more diffuse and slower than elsewhere. Beginning with the first millennium BCE, the conquest of agriculture from the fringes of the Sahara spread over the continent only very slowly and proceeded irregularly, all the more so as it might go from the casual use of cultivation to the systematization of food producing. Cultivation perhaps reached some of the central regions barely before the tenth century and, in some cases, even later. It is thus no surprise that urban forms emerged slowly in those areas.

This contradicts the traditional opposition that both Western historians and anthropologists working in Africa have argued exists between ancient or even medieval cities and economic cities. The former would be essentially religious and political centers based on their military power; the latter, which appeared in mercantile form at the dawn of early modernity, were linked to the establishment of capitalism and later gave birth to the industrial metropolis.[3]

Ancient cities would be characterized by the juxtaposition of the great powers revealed in their monumental architecture: political power in the palace, religious in the temple, mosque, or church, and military in the camp.[4] Of course, this schema has often been used in socio-anthropological studies of precolonial African cities. The dominant element would be of a ritual and cosmological origin, mirrored in the spatial organization of the city, a symbolic reflection of the religious thought presiding over its destiny. In fact, such hypotheses have more often been proven true of villages (Dogon,[5] Sao in Chad[6]) than of cities. Indeed, one of the rare examples that has been analyzed is that of Musumba, capital of the Lunda empire. Musumba's design and resulting layout seem to be an anthropomorphic representation related, for reasons that are not quite clear, with the animal symbolism of the turtle.[7] A series of subclassifications of ancient African cities has been proposed on the basis of this hypothesis. Cities have been classified as "ritual," "administrative," or "mercantile," with the accent always on ideological presuppositions about economics and trade.[8] The traditional city would have been a religious and political center and the seat of the dominant line of the reigning family, which surrounded itself with protected and favored clients.

Certainly, the urban aspect of politics is strong. Most often, especially in central Africa, the major city was first the state capital. Two examples of this have been suggested. In the interlacustrine kingdoms, the aristocracy was made up of originally migratory herders who had possibly arrived from the north and come to rule the farmers already living in the area. These were the Hima herders of the Chwezi kingdom in Rwanda and northern Uganda. Later, in the seventeenth or eighteenth centuries, pastoral so-called Tutsi from Rwanda and Burundi took over political authority at the expense of the "Hutu" peasants. Ankole and Buganda kingdoms were also established. The capital city tended to blend into the royal camp or palace, which was always located in the center. The urban setting remained unstable because each new sovereign had to build a new palace, and thus a new capital, on a new hilltop. These settlements were more like camps than cities.[9]

A later example is that of Foumbam, capital of the Bamum in Cameroon. Claude Tardits shows the extent to which the settlement and urbanism, in the form of concentric lineage-based circles (with the closest circle to the palace indicating closest kinship with the sovereign), were designed to portray the royal power and its views on lineage.[10] In short, the layout of the city, which reproduced that of the palace, always relegated to the periphery the members of society who were least integrated into the hierarchy of power. It thereby reflected the hierarchized kinship structure of the society as a whole, in both the countryside and the city. The king could exercise power only if he guaranteed maintenance of the strata so defined. Procurement of supplies for the city was supposed to follow directly from this, with each house relying on supplies from its dependents and slaves in its rural holdings. Elsewhere, the same type of political-kinship vision of society tended to obliterate or marginalize the key problem of supplying cities, which was initially seen as secondary. The argument has been used, for example, to deny that Yoruba cities were "true" cities.[11]

Politics was a potent force in African cities, partly because it very often merged with economic power. The sovereign or chief controlled long-distance trade; artisans, slaves, and members of other castes, who produced luxuries and items for trade, depended directly on him. At the beginnings of history, like today, the city's power, control, and fame were inseparable from its economic ability to survive and grow. The question of what was the initial trigger is a perfect example of a false dilemma (which came first, the chicken or the egg?), because clearly everything occurred at the same time. Likewise, even historians who do not specialize in antiquity can assert that Athens and Rome were great political and religious metropolises because they were also major economic centers, albeit of an essentially mercantile economy.

It has also been argued that a preindustrial city is not an economic center because it is unproductive, in contrast with an industrial city, which becomes the main focus of the country's productive activities.[12] The "consumer" city is considered a parasite and dismissed as an economic force. This tendency, strongly expressed in relation to Western cities (for example, Paris and London in the seventeenth and eighteenth centuries), has been taken up again by certain specialists on African history.[13] Of course, cities that are the residences of the aristocracy and the military may seem like centers for the "passive" concentration of "parasitical" social groups that receive their income and subsistence from elsewhere (such as their seignorial and rural domains). From this point of view, the city is made up of unproductive residents, such as individuals living on annuities, bureaucrats, soldiers, courtiers, and lords, all of whom confiscate the work of others for their own benefit through slavery, annuities, taxes, and other methods. Nonetheless, these privileged classes generate considerable activity, and not only through the circulation of goods. They attract a wide range of workers who support them and supply them with everything they request, such as food, but also artisanal products made in the city, slaves, servants, merchants, artisans, financiers, lenders, innkeepers, lobbyists, and masons. In turn, all these people increase the need for urban supply systems and markets. It cannot be denied that they play a strategic role in stimulating the economy, and it seems a little too convenient not to take this into account.

So, where shall we draw the line with respect to *modern* cities? There are as many proposals as there are historians. Theories are related both to the period studied by the researcher and to the theoretical components suggested by his or her field.

Gordon Childe proposed using the English range of terms. He reserves *city* for "true" cities meeting his ten criteria, and uses *town* to designate the set of transitional forms that occurred throughout what he calls, by analogy with agriculture's "Neolithic revolution," the "urban revolution," which was a slow, gradual process lasting several decades or even centuries before coming to term.[14] Georges Duby essentially defines the preindustrial city by its political function. He nevertheless tends to distinguish the *cité antique* (ancient city) from the medieval (premodern) *ville* that emerged between the eleventh and thirteenth centuries. Such towns gave a greater role to merchants and artisans and were centers of production and exchange born from the beginnings of the West's economic growth.[15]

The medievalist Guy Blois, to whom we will return because his suggestions are valuable, defines the content of this new urban revolution[16] as the genesis of a new distinction between the city and the countryside, not based on the city simply siphoning off supplies but on complementary bilateral exchanges involving constant circulation in both directions of people and goods, and reciprocal stimulation of the urban and rural economies. The Africanist historian Fred Cooper expresses this in a more theoretical and apparently less dated (or at least more recent) manner: the threshold is crossed when the city is no longer simply a marketplace and becomes the economic center of the market.[17] Prior to that, rural and urban economies are somewhat independent. It is even possible to imagine, in the case of cities with an abusively demanding slave or tribute system, such as the Roman Empire, agrarian relief obtained by the nonexistence or shrinking of the city, as was the case in the early Middle Ages in Europe.

This idea allows us to differentiate the substance of the capital cities that were still faltering in ancient central Africa from the network of mid-sized and small cities that were part of a structured regional economy, such as in the Ghanaian backcountry in the seventeenth century. Guy Bois always makes the distinction between cities that were "parasites" and those that were "economic leaders," but he considers the West to have crossed the threshold much later than usually thought, around 1000 CE. Prior to that, there was the end of the ancient city, then the genesis of the city as the center of the market economy. Of course, here we are concerned less with the date, established on the basis of European history, than with the criterion.

G. Sjoberg took a different approach and proposed to distinguish the "preindustrial" city (which he leaves debatably vague and timeless) from the "modern" economic city. The suggested threshold is later and would correspond to another "revolution": that of the technology underlying each form of city. He focused on the sources of energy used by the city, as a center of culture and civilization, to ensure that it obtains the surpluses needed for growth. A major difference between preindustrial and industrial societies is indeed that for the former the main form of production involves human and animal power (portage, draught, pack) instead of the inert sources of energy used by technologically advanced societies (steam, electricity, nuclear energy).[18] Even though it reduces preindustrial variations to a single category of at least two thousand years of urban history, this opposition has its consistency. It has the advantage of taking the emphasis off the artificial dichotomy of political versus economic, since the emphasis on technology no longer excludes economics from the ancient city.

## Different Types of Cities

During the early Middle Ages in Europe and in precolonial non-Islamized Africa, cities were rare. This was because a city and its related activity depend on the socioeconomic level of the surrounding area. A predominantly subsistence economy has little or (if the agrarian model stagnates or regresses) no need for cities. On the contrary, Henri Pirenne has demonstrated the degree to which the resurgence of medieval cities in the West in the tenth and eleventh centuries went hand in hand with the resurgence of European trade.[19] Leaving aside the controversial problem of cause and effect, let us simply note that the renewal of trade at the time corresponded to an urban revolution that was, in a way, analogous to the much later synchronicity between industrial progress and changes in nineteenth-century cities. The reason for this is that the role of cities was analogous: they were the centers of accumulation of capital, first through trade and later through industry.

Similar reasoning can be applied to the first generations of African cities. It is possible that merchants and peasants looked to the city for the military, and therefore political, safety needed to ply their trades. Permanent quarters of merchants and guilds of artisans were established, as in medieval Sahel. They attracted more and more products from nearby, from the region, and from afar, as well as ideas and people, whose deeds were officially protected or even confiscated by the "prince."[20] Sometimes things remained virtually unchanged for a long time. Urban development was slow enough for previously rural inhabitants to get used to it without any major shock, and thus not rebel or feel threatened by exceptional requirements or creative initiatives. The cities were tailored to the needs and scale of the region and its population. They were, as Western urbanists tend to say today, "not very urban," in other, plainer words, not comparable with what they too often call "true cities" (read: western industrial city).

Thus, there are forms of urbanization adapted to each era and every set of socioeconomic features. This is why, despite a general definition with universal scope, there are as many types of cities and nuances and transitions between these types as there are geocultural areas in Africa and elsewhere. Throughout time and across space, we can systematically identify the following: (1) dominant forms of production and exchange (known as "modes of production" as late as the 1970s), which include either a *domestic* lineage system based on subsistence or a slave-based system of production, combined with an elitist society that consumes or exports (or more often both); a mercantile economy based on commercial capitalism; a proto-industrial society in transition from the preceding; and an industrial capitalist society; (2) to each of these correspond sets of social structures and institutions, and ways of life and thought linked to models of power, all of which are part and parcel of an ideology (with religious roots in a prescientific context and with philosophical-technological roots otherwise) that underlies and supports the whole; (3) to each of these societies, that is, these structures made up of interlocking economic data, power, and thought (that Guy Bois suggests we call "social systems"), correspond specific forms of cities, which thus seem to reveal the organization of the society as a whole; (4) the urban planning that emerges is therefore the *reflection in space of the social process of urbanization*.

For it is first a process. Of course, all these elements occur over time. Even in the case of a brutal, rapid upheaval such as the shock of colonial conquest, the interaction between the old and the new is a constant, and constantly dynamic. In history there is never a complete jump from one set of social structures to another, no matter what the area (institutional, economic, let alone ideological and mental).[21]

Like other processes, urbanization should not always be seen as a process of adaptation to the city. Africans have not had to adapt to cities because it is they who made the cities what they have become over the centuries, including the most recent ones. The cities did not make those who live there. This clarifies the meaning and limitations of the concept of Africans who are "strangers to the city."[22] Africans have felt themselves to be strangers to the city only when it was modeled on politics, economics, and culture (for example, the colonial model or the Western model) that were not their own, or rather not what used to be theirs. In the relatively brief phase in which the colonial urban model was imposed in an authoritarian manner, Africans found themselves dispossessed of part of their universe and required, truly, to adapt, in other words to both cope with the imposed paradigm and create and invent novel strategies for survival in the city by combining old and new. Thus, before the end of the colonial era, Africans, who accounted for the vast majority of the urban population, largely reinvented their cities. Today, cities have become again, in whole or in part, what Africans have made them and what they will make of them in the future. Once again, it is not the city that makes the African but the African who makes the city. Keeping this simple observation in mind could be useful to many international experts.

## Urbanization and Colonization

As special as it might be, the colonial city should not be considered a historical exception. On the contrary, it could be argued that all cities, no matter what the society, location, or point in history, have always been tools for colonization. Since they are places where contact is unavoidable between many different cultures and constantly changing living beings, cities have played a major role as social mixing pots and cultural disseminators by influencing the entire area under their control. A city's power could go from one extreme to another: coercive and brutal in conquering military cities or colonial cities, or progressive and attractive where the cultural (for example, religious, artistic, and technological) influence of the city was its primary strength. The result is clearly the same. Through its growth, the dominant city upsets and reorganizes the entire region to its advantage. The countryside is soon crisscrossed by a structured urban network, of which the city is the focus.

Why speak of colonization? Because the city dwellers who control the surroundings are, by definition, new inhabitants from elsewhere, such as the countryside, another village, or abroad. The city therefore brings a number of civilizations into symbiosis, especially that of the people who initially lived there and that of the conquerors. This was the case, for example, in Roman cities in North Africa, and in Gallo-Roman cities also.[23] However, it was also most probably the case with Yoruba cities, which is why it is useful to investigate analogies and differences between Yoruba colonization and colonization in general.

The Yoruba seem to be the product of a series of population movements toward the south between the seventh and tenth centuries. The people in question began by founding the mother city of Ile-Ife. The dynamism that led to their domination and even exploitation of local populations that were not yet very structured seems have been partially due to their mastery of iron metallurgy (which was already known locally) and their vocation as traders and intermediaries between the Chad region (Kanem, Bornu) and the area around their southern settlement. We have seen that there is little evidence of a structured urban network before the nineteenth century, but it must have been in operation for a long time. The Sahelian links go back to the Hausa and Nupe caravans, and the Atlantic link clearly existed in the sixteenth century. Living in a city guaranteed safety and made it possible to concentrate government and trade. Oral traditions report many cases of hamlets required to merge with the city, a trend that was accentuated in the nineteenth century under the pressure of the "Yoruba wars" among neighboring cities and against Fulbe invaders. From then on, cities were considered strongholds that brought together rural populations from up to 20 miles away.[24] Ife, Oyo, and many other lesser centers tended to creep southward over the centuries, and the apparent ease with which the Yoruba, aided by the temporary nature of their construction materials, moved their cities as needed, most often because of a military threat, has reinforced the tendency of some authors to mistakenly cast doubt on the eminently urban nature of Yoruba culture.[25] As we saw in chapters 1 and 5 from the vocabulary used, the city was considered more as a living community than a given physical location. As far back as we can see, the raison d'être of this urban civilization was to dominate the region politically and organize it economically. This was legitimized and exalted by subsuming a religious tradition about the foundation.

The Asante example could be analyzed in a similar manner. The expansion of urban centers of power and trade such as Kumasi, Salaga, and Bonduku seems to have happened in response to the same process of colonization—in other words, the imposition and spread of a new system of economic and political values over a subjected and dependent preexisting environment. First, Begho, north of the future Asante, seems to have been an outpost of the central Niger civilization, a Manding colony located near the forested areas that produced gold and kola nuts.[26] Of course, as in Yoruba country, the northern influences were combined with input from the Atlantic coast. Ray A. Kea has provided an admirable exposition of how an urban trading culture spread inland as early as the Portuguese arrival in Elmina in 1471.[27] When it was founded at the crossroads of the main trade routes a few centuries later, Kumasi in turn became the dominant cultural focus of a conquering civilization.

Let us end the revisionist parallel here. Of course, our goal is not to minimize the importance of the colonial episode but to point out that we should also avoid exaggerating the differences in nature with another period of history. The colonial cities of the nineteenth and twentieth centuries were extreme cases of overwhelming and especially anomalous coercive power, since the real power was located in the metropolis. Power (administrative, economic, and even to a certain extent religious) was exaggerated to an extreme. It was both foreign and had stronger institutions than the local people, and thus was able to make the culture and economy dependent because they were oriented to the outside. However, despite these excessive aspects, European culture in colonial cities was not imposed on the excluded middle except in the way described above. Relatively speaking, the original population was more numerous than ever and the urban cultural melting pot was bubbling.

Yet there is more. In the end, analysis shows that there was another point of convergence for African cities all over the continent. In the nineteenth century, well before the period of colonial imperialism, there was really a second urban revolution. Throughout this work, we have tried to identify both internal and external signs and factors in the social, political, religious, economic, and even military domains that combined and led to the turning point. The original processes were either destroyed, as in the case of the abandoned stone cities in eastern Africa, or radically transformed, in the west, east, and south. The result was a new common point of departure. For example, as different as virtually all of Cape Town's history may seem from that of Addis Ababa, Dar es Salaam, St. Louis in Senegal, and Lagos, and even more so from that of Ibadan and Abeokuta, in every case the same event clearly occurred: a city emerged that was part of the dominant process at the time, namely, the technological and socioeconomic revolution that was more or less orchestrated by the Western capitalist world.

In short, on the eve of colonial imperialism, African urbanization already had the foundations of its transformation toward the modern city. Whether they were already bases for international mining and banking interests (such as Cape Town and Johannesburg) or remained small administrative centers or modest market towns (such as Ouagadougou and Libreville), African cities became the footholds of new powers, namely the economic and political interests of the Europeans, who came to own virtually all of the continent within a few years, a process completed in 1900. As bank headquarters, business centers, and major labor markets, cities became even more effective in one of their most ancient roles: *as centers for colonization.*

Cities, but not all cities. Until now, the focus has generally been on the supposedly decisive role of the Western initiative. The colonizers are supposed to have created their cities, which were often ports, such as Dakar, Bathurst, Abidjan, Conakry, Cotonou, Port Harcourt, Port Gentil, Dar es Salaam, Beira, and Port Natal (Durban), or at strategic crossroads, out of nothing or at best from tiny villages at the heart of an area to be conquered and exploited, for example, Johannesburg, Lusaka, Nairobi, Leopoldville, Brazzaville, Fort Lamy (N'Djamena), Yaounde, and Bamako. This is partially true. But only very partially. Most of the time, the Europeans were few in number and interested in speed and efficiency, so they mainly used existing centers. What they did change, in accordance with their outward-looking interests, were the transportation and trade networks. Moreover, the African cities that they chose became their bases. Which ones were chosen? Certainly the most advantageous, in other words, those that had a good site, a dynamic and diversified urban society that was ready for use, so to speak, or leaders who controlled the region and therefore embodied and held power. Colonizers had the choice between destroying or at least abandoning ancient cities to neglect and deterioration so as to eradicate a challenge to their authority, or seizing them for their own use. The former solution was relatively unusual since it was militarily and politically costly. There are some examples of it, however, since it was sooner or later the fate of Gorée, Abomey, Kilwa, Sofala, Omdurman, Jenne, Timbuktu, Musumba, and, generally, most of the ancient Bantu capitals. The sites rarely disappeared from the map. Most often, colonizers were ready to jump at the opportunity offered by cities that were ready to change, in particular those that were already strong enough to keep or reclaim power, such as Addis Ababa, Mombasa, Khartoum, São Salvador (Mbanza-Kongo), Lagos, Ibadan, Ife, Porto Novo, Kumasi, Bobo Dioulasso, and Ouagadougou. Let us turn the dominant current on its head and ask not which cities were *created by* the colonizers, but which were *imposed on* them, if only by their open willingness to collaborate with the new order.

Whites came to depend more and more completely on cities, where most of them lived.[28] Colonial capitals, like the capitals that preceded them, remained the strategic centers of military, political, and economic decisions. Initially garrison headquarters, but soon the seats of government, cities were naturally chosen by Western companies for their main offices. Increasingly, they provided the greatest labor markets, not because they became production centers (though there was always job growth in the service industries, in which interpreters, administrative clerks, postal workers, small merchants, and unskilled laborers were employed),[29] but because they controlled supply and demand. Nevertheless, they did nothing to ensure maintenance of production, which always remained in the countryside. This is why the cities attracted not only products but also people and labor.[30] They received more and more migrants, who were always ready to bring back and disseminate in their original homes all they had learned and absorbed in the city. Thus, while they had always been vectors for modernization, cities became synonymous with openness to colonization, in other words, dependency on the West.

In Africa, this was conducive to the premature (given the level of development at the time) emergence of precursor signs of major third-world cities today. Such precursors include temporary shelter (incorrectly labeled "spontaneous") and "informal" social structures and work, which are phenomena much older than their recent "discovery" by experts; they could already be seen at least in the precolonial cities of the nineteenth century.[31]

## Culture and Cities

My last general observation is that the cities were extraordinary cultural mediators. They have always been rich centers for the encounter and combination, if not synthesis, of values considered traditional (in other words, previously belonging to the local people) and the dominant imported values of the time. This is why the standard dichotomy between "traditional" and "modern" is mistaken. This book provides many examples showing that the process has instead always consisted of combining old and new, more or less successfully, by adapting established heritages to the need for change.

Throughout it all, city dwellers, integral parts of the new society, navigated by feel among the cultures, routinely inventing ways of adapting that implicitly favored the powers that were the most aggressive, politically effective, ideologically convincing, technologically developed, and socially promising. Western culture quickly dominated. Social practices, technology, lifestyles, and ways of thinking changed, and urbanites helped to spread the changes around them, including in the surrounding countryside. In one way or another, they acted as mediators and brokers. When city dwellers returned to their villages in the farthest reaches of the bush, they brought new knowledge and new technology and know-how—in short, a new way of seeing the world. They became innovators. The spread of new ideas, religions, and technology had no other cause. This process of popular mediation had not been studied until the past twenty years at most, perhaps because the methodology required for such research is far from obvious.[32]

The major difference between the precolonial and colonial periods was one of degree: colonial hegemony accelerated the process by imposing a direct, brutal confrontation between those who were dominant and those who were dependent. However, the process had begun long before in an apparently more neutral way, in a more insidious and casual manner that was less likely to give rise to resistance. It occurred on the coasts at the beginning of Portuguese, Dutch, Danish, British, and French sea exploration. Earlier, it operated in the same way when Africans first came into contact with Arabs and Islam: new skills, concepts, and technologies spread quickly. Ports and mercantile cities soon became extraordinary tools of mediation. Urban life acquired specific features and a culture that distinguished it from rural life. Urban culture was characterized by different social classes and specific lifestyles, of which the political and recreational social interactions (military parades, processions, celebrations, art) should be studied in greater depth, for, as a major source of mediation, the city was therefore probably also a wellspring of African creativity. Unfortunately, we do not know much about ancient times, aside from what was preserved thanks to the princes' classical roles as benefactors and entrepreneurs, for example, Ife and Benin bronzes, Bakuba masks, Friday mosques, and the façades of houses in Kumasi or elsewhere. A later sign, which does not mean that nothing existed before, was the emergence of popular arts, including painting that shows the genesis of a veritable cultural symbiosis: it is a borrowed technique that was virtually unknown in ancient African societies except for Christian art in Ethiopia but has recently undergone a remarkable development in cities. Since the end of the nineteenth century, Addis Ababa has been famous for paintings that celebrate the high point of the battle of Adowa (1896), which spared the country from colonial humiliation. The city thus seems to be particularly conducive to popular memory and art, in contrast with the countryside, which is the location par excellence of "traditional" art and folklore.[33] We have also tried to restore this social and cultural aspect of the city to the history of Africa.

# Notes

## Preface, Introduction, and Note on Transcription

1. Cambridge University Press, forthcoming.
2. Davidson, *Lost Cities of Africa;* R. W. Hull, *African Cities and Towns before the European Conquest.*
3. D. M. Anderson and R. Rathbone, eds., *Africa's Urban Past* (Portsmouth, N.H.: Heinemann, 2000). A similar publication is forthcoming: Toyin Falola and Steven J. Salm, eds., *African Cities: History and Culture* (Rochester, N.Y.: University of Rochester Press). It contains 16 articles out of 140 papers, most of the others to be published under the title *African Urban Culture. A History* (Durham, N.C.: Carolina Academic Press). Both introductions are written by Coquery-Vidrovitch.
4. V. Luling, *A Somali Sultanate. The Geledi City-State over 150 Years* (London: Haan, 2001). Geledi was a Somali sultanate located around Afgooye, inland from Mogadishu, that flourished from the mid-nineteenth century through the twentieth century.
5. The title of L. Plotnicov's 1967 book on the city of Jos, Nigeria.
6. I assume that the reader is generally familiar with these aspects. See any of many overviews of African history and culture, such as P. Curtin et al., *African History: From Earliest Times to Independence,* 2nd ed. rev. (London and New York: Longman, 1995).
7. In 1990, the average urbanization rate in Africa was probably 39 percent.
8. I began collecting these references in 1987 thanks to a six-month fellowship at the Woodrow Wilson Center for International Scholars, Washington, D.C. See C. Coquery-Vidrovitch, "Process of urbanization."
9. Centre national de la Recherche scientifique, the general funding and evaluating organization in France for research, all disciplines concerned.
10. The former name of this institute, co-tutored by CNRS and Université Paris-7-Denis Diderot, was Tiers Mondes, Afrique. Les sociétés dans leur histoire et leur environnement, now SEDET, Sociétés en Dévelop-

pement dans l'Espace et le Temps.

11. See several of these papers published in Coquery-Vidrovitch, ed., *Processus d'urbanisation*; Cahen, ed., *Bourgs et villes en Afrique lusophone*; S. Dulucq et O. Goerg, eds, *Les investissements français en Afrique de l'Ouest* (Paris: L'Harmattan, 1990); Coquery-Vidrovitch et al., eds, *Les échanges ville-campagne en Afrique francophone: mobilité des hommes, circulation des biens, diffusion des modèles* (Paris, L'Harmattan, 1996); Coquery-Vidrovitch and O. Goerg, eds., *La ville européenne outre mers: un modèle conquérant?* (Paris: L'Harmattan, 1996). See also Coquery-Vidrovitch, *Villes coloniales*, 47–68, and Coquery-Vidrovitch, "Villes africaines anciennes," 62–77.

12. Cf., among others who criticized old views on African tradition, authenticity, etc., T. O. Ranger and E. Hobsbawm, *The Invention of Tradition* (Cambridge: Cambridge University Press, 1983); V. Mudimbe, *The Invention of Africa* (Bloomington: Indiana University Press, 1988); J. L. Amselle, *Logiques métisses* (Paris: Payot, 1989), English translation, *Mestizo Logics: Anthropology of Identity in Africa and Elsewhere* (Stanford, Calif.: Stanford University Press, 1998); Leroy Vail, ed., *The Creation of Tribalism in Southern Africa* (London: James Currey, 1989).

13. On the difficulties involved in translating an African toponym into French or English, see a provocative short article by Michel Cahen: "Vive le Zimbaboué! Histoire de mots et européocentrisme classificatoire," *Politique africaine* 46 (1992): 117–19.

## Chapter One

1. F. Braudel, *Grammaire des civilisations* (Paris: Flammarion, 1963), 40–68.

2. *Blue Book* 193 (Wakefield, U.K.: Microform Academic Publishers, Microfilm 96 995/40).

3. R. de Maximy, "Tous les chemins ne mènent pas à Tombouctou . . .," in *Processus d'urbanisation*," edited by C. Coquery-Vidrovitch, 1:11–25.

4. E. Lampard, "The Nature of Urbanization," in *The Nature of Urbanization*, edited by E. Lampard, 3–53.

5. Davis, "The Urbanization of the Human Population," 43.

6. E. Skinner, *African Urban Life. The Transformation of Ouagadougou* (Princeton, N.J.: Princeton University Press, 1974), 5.

7. Childe, "The Urban Revolution."

8. Wirth, "Urbanism as a Way of Life."

9. For a dense and concise summary of knowledge in the field at the beginning of the 1960s, see "Histoire et urbanisation," *Annales* 4 (1970, special issue): 829–1208.

10. Davidson, *The Lost Cities of Africa*.

11. Hull, *African Cities and Towns.*

12. Sjoberg, *Preindustrial City.*

13. Bairoch, *De Jericho*; Rossi, *Modelli di Città.*

14. Winters, "Traditional Urbanism," 518n 83.

15. Tardits, *Le Royaume Bamoum*, 287–88.

16. Bakari, "L'Afrique Occidentale," 76.

17. A. Dillman, *Lexicon Linguæ Aethiopicæ* (Lipsiae, O. Wiegel, 1865; Osnabrück, 1970), 851–52 and 1007; C.W. Isenberg, *Dictionary of the Amharic Language* (London, 1941), 142; A. d'Abbadie, *Dictionnaire de la langue Amarenne* (Paris, 1881), 622–23; comment in D. Crummey, "Towns: A Review of the Evidence" (1987 revision of paper presented to the International Symposium on the African Horn of Africa, Cairo, January 1985).

18. P. S. Garlake, *Great Zimbabwe*, 11, quoting, among others, João de Barros (1552). This etymology was discussed more recently (see chapter 3 of this book).

19. P. Gutkind, "Notes on the Kibuga," 30–31.

20. W. E. Cousins, "The Great Hova City," 369.

21. R.S. Rattray, *Religion and Art in Ashanti* (London: Oxford University Press, 1987); K. Arhin, "West African Trading Settlements in the Asante Hinterland in the Nineteenth Century" (paper presented at Symposium on Indigenous African Towns, University of California at Los Angeles, 1980), 27–28.

22. Rattray, *Ashanti proverbs (the primitive ethics of a savage people)* (Oxford: Clarendon Pres, 1916), 25.

23. Kea, *Settlements*:28–34.

24. E. Krapf-Aspari, *Yoruba Towns and Cities*, 25

25. Mabogunje, *Urbanization in Nigeria*, 33.

26. Wirth, "Urbanism," 8.

27. Hull, "Urban Design and Architecture," 388.

28. Berry, *Urbanization*; Salau, "Urban Process," 27.

29. See Mumford, *City in History*, 93.

30. G. Sautter, *Une géographie du sous-peuplement. République du Congo, République Gabonaise* (Paris/The Hague: Mouton, 1966), 209–78; Coquery-Vidrovitch, *Brazza et la prise de possession du Congo* (Paris/The Hague: Mouton, 1966), 93–112.

31. C. D. Forde, *Yakö Studies* (London: Oxford University Press and I.A.I, 1964).

32. Balandier, *Daily Life in the Kingdom of the Kongo*, 132, quoting a missionary report of the eighteenth century.

33. J. Leclerc, *Aux sources du Nil par le chemin de fer de l'Ouganda* (Paris: Plon-Nourrit, 1913), 156.

34. Connah, *Archeology of Benin*, 105.
35. Randles, "Precolonial Urbanization in Africa South of the Equator," 891–97.
36. (1) A more extensive and denser population. (2) Full time specialist craftsmen, transport workers, merchants, officials and priests who do not themselves procure their own food by agriculture, stock-breeding, fishing or collecting. (3) The tiny surplus being used as tithe or tax concentrated in the capital. (4) Truly monumental public buildings. (5) A ruling class of priests, civil and military leaders and officials not engaged in food production. (6) Therefore compelled to invent systems of recording and exact, but practically useful, sciences (writing and numeral notation). (7) And to elaborate arithmetic, geometry, and astronomy. (8) Full-time sculptors, painters or seal-engravers generated conceptualized and sophisticated styles of artistic expressions. (9) Regular foreign trade over long distances was financed by the concentrated social surplus. (10) Craftsmen were both provided with raw materials and guaranteed security by the State, the city being a community to which one could belong politically as well as economically. Childe, *Social Evolution*, 36–38.
37. Braudel, *Les structures du quotidien* (Paris: Seuil, 1979), 423. In English, *Civilization and Capitalism, 15th–18th century*, vol. 1, *The Structures of Everyday Life: The Limits of the Possible* (New York: Harper and Row, 1982).
38. Ibid., 450.
39. Gideon Sjoberg, an American sociologist, took this thesis to the absurd. His mechanical mode of reasoning equaled his ignorance of the realities of African history: by asserting that writing was required for a city to emerge, he excluded the possibility that ancient African societies included any form of urbanization. The same applied to American Indian communities, except the Mayas, because "our definition relegates to a marginal or transitional status the Inca communities that most anthropologists stubbornly insist were urban centers, foci of civilization." Sjoberg, *Preindustrial City*, 33.
40. Max Weber suggested that a city be defined as a settlement where the inhabitants are mainly involved in non-productive activities. Historically, this "majority" was often actually a minority, including in medieval Europe. Weber, *The City*, 18.
41. According to Toynbee, *Cities on the Move*, the criterion of a city as not being self-sufficient was common to all cities from Jericho to Megalopolis. On urban accessibility, see Morton-Williams, "Some Factors in the Location, Growth and Survival of Towns in West Africa," in *Man, Settlement and Urbanism*, edited by Ucko et al., 284.
42. Mabogunje develops these points in *Urbanization in Nigeria*, ch. 2.
43. C. S. Coon, *Caravan: The Story of the Middle East* (New York: Holt, 1958),

231. See also, on Africa South of the Sahara, Coquery-Vidrovitch and Lovejoy, *The Workers of African Trade* (London: Sage, 1985), 304.

44. Griffeth, "The Hausa City-States."

45. Hugh Clapperton, *Journal of a second expedition into the interior of Africa, from the Bight of Benin to Soccatoo; to which is added the Journal of Richard Lander from Kano to the sea-coast, partly by a more eastern route* (London: F. Cass, 1829); Heinrich Barth, *Travels and discoveries in North and Central Africa: being a journal of an exhibition undertaken under the auspices of H. B. M.'s Government in the years 1849–1855*, 3 vols. (1857; London: F. Cass, 1965).

46. Mabogunje, *Urbanization in Nigeria*, 69–71.

47. Ibid., 78.

48. Akorede, "The Impact of Socio-cultural Changes," 71.

49. Kea, *Settlements, Trade and Polities*, 32–94.

50. A. M. O'Connor, *The African City*.

## Chapter Two

1. N. Lambert, "Les industries du cuivre dans l'Ouest saharien," *West African Journal of Archaeology* 1 (1971): 9–21 (Mauretania); D. S. Calvocoressi and N. David, "A New Survey of Radiocarbon and Thermoluminescence Dates for West Africa," *Journal of African History* 20, no. 1 (1979): 1–20 (Azelik, Aïr); N. Echard, ed., "Métallurgies africaines, nouvelles contributions," in *Mémoire de la Société des Africanistes* (Paris, 1983), vol. 9. For later archaeological updatings, see *The African Archeologist Review*, published by Cambridge University Press from 1983 to 1994 and by Plenum Press since 1996. Recent archaeological studies try to connect censuses and results of excavations to theoretical and cultural issues so as to explore the social background of historical societies.

2. P. J. Munso, "Archaeological Data on the Origin of Cultivation in the Southwestern Sahara and their Implication for West Africa," in *Origins of African Plant Domestication*, edited by J. R. Harlan, J. M. J. de Wet, and A. Stealer (The Hague: Mouton, 1976), 187–209.

3. J. Atherton, "Excavations at Kamabal and Yagala Rock Shelter," *West African Journal of Archaeology* 2 (1972): 39–74; C. Gabel, "Microlith Occurrences in the Republic of Liberia," *West African Journal of Archaeology* 6 (1976): 21–37.

4. J. Atherton, "A Hypothesis on Sierra-Leone by Atherton 1972. Protohistoric Habitations Sites in North East Sierra Leone," *Bulletin de la Société Royale Belge d'Anthropologie et de Préhistoire* 83 (1972): 5–17. A similar hypothesis may be valuable in Central Africa.

5. J. Yoyotte, "Pharaonic Egypt: Society, Economy and Culture," in *General History of Africa*, vol. 2, *Ancient Civilizations of Africa*, edited by G. Mokhtar (Berkeley: University of California Press, 1981), 112.

6. F. Geus, "La section française de la Direction des Antiquités du Soudan. Travaux de terrain et de laboratoire en 1982–1983," *Archéologie du Nil moyen* 1 (1986): 13–58; also Geus, "Franco-Sudanese Excavations in the Sudan (1982–83)," *Nyame Akuma* 23 (1983): 23–25.

7. J. Leclant, "The Empire of Kush: Napata and Meroe," in *General History of Africa*, vol. 2, *Ancient Civilizations of Africa*, chapter 10, pp. 278–97.

8. Cf. Shinnie, *Meroe*, chapter 3, "Towns, Temples and Cemeteries."

9. V. M. Fernandez, "Spanish Excavations in the Sudan: 1978–1981," *Nyame Akuma* 23 (1983): 20–22. Cf. A. E. Close, "Current Research and Recent Radiocarbon Dates from Northern Africa, III," *Journal of African History* 29, no. 2 (1988): 158.

10. H. Amborn, "Die Problematik der Eisenverhüttung im Reiche Meroe." Quoted by Leclant, "The Empire of Kush," 332–333.

11. P. L. Shinnie and F. Y. Kense, paper presented at Third International Meroïtic Conference, Toronto.

12. See also, on Meroë: S. Danadeni and S. Wenig, *Studia Meroitica 1984* (Meroitica 10) (Berlin: Akademie Verlag, 1989); and most of the papers given at the Sixth International Meroitic Conference, Khartoum.

13. Mathew, "The Dating and the Significance of the Periplus of the Erythrean Sea."

14. Y. M. Kobishanov, "Aksum: Political System, Economics and Culture, First to Fourth Century," in *General History of Africa*, vol. 2, chapter 15, 381–400. See also E. Phillips and D. Phillipson.

15. S. C. Munro-Hay, "Excavations at Aksum." See also: Y. M. Kobishanov and J. W. Michels, eds., *Axum* (University Park: Pennsylvania State University Press, 1979); S. A. Sellassie, *Ancient and Medieval Ethiopian History to 1270* (Addis Ababa: United Printers, 1972); Y.M. Kobishanov, "Aksum: Political System, Economics and Culture, First to Fourth Century," in *General History of Africa*, vol. 2, *Ancient Civilizations of Africa*, edited by G. Mokhtar (Berkeley: University of California Press, 1981), chapter 15, 381–400; and D.W. Phillipson, *Archaeology at Aksum, Ethiopia, 1993–7.*

16. Cf. A. M. H. Sheriff, "The East African Coast and Its Role in Maritime Trade," in *General History of Africa*, vol. 2, chapter 22, 551–67.

17. M. C. Smith and H. T. Wright, "Notes on a Classical Maritime Site: The Ceramics from Ras Hafun, Somalia," *Azania* 13 (1988): 115–42. For further details, see: J. J. Sinclair, "Archaeology in Eastern Africa: an Overview of Current Chronological Issues," *Journal of African History* 32, no. 2 (1991): 179–220.

18. H. N. Chittick, "The Shirazi Colonization of East Africa," *Journal of Afri-*

*can History* 6, no. 3 (1965): 275–97; and J. Fage and R. Oliver, eds., *Papers in African Prehistory* (Cambridge: Cambridge University Press, 1970), 257–76.

19. Horton, "The Swahili Corridor," 86.

20. V. Grotannelli, "A Lost African Metropolis (Shungwaya)," in *Afrikanistische Studien*, edited by J. Lukas (Berlin: Akademie-Verlag, 1955); see R. A. Obudho and Johnson and Johnson, "Urbanization and Development Planning in Kenya. An Historical Appreciation," *African Urban Notes*, ser. B, 1, no. 5 (1975).

21. *The Periplus Maris Erythraei.*

22. B. A. Datoo, "Rhapta. The Location and Importance of East Africa's First Port," *Azania* 5 (1970): 65–75; G. Mathew, "The East Africa Coast until the Coming of the Portuguese," in *History of East Africa*, edited by R. Oliver and G. Mathew (Oxford: Clarendon Press, 1963), 1:94–128.

23. R. C. Soper, "Iron Age Sites in North Eastern Tanzania," *Azania* 2 (1967): 19–36; and Soper, "A General Review of the Early Iron Age in the Southern Half of Africa," *Azania* 6 (1971): 5–37.

24. T. M. Ricks, "Persian Gulf Seafaring and East Africa. 9th–12th centuries," *African Historical Studies* 3 (1970): 339–58; S. A. Rizvi, "Zanj. Its First Known Use in Arabic Literature," *Azania* 2 (1967): 200-201; A. Popovic, *La révolte des esclaves en Iraq au IIIe/IXe siècle* (Paris, 1976), translated by Léon King under the title *The Revolt of African Slaves in Iraq in the 3rd/9th Century* (Princeton: Markus Wiener, 1999); O. Lara, "Esclavage et révoltes négro-africaines dans l'Empire musulman du haut Moyen Âge," *Présence Africaine* 98 (1976): 50-103.

25. P. J. Munson, "Recent Archaelogical Research in the Dhar Tichitt Region of South Central Mauretania," *West African Archaelogical Newsletter* (Ibadan) 10 (1968): 6–13; and Munson, "Connections and Additional Comments concerning the Tichitt Tradition," *West African Archaelogical Newsletter* (Ibadan) 12 (1970): 47–48; J. D. Fage, *History in Africa* (1978), 67–68; A. E. Close, "Current Research III," 145-76; Holl, "Economie et société."

26. Prehistorical data are expressed as "BP" (Before Present), which conventionally means "before 1950 CE." In other words, the most remote data here is from 1880 BCE.

27. A. Holl, "Subsistence Patterns of the Dhar Tichitt Neolithic, Mauretania," *African Archaeology Review* 3 (1985): 151–62.

28. This hypothesis was proposed by Devisse, "Histoire et tradition," 9.

29. D. Grébénart, "Characteristics of the Final Neolithic and Metal Ages in the Region of Agadez (Niger)," in Close, *Prehistory of Arid North Africa. Essays in Honor of Fred Wendorf* (Dallas: Southern Methodist University Press, 1987), 287-316.

30. T. Shaw, "Nok Statuettes of Nigeria," *Scientific American*, April 1981.

31. Shaw, *Igbo Ukwu*.

32. McIntosh and McIntosh, *Prehistoric Investigations*.

33. J. Devisse, "Routes de commerce et échanges en Afrique occidentale en relation avec la Méditerranée," *Revue d'Histoire économique et sociale* 50 (1972): 42-73, 51 (1972): 357-97. On pre-Islamic copper in Niger, see Posnansky and McIntosh, "New Radio-Carbon Dates"; McIntosh and McIntosh, *Prehistoric Investigations*, 413-42; and A. E. Close, "Current Research and Recent Radiocarbon Dates from Northern Africa," *Journal of African History* 21, no. 2 (1980): 145-67, and Close, "Current Research and Recent Radiocarbon Dates from Northern Africa, *Journal of African History* 25, no. 1 (1984): 1-24.

34. Posnansky, "Aspects of Early West African Trade"; B. Chavanne, *Villages anciens du Tekrour* (Paris: Karthala-CRA, 1985).

35. Unfortunately, they are often the result of worse than amateur methods in surrounding areas by local people, who excavate without control to sell their findings to foreign visitors, and see a means of survival in the site's success as a tourist attraction, to the great dismay of archaeologists in Mali. Fortunately, the site of Jenne Jeno is now protected: you need an authorization to visit it.

36. Devisse, "L'apport de l'archéologie."

37. On Tegdaust excavations, five volumes were published by a team directed by J. Devisse (D. Robert and S. Robert, C. Vanacker, J. Polet, D. Robert-Chaleix, and B. Saison, *Tegdaoust*, vols. 1–5 (Paris: Éditions Recherches sur les civilisations, 1970, 1979, 1983, 1985, 1989); see especially vol. 3, *Enquêtes générales*.

38. J. O. Hunwick. "The Mid-14th Century Capital of Mali," *Journal of African History* 14, no. 2 (1973): 195-208.

39. Filipowiak, "Expédition archéologique."

40. McIntosh and McIntosh, *Prehistoric Investigations*, 1:20; Close, "Current Research" 166-67; J. M. Abun-Nasr, *A History of the Maghrib in the Islamic Period* (Cambridge: Cambridge University Press, 1987), 29.

41. Devisse, *Recherches sur Aoudaghost*, 3:7.

42. Ibid.

## Chapter Three

1. Davidson, *Lost Cities of Africa.*

2. Ibid., 233.

3. Sassoon, "New Views," 201-18.

4. Sutton, "Ancient Civilizations."

5. Whitty, "Classification of Prehistoric Stone Buildings," 959.

6. R. Summers, "The Rhodesian Iron Age," in Fage and Oliver, *Papers in African Prehistory*, 169.

7. Whitty, "Zimbabwe and Inyanga," in *Man, Settlement and Urbanism*, edited by Ucko et al. (London: Duckworth, 1972), 901.

8. P. Sinclair, "Some Aspects of the Economic Level of the Zimbabwe State," in *Papers Presented in Honour of Miss G. Caton-Thompson, Zimbabwea 1* (National Museums and Monuments of Zimbabwe, 1984), 48–53. Quoted by Connah, *African Civilizations*, 197, with a useful summary of recent archaeological conclusions on Zimbabwe.

9. Cf. Garlake, *Great Zimbabwe*.

10. See Randles, *L'Empire du Monomotapa*, 19–22. He refers to João de Barros's description of the hinterland.

11. Sinclair, "Some Aspects," 210.

12. Dhlo-Dhlo probably was first settled at the end of the sixteenth century (date based on the discovery of Chinese pottery and a bottle of Dutch gin). Khami probably was older. Perhaps the first inhabitants settled there as early as the eleventh century. A culture would have developed there more or less at the same time as in Zimbabwe. Summers, *Ancient Ruins and Vanished Civilizations*.

13. Ibid.

14. T. N. Huffman, "Archaeology and Ethnohistory of the African Iron Age," *Annual Review of Anthropology* 11 (1982): 146.

15. On the *Mfecane* and *Difaqane* (a Nguni word meaning "forced migrations"), and related discussion, see, among others, L. Thompson and M Wilson, eds., *The Oxford History of South Africa* (New York: Oxford University Press, 1970), vol. 1, chapter 8, and C. Hamilton, ed., *The Mfecane Aftermath. Reconstructive Debates in Southern African History* (Johannesburg: Witwatersrand University Press, 1995).

16. Whitty "Classification of Prehistoric Stone Buildings."

17. Summers, *Ancient Ruins and Vanished Civilizations*.

18. J. Campbell, *Travels in South Africa (Second Journey)* (London: Missionary Society, 1822), 1:220–227. See also chapters 19 to 23.

19. "The ruins of innumerable towns, some of amazing extent …"J. P. R. Wallis, ed., *The Matabele Mission, a Selection from the Correspondence of John and Emily Moffat, David Livingstone and Others, 1858–1878* (Cape Town: C. Struik, 1974), 1:8.

20. "They [the towns] are shrouded in mystery." A. A. Anderson, *Twenty-five Years in a Waggon; Sport and Travel in South Africa*, 2nd ed. (London: Chapman and Hall, 1988), 29.

21. Mworoha, *Peuples et rois d'Afrique*, chapter 1.

22. This enigma was willingly, but perhaps unconsciously, transmitted by

the Tutsi tradition. This does not guarantee its value, as J. Vansina notes: "Burundi oral traditions were completely distorted by a cyclical conception, the negation of a linear succession of events all over time, the denial of a causal chain, in short the absence of an historical understanding." J. Vansina, *La légende du passé; traditions orales du Burundi* (Tervuren: Musée royal de l'Afrique centrale, 1972). On our current knowledge, see, among others, J.-P. Chrétien, *The Great Lakes of Africa*. And, above all, Vansina, *L'évolution du royaume Rwanda des origines à 1900* (Brussels: Académie royale des Sciences d'outre-mer, 2000), and Vansina, *Le Rwanda ancien: Le Royaume Nyiginya* (Paris: Karthala, 2001).

23. Denyer, *African Traditional Architecture*, 37–38. R. Shaw quoted in Sinclair, "Some Aspects," 201–202.

24. Hull, "Urban Design," 390.

25. J. P. Chrétien, "Le passage de l'expédition d'Oscar Baumann au Burundi (Sept.–Oct. 1892)," *Cahiers d'Études africaines* 8, no. 29 (1968): 48–95.

26. Mworoha, *Peuples et rois d'Afrique*, 116–26.

27. Cf. Reyher, *Zulu Woman*.

28. Lugan, *Nyanza*, 2–3.

29. R. Kandt, *Caput Nili* (Berlin: D. Reimer (E. Vohsen), 1904), letter 18. Quoted in Lugan, *Nyanza*.

30. Chalux, *Un an au Congo belge* (Brussels: A. Dewit, 1925), 490–91.

31. From royal genealogies, Ntare the First's reign has been dated 1555–1588, plus or minus 52, which means circa between 1476 and 1607.

32. R. Oliver, "Ancient Capital Sites," 51–54. R. Oliver's excavation locations were inspired by oral Ankole traditions, transcribed in 1955 from the late Nuwa Mbaguta's papers. Nuwa Mbaguta was a royal officer, or *Nganzi*, in Ankole from 1895 to 1937. He died in 1944. Oliver's proposals were revised by A. Reid and P. Robertshaw, "A New Look at Ankole Capital Sites," *Azania* 22 (1987): 83–88.

33. Gutkind, "Notes on the Kibuga," 137–38. Cf. chapter 1 of this book.

34. Another possible meaning would be: *dzimba woye* (venerable houses): Garlake, *Great Zimbabwe*, 11. Linguists are not convinced by this hypothesis for, in Shona, the meaning of *dzimbahwe* is a chief's "enclosure," "house," or "tomb": T. N. Huffman, personal information conveyed to Connah in 1985 and published in *African Civilizations*, 192.

35. Garlake, *Great Zimbabwe*, 51.

36. Pedro João Batista, "Exploraçãoes dos Portugueses no interior d'Africa meridional . . . Documentos relativos à viagem de Angola para Rios de Senna," *Annaes Maritimos e Coloniaes* 3, no. 5 (1843): 162–90; 3, no. 6 (1843): 223–40; 3, no. 7 (1843): 278–97; 3, no. 9 (1843): 423–40; 3, no. 10 (1843): 493–506; 3, no. 11 (1843): 538–52. Quoted by A. Margarido, "La capitale de l'Empire Lunda." Gaça went to Musumba in the mid-

nineteenth century (J. R. Graça, "Expedição ao Muataiânvua," *Boletim da Sociedade de Geografia de Lisboa* 9, no 1 (847): 454. P. Pogge went there only in 1880. Randle, "Pre-colonial Urbanization."

37. J. Miller, "Cokwe Trade and Conquest in the 19th century," in *Precolonial African Trade. Essays on Trade in Central and Eastern Africa before 1900*, edited by R. Gray and D. Birmingham (London: Oxford University Press, 1970), 175–201.

38. Denyer, *African Traditional Architecture*, 38.

39. John Roscoe (1861–1932) brought back a report and published his work: *The Soul of Central Africa; a general account of the Mackie Ethnological Expedition* (London and New York: Cassell and Co Ltd.); Roscoe, *The Baganda; An Account of Their Native Customs and Beliefs*, 2nd ed. (New York: Barnes and Noble, 1966). J. H. Speke, *Journal of the Discovery of the Sources of the Nile* (London: Blackwood, 1864). They are used by Gutkind, "Notes on the Kibuga." See also Gutkind, *The African Administration of the Kibuga*, and R. Reid and H. Médard, "Merchants, Missions and the Remaking of the Urban Environment in Buganda," in Anderson and Rathbone, pp. 98–108.

40. Gutkind, *The African Administration of the Kibuga*, 10–11.

41. Tardits, *Le royaume Bamoum*, chapter 13.

42. When we think that the *kibuga* still had barely 35,000 inhabitants in 1948 (but had lost, it is true, its status as capital city since the colony's capital was then at Entebbe), we cannot help but be struck by the stability of the numbers. In 1958, there were 52,673 African inhabitants settled in the kibuga, while the total population of the city of Great Kampala (including the kibuga) had over 100,000 habitants.

43. Cf. Balandier, *Daily Life in the Kingdom of the Kongo*, chapter 2.

44. Proyart, *Histoire de Loango*. See also Randles, *L'ancien royaume de Congo*, 168.

45. c. 1624. *Historia do reino do Congo*. Translated by F. Bontinck *Études d'histoire africaine*, vol. 4, *Histoire du royaume du Congo* (Leuven: Nauwelaerts, 1972), 97.

46. Ibid., 104.

47. Antonio Pigafetta, who lived between 1480/91 and 1534, wrote the story of Magellan's travels (first published in 1536): *The First voyage round the world, by Magellan, translated from the accounts of Pigafetta, and other contemporary writers; accompanied by original documents, with notes and an introduction*, by Lord Stanley of Alderley (London: Printed for the Hakluyt Society, 1874).

48. Thornton, *Kingdom of Kongo*, 79.

49. Domingos Erispinus Barreiros quoted by Thornton: 64n61.

50. Randles, *L'ancien royaume de Congo*, 170.

51. Thornton proposes the highest estimate (*Kingdom of Kongo*, 91).

52. Randles, *L'ancien royaume du Congo,* and Thornton, "Demography and History in the Kingdom of Kongo, 1550-1750," *Journal of African History* 18, no. 4 (1977): 526; Thornton, "The Kingdom of Kongo, ca. 1390-1678: The Development of an African Social Formation," *Cahiers d'Études Africaines* 22, nos. 87-88 (1982): 325-42.

53. Thornton, *The Kingdom of Kongo*, 1983.

54. Ibid., 18-19.

55. Ibid., chapter 4, 38-55.

56. "It was a true city," J. Vansina, *The Children of Woot* (Madison: University of Wisconsin Press, 1978), 137.

57. All above quotations are translated from G. Bois, *La mutation de l'an Mil. Lourmand, village mâconnais, de l'Antiquité au féodalisme* (Paris: Fayard, 1989), 130-32. They show the universality of the process of urbanization, and how varied the legal, political and social backgrounds can be. See also M. M. Dufeil, "La ville bantu dans l'histoire urbaine de l'Afrique," *Muntu* (Libreville) 2 (1985): 121-40.

## Chapter Four

1. Chirot, "Urban and Rural Economies," 547-50.

2. G. Marçais, "L'islamisme et la vie urbaine," *Comptes-rendus de l'Académie des Inscriptions et Belles-Lettres* (Paris) (January–March 1928): 86-100. A more pertinent revision of the historiography of the concept was proposed by J. Abu-Lughod, "The Islamic City. Historic Myth, Islamic Essence, and Contemporary Relevance," *International Journal of Middle East Studies* 19, no. 2 (May 1987): 155-76. Based on an impressive bibliography of theoretical studies on the Muslim city, she argues that the usual examples are Fez in Morocco, and Damas and Alep under the Mamluk empire: general laws cannot be inferred from case studies that are so specific in time and space.

3. Berque, "Medinas, villes neuves et bidonvilles," *Les Cahiers de Tunisie* (1958): 5-42; G. Marçais, "L'urbanisme musulman," 5th congress, Fédération des sociétés savantes de l'Afrique du nord, Alger, 1940.

4. Marçais, "La conception des villes dans l'Islam," *Revue d'Alger* 2 (1945): 517-33. It is repeated nearly word for word in G. von Grunebaum, "The Structure of the Muslim Town," *Islam. Essays in the Nature and Growth of a Cultural Tradition* (Ann Arbor: University of Michigan, 1955), 141-245. (Republished in 1961 by Routledge and Kegan Paul.)

5. A. Hourani Ibert and S. M. Stern, eds., *The Islamic City: A Colloquium*

[held at All Souls College, Oxford, June 28–July 2, 1965] (Philadelphia: University of Pennsylvania Press, 1970).

6. Y. Thébert and J.-L. Biget, "L'Afrique après la disparition de la cité classique: cohérence et ruptures dans l'histoire maghrébine," *L'Afrique dans l'Occident romain (Ier siècle av.J.C.–IVè siècle ap. J.C.): actes du colloque organisé par l'Ecole française de Rome sous le patronage de l'Institut national d'archéologie et d'art de Tunis (Rome, 3–5 décembre 1987)* (Rome: École Française de Rome, Palais Farnèse, 1990), 575–602.

7. I. M. Lapidus, *Muslim Cities* (on Mesopotamian cities).

8. A. Miquel, *La géographie humaine du monde musulman jusqu'au milieu du XIe siècle. IV. Les travaux et les jours* (Paris: EHESS, 1988), 201–254.

9. See chapter 3 of this book and S. Berthier, *Recherches archéologiques sur la capitale de l'empire de Ghana: étude d'un secteur d'habitat à Koumbi Saleh, Mauritanie: campagnes II–III–IV–V, (1975–1976)–(1980–1981)* (Oxford: Archaeopress, 1997).

10. M. Agier, *Commerce et sociabilité. Les négociants soudanais du quartier zongo de Lomé* (Paris: ORSTOM, 1993).

11. Cf. Callaway, "Nigeria's Indigenous Education."

12. Romero Curtin, "The Sacred Meadows," 342.

13. Prussin, *Hatumere*.

14. F .W. Schwerdtfeger, review of L. Prussin, *Hatumere* (1986), in *Africa* 60, no. 1 (1990): 150–53.

15. Devisse, "Histoire et tradition urbaine," referring to L. Prussin, "Building Technologies in the West African Savannah," in *Le sol, la parole et l'écrit* (Paris: Société française d'Histoire d'Outre-Mer, 1981): 227–45.

16. See works by Devisse, Robert, and Vanacker, *Tegdaoust* (cf. chapter 2, n. 37). As for the decline and disappearance of Awdaghust houses beginning in the mid-twelfth century due to the accumulation of sand and the caravans shifting towards the east, see Robert-Chaleix, *Tegdaoust V.*

17. Devisse, "Histoire et tradition urbaine," 5–7.

18. Shinnie and Ozanne, "Excavations at Yendi Dabari."

19. Devisse, "Histoire et tradition urbaine."

20. See Djibo M. Hamani, Boubé Gado, et al., "Le Niger," a photocopied report: "Programme c/4, Publications d'ouvrages de référence sur la culture et la civilisation islamiques dans les pays membres" (Morocco: ISSESCO, c.1987 [n.d]).

21. D. Lange and S. Berthoud, "Al-Qasaba et d'autres villes de la route centrale du Sahara," *Païdeuma* 23 (1977): 21–25.

22. N. Levtzion and J. F. P. Hopkins, *Corpus of Early Arabic Sources for West African History* (Cambridge and New York: Cambridge University Press, 1981; reprint, Princeton: Markus Wiener Publishers, 2000), 22.

23. J. M. Cuoq, *Recueil de sources arabes*, 187.

24. In 1124, Al-Idrisi described "the city of Tamalma . . . , a small town of Kawarland, which is populated, with many people coming there, but without walls." Ibid., 156–57.

25. Chronological list of the Kings of Bornu in D. Lange, *Le Diwan des Sultans du (Kanem-) Bornu. Chronologie et histoire d'un royaume africain de la fin du Xe siècle jusqu'à 1808* (Wiesbaden: F. Steiner, 1977), 67.

26. In the Kori Mammamet area, fifty miles northeast of Arlit, between 640 and 880 CE. F. Paris, J. P. Roset, and J.F. Saliège, "Une sépulture musulmane ancienne dans l'Aïr septentrional (Niger)" [Note by T. Monod], *Comptes-rendus de l'Académie des Sciences de Paris* 303, series 3, no. 12 (1983): 513–18.

27. It was already influenced by Islam when Al-Bakri (who died in 1094) went there. Cuoq, *Recueil de sources arabes*, 217.

28. T. Lewicki, "Les origines et l'islamisation de la ville de Tadmakka d'après les sources arabes," *Revue Française d'Histoire d'Outre-Mer* 66, nos. 242–43 (1979): 163–67.

29. S. Sidibé, "Es-Souk Tadmekka," *L'Universo* 64, no. 5 (1984): 103–14; and Sidibé, "Es-Souk, l'ancienne Tadmekka. Quelques réflexions sur la cité commerciale du Moyen Âge," in *L'histoire du Sahara et des relations transsahariennes entre le Maghreb et l'ouest africain du Moyen Âge à la fin de l'époque coloniale. Actes du IVe Colloque eurafricain* (Bergama: Gruppo Walk Over, 1984), 110–14.

30. P. Cressier, "La grande mosquée d'Assodé," *Journal des Africanistes* 59, nos. 1–2 (1989): 139.

31. Cuoq, *Recueil de sources arabes*, 317.

32. Cressier and Bernus, "La grande mosquée d'Agades: architecture et histoire," *Journal de la Société des Africanistes* 54, no. 1 (1954): 5–44.

33. Djibo Hamani, "Au carrefour du Soudan et de la Berbérie: le sultanat Tuareg de l'Ayar" (Ph.D. thesis, Université Paris, 1985).

34. Aboubacar Adamou, "Agadez et sa region," *Études Nigériennes* 44 (1979): 48 (Niamey: Institut de Recherches en Sciences humaines).

35. Agades is known thanks to written chronicles: Y. Urvoy, "Chroniques d'Agadez," *Journal de la Société des Africanistes* 4 (1934).

36. Hamani, "Au carrefour du Soudan."

37. Urvoy, "Chroniques d'Agadez," 154.

38. Leo Africanus (ca. 1492–ca. 1550), *A Geographical Histories [sic] of Africa written in Arabic and Italian by John Leo, a Moor born in Granada brought up in Barbarie*, translated and collected by John Pory, edited by Luther Jones (Pittsburgh: Jones' Research and Publishing, 1994); *Description de l'Afrique* (Paris: Maisonneuve, 1956), 2:473–74.

39. Cressier, "La grande mosquée d'Assodé," 133–162.

40. H. Barth, *Travels and Discoveries in North and Central Africa: being a jour-*

*nal of an expedition undertaken under the auspices of H. B. M.'s Government in the years 1849–1855* (1857. London: F. Cass, 1965), vol. 1, chapter 6, "Excursion to Agades."

41. F. Foureau, *D'Alger au Congo par le lac Tchad. Mission saharienne Foureau-Lamy* (Paris: Masson, 1902), 377–81.

42. A.A. Boahen, *Britain, the Sahara and the Western Sudan, 1788–1861* (London: Oxford University Press, 1964).

43. Bivar and Shinnie, "Old Kanuri Capitals."

44. D. Lange, *A Sudanese Chronicle: The Bornou Expeditions of Idris Alauma (1564–1576) according to the account of Ahmad b. Furtu* (Arabic Text, English Translation and Geographical Gazetteer) (Stuttgart: Franz Steiner Verlag Wiesbaden, 1988). See also Lange, "Trois hauts dignitaires Bornouans du 16e siècle: le Digma, le grand Jarma et le Cikama," *Journal of African History* 29, no. 2 (1988): 177–90.

45. The visitor's name is not given by the author of this description, A. Mahadi, "The Cities of Bornou," in *Cities of the Savannah*, 14.

46. Ibid., 9–26.

47. S. B. Aradeon, "Al-Sahili. The Historians' Myth of Architectural Technology Transfer from North Africa," *Journal des Africanistes* 59, nos. 1–2 (1989): 99–131.

48. C. Monteil, *Djenné, métropole du delta du Niger* (Paris: Société d'Éditions géographiques, maritimes et coloniales, 1927; republished 1971), 193.

49. Ibid., 189.

50. The most famous chronicles are the Tarikhs: *Tarikh el-fettach* and *Tarikh al-Sudan*, discovered and translated at the beginning of the twentieth century: Mahmûd Kâti, *Tarikh el-fettach, ou Chronique du chercheur, pour servir à l'histoire des villes, des armées et des principaux personnages du Tekrour* (Paris: Leroux, 1913; republished 1980); Hunwick's 1999 translation of Sa'di's Ta'rikh. Also see: J. O. Hunwick, *Shari'a in Songhay: The Replies of al-Maghili to the Questions of Askia al-Hajj Muhammad* (London: M. A. Cherbonneau, 1985); *Essai sur la littérature arabe au Soudan d'après le Tekmilat ed-Dibadje d'Ahmed Baba le Tombouctien* (Paris: Société archéologique de la Province de Constantine, 1985). An indispensable work is R. Mauny, *Tableau géographique de l'ouest africain au Moyen Âge, d'après les sources écrites, la tradition orale et l'archéologie* (Dakar: IFAN, 1961).

51. This view is corrected and discussed in several works: Cissoko, "L'intelligentsia"; Dramani-Issifou, "Islam et société dans l'Empire Songhaï"; Saad, *Social History of Timbuktu*; Gomez, "Timbuktu under Imperial Songhay"; Hunwick, "Secular Power and Religious Authority in Muslim Society," and Hunwick, *Timbuktu and the Songhay Empire*.

52. Cissoko, "L'intelligentsia."

53. Abitbol, *Tombouctou et les Arma*, and Abitbol, *Tombouctou au milieu*.

54. *Ta'rikh al-Sudan*: text in Arabic quoted by Abitbol, *Tombouctou au milieu*, 163n42.

55. R. Caillié, *Travels through Central Africa to Timbuctoo, and across the Great Desert, to Morocco, Performed in the years 1824–1828* (London: Cass, 1968).

56. Quoted by Kerjean, *La piste interdite*.

57. Milner, "The Folk-Urban Continuum," 14.

58. Nevertheless see F. Iroko, "Gao des origines à 1591" (thesis, Université Paris-1, 1974). See also Insoll, "Iron Age Gao."

59. Iroko quoted by Dramani-Issifou, "Islam et société."

60. H. Lhote, "La route des chars de guerre libyens Tripoli-Gao," *Archeologia* 9 (1966): 28–36. His datation of 500 BCE was recently postponed.

61. Cissoko, "L'intelligentsia," 64.

62. See also J. Hunwick, "Secular Power and Religious Authority"; Boulnois and Boubou Hama, *L'Empire de Gao. Histoire, coutumes et magie des Son-rhaï* (Paris: Maisonneuve, 1954). We hear echoes of these descriptions in Cà da Mosto (1455), Pacheco Pereira (1506–1508), Valentim Fernandes (1506–1507), and João de Barros (1552).

63. Kerjean, *La piste interdite*.

64. J. D. Fage, *A History of Africa* (New York: Routledge, 1978 and 2002), 66–70.

65. *Yaarse* was the name used for Jula people settled in the Mosi country.

66. Valentim Fernandes, *Description de la côte occidentale d'Afrique (Sénégal du Cap de Monte, Archipels)*, edited by Th. Monod, A. Teixeira da Mota, and R. Mauny (Bissau: Publicações do Centro de Estudos da Guiné Portuguesa, no. 11, 1951). Fernandes did not travel himself, but he obviously had good informers.

67. Quoted by Fage, *History of Africa*, 91.

68. *Ton* and *Tonawa* were used in Mande and Hausa to signify *Akan*, and *Bitu* was the Hausa name for *Begho*. Ibid.

69. H. P. J. Renaud, "La première mention de la noix de kola dans la matière médicale des Arabes," *Hesperis* 8 (1928): 51–52.

70. M. Posnansky, "Archaeological Aspects of the Brong-Ahafo Region," in *West African Traders in the 19th and 20th Centuries*, edited by K. Arhin (London: Longman, 1979), 24.

71. Crossland, *Pottery*.

72. Posnansky, "Archaeological Aspects of the Brong-Ahafo Region"; Posnansky, "Excavations at Begho, Ghana," *Nyame Akuma* 15 (1981). *Bono-Mansu* perhaps meant "Mande settlement in Boboland." Fage, *History of Africa*, 95. See also Posnansky, "Ghana and the Origins of West African Trade," and Posnansky, "Aspects of Early West African Trade."

73. Bobo Dioulasso means "Jula settlement in Boboland."

74. Mabogunje, *Urbanization in Nigeria*, 54.

75. P. Bonte, "Fortunes commerciales à Shingîti (Adrar mauritanien) au dix-neuvième siècle," *Journal of African History* 39, no. 1 (1998): 1–13.

76. Griffeth, "The Hausa City-States from 1450 to 1804," 143–80.

77. The tradition of seven mother cities first appeared in the *Kano Chronicle*, the oldest known text on the area. It probably resulted from a collection of diverse local traditions written in Arabic in the seventeenth century by scholars belonging to the Muslim community. Most of them were compiled by a British colonial officer at the beginning of the twentieth century: H. R. Palmer, *Sudanese Memoirs*, 3 vols. (Lagos: Government Printer, 1928). On the Hamitic myth propagated by the Hausa, see D. Lange, "The Evolution of the Hausa Story: From Bawo to Bayajidda," *Afrika und Übersee* 70 (1987): 195–209.

78. J. E. G. Sutton, "Towards a Less Orthodox History of Hausaland," *Journal of African History* 20, no. 2 (1979): 179–201.

79. G. Nicolas, *Dynamique sociale et appréhension du monde au sein d'une société hausa* (Paris: Institut d'Ethnologie/CNRS, 1975).

80. C. Meillassoux, ed., *The Development of Indigenous Trade and Markets in West Africa* (London: International African Institute/Oxford University Press, 1971).

81. *Birni* first meant "a fortified wall," then came to mean the space inside the wall, i.e., the city (cf. chapter 1 of this book).

82. M. G. Smith, "The Kano Chronicle as History," in *Studies in the History of Kano*, edited B. M. Barkindo, 41.

83. Leo Africanus, *Description de l'Afrique*, 476.

84. Historical traditions of Katsina quoted in 1979. *Le Niger, Textes et documents d'histoire du 16e au 20e siècle* (Niamey: INDRAP, no. 123, 1979), 26.

85. M. Last, "Historical Metaphors in the Intellectual History of Kano before 1800," *History in Africa* 7 (1980): 161–62.

86. I. S. Halil, "Notes on Taxation as a Political Issue in the 19th century Kano," in *Studies in the History of Kano*, edited by B. M. Barkindo.

87. See chapter 5 of this book.

88. Last, "From Sultanate to Caliphate: Kano c. 1450–1800," in *Studies in the History of Kano*, edited by B. M. Barkindo.

89. Frishman, "Population Growth of Kano," 224–25.

90. M. G. Smith, *Government in Zazzau, 1800–1950* (London: Oxford University Press, 1966); and M. G. Smith, *The Affairs of Daura* (Berkeley: University of California Press, 1978). Also M. G. Smith, "Pluralism in Precolonial African Societies," in *Pluralism in Africa*, edited by L. Kuper and M. G. Smith (Berkeley: University of California Press, 1969), 91–151.

91. Logan, "The Walled City of Kano"; Schwerdtfeger, "Urban Settlement Patterns in Northern Nigeria (Hausaland)," in Ucko, Tringham, and Dimbley, *Man, Settlement, and Urbanism*, 547–56.

92. Last, "From Sultanate to Caliphate."

93. Barkindo, "The Gates of Kano City."

94. Chittick, "The Shirazi colonization," 257–76.

95. Horton, *Early Settlements*.

96. Horton, "Swahili Corridor." On the earliest dating of the building of a mosque in Shanga, Lamu islands, see Horton, *Early Settlements*, and Horton, "Early Muslim Trading Settlements on the East African Coast," *Antiquaries Journal* 68 (1986): 290–323.

97. Curle, "The Ruined Towns"; G. W. B. Huntingford, "The Town of Amud, Somalia," *Azania* 13 (1978): 181–86.

98. A. Nègre, "A propos de Mogadiscio au Moyen Âge," *Annales de l'Université d'Abidjan*, Série 1, 5 (1977): 5–38.

99. E. G. Ravenstein, "Somali and Galla Land, Embodying Information collected by Rev. Thomas Wakefield," *Proceedings of the Royal Geographical Society* 6 (1984): 266–67.

100. Nurse and Spear, *The Swahili*, chapter 5, "The Rise of the Swahili Town-States 1100–1500," 83.

101. Kirkman, in Chittick and Rotberg, *East Africa and the Orient*, 239.

102. B. J. Walter, "Spatial Diffusion Perspective."

103. F. J. Berg, "The Swahili Community of Mombasa." See also Vernet, "Les cité-Etats Swahili."

104. Chittick, *Kilwa*, and Chittick, "Kilwa and the Arab Settlement."

105. According to the *Kilwa Chronicle* in Arabic, there was a mosque on Kilwa Island where only one Arab family is reported to have lived. Similar myths are found in Zanzibar, Comoro Islands, and Madagascar.

106. R. Summers, "Ancient Mining in Rhodesia," in *Memoirs of the National Museums and Monuments of Rhodesia* (Salisbury, 1969), 195.

107. J .J. Sinclair, "Archaeology in Eastern Africa: an Overview of Current Chronological Issues," *Journal of African History* 32, no. 2 (1991): 187.

108. Garlake, *Early Islamic Architecture*.

109. Quoted by Devisse, "Africa in Intercontinental Relations," in *General History of Africa* (Berkeley: University of California Press, 1985), 4: 635–72.

110. "Kilwa, we are told, was a mass of wooden huts for some 200 years, till the reign of the Amir Sulayman Hasan who, 198 or 200 years after Sulayman bin Hasa, built it of stone, embellished it with mosques, and strengthened it with forts and towers of coralline and lime." In J. F. Burton, *Zanzibar. City, Island and Coast* (London: Tinsley Brothers, 1872), 2:358–60.

111. C. H. Stigand, *The Land of Zenj* (London: Frank Cass, 1966). R. L. Pouwels, "The Battle of Shela. Point of Departure in the Modern His-

tory of the Kenyan Coast," *Cahiers d'Études africaines* 31–3 (123) (1991): 323–90.

112. Chittick, "Medieval Mogadishu."

113. J. de V. Allen, "Swahili Culture Reconsidered: Some Historical Implications of the Material Culture of the Northern Kenya Coast in the 18th and 19th centuries," *Azania* 9 (1974): 129–31. The Lamu revival resulted in the Sheila battle (between 1807 and 1813?). Lamu defeated the coalition of its two permanent rivals, the cities of Pate and Mombasa. Pouwels, "The Battle of Shela."

114. Eastman, "Women, Slaves and Foreigners."

115. Nurse and Spear, *The Swahili*, 95–96.

116. Pouwels, "The Battle of Shela."

117. Pouwels, *Horn and Crescent*.

## Chapter Five

1. C. Coquery-Vidrovitch, "Villes africaines anciennes."

2. "Cabo verde," *Boletim de Informaçao e Propaganda* 9, no. 106 (1958): 8; E. Andrade, "La formation des villes au Cap-Vert," in Cahen, ed., *Bourgs et villes*, 23–39; and J. Estevão, "Peuplement et phénomènes d'urbanisation au Cap-Vert pendant la période coloniale," in Cahen, ed., *Bourgs et villes*, 23–62.

3. J. Boulègue, "Relation de Francisco d'Andrade sur les îles du Cap-Vert et la côte occidentale d'Afrique," *Bulletin de l'IFAN-B* 29, nos. 1 and 2 (1967).

4. Most settlements were Portuguese, but also Spanish because of the union of the two kingdoms from 1580 to 1604. There were a few Dutch ones as of 1596, then English, French, Brandenburgian, Swedish, and Danish trading forts and castles. As late as the eighteenth century, Denmark was the main maritime empire in the north of Europe. Danish traders visited the Guinean coast for the first time during the reign of Christian II (1588–1644). They brought back ivory, gold, and sugar. In 1656, Frederick III founded a chartered company to trade on the Guinean coast. In 1659 the Danish bought their first plot of land on the gold coast. In 1666 they founded Christianborg (Accra). Then they established a number of trading posts or "lodges" in the Volta River delta. Danish expeditions on the African coast continued as late as 1850. Grove and Johansen, "Historical Geography," 1376–77.

5. See, for example, Lawrence, *Trade Castles and Forts*; Fage, *History in Africa*, 65; Van Dantzig and Pridy, *Short History*; Gayibor, *Les villes négrières*.

6. Lawrence, *Trade Castles and Forts*, 16–17.

7. A. Van Dantzig, "La juridiction du fort Saint Antoine d'Axim," *Revue Française d'Histoire d'Outre-Mer* 66, nos. 242–43 (1979): 223–35.

8. A number of old case studies exist, which are used to varying degrees by more recent writers. See Correia Lopes, *São João,* and also notes 4, 10, 15, and 22 in this chapter.

9. Van Dantzig, "La juridiction," 233.

10. Lawrence, *Trade Castles and Forts,* 29.

11. C. Agbo (nicknamed Alidji), *Histoire de Ouidah.* He began to write the chronicle as early as 1945.

12. On the progressive organization by the British of the Fante protectorate, see D. Kimble, *A Political History of Ghana. The Rise of Gold Coast Nationalism, 1850–1928* (Oxford: Clarendon Press, 1963).

13. In 1682, the Brandenburg Company ordered that supplies sufficient for sixteen months had to be stored; these supplies included bread, flour, oil, salt, soap, brandy, meat and delicatessen, shoes, stockings, hats, shirts, and other pieces of cloth. Lawrence, *Trade Castles and Forts,* 86.

14. Agbo, *Histoire de Ouidah,* 89.

15. The biggest structure was discovered at Elmina. It was built in the Portuguese style, using big red bricks and square pipes to collect water flowing from neighboring roofs through gutters running along the pavement towards a hole located at the top of the tank. Agbo, *Histoire de Ouidah,* 91. On the process of cultural influences, from the Portuguese to the British culture from 1400 to 1900, see C. R. DeCorse, *An Archaeology of Elmina.*

16. Agbo, *Histoire de Ouidah,* 104. The first description was proposed by Pina, the second by João de Barros, who wrote his in the 1550s: *Asia de João de Barros. Dos feitos que os Portugueses fizeram no descobrimento e conquista dos mares e terras de Oriente* (Lisbon: Colonial Office, 1945). See also Ballong-wen-Mewuda, *Saint-Georges-de-la-Mine.*

17. See Henri's citadel, built from 1808 to 1820 in the north of Haiti. It was never completed; this was the very first independent black state in American history and had just won a war of independence.

18. Quoted by Lawrence, *Trade Castles and Forts,* 85.

19. Ibid., 185.

20. The Danish fort of Whydah was sold early to the French Fabre Company.

21. The Fabre Company was expelled from Dahomey during World War I.

22. See Kea, *Settlements, Trade, and Polities,* based on Dutch archives. This book is extremely valuable, and it is largely used here, despite the fact that it contains so much information that it could be difficult to absorb. See also J. M. Postma, *The Dutch in the Atlantic Slave Trade 1600–1815* (Cambridge; New York: Cambridge University Press, 1990).

23. Johnson, "Indigenes or Invaders?"

24. W. Bosman, *A new and accurate description of the coast of Guinea, divided into the Gold, the Slave, and the Ivory Coasts*, edited by J. R. Willis, J. D. Fage, and R. E. Bradbury (London: F. Cass, 1967). The book was first published in Dutch in 1704.

25. T. F. Garrard, "Study in Akan Goldweights: The Origins of the Gold-weight System," *Transactions of the Historical Society of Ghana* 13, no. 1 (1972).

26. Estimates of *dumba* weights vary widely from one source to the next: Fante *dumbas* or *dummas* could vary between 1.8 and 3.6 grams. Akyem and Baule dumbas or dammas weighed 0.074 grams. These units of measurement may or may not refer to the same actual weight. There were also dumbas or dammas varying between 62.2 and 170.7 grams. Therefore it may be impossible to calculate how much one would be worth today. Garrard, *Transactions* 13, nos. 1 and 2 (1972) and 14, nos.1 and 2 (1973). Kea suggests that 384 dambas be considered equal to one English gold ounce (31,1035 gr.); this would mean 0.08 gr. for one dumba. Kea, *Settlements, Trade, and Polities*, 339n30.

27. Guy Bois, *La mutation de l'an Mil. Lournand, village mâconnais de l'Antiquité au féodalisme* (Paris: Fayard, 1989).

28. I. Wilks, "Northern Factor"; Arhin, "The Structure of Greater Ashanti."

29. Thus Bois describes the urban revolution emerging in the French Mâconnais area from the eleventh century onwards. Bois, *La mutation*, 125-26.

30. Ibid., 127.

31. Oral information from Jean-Loup Amselle.

32. P. C. W. Gutkind, "The Canoemen of the Gold Coast (Ghana). A Survey and an Exploration in Precolonial Labour History," *Cahiers d'Études africaines* 29, nos. 3-4 (115-16) (1989): 339-76.

33. Danish sources quoted by Kea, *Settlements, Trade, and Polities*, 44–45 and 48.

34. Ibid., 19. The word *millie* was used indiscriminately for all kinds of cereals: millet, sorghos and maize.

35. Bois, *La mutation*, 144.

36. Benin City should not be confused with the modern state of Benin, former colonial Dahomey.

37. 1486. Portuguese report by João de Barros. *Decada* I, III: chapter 4.

38. Duarte Pacheco Pereira, *Esmeraldo de Situ Orbis* (Lisbon: A. E. da Silva Dias, 1905; English translation, London: Hakluyt Society, 1937), 117. The original text was written in 1506–1508.

39. John Adams gives the city the name of Jabu. The city can be reached from the river (lagoon) of Lagos. J. Adams, *Remarks on the Country Extending from Cape Palmas to the River Congo. . .* (London: G. and W. B. Whitaker, 1823). See also P. A. de Sandoval, *De Instauranda Aethiopium Salute*

(1657). Translated: *Un Tratado sobre la esclavitud,* Introducción, transcripción y traducción de Enriqueta Vila Vilar (Madrid: Alianza Editoria, 1987).

40. H. Bascom, "Les premiers fondements historiques de l'urbanisme Yoruba," *Présence Africaine* (23) (Dec. 1958/Jan. 1959): 22–40. Wheatley, "Significance of Traditional Yoruba Urbanism," 397–98. In 1729, d'Anville localized Oyo too far to the west. A map of 1843 is reproduced in E. Foa, *Le Dahomey: histoire, géographie, mœurs, coutumes, commerce, industrie, expéditions françaises (1891–1894)* (Paris: A. Hennuyer, 1895), 10.

41. A most useful history of the Yoruba remains R. Smith, *Kingdoms of the Yoruba* (London: Methuen, 1969).

42. R. Smith, "The Alafin in Exile," 109–53. Peel, "Kings, Titles, and Quarters."

43. F. Willett, "On the Funeral Effigies of Owo and Benin and an Interpretation of the Life-size Bronze Heads from Ife, Nigeria," *Man* 1, no. 1 (1966); and Willet, "A Survey of Recent Results in the Radio-carbon Chronology of Western and Northern Africa," *Journal of African History* 12, no. 3 (1971): 339–70.

44. Wheatley, "Significance of Traditional Yoruba Urbanism," 402–404.

45. P. Morton-Williams, "The Influence of Habitat and Trade on the Policies of Oyo and Ashanti," *African Notes* 4, no 3 (1968): 39–52.

46. G. J. Afolabi, *Yoruba Palaces. A Study of Afins of Yorubaland* (London: University of London Press, 1966).

47. Caboceer was the title given to the king's ministers.

48. H. Clapperton, *Journal of a Second Expedition into the Interior of Africa, from the Bight of Benin to Soccatoo* (1829; London: F. Cass, 1966), 58.

49. R. Lander and J. Lander, *Journal of an Expedition to Explore the Course and Termination of the Niger* (New York: J. & J. Harper, 1833), vol. 1, chapter 4.

50. Willett, *Ife in the History of West African Sculpture* (London: Thames and Hudson, 1967).

51. Mabogunje and Omer-Cooper, *Owu in Yoruba History.*

52. Ozanne, "New Archeological Survey."

53. Law, *Towards a History,* 260–71; P. C. Lloyd, "The Yoruba: An Urban People?" in *Urban Anthropology,* edited by A. W. Southall, 107–23.

54. Lloyd, *Yoruba Land Law.*

55. Journal of Reverend D. Hinderer, 13–14 December 1854, *Christian Missionary Society,* CA2/049 (b). Quoted by Law, *Towards a History,* 263.

56. Mabogunje, *Urbanization in Nigeria,* 76–78.

57. The case was discussed in chapter 1 of this book.

58. Morton-Williams, "The Influence of Habitat and Trade."

59. Wilks, "Northern Factor."

60. See *The Kano Chronicle,* which refers to Muslim *Wongarawa* (Mande-speaking people) under the reign of the eleventh *sarkin* (1349–85).

61. On bead making in Oyo, see Willett, *Ife.*

62. See R. Law, *The Oyo Empire c. 1600–c.1836. A West Imperialism in the Era of the Atlantic Slave Trade* (London: Oxford Clarendon Press, 1977).

63. Exact references in Law, "Trade and Politics," 324-327.

64. A. F. C. Ryder, *Benin and Its Europeans,* is an historical account of the re-lationships between the Europeans and Benin City. J. Egharevda, *A Short History of Benin* (1934; Ibadan: Ibadan University Press, 1968), mostly uses more or less convincing oral traditions. For precise archaeological information, see G. Connah, "Archaeology in Benin," *Journal of African History* 13, no. 1 (1972): 25–38, and, mainly, Connah, *The Archeology of Benin*; also P. J. Darling, "Notes on the Earthworks of the Benin Empire," *West African Journal of Archaeology* 6 (1976): 143–49, and Darling, *Archae-ology and History in Southern Nigeria* (Cambridge: Cambridge University Press, 1984). See also Onokerhoraye, "Urbanism as an Organ." A useful summary is in Connah, *African Civilizations,* 130–35.

65. D. Pacheco Pereira, *Esmaraldo de Situ Orbis,* 134.

66. 1694 text quoted by Ryder, *Benin and Its Europeans,* 113n3.

67. Connah, "New Light."

68. For further information, see R. E. Bradbury, "The Kingdom of Benin," in *West African Kingdoms in the Nineteenth Century,* edited by Daryll Forde and P. M. Kaberry (London: Oxford University Press, 1967), 1–35.

69. See, among others, C. Tabutin, ed., *Population et sociétés en Afrique au sud du Sahara* (Paris: L'Harmattan, 1988).

70. For a not definitive but nevertheless impressive overview on the ques-tion: P. Lovejoy, *Transformations in Slavery. A History of Slavery in Africa* (Cambridge: Cambridge University Press, 1983; 2nd ed., 2000). See other more detailed studies, such as C. Becker, "Note sur les chiffres de la traite atlantique française au XVIIIᵉ siècle," *Cahiers d'Etudes Africaines* 26, no. 4 (104) (1986): 633–79; D. Cordell and J. Gregory, eds., *African Population and Capitalism. Historical Perspectives* (Boulder, Colo.: Westview Press, 1987; D. Eltis, *Economic Growth and the Ending of the Transatlantic Slave Trade* (London: Oxford University Press, 1987); P. Manning, *Slavery and African Life* (Cambridge: Cambridge University Press, 1990); M. A. Klein, *Slavery and Colonial Rule in French West Africa* (Cambridge and New York: Cambridge University Press, 1998); David Eltis, Stephen D. Behrendt, and David Richardson, eds., *The Transatlantic Slave Trade: A Database on CD-ROM* [computer file] (Cambridge and New York: Cam-bridge University Press, 1999).

71. C. Meillassoux, *The Anthropology of Slavery: The Womb of Iron and Gold* (Chicago: University of Chicago Press; London: Athlone Press, 1991).

72. A. Ly, *Les noctuelles vivent de larmes* (Paris: L'Harmattan, 1989).

73. On this traumatic history of Africa in the nineteenth century, see, among others, Coquery-Vidrovitch, *L'Afrique et les Africains au 19ème siècle. Mutations, révolutions, crises* (Paris: A. Colin, 1999). On the eastern coast: S. Daget and P. Renault, *Les traites négrières en Afrique* (Paris: Karthala, 1985). There are many other excellent books in English. See note 70.

74. Kea, *Settlements, Trade, and Polities*, 90, and 363n156.

75. I. Wilks, *Asante in the Nineteenth Century. The Structure and Evolution of a Political Order* (Cambridge: Cambridge University Press, 1975).

76. Ibid.

77. A large bibliography has long been available on the topic. See among others: C. Coquery-Vidrovitch, "La fête des coutumes au Dahomey. Historique et essai d'interprétation," *Annales* 29, no. 4 (1964): 696–716; G. M. Ahananzo, *Le Danxome* (Paris: Nubia, 1964); I. A. Akinjogbin, *Dahomey and Its Neighbours 1708–1818* (Cambridge: Cambridge University Press, 1967); Law, *Ouidah*.

78. A. Akindele and C. Aguessy, "Contribution à l'etude d'histoire"; A. Sinou, B. Oloudé, A. Gnacadja et al., *Porto-Novo, Atlas historique* (Paris: OR-STOM, 1985), largely used by B. Oloudé and A. Sinou, *Porto-Novo, Ville d'Afrique noire* (Marseille: Parenthèses, 1985).

79. B. Barry, *Le royaume du Waalo 1659–1859* (Paris: Maspero, 1972; republished, L'Harmattan, 1989), and Barry, *Senegambia and the Atlantic Slave Trade* (Cambridge and New York: Cambridge University Press, 1998).

80. D. T. Niane, *Histoire des Mandingues de l'ouest. Le royaume de Gabou* (Paris: Karthala-Arsan, 1989).

81. Udo, "Growth and Decline of Calabar"; Hackett, *Religion in Calabar*; R. K. Udo and B. Ogundana, "Factors Influencing the Fortunes of Ports in the Niger Delta," *Scottish Geographical Magazine* 82 (1966): 169–83.

82. Brazil and especially the Caribbean islands were the primary locations for sugar-cane slave plantations in the seventeenth and eighteenth centuries. At the time, petty agrarian capitalism progressed there in the nineteenth century: D. Tomich, *Slavery in the Circuit of Sugar. Martinique and the World Economy 1830–1848* (Baltimore, Md.: The Johns Hopkins University Press, 1990). Only in the first part of the nineteenth century did slave cotton plantations emerge in the American South. But, although American slavery was by no means looked at as illegitimate at that time, it had little effect on African slave-trading kingdoms. Since slave trading was outlawed by the British as early as 1807, American slaves were mostly imported from the Caribbean islands. Slaves' death rates declined, while health care improved thanks to a less deadly climate, and breeding slaves locally was favored.

83. Gayibor, "Les villes négrières." On the Nigerian and Dahomean coasts:

Law, "Trade and Politics" and *Ouidah*.

84. A study by S. Berbain appeared as early as 1942 (*Le comptoir français*).

85. A. Delcourt, *La France et les établissements français du Sénégal entre 1713 et 1763* (Dakar: Mémoire de l'IFAN, 1952).

86. Biondi, *Saint-Louis du Sénégal*.

87. Originally, in French, *mulâtre* meant African metissage, while *métis* meant Asian.

88. See the huge but unpublished dissertation by R. Pasquier (University of Paris-I, 1988) on Saint-Louis trading people between 1830 and 1848 (the year of emancipation in French colonies). By the same author, a useful article: "Villes du Sénégal." See also L. Marfaing, *L'évolution du commerce au Sénégal: 1820–1930* (Paris: L'Harmattan, 1991). See also L. Harding and P. Kipré, eds., *Commerce et commerçants en Afrique de l'ouest* (Paris: L'Harmattan, 1992).

89. Pasquier, "Villes du Sénégal," 393.

90. Brews archives, Letter of 1792, quoted by Margaret Priestly, *West African Trade and Coast Society. A Family Study* (London: Oxford University Press, 1969), 121.

91. Priestley, *West African Trade and Coast Society*.

92. P. Verger, *Flux et reflux de la traite des nègres entre le golfe du Bénin et Bahia de todos os santos du 17è au 19è siècles* (Paris/The Hague: Mouton, 1968), ch. 16. See also Verger, "Afro-américains. Influence du Brésil dans le Bénin," *Bulletin de l'IFAN-B* 27 (1953). More recently: J. Thornton, *Africa and Africans in the Making of the Atlantic World, 1400–1800* (Cambridge: Cambridge University Press, 1992); K. Mann and E. G. Bay, eds., *Rethinking the African Diaspora. The Making of a Black Atlantic World in the Bight of Benin and Brazil* (London: Frank Cass, 2001); L. M. Heywood, ed., *Central Africans and Cultural Transformations in the American Diaspora* (Cambridge: Cambridge University Press, 2002).

93. Verger, *Flux et reflux*, 605–606. Law, *Ouidah*.

94. D. Ross, "The Career of Domingo Martinez in the Bight of Benin," *Journal of African History* 6, no. 1 (1965): 79–90.

95. C. Tardits, *Porto-Novo. Les nouvelles générations africaines entre leurs traditions et l'Occident* (Paris/The Hague: Mouton, 1958).

96. H. Brunschwig, *Noirs et Blancs dans l'Afrique noire française ou comment le colonisé devint colonisateur (1870–1914)* (Paris: Flammarion, 1983), 92–93.

97. G. Brooks, *Eurafricans in Western Africa. Commerce, Social Status, Gender, and Religious Observance from the Sixteenth to the Eighteenth Century*, Western African Studies (Athens: Ohio University Press and Oxford: J. Curry, 2003).

98. Cameiro da Cunha and P. Verger, *From Slave Quarters to Town Houses*.

*Brazilian Architecture in Nigeria and the People's Republic of Benin* (São Paulo: Nobel Edusp, 1985). Recently, Peter Mark, *Portuguese Style and Luso-African Identity* (Bloomington: Indiana University Press, 2002), argued that the Brazilian architectural model was not born in Brazil but rather was brought back to Africa, from where it had come two centuries earlier, when former Luso-Africans popularized it before the start of slave trading.

99. Sinou et al., *Atlas historique*, 64–65.
100. F. Raison-Jourde, *Bible et pouvoir à Madagascar au XIXe siècle* (Paris: Karthala, 1991).
101. J. Gubler, "Architecture and Colonialism. A Historical Safari," *Lotus International* 26 (1980): 5–19.
102. Described by Peter Mark, *Portuguese Style*.
103. The urban habitat, especially on the eastern part of the coast populated by Yoruba people (Benin and Nigeria of today), resulted from the nineteenth century on, from blending the local housing with a mix of Brazilian and Indian architectural styles. The influence of the bungalow, brought from India to England in the eighteenth century, and re-exported from England to Nigeria at the end of the nineteenth century, was studied by A. D. King, *The Bungalow. The Production of a Global Culture* (London: Routledge and Kegan Paul, 1984). The cultural meeting between these two types (Indian and Luso-Africano-Brazilian) of veranda houses has not yet been studied.
104. Adandé, "Abomey."
105. Houseman, Crépin, et al., "Notes sur la structure."
106. R. Norris, *Memoirs of the Reign of Bossa Ahádee, King of Dahomy* (1789; London: F. Cass, 1968), 92.
107. Houseman, Crépin, et al., "Notes sur la structure," 541–42.
108. Ibid., 542–44.
109. S. C. Anignikin and M. B. Anignikin, *Étude sur l'évolution historique, sociale et spatiale de la ville d'Abomey*. Partially published in Coquery-Vidrovitch, ed., *Processus d'urbanisation*, "Perception du phénomène urbain en Afrique noire pré-coloniale: l'exemple d'Abomey, capitale du Danxome," 1:36–40.
110. W. Snelgrave, *A New Account of Some Part of Guinea, and the Slave Trade* (London: J. Knapton, 1734).
111. Verger, *Flux et reflux*.
112. Adams, *Remarks on the Country*.
113. Sinou and Oloude, *Porto-Novo*, 52–53.
114. M.-J. Pineau-Jamous, "Porto-Novo: royauté, localité et parenté," *Cahiers d'Études Africaines* 26, no. 4 (104) (1986): 547–76. We have more doubts than the author about the oral traditions she accounts for and rebuilds.

115. Akindele and Aguessy, "Contribution à l'étude."

116. Marguerat, "Kumasi." I owe much to this excellent article.

117. Ibid., 8–9.

118. Boutillier, *La ville de Bouna*, 4–6.

119. M. J. Bonnat, "General Description of Salaga," *Liverpool Mercury*, June 12, 1876; A. Olorunfemi, "The Contest for Salaga: Anglo-German Conflict in the Gold Coast Hinterland," *Journal of African Studies* 11, no. 1 (1984): 16–23.

120. According to K. Arhin, "Transit Markets in the Asante Hinterland."

121. T. E. Bowdich, *Mission from Cape Coast Castle to Ashante* (London: J. Murray, 1819; London: F. Cass 1966).

122. Wilks, *Asante in the Nineteenth Century*, 375n11.

123. Marguerat, "Kumasi," 13–15.

124. R. S. Rattray, *Religion and Art in Ashanti* (London: Oxford University Press, 1927).

125. Bowdich, *Mission from Cape Coast Castle*, mentions a village of parasol makers and another of blacksmiths.

126. M. Johnson, "Ashanti Craft Organization," 78–82 and 97.

127. J. Gros, *Voyages, aventures et captivité de J. Bonnat chez les Achantis* (Paris: M. Dreyfous, 1884).

128. Wilks attempts to understand and to draw the old city in *Asante in the Nineteenth Century*, 74–86.

129. Bowdich, *Mission from Cape Coast Castle*, 306 and 323.

130. T. B. Freeman, *Journal of various visits to the kingdoms of Ashanti, Aku, and Dahomi, in western Africa* (1843; London: Cass, 1968), 54–55.

131. J. Dupuis, *Journal of a Residence in Ashantee* (1824; London: F. Cass, 1966), 83.

132. On international trading activities during the period, see Alpers, *Ivory and Slaves*. Unfortunately, he does not speak at all of cities or even of import-export harbors.

133. Connah, *African Civilizations*, 155–58.

134. J. Strandes, *The Portuguese Period in East Africa*, translated from German (Nairobi: East African Literature Bureau, 1961); A. H. Prins, *The Swahili-speaking Peoples of Zanzibar and the East African Coast (Arabs, Shirazi and Swahili)* (London: International African Institute, 1961); F. J. Berg, "The Swahili Community of Mombasa."

135. João de Barros quoted by R. F. Burton, *Wanderings in West Africa*, 2: 25–27.

136. Berg, "The Swahili Community of Mombasa."

137. Burton, *Wanderings in West Africa*, 2:362–67.

138. Elkiss, *The Quest for an African Eldorado*.

139. On the history of the city and island of Mozambique: "Ilha de Moçam-

bique: Nos 170 anos da fundação…," 1988; *Ilha de Moçambique. Relatorio – Report, 1982–1985;* and M. Angius and M. Zamponi, *Ilha de Moçambique.*

140. A. Roberts, "Nyamwezi Trade," in *Precolonial African Trade. Essays on Trade in Central and Eastern Africa before 1900,* edited by Richard Gray and David Birmingham (London: Oxford University Press, 1970), 39–74.

141. Burton, *Wanderings in West Africa,* 2:372.

142. Brown, "Bagamoyo," 70.

143. Abdul Sheriff, "Mosques, Merchants and Landowners in Zanzibar Old Stone Town," in *Histoire sociale de l'Afrique de l'Est (XIXe–XXe siècles)* (Paris: Karthala, 1991), 383–402.

144. C. Le Cour Grandmaison, "Rich Cousins, Poor Cousins: Hidden Stratifications among the Omani Arabs in Eastern Africa," *Africa* 59, no. 2 (1989): 176–84.

145. Le Cour Grandmaison, "Migrations Omani en Afrique centrale: repères historiques et généalogiques," *Revue de civilisation burundaise* (Bujumbura), 1985. This is part of long-term research and a series of French-English conferences on the Swahili people: I. Formal and informal stratification in Eastern Africa (1987). II. Réseaux et échanges dans les sociétés côtières d'Afrique orientale (1989). III. Influences de l'intérieur du continent sur les structures et les stratégies d'autonomie (1992). J. Glassman, *Feasts and Riots.*

146. Alain Ricard, "Zanzibar à l'horizon," *Le Monde,* August 11, 1990, 9–10.

147. J. M. Gray, "Early Connections between the United States and East Africa," *Tanganyika Notes and Records* 22 (1946): 55–86; C. Clendenen, R. Collins, and P. Duignan, *Americans in Africa,* vol. 1, *Up to 1864* (Stanford, Calif.: Stanford University Press, 1964).

148. In 1873, the British obtained from Sultan Bargash a treaty forbidding the slave trade out of his empire. In the empire, slavery was suppressed in 1891; approximately 80 percent of the population—concubines, field-workers, slaves involved in trading business—were enslaved at that time. In 1884, the first stone of an Anglican cathedral to be built was symbolically placed on the former slave marketplace. In 1886, a European commission unilaterally decided that the sultan's possessions would be restricted to the islands of Zanzibar, Pemba, Mafia, and Lamu, plus a ten-mile strip of land along the African coast. F. B. Pearce, *Zanzibar;* J. Gray, *History of Zanzibar from the Middle Ages to 1956* (London: Oxford University Press, 1962); N. R. Bennett, *A History of the Arab State of Zanzibar* (London: Methuen, 1986) and *Arab versus European. Diplomacy and War in the 19th Century East Central Africa* (New York: Africana Publishing Company, 1986); and, above all, Sheriff, *Slaves, Spices and Ivory,* and

Glassman, *Feasts and Riots.*

149. See, quite recently, M. Pearson, *Port Cities and Intruders*, and Chami and Pwiti, *Southern Africa and the Swahili World.*


## Notes to Chapter 6

1. Cf. C. Coquery-Vidrovitch, *L'Afrique et les Africains au 19e siècle* (Paris: Colin, 1999).
2. "Papers on Firearms in Sub-Saharan Africa," *Journal of African History* 2, nos. 2 and 4 (special issues 1971).
3. F. Cooper, *From Slaves to Squatters: Plantation Labor and Agriculture in Zanzibar and Coastal Kenya 1890–1925* (New Haven: Yale University Press, 1980).
4. J. Ford, *The Role of the Trypanosomiases in African Ecology* (Oxford: Clarendon Press, 1971).
5. *East African Explorers*, selected and introduced by C. Richards and J. Place (London: Oxford University Press, 1960), 71.
6. R. F. Burton, *Zanzibar,* vol. 2, ch. 3, pp. 47–50.
7. Ibid., ch. 2.
8. Ibid., 342–43.
9. E. Verdick, *Les premiers jours au Katange (1880–1903)* (Brussels, 1952), quoted by M. Wright, "Bwanika: Consciousness and Protest among Slave Women in Central Africa 1886–1911," *Women and Slavery in Africa*, edited by C. Robertson and M. Klein (Madison: University of Wisconsin Press, 1983), 246–70.
10. The city of Bunkeya was studied by M. Wright thanks to the testimonies of elderly female slaves. A vibrant novel by a great Malian writer, Adoulaye Ly, tells the life story of a slave woman who lived in West Africa at the end of the nineteenth century. *Les noctuelles vivent de larmes* (Paris: L'Harmattan, 1989): "Add slavery to polygyny, make a woman a slave, and you obtain a supreme human degradation, the worst creature in the divine world: a female slave."
11. Described by F. S. Arnot, *Garenganze; Or, Seven Years' Pioneer Mission Work in Central Africa* (1888; London: Cass, 1969), 194.
12. Quoted by E. Alpers, "Trade, State and Society among the Yao in the Nineteenth Century," *Journal of African History* 10, no. 3 (1969): 405–20.
13. According to R. M. Heanley, *A Memoir of Edward Steere, D.D., LL.D. Third Missionary Bishop in Central Africa* (London: G. Bell, 1888), 145–46, the whole land was cultivated, so that the city looked like a green sea on which the roofs of the huts seemed to float.

14. Y. B. Abdallah, *The Yaos = Chiikala cha Wayao*, compiled by Yohanna B. Abdallah; arranged, edited, and translated by Meredith Sanderson (1919; 2nd ed., London: Cass, 1973), 54.

15. J. de Azevedo Coutinho, *Memorias de um Velho Marinheiro e Soldado de Africa* (Lisbon: Livraria Bertrand, 1941), 181.

16. J. F. Elton, *Travels and Researches among the Lakes and Mountains of Eastern and Central Africa* (1879; London: F. Cass, 1968), 288–89.

17. R. Oliver, *Sir Harry Johnson and the Scramble for Africa* (New York: St. Martin's Press, 1958).

18. Burton, *Zanzibar*, 2:505. Quoted by B. Brown and W. Brown, "East Africa Trade Towns: A Shared Growth," in *World Anthropology. A Century of Change in Eastern Africa*, edited by W. Arens (Paris and The Hague: Mouton, 1976).

19. Cf. A. Roberts, "Nyamwezi Trade," in *Pre-Colonial African Trade*, edited by Richard Gray and David Birmingham, ch. 5, n. 133; also Roberts, "The Nyamwezi," in *Tanzania before 1900*, edited by A. Roberts (Nairobi: East African Publishing House, 1968).

20. Posnansky, "Connections between the Lacustrine People and the Coast," 216-25.

21. Data quoted with their sources by Brown and Brown, "East Africa Trade Towns," 197. See also B. Brown, *Ujiji*, and B. Brown, "Muslim Influence on Trade and Politics," 617-29.

22. H. M. Stanley, *How I found Livingstone* (New York: Scribner, Armstrong, & Co., 1872), 264. Also Burton, *Zanzibar*, 2:7.

23. Burton, *Zanzibar*, 1:327.

24. J. H. Speke, *Journal of the Discovery of the Sources of the Nile* (London: Blackwood, 1864), 91.

25. Report by Father A. Horner, *Bulletin général de la Congrégation du Saint-Esprit* 5 (1868): 495 and 832-51.

26. Habari za Mrima, MS 291, Allen/Knappert Collection, University of Dar es Salaam. Quoted by W. T. Brown, "The Politics of Business," 631-43.

27. Brown, "The Politics of Business," 633 and 640.

28. W. T. Brown, "Bagamoyo," 69-83.

29. *Intelligence Notes on British and German East Africa 1915*, Nairobi, British Report: 6. Quoted in ibid., 83.

30. Glassman, *Feasts and Riots*.

31. A. Germain, "Note sur Zanzibar et la côte orientale d'Afrique," *Bulletin de la Société de Géographie* 16 (1868): 536ff.

32. Tippu Tip, *Maisha ya Hamed bin Muhammed el Murjebi: yaani Tippu Tip, kwa maneno yake mwenyewe*, historical introduction by Alison Smith; translation by W. H. Whitely (Arusha: Beauchamp Printing Co., [1959]). This testimony is to be used cautiously, since Tippu Tib's memoirs were

written thirty years after the events occurred.

33. J. Vincent, "The Dar es Salaam Townsman. Social and Political Aspects of City Life." *Tanzania Notes and Records* 71 (1970): 153–54.

34. Sutton, "Dar es Salam," 4–20, and ibid., 149–56.

35. J. Comaroff, *Body of Power, Spirit of Resistance. The Culture and History of a South African People* (Chicago: University of Chicago Press, 1985), 8–9.

36. U. Monneret de Villard, *Storia della Nubia Cristiana* (Roma: Pont. Institutum Orientalum Studiorum, 1938); O. G. S. Crawford, *The Fung Kingdom of Sennar with a Geographical Account of the Middle Nile Region* (Gloucester, U.K.: John Bellows Ltd, 1951); P. L. Shinnie, "The Culture of Medieval Nubia and its Impact on Africa," in *Sudan in Africa: Studies Presented to the First International Conference Sponsored by the Sudan Research Unit*, edited by Y. F. Hasan (Khartoum: Khartoum University Press, 1968), 42–50; J. L. Spaulding, *Kingdoms of the Sudan* (London: Methuen, 1974).

37. P. M. Holt, *The Mahdist State in the Sudan 1881–1898. A Study of Its Origins, Development and Overthrow* (Oxford: Clarendon Press, 1958), and Holt, *A Modern History of the Sudan from the Funj Sultanate to the Present Day* (London: Weidenfeld and Nicholson, 1961).

38. W. G. Browne, *Travels in Africa, Egypt and Syria, from the year 1792 to 1798* (1799; London: printed for T. Cadell and W. Davies, 1799; 2nd ed., 1806), 284–85.

39. El-S. El-Bushra, "Towns in the Sudan," 63–70. Evaluations are from travelers' accounts of the eighteenth and nineteenth centuries.

40. C. Poncet, *Voyage en Éthiopie effectué dans les années 1698, 1699, et 1700 . . .*, quoted in C. Winters, "Traditional Urbanism in the North Central Sudan," 503–505.

41. Poncet quoted in Winters, ibid.

42. F. Cailliaud, *Voyage à Méroe, au Fleuve Blanc, au delà de Fazoql dans le midi du royaume de Sennar . . .* (Paris: Jomard, 1823), 2:257–58.

43. El-Bushra, "Towns in the Sudan," 65.

44. Ibid., 63–70.

45. W. G. Browne, *Travels in Africa*, 286–87.

46. The tower was not so tall before the nineteenth century. It partially fell down in the early 1820s, probably because the technical knowledge to build such a high building was not yet well mastered. Most of the best houses in Sennar had only two stories.

47. S. O'Fahey and J. L. Spaulding, *Kingdoms of the Sudan* (London: Methuen, 1974), 78–82.

48. These land charts, collected by a researcher in Khartoum, are a major source of documentation on this period. C. Winters, "Traditional Urbanism in the North Central Sudan," 508.

49. J. L. Burckhardt, *Travels in Nubia* (London: Murray, 1819); and F. Cailliaud, *Voyage à Méroe.*

50. Winters, "Traditional Urbanism in the North Central Sudan."

51. W. G. Browne's map, *Travels in Africa,* 179–80.

52. C. G. Gordon, *The Journals of Major-Gen. C. G. Gordon, C. B., at Kartoum* (Boston and New York: Houghton, Mifflin, 1885; Vanguard Press, 1961).

53. P. Rossignoli, *I miei dodici anni di prigiona in mezzo ai Dervisci del Sudan* (Mondovi: B. Graziano, 1898).

54. R. C. Slatin, *Fire and Sword in the Sudan; A Personal Narrative of Fighting and Serving the Dervishes, 1879–1895* (London and New York: E. Arnold, 1896), 500–570.

55. F. Rehfish, "A Sketch of Early History," 42–43.

56. H. Moniot, "Râbih', émir d'un 'empire mobile' aux confins soudanais," in *Les Africains,* edited by C.-A. Julien (Paris: Éditions Jeune Afrique, 1978), 4:289–309.

57. Moniot, "Râbih," 291–92.

58. A. Mahadi, "The Cities of Bornou," in *Cities of the Savannah.*

59. Scholars who have studied northern Nigeria emirates were more interested in political and religious state power and the sultan's prerogatives than in his capital city. S. J. Hogben and A. H. M. Kirk-Green, *The Emirates of Northern Nigeria. A Preliminary Study of Their Historical Traditions* (London: Oxford University Press, 1966); H. A. S. Johnson, *The Fulani Empire of Sokoto* (London: Oxford University Press, 1967); M. D. Last, *The Sokoto Caliphate* (New York: Humanities Press, 1967).

60. *Cities of the Savannah,* 48–51.

61. Clapperton, *Journal of a Second Expedition,* 377–79.

62. J. M. Voisin, *La question religieuse dans la subdivision de Maradi* (Paris: Mémoire ENFOM, 1956); P. David, "Maradi. L'ancien État et l'ancienne ville, site, population, histoire," *Études nigériennes* 18 (1964).

63. J. N. Paden, *Religion and Political Culture in Kano.*

64. J. Moody, "Paul Staudinger. An Early European Traveller to Kano," *Kano Studies* (1967): 47–50.

65. C. A. Robinson quoted by M. Johnson, "Periphery and the Centre: The 19th Century Trade of Kano," in *Studies in the History of Kano,* edited by Barkindo, 132.

66. C. Monteil, *De Saint-Louis à Tripoli par le lac Tchad* (Paris: Société d'Éditions géographiques, maritimes et coloniales, 1894), 282 and 291.

67. According to C. A. Robinson, Kano marketplace was the most important in tropical Africa. Its manufactured goods were sold from the Atlantic Ocean to the River Nile, and even as far as the Red Sea. *Hausaland or Fifteen Hundred Miles through the Central Sudan* (London: Sampson Low,

Marston, 1896), 100 and 111.

68. Barth, *Travels and Discoveries,* 1:511.

69. Robinson, *Hausaland or Fifteen Hundred Miles,* 282. C. Monteil, *De Saint-Louis à Tripoli,* 113.

70. Barth, *Travels and Discoveries,* 1:513.

71. Ibid., 1:512. Barth describes the Kano area as one of the most fertile in the world.

72. Gowers's *Report on Katsina,* Kadina Archives, quoted by M. Johnson, "Periphery and the Centre," 142 and 146.

73. H. K. Said, "Notes on Taxation as a Political Issue in 19th Century Kano," in *Studies in the History of Kano,* edited by Barkindo, 117–26.

74. A. Patton, Jr., "The Ningi Chiefdom and the African Frontier: Mountaineers and Resistance to Sokoto Caliphate, ca 1800–1908" (Ph.D. diss., University of Wisconsin, Madison, 1975).

75. Alan Frishman, "The Population Growth of Kano, Nigeria," in *African Historical Demography,* vol. 1 (Edinburgh: Centre of African Studies, University of Edinburgh, 1977), 212–50.

76. This town's history is known from two records written in Arabic telling Gumbu family stories. C. Meillassoux, "Les origines de Gumbu (Mali)," *Bulletin de l'IFAN (B)* 34, no. 2 (1972): 268–98.

77. Meillassoux, "Le commerce précolonial et l'esclavage à Gubu du Sahel (Mali)," in Meillassoux, *The Development of Indigenous Trade and Markets in West Africa* (London: International African Institute and Oxford University Press, 1971), 182–98.

78. Clapperton, *Journal of a Second Expedition;* and Lander and Lander, *Journal of an Expedition.*

79. T. J. Bowen, *Central Africa: Adventures and Missionary Labour in Several Countries in the Interior of Africa from 1849 to 1856* (Charleston, S.C.: Southern Baptist Publication Society, 1857).

80. M. Johnson, "Periphery and the Centre," 127–46.

81. A. L. Mabogunje and J. D. Omer-Cooper, *Owu in Yoruba History.*

82. Shaka's role in the turmoil of the Southern Africa hinterland was probably largely exaggerated by the Afrikaners' historiography, as was cleverly demonstrated by Carolyn Hamilton, *Terrific Majesty. The Powers of Shaka Zulu and the Limits of Historical Invention* (Cambridge: Harvard University Press, 1998). Missionaries and traders also frequented Port-Natal (later Durban), and the slave trade was largely intensified in the interior throughout the eighteenth and nineteenth centuries. Carolyn Hamilton, ed., *The Mfecane Aftermath. Reconstructive Debates in Southern African History* (Johannesburg: Witwatersrand University Press, 1995).

83. V. E. A. Akorede, "The Impact of Socio-cultural Changes on the Patterns of Urban Land Use," 71–78.

84. G. O. Oguntomisin and T. Falola, "Refugees in Yorubaland in the Nineteenth Century," 165.
85. J. F. A. Ajayi and R. Smith, *Yoruba Welfare in the Nineteenth Century* (Ibadan: Ibadan University Press, 1964). Also see T. Falola and G. O. Oguntomisin, *Yoruba Warlords of the 19th Century* (Trenton, N.J.: Africa World Press, 2001).
86. S. O. Biobaku, *The Egba and their Neighbours, 1842–1872* (Oxford: Clarendon Press, 1957); E. Philips, "The Egba at Abeokuta," 117–31.
87. T. Falola, "Migrant Settlers in Ife Society, 1830–1960," *Calabar Historical Journal* 3, no. 1 (1985): 18–35.
88. Mabogunje, *Urbanization in Nigeria*, 91.
89. H. Wolpe, *Urban Politics in Nigeria. A Study of Port-Harcourt* (Berkeley: University of California Press, 1974), ch. 3.
90. B. Floyd, *Eastern Region. A Geographical Review* (London: Macmillan, 1969).
91. R. K. Udo and B. Ogundana, "Factors Influencing the Fortunes of Ports in the Niger Delta," *Scottish Geographical Magazine* 82 (1966): 169–83.
92. Mabogunje, *Urbanization in Nigeria*, 80–81. On the importance (and a bibliography) of historical urban chronicles written by many Yoruban scholars toward the end of the nineteenth century and the first half of the twentieth century, see T. Falola, *Yoruba Gurus. Indigenous Production of Knowledge in Africa* (Trenton, N.J., and Asmara, Eritrea: Africa World Press, 1999).
93. M. Johnson, "Periphery and the Centre," 104 n. 24.
94. B. W. Holder, "The Markets of Ibadan," in *The City of Ibadan*, edited by Lloyd et al., 173–90.
95. Cf. Landers's description 1832; and Johnson, Martin, and Gollmer quoted in Mabogunje, *Urbanization in Nigeria*, 104 nn. 39, 40, and 41.
96. P. C. Lloyd, "The Yoruba. An Urban People?" in *Urban Anthropology*, edited by A. W. Southall, 107–23.
97. S. Goddard, "Town-Farm Relationships in Yorubaland," 21–29.
98. B. Awe, "Ibadan. Its Early Beginning," in *The City of Ibadan*, edited by Lloyd et al., 11–26.
99. Ibid., 14.
100. T. Falola, "From Hospitality to Hostility: Ibadan and Strangers 1830–1904," *Journal of African History* 26, no. 1 (1985): 51–68; and Falola, *The Political Economy of a Precolonial State*.
101. A. K. Ajisafe, *History of Abeokuta* [a chronicle] (Bungay, Suffolk: Richard Clay & Sons, 1985).
102. Biobaku, *The Egba and their Neighbours*, 52.
103. Philips, "The Egba at Abeokuta," and A. J. Williams-Myers, "Abeokuta: A British Impediment in West Africa: The John Gallagher and Ronald

Robinson Theses," *Journal of African History* 2, no. 1 (1984): 4–14.

104. A. Pallinder-Lax, "Aborted Modernization in West Africa? The Case of Abeokuta," *Journal of African History* 15, no. 1 (1974): 68.

105. On Bonduku: E. Terray, *Une histoire du royaume Abron du Gyaman: des origines à la conquête coloniale* (Paris: Karthala, 1995).

106. B. Kirby, Report of Mission to Kumasi and the Interior Provinces of the Ashanti Kingdom, 1884, Parliamentary Papers c.4477.

107. Dates and references are given by K. Arhin, "West African Trading Settlements in the Asante Hinterland in the Nineteenth Century" (paper presented at Symposium on Indigenous African Towns, University of California, Los Angeles, December 1980), 15.

108. L. G. Binger, *Du Niger au golfe de Guinée par le pays Kong et le Mossi 1887–1889* (Paris: Hachette, 1892), 1:139 and 1:165.

109. K. Arhin, "Transit Markets," 5–22.

110. E. P. Skinner, *The Mossi of the Upper Volta* (Stanford, Calif.: Stanford University Press, 1964), introduction and 204–207, according to *Ta'rikh es-Sudan*, and Barth, *Travels and Discoveries*.

111. See M. Izard, *Gens de pouvoir, gens de terre: les institutions politiques de l'ancien royaume du Yatenga (bassin de la Volta blanche)* (Cambridge: Cambridge University Press; New York: Éditions de la MSH, 1985).

112. Dr. Crozat, "Rapport sur une mission au Mossi (1890)," *Journal officiel de la République française* 5–9 October 1891, 4822–37; and Binger, *Du Niger au golfe de Guinée*, 1:502).

113. Binger, *Du Niger au golfe de Guinée*, 1:467.

114. Dr. Krause, "Krause's Reise," *Mittheilungen aus Justus Perthes' geographischer Anstalt über wichtige neue Erforschungen auf dem Gesammtgebiete der Geographie* (Gotha: Justus Perthes, 1887–88), 32–33.

115. Crozat, "Rapport sur une mission," 4820.

116. Binger, *Du Niger au golfe de Guinée*, 1:460.

117. M. Tymowski, "Le développement de Sikasso, capitale du Kenedugu, en tant que siège du pouvoir politique et centre urbain," *Revue française d'Histoire d'Outre-Mer* 68, nos. 250–53 (1981): 436–45; and M. Collieaux, "Contribution à l'étude de l'histoire de l'ancien royaume de Kénédougou (1825–1898)," *Bulletin du Comité d'Études historiques et scientifiques de l'Afrique occidentale française* (1924): 128–81.

118. T. Bah, *Architecture militaire traditionelle*.

119. Tardits, *Le royaume Bamoum*. The writing was first based on ideograms, and then on an alphabet.

120. Ibid., 161–62.

121. Ibid., 573–76.

122. Tardits, "Njoya, ou les malheurs de l'intelligence chez un sultan Bamoum," in *Les Africains,* edited by Julien (1977), 9:261–96; and Tar-

dits, "L'Écriture, la politique et le secret chez les Bamoum," *Africa* 46, no. 2 (1976): 224–40.

123. The urban history of Ethiopia was studied by R. Pankhurst, "Notes on the Democratiic [sic] History of Ethiopian Towns and Villages," 60–83; Pankhurst, "Menelik and the Foundation of Addis Ababa," 103–17; and Pankhurst, "The Foundation and Growth of Addis Ababa to 1935," *Ethiopian Observer* 6 (1962): 33–61. Most of these papers are collected in Pankhurst, *History of Ethiopian Towns.* See also Horvath, "The Wandering Capitals of Ethiopia," and Horvath, "Addis Abeba's Eucalyptus Forest"; M. Perret, "Villes impériales, villes princières: note sur le caractère des villes dans l'Éthiopie du XVIIIè siècle," *Journal des Africanistes* 56, no. 2 (1986): 55–65; D. Crummey, "Some Precursors of Addis Ababa."

124. Description of Gondar in Perret, "Villes impériales," 57–59.

125. J. Iliffe, *The African Poor,* ch. 2.

126. J. Bruce, *Travels to Discover the Sources of the Nile in the Years 1668 . . .,* 5 vols. (London: G. G. J. and J. Robinson, 1790; Westmead, U.K.: Gregg International, 1972).

127. Pankhurst, "Notes on the Democratiic [sic] History of Ethiopian Towns and Villages," 63.

128. R. Burton, *First Foodsteps in East Africa* (1894; London: Routledge and Kegan Paul, 1966), 2:13–19; Pankhurst, "Notes on the Democratiic [sic] History of Ethiopian Towns and Villages," 75–76.

129. A well-documented novel was written on the topic, with a good description of the capital city of Magdala in the 1860s; the author was trained as a geographer. G. Caban, *Magdalla* (Paris: Le Seuil, 1987).

130. M. Griaule, "Un camp militaire abyssin," 117–22. These urban structures are well described by Portuguese or British sources (and probably Dutch ones) from the sixteenth to the eighteenth century. Horvath, "Wandering Capitals."

131. Bruce, *Travels.*

132. Father F. Alvarez, *The Prester John of the Indies (Narrative of the Portuguese Embassy to Abyssinia during the Years 1520–27),* trans. C. F. Beckingham and G. B. W. Huntingford (Cambridge: Cambridge University Press, 1961), 1:320, 2:331 and 337.

133. On Addis Ababa history, see Pankhurst, *History of Ethiopian Towns.*

134. Guébré Sellassié, *Ministre de la Plume de S. M. l'empereur Ménélik II. Chronique du règne de Ménélik II, roi des rois d'Éthiopie* (Paris: Maisonneuve, 1932).

135. Count Gleichen, *With the Mission to Menelik, 1897* (London: E. Arnold, 1898), 2:190–91.

136. E. Mérab, *Impressions d'Éthiopie (l'Abyssinie sous Ménélik II)* (Paris: Leroux, 1922), 2:116.

137. The public works became necessary when, after a terrible drought in 1910, two-thirds of the wells dried up.

138. F. Rosen, *Deutsche Gesandtschaft in Abessinien* (1907), 278–82, quoted in Pankhurst, "The Foundation and Growth of Addis Ababa," 44.

139. Horvath, "Addis Abeba's Eucalyptus Forests."

140. MacGillivray, working at the Abyssinian Bank. Ibid., 52.

141. A. Brun-Rollet, *Le Nil Blanc et le Soudan. Études sur l'Afrique centrale, mœurs et coutumes des sauvages* (Paris: L. Maison, 1855), 103. Discussed in R. C. Stevenson, "Old Khartoum," 7.

142. H. Déhérain, "Le Soudan égyptien de Mohamed Aly à Ismaïl Pacha," in *Histoire de la nation égyptienne* . . . vol. 6, *L'Égypte de 1801 à 1882*, edited by G. Hanotaux (Paris: Plon, 1936), 430ff.; M.-A. Yagi, "Les origines de Khartoum," *Présence africaine* 22 (1958): 81–85; Stevenson, "Old Khartoum," 1–38; R. L. Hill, "An Unpublished Chronicle of the Sudan 1822–1841," *Sudan Notes and Records* 37 (1956): 2–19.

143. F. Cailliaud, *Voyage à Méroé, au Fleuve Blanc au-delà de Fâzoql, dans le midi du royaume de Sennâr, à Syouah et dans cinq autre oasis, fait dans les années 1819, 1820, 1821 et 1822* (Paris: Imprimerie royale, 1826–27), 2:198.

144. Lord Prudhoe, "Extracts from Private Memoranda kept by Lord Prudhoe on a Journey from Cairo to Sennar in 1829," *Journal of the Royal Geographical Society* (London) 5 (1835): 38.

145. Ibid.

146. Baron F. Callot, *Der Orient und Europa, Erinnerungen und Reisebilder von Land und Meer* (Leipzig, 1855; microfilm, East Lansing: Michigan State University Libraries, 1993). Quoted by Yagi, "Les origines de Khartoum," 84.

147. In 1846, the British ambassador to the Ottoman Empire still used the obsolete denomination of Sennar to mean Sudan. R. L. Hill, "An Unpublished Chronicle."

148. E. Combes, *Voyage en Égypte* (Paris: V. Magen, 1846), 2:124.

149. Prince Herman von Pückler-Muskau, *Aus Muhamad Ali's Reich*, 3 vols. (Stuttgart, 1844); translated by H. E. Lloyd, *Egypt under Mehemet Ali* (London: H. Colburn, 1845), 2:293–94.

150. J. Heyworth-Dunne, *An Introduction to the History of Education in Modern Egypt* (1938; London: F. Cass, 1968), 172–73.

151. Stevenson, "Old Khartoum," 14.

152. The latter seems actually to have been a wealthy Syrian living in the Copt district. Mentioned as early as 1865 as a consular agent paid by the United States, he was murdered in 1898 during the siege of Khartoum.

153. Hamdan, "The Growth and Functional Structure of Khartoum," 21–40.

154. Most data are collected (with their references) by Stevenson, "Old Khartoum," 17.

155. He died in Ondurman in 1918 at the age of 91. Ibid., 18.
156. R. Buchta, *Die Oberen Nil-Länder* (Berlin, 1881), print 4.
157. E. G. Sarsfield-Hall, *A Brief Account of the Siege and Fall of Khartoum* (Khartoum, n.d.). Quoted in Stevenson, "Old Khartoum," 31. See also Sarsfield-Hall, *From Cork to Khartoum: Memoirs of Southern Ireland and the Anglo-Egyptian Sudan, 1886 to 1936* (Keswick: self-published, 1975).
158. A Portuguese league measured 3.83 miles. F. Latour da Veiga Pinto, *Le Portugal et le Congo au XIXe siècle* (Paris: PUF, 1972), 47–65.
159. H. Deschamps, ed., *Histoire de l'Afrique noire* (Paris: PUF, 1970), 1:384.
160. A. da Silva Rego, *O Ultramar português no século XVIII* (Lisbon: Agência geral do Ultramar, 1967), 290–91. On the opposite coast, the port of Lourenço Marques (today Maputo in Mozambique) was long a plain fort just used to protect landings in Delagoa Bay. In 1830, it housed only the governor, eight officers, and seventy-three soldiers, plus a few other people: half a dozen European traders belonging to the Company and one or two independent traders. There were not more than three or four hundred Africans, and among them many were slaves. There was no communal organization. Competition with other European nations was harsh and, in the nineteenth century, there was pressure from the Zulu as well; Chief Dingane attacked the post in 1833. A. Lobato, *Quatro Estudos e une evocação para a Historia da Lourenço Marques* (Lisbon, 1961). Quoted in G. Liesegang, "Dingane's Attack on Lourenço Marques in 1833," *Journal of African History* 10, no. 4 (1969): 565–79.
161. Ultramar archives of Portugal preserved in Lisbon are extremely rich, but they were closed for years during Salazar's dictatorship. They are hardly classified and not easy to consult, so research is slow. Many old travel accounts were published, and they are not so easy to find outside of Portugal. Among others, two surveys are useful: E. A. da Silva Corrêa (especially for the eighteenth century), *Historia de Angola*, 2 vols. (Lisbon: Editorial ática, 1937), and R. Delgado, *Historia de Angola*, 4 vols. (Lobito: Tip. do Jornal de Benguela, 1948–55). See also D. Birmingham, *Trade and Conflict in Angola; the Mbundu and Their Neighbours under the Influence of the Portuguese, 1483–1790* (Oxford: Clarendon Press, 1966); and C. R. Boxer, *The Portuguese Seaborne Empire 1415–1825* (New York: Knopf, 1969).
162. J. J. Lopes da Lima, *Ensalo sobre a Statistica das Possessões Portuguezes* (Lisbon, 1846), 3:88.
163. B. Davidson, *In the Eye of the Storm. Angola's People* (Garden City, N.Y.: Doubleday, 1972), ch. 6.
164. J. C. Miller, *Way of Death. Merchant Capitalism and the Angolan Slave Trade 1730–1830* (Madison: University of Wisconsin Press, 1988), chs. 8 and 9.

165. Lopes da Lima, *Ensalo sobre.*

166. J. K. Thornton, "The Demographic Effects of the Slave Trade on Western Africa 1500–1850," in *African Historical Demography*, vol. 2 (Edinburgh: Centre for African Studies, University of Edinburgh, 1981), 713.

167. Miller, *Way of Death*, 288–91.

168. Ibid., 294. On nineteenth-century creolization, see in French: A. Stamm, "La société créole à Saint Paul de Loanda dans les années 1836–1848," *Revue française d'Histoire d'Outre-Mer* 59, no. 213 (1972): 578–610. Since then, the bibliography on creolization has increased enormously on both sides of the Atlantic Ocean.

169. Letter sent to the Swedish ambassador to London 1925. Quoted in T. N. Goddard, *The Handbook of Sierra-Leone* (New York: Negro Universities Press, 1969), 25.

170. T. M. Winterbottom, *An Account of the Native Africans in the Neighbourhood of Sierra Leone* (1803; London: Frank Cass, 1969), 23 and 275–76.

171. Fugitive black slaves, and their descendants, who formed their own free societies in Jamaica and other parts of the Caribbean. *Maroon* comes from the Spanish word *cimarrón*, which means cattle returned to the wild.

172. *Church Missionary Society*, CAI/E5A/98, Garnon to Pratt, March 5, 1817; and CAI/M1, Fitzerald to Pratt, June 8, 1821. Quoted in J. Peterson, *Province of Freedom*, 91 and 310.

173. G. E. Brooks, *Yankee Traders, Old Coasters and African Middlemen; A History of American Legitimate Trade with West Africa in the Nineteenth Century* (Boston: Boston University Press, 1970).

174. B. E. Harrell-Bond, A. M. Howard, and D. E. Skinner, *Community Leadership and the Transformation of Freetown (1801–1976)*, 20–30.

175. J. Peterson, *Province of Freedom*, 77–80.

176. R. F. Burton, *Wanderings in West Africa*, ch. 4, "A Day at St Mary's, Bathurst."

177. Ibid., 150.

178. Ibid., ch. 5, "Three Days at Freetown, Sierra-Leone." On Freetown architecture and urbanism, see also S. Kande, *Terre, urbanisme et architecture créoles en Sierra Leone.*

179. Harrell-Bond et al., *Community Leadership.*

180. S. Kande, *Terre, urbanisme et architecture créoles*, and O. Goerg, *Pouvoir colonial, municipalités et espace urbains.*

181. *Royal Gazette and Sierra Leone Advertiser*, May 9, 1818.

182. Peterson, *Province of Freedom*, ch. 8.

183. There were 64,500 inhabitants in 1948, and 85,000 inhabitants in 1965. R. Jarrett, "Some Aspects of the Urban Geography of Freetown, Sierra-Leone," *Geographical Review* 46 (1956): 334 and 351.

184. A. J. G. Wyse, "Kriodom: A Maligned Culture," *Journal of the Historical*

*Society of Sierra-Leone* 3, nos. 1–2 (1979): 37–48; and Wyse, *Searchlight on the Krio of Sierra-Leone. An Ethnographical Study of a West African People* (Freetown: Fourah Bay College, 1980), 16–18 (insightfully commented upon and criticized by Kande).

185. D. E. Skinner and B. E. Harrell-Bond, "Misunderstandings Arising from the Use of the Term Creole in the Literature on Sierra-Leone," *Africa* 47, no. 3 (1977): 318 n. 5.

186. M. Last and P. Richards, eds., *Sierra-Leone 1987–1987. Two Centuries of Intellectual Life* (Manchester: Manchester University Press and International African Institute, 1987).

187. B. E. Harrell-Bond, *Modern Marriage in Sierra-Leone: A Study of the Professional Group* (The Hague: Mouton, 1975).

188. Such events were not exceptional; another example was the *Bonfim* picnic, a festival organized by the Afro-Brazilians of Porto-Novo, halfway between carnival and religious festivity, which has been celebrated at least since the second half of the nineteenth century. Goerg, *Pouvoir colonial*, 1: 250–51.

189. O. Goerg, "Between Everyday Life and Exception: Celebrating Pope Hennessy Day in Freetown, 1872–c. 1905," *Journal of African Cultural Studies* 15, no. 1 (2002): 119–31.

190. Studied at large in Goerg, *Pouvoir colonial*.

191. Even relatively recent works on Liberia pay little attention to the city of Monrovia. G. J. Liebenow, *Liberia: The Quest for Democracy* (Bloomington: Indiana University Press, 1987); T. W. Shick, *Behold the Promised Land. A History of Afro-American Settler Society in Nineteenth Century Liberia* (Baltimore, Md.: The Johns Hopkins University Press, 1980).

192. D. McCall, "Liberia: An Appraisal," *Annals of the American Academy of Political and Social Science* 306 (1956): 90. For a good bibliography on Liberia see D. E. Dunn, *Liberia* (Santa Barbara, Calif.: CLIO Press, 1995).

193. M. Ford, *Ethnic Relations and the Transformations of Leadership among the Dan of Nimba, Liberia* (Ann Arbor, Mich.: University Microfilms International, 1990); A. Konneh, *Indigenous Entrepreneurs and Capitalists: The Role of the Mandingo in the Economic Development of Modern-day Liberia* (Ann Arbor, Mich.: University Microfilms International, 1992).

194. R. Pasquier, *Le Sénégal au milieu du XIXe siècle. La crise économique et sociale* (Thèse d'État, Université Paris-4, 1987) (7 vol.); Pasquier, "Villes du Sénégal," and Pasquier, *Le Sénégal*; C. Camara, *Saint-Louis du Sénégal*; F. Brigaud and J. Vast, *Saint-Louis du Sénégal. Ville aux mille visages*. See useful notations in B. Barry, *Le royaume du Waalo* (1972; Paris: Karthala, 1988); A. Sinou, "Saint-Louis du Sénégal. Du comptoir à la ville," *Cahiers d'Études africaines* 29, nos. 3–4 (115–16) (1987): 377–96; R. Bonnardel, *Saint-Louis. Mort ou naissance?* (Paris: L'Harmattan, 1992).

195. Marie-Thérèse Knight-Baylac, "La vie à Gorée de 1677 à 1789," *Revue française d'Histoire d'Outre-Mer* 57, no. 209 (1970): 377–420.

196. Marie-Thérèse Knight, "Gorée au XVIIIè siècle: l'appropriation du sol," *Revue française d'Histoire d'Outre-Mer* 64, no. 234 (1977): 33–34.

197. Out of the ten other women, only six were mentioned by name, while one was "a free negroe woman" and the last three were "liberated slaves." Among the nine men, two were French traders, one a clerk, and one an interpreter. Ibid., 42.

198. Archives du Dépôt des Fortifications des Colonies, Gorée. B22, quoted in Knight-Baylac, "La vie à Gorée de 1677 à 1789," 35.

199. Dr. Cariou, "Promenade à Gorée" (private manuscript), quoted in ibid.

200. Knight-Baylac, 394.

201. On signares: G. E. Brooks, "The signares of Saint-Louis and Gorée: Women Entrepreneurs in Eighteenth Century Senegal," in *Women in Africa: Studies in Social and Economic Change*, edited by N. Hafkin and E. Bay (Stanford, Calif.: Stanford University Press, 1976), 19–44; J.-P. Biondi, *Saint-Louis du Sénégal*.

202. General instructions to Schmaltz, December 31, 1818. Quoted in H. J. Légier, "Institutions municipales et politique coloniale: les communes du Sénégal," *Revue française d'Histoire d'Outre-Mer* 55, no. 204 (1968): 416.

203. M. Crowder, *Senegal. A Study of French Assimilation Policy* (1962; London: Methuen, 1968).

204. Pasquier, "Villes du Sénégal."

205. Brigaud and Vast, *Saint-Louis du Sénégal*, 45.

206. Most monographs offer an introductory chapter dealing with the nineteenth century. Only a few studies have been written by historians. A. B. Aderibigbe, ed., *Lagos: The Development of an African City*; S. O. Asein, "Literature and Society in Lagos"; P.A. Baker, *Urbanization and Political Change. The Politics of Lagos 1917–1967* (Berkeley: University of California Press, 1974); S. T. Barnes, *Patrons and Power. Creating a Political Continuity in Metropolitan Lagos* (Bloomington: International African Institute/Indiana University Press, 1986); P. Cole, *Modern and Traditional Elites in the Politics of Lagos*; T. S. Gale, "The History of British Colonial Neglect of Traditional African Cities," *African Urban Studies* 5 (1979): 11–24; A. G. Hopkins, "The Lagos Strike of 1897," *Past and Present* 35 (1979): 135–55; Hopkins, "Imperialism in Lagos, 1880–1892"; Hopkins, "Property Rights and Empire Building"; E. Krapf-Askari, *Yoruba Towns and Cities*; Mabogunje, *Urbanization in Nigeria*; R. Law, "Trade and Politics Behind the Slave Coast"; M. Peil, *Lagos. The City Is the People* (London: Belhaven Press, 1991); K. Mann, "The Birth of a Colonial City. Trade, Credit and Land in Nineteenth Century Lagos," Symposium on New Perspectives on Colonial Africa, University of Illinois, Urbana-Champaign, 1987.

207. Cf. P. A. Baker, *Urbanization and Political Change*; S. T. Barnes, *Patrons and Power*, and P. Cole, *Modern and Traditional Elites*.

208. Hopkins, "Imperialism in Lagos."

209. The first census was conducted in 1866. Cited in Mabogunje, *Urbanization in Nigeria*, 242–44.

210. S. Adesina, "The Development of Western Education," in *Lagos: The Development of an African City*, edited by A. B. Aderibigbe, 126–27.

211. *Report*, October 18, 1924. Colonial Office of West Africa. Public Record Office CO 586/128.

212. J. Western, *Outcast Cape Town* (Minneapolis: University of Minnesota Press, 1981), ch. 2, "Cape Town before Apartheid."

213. N. C. Pollock, "The Development of Urbanization in Southern Africa," in *Urbanization and Its Problems*, edited by R. P. Beckinsale and J. M. Houston (New York: Barnes and Noble, 1968), 308.

214. *Records of the Cape Colony from February 1793 [to April 1831]. Copied for the Cape Government, from the manuscript documents in the Public Record Office* (London: Printed for the Government of the Cape Colony, 1897–1905), 6:72 and 6:180; R. Elphick and G. Giliome, eds., *The Shaping of South African Society 1652–1820* (Cape Town and London: Longman, 1979); R. Ross, "Cape-Town (1750–1850)."

215. R. Ross, "The Occupation of Slaves in Eighteenth Century Cape-Town," in *Studies in the History of Cape-Town*, edited by C. Saunders, vol. 2.

216. J. Amstrong, "The Slaves, 1652–1780," in Elphick and Giliomee, *The Shaping of South African Society*, 76–79; J. M. Postma, *The Dutch in the Atlantic Slave Trade 1600–1815* (Cambridge: Cambridge University Press, 1990), 111–12.

217. M. F. Valkhoff, *Studies in Portuguese and Creole; with Special Reference to South Africa* (Johannesburg: Witwatersrand University Press, 1966), 146–241.

218. R. Shell, "The Establishment and Spread of Islam at the Cape from the Beginning of Company Rule to 1838" (honours thesis, University of Cape Town, 1974).

219. S. Judges, "Poverty, Living Conditions and Social Relations—Aspects of Life in Cape Town in the 1830s" (M.A. thesis, University of Cape Town, 1977).

220. H. Philips, "Cape Town in 1829," in *Studies in the History of Cape Town*, edited by Saunders, 3:8.

221. Ross, "Cape Town 1750–1850," 115. C. Pama, *Bowler's Cape Town*.

222. *The Buildings of Central Cape Town* (Cape Town: Cape Provincial Institute of Architects, 1978), 10; Pollock, "The Development of Urbanization in Southern Africa," 308.

223. In comparison, Durban was slow to develop. Founded in 1824 as Port

Natal, in 1835 it was given the name of a governor of the Cape Colony. Before 1828, when the Boers (former Dutch settlers) began to prevail, it was a tiny trading post that was more or less controlled by the Zulus. The British made Natal a colony in 1844. Durban remained a small town; it had fewer than four thousand inhabitants in 1870. The colony's only sources of wealth were sugarcane plantations. Only in 1910, when a unified Federation was created, did it open the Rand to the sea.

224. R. F. M. Immelman, *Men of Good Hope. The Romantic Story of the Cape Town Chamber of Commerce* (Cape Town: Cape Town Chamber of Commerce, 1955).

225. Western, *Outcast Cape Town*, 33.

## Conclusion

1. The best-known introduction to this idea is P. Bohannan and G. Dalton, eds., *Markets in Africa* (Evanston, Ill.: Northwestern University Press, 1963).

2. P. Bairoch, *De Jericho à Mexico*. See also J. Desmond Clark and S. A. Brandt, eds., *From Hunters to Farmers: The Causes and Consequences of Food Production in Africa* (Berkeley: University of California Press, 1984).

3. L. Mumford, *The City in History*, 410–11.

4. G. Duby, *Histoire de la France urbaine*, introduction to vol. 1.

5. M. Griaule, *Dieu d'eau* (1948: Paris: Fayard, 1966), 92–94.

6. Lebeuf, *Archéologie tchadienne*, 75–87.

7. A. Margarido, "La capitale de l'Empire Lunda," 857–91, quoting Henrique Augusto Dias de Carvalho, *Ethnographia e historia tradicional dos povos da Lunda* (Lisbon: Impresa nacional, 1890). Margarido suggests another possible explanation, referring to the design of an army on the move.

8. C. Winters, "The Classification of Traditional African Cities."

9. E. Mwohora, *Peuples et rois de l'Afrique des grands lacs*, 116–25.

10. C. Tardits, *Le royaume Bamoum*, ch. 13.

11. P. Lloyd, "The Yoruba: An Urban People?" in *Urban Anthropology*, edited by A. W. Southall, 107–23.

12. M. Weber, *La ville* (Paris: Aubier Montaigne, 1947), 21–24.

13. M. J. Daunton, "Towns and Economic Growth in Eighteenth Century England," in *Towns in Society*, edited by P. Abrams and E. A. Wrigley, 245–78; Wrigley, "Parasite or Stimulus: The Town in a Pre-Industrial Economy" in ibid., 295–310. On African cities: B. F. Hoselitz, "Generative and Parasitic Cities."

14. V. Gordon Childe, "Civilization, Cities and Towns," 36–37.

15. Duby, "La ville médiévale," in *Histoire urbaine*, 2:14.

16. G. Bois, *La mutation de l'an mil. Lournand, village mâconnais de l'Antiquité au féodalisme* (Paris: Fayard, 1989).

17. F. Cooper, ed., 1983. *Struggle for the City. Migrant Labor, Capital and the State in Urban Africa* (London: Sage, 1989), introduction.

18. G. Sjoberg, *The Preindustrial City*.

19. H. Pirenne, *Les villes et les institutions urbaines*.

20. S. M. Blumin, "When Villages Become Towns. The Historical Contexts of Town Formation" in *The Pursuit of Urban History*, edited by Frazer and Sutcliffe, 54–68.

21. On a dialectical relationship between structure, process, and rupture, which is the very basis of historical thinking, see Bois' conclusion, *La mutation*, 248–58.

22. L. Plotnicov, *Strangers to the City*.

23. T. C. McGee, *The Urbanization Process in the Third World*, 171–72.

24. A. Mabogunje, *Urbanization*, ch. 2; E. Krapf-Aspari, *Yoruba Towns and Cities*; Samuel Johnson, *The History of the Yorubas: From the Earliest Times to the Beginning of the British Protectorate* [1897], edited by Obadiah Johnson (1921; reprint, Westport, Conn.: Negro University Press, 1970), must not be forgotten, especially p. 281. The Yoruba colonialism theory was proposed again by J. D. Fage, *A History of Africa* (1978; rev. ed., New York: Routledge, 2001), 102–104.

25. Cf. A. Robert, "Towards a History of Urbanization in Precolonial Yorubaland," in *African Historical Demography*, vol. 1 (Edinburgh, 1977), 260–71.

26. I. Wilks, "The Northern Factor in Ashanti History," 26.

27. R. A. Kea, *Settlements, Trade and Polities in the Seventeenth Century*, ch. 2, "Urban Networks and Central Places."

28. R. Ross and J. Telkamp, *Colonial Cities*, introduction.

29. H. Brunschwig, *Noirs et blancs dans l'Afrique noire française, ou Comment le colonisé devint colonisateur, 1870–1914* (Paris: Flammarion, 1983).

30. From the beginning of colonialism, migrants mainly converged toward urban centers, except for a few areas where there were European or African plantations. Mining compounds, public works (railway stations, harbors), and administrative centers absorbed most of them. C. Coquery-Vidrovitch, *Africa South of the Sahara. Endurance and Change* (Berkeley: University of California Press, 1987), section 4, ch. 10.

31. The "informal sector" is a concept created by the International Labor Office (ILO) in 1971. But the process existed long before, as has been pointed out by a few researchers. See J. Iliffe, *The African Poor*, chs. 2, 6, and 7.

32. Jean Comaroff first introduced a method of historical cultural anthropol-

ogy to study how modes of thinking changed in Tswanaland long before colonialism occurred: missionaries' messages opened people's minds to westernized thoughts from the beginning of the nineteenth century. Comaroff, *Body of Power, Spirit of Resistance. The Culture and History of a South African People* (Chicago: University of Chicago Press, 1985). Later, the analysis was enlarged: Jean Comaroff and John Comaroff, *Of Revelation and Revolution. Christianity, Colonialism and Consciousness in South Africa* (Chicago: University of Chicago Press, 1991).

33. K. Barber, "Popular Arts in Africa," *African Studies Review* 30, no. 3 (1987): 23–32. Today, these intercultural mixed influences explode as urban arts. S. Vogel, ed., *Africa Explorers. Twentieth Century African Art* (New York: Center for African Art, 1991); B. Jewsiewicki, *Mami Wata. La peinture urbaine au Congo* (Paris: Gallimard, 2003).

# Bibliography

This bibliographical survey does not mention all the titles detailed in the endnotes. A number of specialized articles or books that are not readily available or that do not actually focus on the topic of this study were omitted; in these cases the notes include complete references. Archival materials, printed or not printed, are also omitted. Except for a few major studies dealing with general urban history, such as the *General History of Africa* (UNESCO), basic books and collections are not mentioned: these references can be found in many handbooks on Africa. This bibliography focuses on books and major articles dealing specifically with urban African history, particularly precolonial urban history south of the Sahara.

## Listed by Title

*Allo specchio della storia: l'eredità coloniale. Brazzaville 1880–1960.* Torino: AGIP. Recherches Congo, 1990.

"Centenario da cidade de Maputo 1887–1987 (especial)," and "Obras sobre a cidade de Maputo existentes no arquivo historico de Moçambique (supplemento)." *Arquivo, Boletim de Arquivo Historico de Moçambique* (1987): 174 and 207.

*Cités-mémoires du désert. Campagne internationale pour la sauvegarde des villes anciennes de Mauritanie.* Paris: UNESCO, 1989.

*Cities of the Savannah (A History of Some Towns and Cities of the Nigerian Savannah)*. Zaria: Nigeria Magazine and Ahmadu Bello University, ca. 1975.

"Ilha de Moçambique. Nos 170 anos de fundação da primeira cidade de Moçambique." *Arquivo. Boletim do Arquivo Historico do Moçambique* 4 (1988, especial).

*Ilha de Moçambique. Relatorio/Report*. Aarhus, Denmark: Arkitekskolen, 1982.

*Ouidah et son patrimoine*. Paris-Cotonou: ORSTOM/SERHAU, 1991.

*Periplus Maris Erythraei*, edited and translated by L. Casson. Princeton, N.J.: Princeton University Press, 1989.

"Sociétés urbaines en Égypte et au Soudan." *Cahier de Recherches de l'Institut de Papyrologie et d'Egyptologie de Lille* (1986, special issue).

*Trésors cachés du vieux Lomé. L'architecture populaire ancienne de la capitale du Togo*. Lomé: Centre culturel français/ORSTOM, 1991.

"Villes africaines." *Cahiers d'Études Africaines* 13 (1973, special issue): 397–605.

"Villes africaines au microscope." *Cahiers d'Études Africaines* 21 (1–3), nos. 81–83 (1981, special issue): 1–404.

## Listed by Author

Abitbol, M. *Tombouctou et les Arma. De la conquête marocaine (1591) à l'hégémonie de l'Empire Peul du Macina en 1832*. Paris: Maisonneuve and Larose, 1979.

———. *Tombouctou au milieu du 18ᵉ siècle d'après la chronique de Mawlay al-Qasim B. Mawlay Sulayman* [translated and annotated]. Paris: Maisonneuve and Larose, 1982.

Abrams, P., and E. A. Wrigley, eds. *Towns in Society*. Cambridge: Cambridge University Press, 1978.

Acquah, I. *Accra Survey*. Accra: Ghana University Press, 1972.

Adams, M., L. Prussin, et al. "Traditional Asante Architecture." *African Arts* 13 (1980): 57–65, 79–82, 85–87.

Adande, A. "Abomey, Joyau d'un humanisme nègre." *Brousse* 4 (1953): 17–20.

Aderibigbe, A. B., ed. *Lagos: The Development of an African City*. Lagos: Longman, 1975.

Agbanon, F., II. *Histoire de Petit-Popo et du royaume Guin (1934)*. Lomé/Paris: Karthala/Haho, 1991.

Agbo, C. *Histoire de Ouidah du 16ᵉ au 18ᵉ siècles*. Avignon: Presses Universelles, 1959.

Agbola, T. "City Profile: Kaduna." *Cities* 3, no. 4 (1986): 282–89.

Akindele, A., and C. Aguessy. *Contribution à l'étude de l'histoire de l'ancien royaume de Porto-Novo*. Dakar: Mémoire de l'IFAN, nº 25, 1953.

Akinsemoyin, K., and A. Vaughan-Richards. *Building Lagos*. Lagos: F. and A. Service, 1976.

Akorede, V. E. A. "The Impact of Socio-cultural Changes on the Patterns of Urban Land Use: The Case of Ilorin. *African Urban Studies* 5 (1979): 71–84.

Alagoa, E. J., and A. Fombo. *A Chronicle of Grand Bonny*. Nigeria: Onyoma Research Publications, 2000.

Alencastro, Felipe de L. *O trato dos viventes [A History of Angola]*. São Paulo: Ed. Companhia das Letras, 2000.

Allen, J. de V. "Swahili Culture and the Nature of East Coast Settlement." *International Journal of African Historical Studies* 14, no. 2 (1981): 306–34.

———. *The "Shirazi" Problem in East African Coastal History*. Wiesbaden: Paideuma, 1981.

———. *Origins: Swahili Culture and the Shungwaya Phenomenon*. London: J. Currey; Nairobi: EAEP; Athens: Ohio University Press, 1993.

Alpers, E. *Ivory and Slaves. Changing Patterns of International Trade in East Central Africa in the Later Nineteenth Century*. Berkeley: University of California Press, 1975.

Alquier, P. "Saint-Louis du Sénégal pendant la Révolution et l'Empire (1789–1809)." *Bulletin du Comité d'Études historiques et scientifiques de l'AOF* 5 (1922): 277–320 and 411–63.

Amaral, I. de. *Luanda (Estudo de geografia urbana)*. Lisbon: Junta de Investigaçoes do Ultramar, 1968.

Amborn, H. "Die Problematik des Eisenverhüttung im Teiche Meroe." *Paideuma* 16, nos. 10–11 (1970): 71–95.

Ambrose, D. *Maseru: An Illustrated History*. Morija: Lesotho, 1993.

Amin, S., and D. Forde, eds. *Modern Migrations in Western Africa*. Oxford: Oxford University Press/International African Institute, 1974.

Amselle, J.-L. *Les négociants de la savane*. Paris: Anthropos, 1977.

Amselle, J.-L., ed. *Les migrations africaines. Réseaux et processus migratoires*. Paris: Maspero, 1976.

Anderson, D. M., and R. Rathbone, eds. *Africa's Urban Past*. Oxford: James Currey; Portsmouth, N.H.: Heinemann, 2000.

Angius, M., and M. Zamponi. *Ilha de Moçambique. Convergência de povos e culturas*. Saint Marin: AIEP editore, 1999.

Anignikin, S. C., and M. B. Anignikin. "Étude sur l'évolution historique, sociale et spatiale de la ville d'Abomey." In *Projet Plans d'urbanisme en République populaire du Bénin*. Paris: Urbanor, 1986.

Anthony, D. H. I. *Culture and Society in a Town in Transition: A People's History of Dar es Salaam, 1865–1939*. Madison: University of Wisconsin Press, 1983.

Arhin, K. "The Structure of Greater Ashanti (1700–1824)." *Journal of African History* 8, no. 1 (1967): 65–85.

———. "Transit Markets in the Asante Hinterland in the Late Nineteenth Century." *Odu* 9 (1974): 5–22.

Asein, S. O. "Literature and Society in Lagos (late 19th–early 20th Century)." *Nigeria Magazine* nos. 117–18 (1975): 22–32.

Awambeng, C. M. *Evolution and Growth of Urban Centres in the North-West Province (Cameroon). Case studies (Bamenda, Kumbo, Mbengwi, Nkambe, Wum)*. Bern and Frankfurt: European University Studies, 1991.

Bah, T. M. *Architecture militaire traditionnelle dans le Soudan occidental, XIIᵉ –XIXᵉ siècles*. Paris: CEA/ACCT, 1985.

Bairoch, P. *De Jericho à Mexico. Villes et Économies dans l'Histoire*. Paris: Gallimard, 1985.

Bakari, K. "L'Afrique occidentale précoloniale et le fait urbain." *Bulletin de l'IFAN-B* 22 (1958).

Baker, J., ed. *Rural-Urban Dynamics in Francophone Africa*. Uppsala: Nordiska Afrikainstitutet, 1997.

Balandier, G. *Daily Life in the Kingdom of the Kongo from the Sixteenth to the Eighteenth Century.* New York: Pantheon Books, 1968.

———. *Sociologie des Brazzavilles noires.* Paris: Presses des Sciences Politiques, 1985.

Ballong-Wen-Mewuda, J. B. *Saint-Georges-de-la-Mine (1482–1637): la vie d'un comptoir portugais en Afrique occidentale.* Lisbon and Paris: Foundation Gulbenkian/EHESS, 1994.

Banton, M. P. *West African City. A Study of Tribal Life in Freetown.* London: IAI and Oxford University Press, 1957.

Barber, K. *I Could Speak Until Tomorrow. Oriki, Women, and the Past in a Yoruba Town.* Washington, D.C.: Smithsonian Institution Press, 1991.

Barkindo, B. M., ed. *Studies in the History of Kano.* Kano, Nigeria: Heineman, 1983.

Barnes, S. T. *The Urban Frontier in West Africa: Mushin, Nigeria.* Bloomington and Indianapolis: Indiana University Press, 1989.

Barros, P. de. "The Iron Industry of Bassar." Ph.D. dissertation, University of California, Los Angeles, 1985.

Bascom, W. R. "Urbanization among the Yoruba." *American Journal of Sociology* 60, no. 5 (1955): 446–54.

———. "Urbanism as a Traditional African Pattern." *Sociological Review* 7 (1959): 29–43.

———. "Some Aspects of Yoruba Urbanism." *American Anthropologist* 64 (1962): 699–709.

Basham, R. *Urban Anthropology. The Cross-cultural Study of Complex Societies.* Palo Alto, Calif.: Mayfield Publishing, 1978.

Beach, D. N. *The Shona and Zimbabwe 900–1850.* London: Heinemann, 1980.

Becher, J. *Dar es Salaam, Tanga und Tabora: Stadtentwicklung in Tanzania unter deutscher Kolonialherrschaft (1885–1914).* Stuttgart: Franz Steiner Verlag, 1997.

Benet, F. "Sociology Uncertain: The Ideology of the Rural–Urban Continuum." *Comparative Studies in Society and History. An International Quarterly* 6, no. 1 (1963): 1–23.

Benjaminsen, T. A., and Berge, G. *Une histoire de Tombouctou.* Paris: Actes Sud, 2004 (translated from Norwegian).

Berbain, S. *Le comptoir français de Juda au XVIIIᵉ siècle*. Dakar: Mémoire de l'IFAN, n° 3, 1942.

Berg, F. J. "The Swahili Community of Mombasa, 1500–1900." *Journal of African History* 9, no. 1 (1968): 35–56.

Bernus, S. *Particularismes ethniques en milieu urbain: l'exemple de Niamey.* Paris: Institut d'Ethnologie, Musée de l'Homme, 1969.

Berry, B. J. L., ed. *Urbanization and Counterurbanization*. London: Sage, 1976.

Betts, R. F. *Dakar, Ville impériale (1857–1960)*. Leiden: Martinus Nijhof for the Leiden University Press, 1985.

Béti, M. (Éza Boto). *Ville cruelle*. Paris: Présence Africaine, 1954.

Bickford-Smith, V. *Ethnic Pride and Racial Prejudice in Victorian Cape Town*. London and New York: Cambridge University Press, 1995.

Biobaku, S. O. "An Historical Sketch of Egba Traditional Authorities." *Africa* 22 (1952): 35–49.

Biondi, J.-P. *Saint-Louis du Sénégal, mémoires d'un métissage*. Paris: Denoël, 1987.

Bivar, A. D. H., and P. L. Shinnie. "Old Kanuri Capitals." *Journal of African History* 3, no. 1 (1962): 1–10.

Bler, S. P. *The Anatomy of Architecture: Ontology and Metaphor in Batammaliba Architectural Expression*. New York: Cambridge University Press, 1987.

Blévin, C., and J. Bouczo, 1997. "Nairobi: un siècle d'histoire (1898–1997)." *Les Cahiers de l'IFRA (Institut français d'Afrique noire)* (5): 64.

Bolande, A. "Militarism and Economic Development in Nineteenth Century Yoruba Country: The Ibadan Example." *Journal of African History* 14, no. 1 (1973): 65–78.

Boutillier, J.-L. *La ville de Bouna de l'époque précoloniale à aujourd'hui*. Paris: ORSTOM, 1972.

———. *Bouna, royaume de la savane ivoirienne. Princes, marchands et paysans*. Paris: Karthala/ORSTOM, 1993.

Bozzoli, B., ed. *Town and Countryside in the Transvaal*. Johannesburg: Ravan Press, 1983.

Brasio, A. *Histoire du Royaume du Congo (c.1624)*. Louvain and Paris: Nauwelaerts, 1972.

Brasseur, G., and P. Brasseur-Marion. *Porto-Novo et sa palmeraie*. Dakar: IFAN, 1953.

Braudel, F. *Towns*. London: Longman, 1976.

Brian, Y., and T. Raftopoulos. *Sites of Struggle. Essays in Zimbabwe's Urban History*. Harare: Weaver Press, 1999.

Bricker, G., and S. Traore, *Transitional Urbanization in Upper Volta: The Case of Ouagadougou, a Savannah Capital*. New York: Praeger, 1979.

Brigaud, F., and J. Vast. *Saint-Louis du Sénégal, ville aux mille visages*. Dakar: Clairafrique, 1987.

Brokensha, D. *Social Change at Larteh, Ghana*. Oxford: Clarendon Press, 1966.

Brown, B. B. "Muslim Influence on Trade and Politics in the Lake Tanganyika Region." *African Historical Studies* 4, no. 3 (1971): 617–29.

———. "Ujiji. The History of a Lakeside Town 1800–1914." Ph.D. dissertation, Boston University, 1972.

Brown, James Wilson. "Kumasi 1896–1923: Urban Africa during the Early Colonial Period." *African Urban Studies* 1 (1978): 57–66.

Brown, W. T. "Bagamoyo. An Historical Introduction." *Tanzania Notes and Records* 71 (1970): 69–83.

———. "The Politics of Business: Relations between Zanzibar and Bagamoyo in the Late Nineteenth Century." *African Historical Studies* 4, no. 3 (1971): 631–43.

———. *Bagamoyo*. Boston: Boston University, 1972.

Burstein, Stanley, ed. *Ancient African Civilizations: Kush and Axum*. Princeton: Markus Wiener, 1997.

Burton, Andrew, ed.. *The Urban Experience In Eastern Africa c. 1750–2000*. Nairobi: British Institute in Eastern Africa, 2002.

Burton, R. F. *Wanderings in West Africa from Liverpool to Fernando Po*. London: Tinsley Brothers, 1863.

———. *Zanzibar. City, Island and Coast*. London: Tinsley Brothers, 1872.

Busia, K. A. *Report on a Social Survey of Sekondi-Takoradi*. Accra: Crown Agents for the Colonies, Government of Gold Coast, 1950.

Cahen, Michel, ed. *Bourgs et villes en Afrique lusophone*. Paris: L'Harmattan, 1989.

Calas, B. *Kampala. La ville et la violence (1880–1993).* Paris: Karthala/ Institut français de Recherches africaines, 1998.

Caldwell, J. C. *Population Growth and Family Change in Africa. The New Elite in Ghana.* London: Hurst, 1968.

———. *African Rural–Urban Migration: The Movement to Ghana's Towns.* Canberra: ANU Press; London: Hurst, 1969.

Callaway, A. "Nigeria's Indigenous Education: The Apprenticeship System." *Odu* 1, no. 1 (1964): 62–79.

Callaway, B. J. *Muslim Hausa Women in Nigeria: Tradition and Change.* Syracuse, N.Y.: Syracuse University Press, 1987.

Camara, C. *Saint-Louis du Sénégal.* Dakar: IFAN, 1968.

———. "Une ville précoloniale au Nigeria: Ondo." *Cahiers d'Études Africaines* 51 (1973): 417–41.

Carter, H. "Urban Origins: A Review." *Progress in Human Geography* 1 (1977): 12–32.

Castells, M. *The Urban Question. A Marxist Approach.* London: Edward Arnold, 1977.

Castro, Henriques I. *Espaços e cidades em Moçambique.* Lisbon: Comissaõ nacional para as Comemorações dos Descobrimentos Portugueses, 1998.

Champaud, J. *Villes et campagnes du Cameroun de l'Ouest.* Paris: ORSTOM, 1983.

Charpy, J. *La fondation de Dakar.* Paris: Larose, 1958.

Chami, F., and G. Pwiti. *Southern Africa and the Swahili World.* Dar es Salaam: Dar es Salaam University Press, 2002.

Chemain, R. *La Ville dans le roman africain.* Paris: L'Harmattan, 1981.

Childe, V. G. "The Urban Revolution." *Town Planning Review* 21, no. 1 (1950): 3–17.

———. "Civilization, Cities and Towns." *Antiquity* 121 (1957): 36–38.

Chirot, D. "Urban and Rural Economies in the Western Sudan: Birni N'Konni and Its Hinterland." *Cahiers d'Études Africaines* 8 no. 4 (1968): 547–65.

Chittick, H. Neville. "Kilwa and the Arab Settlement of the East African Coast." In *Papers in African Prehistory,* edited by Fage and Oliver. Cambridge: Cambridge University Press, 1970.

———. *The Shirazi Colonization of East Africa.* Cambridge: Cambridge University Press, 1970.

———. *Kilwa. An Islamic Trading City on the East African Coast. I. History and Archaeology.* Vol. 2, *The Finds.* Nairobi: British Institute in Eastern Africa, 1974.

———. "Medieval Mogadishu." *Paideuma* 28 (1982): 44–46.

———. "Manda: Excavations at an Island Port on the Kenya Coast." Nairobi: British Institute in Eastern Africa, 1984.

Chittick, H. N., and R. I. Rotberg, eds. *East Africa and the Orient. Cultural Syntheses in Precolonial Times.* London and New York: Africana Publishing, 1975.

Chrétien, Jean-Pierre. *The Great Lakes of Africa: Two Thousand Years of History.* New York: Zone Books, 2003.

Christopher, A. J. "Continuity and Change of African Capitals." *Geographical Review* 75, no. 1 (1985): 44–57.

Christopher, G. *Urbanization, Rural to Urban Migration and Development Policies in the Ivory Coast.* New York: Praeger, 1979.

Cissoko, Sekene Mody. "L'intelligentsia de Tombouctou aux XV–XVIe siècles." *Présence Africaine* 72 (1969): 48–72.

———. *Tombouctou et l'Empire Songhay.* Dakar-Abidjan: Nouvelles Éditions Africaines 1975.

Clément, C. "Espaces de vie, espaces en ville. Parcours migratoires, représentations et pratiques de l'espace urbain à Niamey." Doctorat ès sciences économiques, Université Lyon-II, Lyon, 2000.

Cohen, A. *Customs and Politics in Urban Africa. A Study of Hausa Migrants in Yoruba Towns.* London: Routledge and Kegan Paul, 1969.

Cohen, M. A. *Urban Policy and Political Conflict in Africa. A Study of the Ivory Coast.* Chicago: University of Chicago Press, 1974.

Cole, P. *Modern and Traditional Elites in the Politics of Lagos.* Cambridge: Cambridge University Press, 1975.

Connah, Graham. "New Light on the Benin City Walls." *Journal of the Historical Society of Nigeria* 3 (1968): 15–20.

———. *The Archaeology of Benin: Excavations and Other Researches in and around Benin City, Nigeria.* London: Oxford University Press, 1975.

————. *African Civilizations. Precolonial Cities and States in Tropical Africa: An Archaeological Perspective.* Cambridge: Cambridge University Press, 1987. Rev. ed. 2001.

————. *Forgotten Africa: An Introduction to Its Archaeology.* London: Routledge, 2004.

Conrad, D. C. "A Town Called Dakalajan: The Sunjata Tradition and the Question of Ancient Mali's capital." *Journal of African History* 35, no. 3 (1994): 355–78.

Coquery-Vidrovitch, C. "Villes coloniales et histoire des Africains." *Vingtième siècle. Revue d'Histoire* 20 (1988): 47–68.

————. "The Process of Urbanization in Africa. From the Origins to the Beginning of Independence. An Overview Paper." *African Studies Review* 34, no. 1 (1991): 1–98.

————. "Villes africaines anciennes: une civilisation mercantile pré-négrière dans l'ouest africain, XVIème et XVIIème siècles." *Annales* 6 (1991): 62–77.

————. *Histoire des villes africaines des origines à la colonisation.* Paris: Albin Michel, 1993.

————. "La ville coloniale: lieu de colonisation et métissage culturel." *Afrique contemporaine* 168 (1993): 11–22.

Coquery-Vidrovitch, Catherine, ed. *Histoire des villes et des sociétés urbaines en Afrique noire. 1. Les villes précoloniales.* Cahier Afrique noire 5. Paris: L'Harmattan, 1982.

————, ed. *Processus d'urbanisation en Afrique.* 2 vols. Paris: L'Harmattan, 1988.

Correia Lopes, E. C. *São João Batista de Ajuda.* Lisbon: Agência Geral das Colónias, 1939.

Courrèges, G. *Grand Bassam et les comptoirs de la côte.* Clermont-Ferrand: L'Instant durable, 1987.

Cousins, W. E. "The Great Hova City." *The Antanarivo Annual and Madagascar Magazine* 4, no. 3 (1891): 368–73.

Coutouly, de F. "Timbo la morte." *Afrique française* 10 (1912): 406–409.

————. "Une ville soudanaise de la Haute-Volta." *Bulletin du Comité des Études Historiques et Scientifiques de l'AOF* (1926): 487–97.

Cox, Oliver C. "The Preindustrial City Reconsidered." *Sociological Quarterly* 5 (1964): 133–47.

Crossland, L. B. *Pottery from the Begho-B2 Site, Ghana.* Calgary: University of Calgary Press, 1989.

Crummey, D. "Some Precursors of Addis Abäba: Towns in Christian Ethiopia in the Eighteenth and Nineteenth Centuries." Revised paper (originally presented to the International Symposium on the African Horn of Africa, Cairo, January 1985), New Trends in Colonial History, University of Illinois at Champaign-Urbana, April 1987.

Culot, M., and J.-M. Thiveaud, eds. *Architectures françaises outre-mer. Abidjan, Bangui, Brazzaville, Conakry, Dakar, Libreville, Niamey, Ouagadougou, Tananarive, Yaoundé.* . . . Liège: Pierre Mandaga, 1992.

Cunha, Mariano Carneiro da. *Da Senzala ao Sobrado. Arquitetura Brasileira na Nigéria e na República Popular do Benim (From Slave Quarters to Town Houses. Brazilian Architecture in Nigeria and the People's Republic of Benin).* São Paolo: Nobel Edusp, 1985.

Cunha, Manuela Carneiro da. *Negros, Estrangeiros: os escravos libertos e sua volta à Africa.* São Paolo: Nobel Edusp, 1986.

Cuoq, J. *Recueil des sources arabes concernant l'Afrique occidentale du VIIIᵉ au XVIᵉ siècle.* Paris: Éditions du CNRS, 1975.

Curle, A. J. "The Ruined Towns of Somaliland." *Antiquity* 11 (1937): 315–27.

Curtin, P. "African Enterprise in the Mangrove Trade: The Case of Lamu." In *Entreprises et Entrepreneurs en Afrique, XIXᵉ et XXᵉ siècles,* edited by C. Coquery-Vidrovitch, 1:129–40. Paris: L'Harmattan, 1983.

Daunton, W. J. *Towns and Economic Growth in Eighteenth Century England.* Cambridge: Cambridge University Press, 1978.

David, P. *Maradi. L'ancien État et l'ancienne ville.* Niamey and Bordeaux: Institut de recherches nigériennes, IFAN, 1964.

Davidson, B. *The Lost Cities of Africa.* Boston: Little Brown, 1970. First published in 1969 as *Old Africa Rediscovered.*

Davies, D. H. "Harare, Zimbabwe: Origins, Development and Post-Colonial Change." *African Urban Quarterly* 1, no. 2 (1986): 131–38.

Davies, K. "The Urbanization of the Human Population." *Scientific American* 213, no. 3 (1965): 41–63.

DeCorse, C. R. *An Archaeology of Elmina: Africans and Europeans on the Gold Coast, 1400–1900.* Washington, D.C.: Smithsonian Institution Press, 2001.

Deffontaine, Y. *Guerre et société au royaume de Fetu. Ghana 1471–1720. Des débuts du commerce atlantique à la constitution de la fédération fanti.* Ibadan: IFRA-Karthala, 1993.

Delcourt, J. *La turbulente histoire de Gorée.* Dakar: Editions Clairafrique, 1982.

———. *Naissance et croissance de Dakar.* Dakar: Clairafrique, 1983.

Denis, J. "Les Villes d'Afrique tropicale." *Civilisations* 16 (1966): 22–44.

———. *Le Phénomène urbain en Afrique centrale.* Brussels: Mémoires de l'Académie royale des sciences coloniales, 1968.

Denyer, S. *African Traditional Architecture: An Historical and Geographical Perspective.* London: Heinemann, 1978.

Deroure, F. "La vie quotidienne à Saint-Louis par ses archives (1779–1809)." *Bulletin de l'IFAN-B* 26 (1964): 397–439.

Devisse, J. "L'apport de l'archéologie à l'histoire de l'Afrique occidentale entre le Vᵉ et le XIIᵉ siècle." *Comptes rendus de l'Académie des Inscriptions et Belles-Lettres* (1982): 156–77.

———. "Histoire et tradition urbaine au Sahel." In *Lectures de la ville africaine contemporaine. Transformations de l'architecture dans le monde islamique.* Singapore: Concept Media Pte Ltd., 1983.

Devisse, J., ed., *Recherches sur Aoudaghost,* vol. 3, *Campagne 1960–1965.* Paris: Recherches sur les Civilisations, 1983.

Devisse, Jean, Denise Robert, and Serge Robert. *Tegdaoust-I. Recherches sur Aoudaghost.* Paris: Arts et Métiers Graphiques, 1970.

Dickson, K. B. "Evolution of Seaports in Ghana: 1800–1908." *Annals of the Association of American Geographers* 55, no. 1 (1965): 96–111.

Dihoff, G. *Katsina, Profile of a Nigerian City.* New York: Praeger, 1970.

Dike, A. A. *Misconceptions of African Urbanism: Some Euro-American Notions.* New York: Praeger, 1979.

Diop, A. B. *Société Toucouleur et Migration.* Dakar: IFAN, 1965.

Domian, S. *Architecture soudanaise. Vitalité d'une tradition urbaine et monumentale. Mali, Côte d'Ivoire, Burkina Faso, Ghana.* Paris: L'Harmattan, 1989.

Dramani-Issifou, Z. "Islam et société dans l'Empire Songhaï: sur quelques aspects des relations entre Gao et Tombouctou aux XV<sup>e</sup>–XVI<sup>e</sup> siècles d'après les Ta'rikh soudanais." *L'Information historique* 45 (1983): 244–52.

Driver, F., and D. Gilbert, eds. *Imperial Cities: Landscape, Display and Identity*. Manchester, U.K.: Manchester University Press, 1999.

Du Toit, Brian M., and Helen I. Safa, eds. *Migration and Urbanization. Models and Adaptative Strategies*. Paris and The Hague: Mouton, 1975.

Dubois, F. *Tombouctou la Mystérieuse*. Paris: Flammarion, 1897.

Duby, G. "Les pauvres des campagnes dans l'Occident médiéval jusqu'au XIII<sup>e</sup> siècle." *Revue d'Histoire de l'Église de France* 52 (1966): 25–32.

————, ed. *Histoire de la France urbaine*. Paris: Seuil, 1980.

Dunn, J., and A. F. Robertson. *Dependence and Opportunity. Political Change in Ahafo*. Cambridge: Cambridge University Press, 1973.

Dutto, C. A. *Nyeri Townsmen, Kenya*. Nairobi: East African Literature Bureau, 1975.

Eastman, C. M. "Women, Slaves and Foreigners: African Cultural Influences and Group Processes in the Formation of Northern Swahili Coastal Society." *International Journal of African Historical Studies* 21, no. 1 (1988): 1–20.

Edwards, D. N. "Meroe and the Sudanic Kingdoms." *Journal of African History* 39, no. 2 (1998): 175–94.

Ehret, C. *The Civilizations of Africa: A History to 1800*. Charlottesville: University Press of Virginia, 2002.

El-Bushra, El-S. "Towns in the Sudan in the Eighteenth and Early Nineteenth Centuries." *Sudan Notes and Records* 52 (1971): 63–70.

————. *Urbanization in the Sudan*. Khartoum: Philosophical Society of the Sudan, 1972.

El-Shaks, S., and R. A. Obudho, eds. *Urbanization, National Development and Regional Planning in Africa*. New York: Praeger, 1974.

Ela, J. M. *La ville en Afrique noire*. Paris: Karthala, 1983.

Elkiss, T. H. *The Quest for an African Eldorado: Sofala, Southern Zambezia and the Portuguese, 1500–1868*. Waltham, Mass.: Crossroads Press, 1981.

Epstein, A. L. *Politics in an Urban African Community [Luanshya].* Manchester, U.K.: Manchester University Press, 1958.

———. "Urbanization and Urban Change in Africa." *Current Anthropology* 8 (1967): 275–96.

Fagan, B. *Zambezi and Limpopo Basins.* London and Berkeley: Heinemann and University of California Press, 1985.

Fage, J. D., ed. "A New Checklist of the Forts and Castles of Ghana." *Transactions of the Historical Society of Ghana* 4, no. 1 (1969): 65.

Fair, T. D. J., and R. J. Davies. *Constrained Urbanization: White South Africa and Black Africa Compared.* Beverly Hills, Calif.: Sage, 1976.

Falola, Toyin. *The Political Economy of a Precolonial African State: Ibadan 1830–1900.* Ile-Ife: University of Ife Press, 1984.

Falola, Toyin, and Steven J. Salm, eds. *Urbanization and African Cultures.* Durham, N.C.: Carolina Academic Press, 2005.

———., eds. *African Urban Spaces in Historical Perspective.* Rochester, N.Y.: University of Rochester Press, 2005.

———, eds. *Nigerian Cities.* Trenton, N.J.: Africa World Press, 2004.

Filipowiak, W. "Expédition archéologique polono-guinéenne à Niani." *Africana Bulletin* 4 (1964): 116–27 and 11 (1966): 107–17.

———. "Results of Archaeological Research at Niani." *Nyame Akuma* 11 (1977): 32–33.

———. *Etudes archéologiques sur la capitale médiévale du Mali.* Szcezcin, Poland: Museum Narodowe, 1979.

———. *Le Complexe du palais royal de Mali.* Paris: Société Française d'Histoire d'Outre-Mer, 1981.

Fisher, H. J. *Slavery in the History of Muslim Black Africa.* New York: New York University Press, 2001.

Fitch, J. M., and D. P. Branch. "Primitive Architecture and Climate." *Scientific American* 203 (1960): 134–44.

Fox, R. G. *Urban Anthropology: Cities in Their Cultural Settings.* Englewood Cliffs, N.J.: Prentice-Hall, 1977.

Fraenkel, M. *Tribe and Class in Monrovia.* London: Oxford University Press for International African Institute, 1964.

Frazer, D., and A. Sudcliffe, eds. *The Pursuit of Urban History.* London: Edward Arnold, 1983.

Frishman, Alan. "The Population Growth of Kano, Nigeria." In *African Historical Demography*, vol. 1, 212–50. Edinburgh: Centre of African Studies, University of Edinburgh, 1977.

Gallay, A., E. Huysecom, et al. *Hamdallahi, capitale de l'empire Peul du Massina, Mali*. Stuttgart: Franz Steiner Verlag, 1990.

Gardi, B., P. Maas, and G. Mommersteeg. *Djenné, il y a cent ans*. Amsterdam: KIT Publications; Paris: Karthala, 1995.

Garlake, P. S. *The Early Islamic Architecture of the East African Coast*. London and Nairobi: Oxford University Press, 1966.

———. *Great Zimbabwe*. Harare: Zimbabwe Publishing House, 1973.

———. *Life at Great Zimbabwe*. Harare: Mambo Press, 1982.

Garretson, P. P. "A History of Addis-Ababa from Its Foundation in 1886 to 1910." Ph.D. diss., University of London, 1974.

Gayibor, N. "Les villes négrières de la côte des esclaves au XVIII$^e$ siècle." In *Processus d'urbanisation*, edited by C. Coquery-Vidrovitch, 1:50–58.

Ghaidan, U. *Lamu: A Study of the Swahili Town*. Nairobi: East African Literature Bureau, 1975.

Glassman, J. *Feasts and Riots. Revelry, Rebellion, and Popular Consciousness on the Swahili Coast, 1856–1888*. Portsmouth, N.H.: Heinemann, 1995.

Goddard, S. "Town-Farm Relationships in Yorubaland: A Case Study from Oyo." *Africa* 35 (1965): 21–29.

Goerg, O. *Pouvoir colonial, municipalités et espaces urbains: Conakry-Freetown des années 1880 à 1914*, 2 vols. Paris: L'Harmattan, 1997.

Goglin, J.-L. *Les misérables dans l'Occident médiéval*. Paris: Le Seuil, 1976.

Gomez, M. A. "Timbuktu under Imperial Songhay: A Reconsideration of Autonomy," *Journal of African History* 31, no. 1 (1990): 5–24.

Goody, J. "Ethnohistory and the Akan of Ghana." *Africa* 29, no. 1 (1959): 67–81.

Gouellain, R. *Douala, Ville et Histoire*. Paris: Musée de l'Homme, 1975.

Graham, C. *The Archaeology of Benin: Excavations and Other Researches in and around Benin City, Nigeria*. Oxford: Oxford University Press, 1975.

Grégoire, E. *Les Alhazai de Maradi (Niger). Histoire d'un groupe de riches marchands sahéliens.* Paris: ORSTOM, 1986.

Griaule, M. "Un camp militaire abyssin." *Journal de la Société des Africanistes* 4 (1934): 117–22.

Griffeth, R. "The Hausa City-States from 1450 to 1804." In *The City-State in Five Cultures,* edited by R. Griffeth and C. G. Thomas, 143–80. Santa Barbara, Calif., and Oxford: Clio Press, 1984.

Grove, J. M., and A. M. Johansen. "The Historical Geography of the Volta Delta, Ghana, During the Period of Danish Influence." *Bulletin de l'IFAN, B* 30, no. 4 (1968): 1374–1421.

Grunebaum, G. E. von. *Islam. Essays in the Nature and Growth of a Cultural Tradition.* Westport, Conn.: Greenwood Press, 1961.

Gugler, J., ed. *Urban Growth in Subsaharan Africa.* Kampala: Makerere University Press, 1970.

Gugler, J., and W. G. Flanagan. *Urbanization and Social Change in West Africa.* Cambridge and London: Cambridge University Press, 1978.

Guitart, F. "Les conditions de l'évolution du commerce d'une ville nord-sahélienne du début du XIX$^e$ siècle aux années 1970: Agadez (République du Niger)." Thesis, University of Paris-1, Paris, 1988.

Gutkind, P. C. W. "Notes on the Kibuga of Buganda." *Uganda Journal* 24 (1960): 29–43.

———. *The African Administration of the Kibuga of Buganda.* The Hague: Mouton, 1963.

———. *Bibliography on Urban Anthropology.* New York, London, Toronto: Oxford University Press, 1973.

Gutton, J. P. *La société et les pauvres: l'exemple de la généralité de Lyon 1534–1789.* Paris: Les Belles Lettres, 1971.

Hackett, I. J. *Religion in Calabar: the Religious Life and History of a Nigerian Town.* Berlin and New York: Mouton de Gruyter, 1989.

Hacquart, M. *Monographie de Tombouctou.* Paris: Société d'Éditions maritimes et coloniales, 1900.

Hall, J. *Speak Manzini: An Autobiography of an African City.* Manzini, Swaziland: Landmark Publishers, 2000.

Hama, B. *Textes et documents sur la ville de Niamey.* Niamey: IFAN, 1955.

Hamdan, G. "The Growth and Functional Structure of Khartoum." *Geographical Review* 50, no. 1 (1960): 21–40.

Hance, W. A. "The Economic Location and Function of Tropical African Cities." *Human Organization* 19, no. 3 (1960): 135–36.

———. *Population, Migration and Urbanization in Africa*. New York: Columbia University Press, 1970.

Hanna, W. J., and J. L. Hanna. "The Integrative Role of Urban Africa's Middle Places and Middlemen." *Civilisations* 7, no. 1–2 (1967): 12–29.

Hannerz, U. *Explaining the City: Inquiries towards an Urban Anthropology*. New York: Columbia University Press, 1980.

Harrell-Bond, B. E., A. M. Howard, and D. E. Skinner. *Community Leadership and the Transformation of Freetown (1801–1976)*. The Hague: Mouton, 1978.

Harrison, P. "The Policies and Politics of Informal Settlement in South Africa: A Historical Perspective." *Africa Insight* 1 (1992): 14–22.

Hasan, Y. F. *Sudan in Africa [Napata, Meroe, Nubia]*. Khartoum: Khartoum University Press, 1971.

Hinchman, M. "African Rococo: House and Portrait in Eighteenth-Century Senegal." Dissertation, University of Chicago, 2000.

Hinderink, J., and J. Sterkenburg. *Anatomy of an African Town. A Socio-Economic Study of Cape-Coast, Ghana*. Utrecht: Geographical Institute, State University of Utrecht, 1975.

Hirsch, Bertrand, ed. "Aksum, Ethiopie musulmane." *Annales d'Ethiopie* 17 (special issue, *2001*). Paris: Maisonneuve et Larose / Servedit.

Holder, Gilles, and Anne-Marie Peatrik, eds. "Cité-Etat et Statut Politique de la ville en Afrique et ailleurs," *Journal des Africanistes* 74 (1–2) (special issue, 2004): 9–483.

Holl, A. *Economie et société néolithique du Dhar Tichitt (Mauritanie)*. Paris: Recherches sur les Civilisations, 1986.

Hopkins, A. G. "Imperialism in Lagos, 1880–1892." *Economic History Review* 21, no. 3 (1968): 580–606.

———. "Property Rights and Empire Building: The British Annexation of Lagos, 1861." *Journal of Economic History* 40 (1980): 777–98.

Hopkins, N. S. *Popular Government in an African Town: Kita, Mali*. Chicago: University of Chicago Press, 1972.

Horton, M. C. "The Early Settlements of the Northern Swahili Coast." Ph.D. dissertation, University of Cambridge, 1984.

———. "The Swahili Corridor." *Scientific American* 225, no. 9 (1987): 86–93.

Horton, M., and J. Middleton. *The Swahili: The Social Landscape of a Mercantile Society.* Malden, Mass.: Blackwell Publishers, 2000.

Horvath, R. J. "Addis Abeba's Eucalyptus Forest." *Journal of Ethiopian Studies* 5, no. 6.1 (1968): 15–19.

———. "The Wandering Capitals of Ethiopia." *Journal of African History* 10, no. 2 (1969): 205–19.

Hoselitz, B. F. "Generative and Parasitic Cities." *Economic Development and Cultural Change* 3 (1954): 278–94.

Houseman, M., X. Crépin, et al. "Note sur la structure évolutive d'une ville historique. L'exemple d'Abomey (République populaire du Bénin)." *Cahiers d'Études Africaines* 24-4 (104) (1986): 527–46.

Houssay-Holzschuch, M. "Mother City: une géographie historique de Cape Town, de la colonisation européenne à la veille de la ségrégation (1652–1900)." *Clio en Afrique* (Web) 3 (1997): 20.

Howaed, A. "Pre-colonial Centres and Regional Systems in Africa." *Pan-African Journal* 8, no 3 (1975): 247–70.

Hull, R. W. *African Cities and Towns before the European Conquest.* New York: W. W. Norton, 1976.

———. "Urban Design and Architecture in Precolonial Africa." *Journal of Urban History* 2, no. 4 (1976).

Hunwick, J. O. "Gao and the Almoravids Revisited: Ethnicity, Political Change and the Limits of Interpretation." *Journal of African History* 35, no. 2 (1994): 251–74.

———. "Secular Power and Religious Authority in Muslim Society: The Case of Songhai." *Journal of African History* 37, no. 2 (1996): 175–94.

———, ed. and trans. *Timbuktu and the Songhay Empire. Al-Sa'di's Ta'rikh al-Sudan down to 1613 and Other Contemporary Documents.* Leyden: E. J. Brill, 1999.

Igbafe, P. A. *Benin under British Administration. The Impact of Colonial Rule on an African Kingdom 1897–1938.* Atlantic Highlands, N.J.: Humanities Press, 1979.

Iliffe, J. "Poverty in 19th Century Yorubaland." *Journal of African History* 25, no. 1 (1984): 43–57.

———. *The African Poor. A History*. Cambridge: Cambridge University Press, 1987.

Insoll, T. "Iron Age Gao: An Archaeological Contribution." *Journal of African History* 38, no. 1 (1997): 1–30.

———. *The Archeology of Islam in Sub-Saharan Africa*. Cambridge: Cambridge University Press, 2003.

Iroko, A. F. *Gao des origines à 1591*. Thesis, Université de Paris-1, 1974.

———. "Le commerce caravanier, facteur de naissance et de développement de Djougou dans l'Atacora." In *Processus d'urbanisation en Afrique*, edited by C. Coquery-Vidrovitch, 1:41–50. Paris: L'Harmattan, 1988.

Iroko, Abiola Felix, and Ogunsola John Igue. "Les Villes Yoruba du Dahomey. L'exemple de Ketu." Université du Dahomey (now Université nationale du Bénin), 1975.

Isaacman, Allen F. *The Tradition of Resistance in Mozambique: Anti-colonial Activity in the Zambezi Valley, 1850–1921*. Berkeley: University of California Press, 1976.

Janmohamed, Karim K. "A History of Mombasa, c. 1895–1935: Some Aspects of Economic and Social Life in an East African Port Town during Colonial Rule." Ph.D. dissertation, Northwestern University, Evanston, Ill., 1977.

Johnson, L. L. "Luanda, Angola: The Development of Internal Forms and Functional Patterns." Ph.D. dissertation, University of California at Los Angeles, 1970.

Johnson, M. "Indigenes or Invaders?" *Antiquity* 39 (1965): 59–60.

———. "Migrants' Progress." *Bulletin of Ghana Geographical Association* 9, no. 2 (1964): 4–27, and 10, no. 1 (1965): 13–40.

———. "Ashanti Craft Organization." *African Arts* (1979): 60–63, 78–82, 97, 442.

Kande, S. *Terres, urbanisme et architecture créoles en Sierra Leone: XVIII*$^e$*–XIX*$^e$ *siècles*. Paris and Montreal: l'Harmattan, 1998.

Kea, R. A. *Settlements, Trade, and Polities in the Seventeenth-Century Gold Coast*. Baltimore, Md.: The Johns Hopkins University Press, 1982.

Kendall, T. *Kerma and the Kingdom of Kush, 2500–1500 B.C.: The Archaeological Discovery of an Ancient Nubian Empire.* Washington, D.C.: National Museum of African Art, Smithsonian Institution, 1997.

Kerjean, Alain. *La piste interdite de Tombouctou.* Paris: Flammarion, 1985.

Kirk-Greene, A. H. M. "Capitals of Bornou." *West African Review* 33 (1962): 37–45.

Krapf-Askari, Eva. *Yoruba Towns and Cities. An Enquiry into the Nature of Urban Social Phenomena.* Oxford: Clarendon Press, 1969.

Lampard, E. E. *The Nature of Urbanization.* London: Edwards Arnold, 1983.

Lange, D. "From Mande to Songhay: Towards a Political and Ethnic History of Medieval Gao." *Journal of African History* 35, no. 2 (1994): 275–302.

Lapidus, Ira M. *Muslim Cities in the Later Middle Ages.* London and New York: Cambridge University Press, 1984.

Largueche, A. *Les ombres de la ville: Pauvres, marginaux et minoritaires à Tunis (XVIIème et XIXème siècles).* Manouba, Tunisia: Publication Universitaire, Faculté des Lettres, 1999.

Launay, R. *Beyond the Stream: Islam and Society in a West African Town.* Berkeley: University of California Press, 1992.

Law, Robin. "Towards a History of Urbanization in Pre-colonial Yorubaland." In *African Historical Demography*, vol. 1, 260–71. Edinburgh: Centre for African Studies, University of Edinburgh, 1977.

———. "Trade and Politics behind the Slave Coast: The Lagoon Traffic and the Rise of Lagos, 1500–1800." *Journal of African History* 24, no. 3 (1983): 321–48.

———. *Ouidah: The Social History of a West African Slaving Port, 1727–1892.* London: James Currey, 2004.

Lawrence, A. W. *Trade Castles and Forts of West Africa.* Stanford, Calif.: Stanford University Press, 1964.

Lebeuf, Jean-Paul. *Archéologie tchadienne. Les Sao du Cameroun et du Tchad.* Paris: Herman, 1962.

Lebeuf, Jean-Paul, Immo Kirsch, and Johannes Hermann. *Ouara, ville perdue (Tchad).* Paris: Editions Recherches sur les Civilisations, 1989.

Lefebvre, Henri. *La Révolution urbaine*, 1970. Paris: Gallimard, 1970. Translated by Robert Bononno under the title *The Urban Revolution* (Minneapolis: University of Minnesota Press, 2003).

Lhote, Henri. "Sur l'emplacement de la ville de Tadmekka, antique capitale des Berbères soudanais." *Notes Africaines* 51 (1951): 65–69.

———. "Recherches sur Takkeda, ville décrite par le voyageur arabe Ibn Battouta et située en Aïr." *IFAN-B* 34 (1972): 429–70.

———. "Découverte des ruines de Tadeliza, ancienne résidence des sultans de l'Aïr." *Notes Africaines* 137 (1973): 3–16.

Little, K. *West African Urbanization.* Cambridge: Cambridge University Press, 1965.

Lloyd, Peter C. *Yoruba Land Law.* London: Oxford University Press, 1962.

Lloyd, Peter C., Akin Mabogunje, and B. Awe, eds. *The City of Ibadan.* London: International African Institute and Cambridge University Press, 1967.

Lobato, Alexandre. *Lourenço Marques. Xilunguine: Biografia da Cidade.* Lisbon: Agencia Geral do Ultramar, 1970.

Lobban, Richard A. "Class, Endogamy and Urbanization in the 'Three Towns' of the Sudan." *African Studies Review* 22, no. 3 (1979): 99–113.

———. "Class and Kinship in Sudanese Urban Communities." *Africa* 52, no. 2 (1982): 51–76.

Logan, Philip N. "The Walled City of Kano." *Journal of the Royal Institute of British Architects* 23 (1929): 402–406.

Lombard, Jacques. "Cotonou, ville africaine. Tendances évolutives et réactions des coutumes traditionnelles." *Bulletin de l'IFAN-B* 16, no. 3/4 (1954): 341–77.

Luling, Virginia. *A Somali Sultanate. The Geledi City-State over 150 Years.* London: Haan Associates, 2001.

Maas, P. M., and G. Mommersteeg. *Djenne. Chef-d'œuvre architectural.* Bamako and Eindhoven: Institut des Sciences humaines/Université de Technologie, 1992.

Mabogunje, Akin L. *Yoruba Towns.* Ibadan: Ibadan University Press, 1962.

———. *Urbanization in Nigeria.* London: Africana Publishing, 1968.

Mabogunje, Akin L., and J. D. Omer-Cooper. *Owu in Yoruba History*. Ibadan: Ibadan University Press, 1971.

Marcus, Harold G., ed.; Grover Hudson, assoc. ed. *New Trends in Ethiopian Studies: Papers of the 12th International Conference on Ethiopian Studies, Michigan State University, 5–10 September 1994*. 2 vols. Lawrenceville, N.J.: Red Sea Press, 1994.

Margarido, Alfredo. "La capitale de l'Empire Lunda: un urbanisme politique." *Annales* 4 (1970): 857–61.

Marguerat, Yves. "Kumasi: l'espace et le temps. Trois siècles d'évolution d'une grande ville africaine." In *Processus d'urbanisation en Afrique*, edited by C. Coquery-Vidrovitch, 1: 9–21.

———. "La naissance d'une capitale africaine: Lomé." *Revue française d'Histoire d'outre-mer* 81, no. 302 (1994): 71–95.

Mark, Peter. "Constructing Identity: Sixteenth and Seventeenth-Century Architecture in the Gambia-Geba Region and the Articulation of Luso-African Ethnicity." *History in Africa* 22, no. 2 (1995): 307–27.

———. *Portuguese Style and Luso-African Identity. Precolonial Senegambia, Sixteenth-Nineteenth Centuries*. Bloomington: Indiana University Press, 2002.

Masson-Detournet-Lebeuf, Annie. "Boum-Massénia, capitale de l'ancien royaume du Baguirmi." *Journal de la Société des Africanistes* 37, no. 2 (1967): 215–44.

Mathew, G. *The Dating and Significance of the Periplus of the Erythrean Sea*. London: Africana Publishing, 1975.

Mauny, Raymond. "Notes d'archéologie au sujet de Gao." *Bulletin de l'IFAN* 13 (1951): 837–52.

———. "Notes d'archéologie sur Tombouctou." *Bulletin de l'IFAN* 14 (1952): 899–918.

———. *Tableau géographique de l'ouest africain au Moyen Âge d'après les sources écrites, la tradition et l'archéologie*. Dakar: Mémoires de l'Institut d'Afrique noire, 1961.

McGee, T. C. "The Rural-Urban Continuum Debate, the Pre-industrial City and Rural-Urban Migration." *Pacific Viewpoint* 5, no. 2 (1964): 159–79.

———. *The Urbanization Process in the Third World*. London: C. Bell, 1971.

McIntosh, R. J. "Clustered Cities of the Middle Niger. Alternative Routes to Authority in Prehistory." In *Africa's Urban Past*, edited by Anderson and Rathbone, 19–35.

McIntosh, Susan Keech, and Roderick J. McIntosh. *Prehistoric Investigations in the Region of Jenne, Mali. A Study in the Development of Urbanism in the Sahel*. I. *Archaeological and Historical Background and the Excavations at Jenne-Jeno*. Oxford: BAR, 1980.

———. "The Inland Niger River Delta before the Empire of Mali: Evidence from Jenne-Jeno." *Journal of African History* 22 (1981): 1–22.

———. "Recent Archaeological Research and Dates from West Africa." *Journal of African History* 27, no. 3 (1986): 413–42.

McQuillan, D. Aidan, and Royce Lanier. "Urban Upgrading and Historic Preservation. An Integrated Development Plan for Zanzibar's Old Stone Town." *Habitat International* 8, no. 2 (1984): 43–59.

Meillassoux, Claude. "Plans d'anciennes fortifications (Tata) en pays Malinké." *Journal de la Société des Africanistes* 36 (1966): 29–43.

———, ed. *The Development of Indigenous Trade and Markets in West Africa*. London: Oxford University Press for the International African Institute, 1971.

Meillassoux, C., A. Locati, and S. Spini. "I Bozo del Niger (Mali): insediamento e architettura." *Storia della Città* 25 (1984).

Miner, Horace. "The Folk-Urban Continuum." *American Sociological Review* 17, no. 5 (1952): 529–37.

———. *The Primitive City of Timbuctoo*. Princeton, N.J.: Princeton University Press, 1953.

Mollat, M. *Les pauvres au Moyen-Age: étude sociale*. Paris: Hachette, 1978.

Monteil, Charles. *Une cité soudanaise: Djenné, métropole du delta central du Niger*. Paris and London: Anthropos for the International African Institute, 1971.

Mortimore, M. J. *Zaria and Its Region; A Nigerian Savanna City and Its Environs*. Edited by M. J. Mortimore, with a foreword by I. S. Audu. Zaria, Nigeria: Department of Geography, Ahmadu Bello University, 1970.

Morton-Williams, Peter. "The Yoruba Ogboni Cult in Oyo." *Africa* 30 (1960): 362–74.

———. "An Outline of the Cosmology and Cult Organization of the Oyo Yoruba." *Africa* 34 (1964): 243–61.

———. "Some Factors in the Location, Growth and Survival of Towns in West Africa." In *Man, Settlement and Urbanism*, edited by Peter J. Ucko et al. London: Duckworth, 1972.

Moughtin, J. C. *Hausa Architecture*. London: Ethnographica, 1985.

Mumford, Lewis. *The City in History. Its Origins, Its Transformations, and Its Prospects*. New York: Harcourt, Brace and World, 1961.

Munro-Hay, S. C., ed. *Excavations at Aksum*. London: Memoirs of the British Institute in Eastern Africa, no. 10, 1989.

Munson, P. J. "The Tichitt Tradition. A Late Prehistoric Occupation of the Southwestern Sahara." Ann Arbor, Mich.: University Microfilms International, 1979.

Mworoha, Émile. *Peuples et rois de l'Afrique des grands lacs*. Paris, Bujumbura: Nouvelles Editions Africaines, 1977.

Nadel, S. F. *A Black Byzantium: the Kingdom of Nupe in Nigeria*. London: Oxford University Press, 1942.

Nurse, Derek, and Thomas Spear. *The Swahili: Reconstructing the History and Language in an African Society, 800–1500*. Philadelphia: Philadelphia University Press, 1985.

O'Connor, Anthony M. *Urbanization in Tropical Africa: An Annotated Bibliography*. Boston: G. K. Hall, 1981.

———. *The African City*. London: Hutchinson University Library for Africa, 1983.

O'Hear, Ann. "Craft Industry in Ilorin: Dependency or Independence?" *African Affairs* 86, no. 345 (1987): 505–22.

O'Loughlin, C. "What is the Village? The Relevance of 'Village Studies' in West African Social Research." *Ghana Social Science Journal* 2, no. 1 (1972): 19–26.

Ogunremi, G. O., M. O. Opeloye, and S. Oyeweso. *Badagry. A Study in History, Culture and Tradition of an African City*. Ibadan: Rex Charles Publications, 1994.

Oguntomisin, G. O., and Toyin Falola. "Refugees in Yorubaland in the Nineteenth Century." *Asian and African Studies* 21, no. 2 (1987): 165–85.

Ojo, G. J. Afolabi. *Yoruba Culture. A Geographical Analysis.* London: University of Ife and University of London Press, 1966.

———. *Yoruba Palaces.* London: University of London Press, 1966.

Oliver, Roland. "Ancient Capital Sites of Ankole." *Uganda Journal* 23 (1959): 51–64.

Oliver, Roland, and B. M. Fagan. *Africa in the Iron Age.* Cambridge: Cambridge University Press, 1975.

Onokerhoraye, Andrew Godwin. "Urbanism as an Organ of Traditional African Civilization: the Example of Benin, Nigeria." *Civilization* 25, no. 314 (1975): 294–306.

Orme-Smith, R. "Maïduguri Market, Northern Nigeria." *Journal of the Royal African Society* (July 1938): 318–25.

Ozanne, Paul. "A New Archaeological Survey of Ife." *Odu* 1 (1969): 28–45.

Paden, John N. *Religion and Political Culture in Kano.* Berkeley: University of California Press, 1973.

Pama, C. *Bowler's Cape Town: Life at the Cape in Early Victorian Times, 1834–1868.* Cape Town: Tafelberg, 1977.

Pâques, V. "Origines et caractères du pouvoir royal au Baguirmi." *Journal de la Société des Africanistes* 37, no. 2 (1967): 183–214.

Pankhurst, Richard. "Menelik and the Foundation of Addis Ababa." *Journal of African History* 2, no. 1 (1961): 103–17.

———. "Notes on the Democratiic [sic] History of Ethiopian Towns and Villages." *Ethiopian Observer* 9, no. 1 (1965): 60–83.

———. *History of Ethiopian Towns.* I. *From the Middle Ages to the Early Nineteenth Century.* II. *From the Nineteenth Century to 1935.* Wiesbaden: Franz Steiner Verlag, 1982.

Parker, J. *Making The Town: Ga State and Society In Early Colonial Ghana.* London: James Currey, 2001.

Pasquier, Roger. "Villes du Sénégal au XIXᵉ siècle." *Revue Française d'Histoire d'Outre-Mer* (3rd & 4th trim. 1968): 387–426.

————. "Un aspect de l'histoire des villes du Sénégal: les problèmes de ravitaillement au XIXᵉ siècle." *Cahiers du Centre de Recherches Africaines* 5 (1987): 177–221.

Pauty, E. "Villes spontanées et villes créées en Islam." *Annales de l'Institut d'Etudes Orientales, Université d'Alger* 9 (1951): 52–75.

Pearce, F. B. *Zanzibar. The Island Metropolis of Eastern Africa.* London: T. F. Unwin, 1920; New York: F. Cass, 1967.

Pearson, M. N. *Port Cities and Intruders: The Swahili Coast, India, and Portugal in the Early Modern Era.* Baltimore, Md.: The Johns Hopkins University Press, 2003.

Peel, J. D. Y. "Kings, Titles, and Quarters: a Conjectural History of Ilesha. I. The Traditions Reviewed." *History in Africa* 6 (1979): 109–53.

————. "Urbanization and Urban History in West Africa." *Journal of African History* 21, no. 2 (1980): 269–78.

Péfontan, Commandant. "Histoire de Tombouctou de sa fondation à l'occupation française (XIIIᵉ s.–1893)." *Bulletin du Comité d'Etudes Historiques et Scientifiques de l'AOF* (1922): 81–113.

Peterson, J. *Province of Freedom. A History of Sierra-Leone, 1787–1870.* London: Faber and Faber, 1969.

Phillips, Earl. "The Egba at Abeokuta: Acculturation and Political Change, 1830–1870." *Journal of African History* 10, no. 1 (1969): 117–31.

————. "The Egba at Ikorodu, 1865: Perfidious Lagos?" *African Historical Studies* 3, no. 1 (1970): 23–35.

Phillips, J. "Punt and Aksum: Egypt and the Horn of Africa." *Journal of African History* 38, no. 3 (1997): 423–58.

Phillipson, D. W. *African Archeology.* Cambridge: Cambridge University Press, 1993.

————. *Ancient Ethiopia: Aksum: Its Antecedents and Successors.* London: British Museum Press, 1998.

————. *Archaeology at Aksum, Ethiopia, 1993–7.* 2 vols. London: British Institute in Eastern Africa, 2001.

Pirenne, Henri. *Les villes et les institutions urbaines.* 2 vols. Paris and Brussels, 1939.

Pikirayi, I. "The Archaeological Identity of the Mutapa State: Towards an Historical Archaeology of Northern Zimbabwe." Ph.D. diss., Uppsala University, Uppsala, Sweden, 1994.

――――. *The Zimbabwe Culture: Origins and Decline of Southern Zambezian States.* Walnut Creek, Calif.: AltaMira Press, 2001.

Plotnicov, L. *Strangers to the City. Urban Man in Jos, Nigeria.* Pittsburgh, Pa.: University of Pittsburgh Press, 1967.

Poinsot, Jacqueline, Alain Sinou, and Jaroslav Sternadel. *Les Villes d'Afrique noire entre 1650 et 1960. Politiques et opérations d'urbanisme et d'habitat.* Paris: Ministère de la Coopération et du Développement/ Documentation française, 1989.

Polet, Jean, ed. *Tegdaoust. 4. Fouille d'un quartier de Tegdaoust. Mauritanie orientale. Urbanisation, architecture, utilisation de l'espace construit.* Paris: Éditions Recherche sur les civilizations, 1985.

Posnansky, Merrick. "Ghana and the Origins of West African Trade." *Africa Quarterly* 5, 2, no. 2 (1971): 110–25.

――――. "Aspects of Early West African Trade." *World Archaeology* 5, no. 2 (1973): 149–62.

――――. "Connections between the Lacustrine Peoples and the Coast." In *East Africa and the Orient. Cultural Syntheses in Precolonial Times,* edited by Chittick and Rotberg, 216–25.

Posnansky, Merrick, and R. J. McIntosh. "New Radio-Carbon Dates for Northern and Western Africa." *Journal of African History* 17, no. 2 (1976): 161–95.

Pouwels, Randall L. *Horn and Crescent: Cultural Change and Traditional Islam on the East African Coast, 800–1900.* Cambridge: Cambridge University Press, 1987.

Prévaudeau, M.-M. *Abomey la mystique.* Paris: Editions Albert, 1936.

Proyart, Abbé. *Histoire de Loango, Kakongo et autres royaumes d'Afrique.* Paris: C. P. Berton, 1776. (*History of Loango, Kakongo, and other kingdoms in Africa. A general collection of the best and most interesting voyages and travels in all parts of the world,* edited by J. Pinkerton, 548–97. London: Longman, Hurst, Rees, and Orme.)

Prussin, Labelle. "The Architecture of Islam in West Africa." *African Arts* 1, no. 2 (1967): 32–35 and 70–74.

————. "Islamic Architecture in West Africa. The Fulbe and Manding Models." *Viq. The Journal of the Graduate School. Fine Arts. The University of Pennsylvania* 5 (1982): 52–69.

————. *Hatumere: Islamic Design in West Africa.* Berkeley: University of California Press, 1986.

————, ed. *African Nomadic Architecture. Space, Place and Gender.* Washington, D.C.: Smithsonian Institution Press, 1995.

Prussin, Labelle, and David Lee. "Architecture in Africa: An Annotated Bibliography." *Africana Library Journals* 4, no. 3 (1973): 3–32.

Pulvenis, C. "Une épidémie de fièvre jaune à Saint-Louis du Sénégal (1881)." *Bulletin de l'IFAN-B* 30, no. 4 (1968): 1353–73.

Raftopoulos, B., and Yoshikuni, Tsuneo, eds. *Sites of Struggle: Essays In Zimbabwe's Urban History.* Zimbabwe: Weaver Press, 1999.

Raharijaona, B. and J. "Anciennes résidences royales. Essai de monographies sur Ambohimanga et Ambositra." *Bulletin de l'Académie Malgache* 14 (1931): 111–30.

Rainitovo, I. *Antananarivo Fahizay [Tananarive d'autrefois].* Tananarive: FFMA, 1928.

Rajaonah-Esoavelomandroso, F. "Élites et notables à Antananarivo dans la première moitié du XXᵉ siècle." Thèse d'État, Université de Lyon-II, 1997.

Randles, W. G. L. *L'ancien royaume de Congo des origines à la fin du XIXᵉ siècle.* Paris and The Hague: Mouton, 1968.

————. "Pre-colonial Urbanization in Africa South of the Equator." In *Man, Settlement and Urbanism,* edited by Ucko et al., 891–97.

————. *L'Empire du Monomotapa du XVᵉ au XIXᵉ siècle.* Paris and The Hague: Mouton, 1975.

Redfield, Robert. "The Folk Society." *American Journal of Sociology* 52, no. 4 (1947): 293–308.

Redfield, Robert, and Milton B. Singer. "The Cultural Role of Cities." *Economic Development and Cultural Change* 3 (1954): 53–73.

Rehfish, F. "A Sketch of Early History of Omdurman." *Sudan Notes and Records* 45 (1964): 35–47.

Reyher, Rebecca Hourwich, ed. *Zulu Woman: The Life Story of Christina Sibiya.* 1947; New York: Feminist Press, 1999.

Robert-Chaleix, Denise. *Tegdaoust V. Une concession médiévale à Teg-daoust: implantation, évolution d'une unité d'habitation.* Paris: Éd. Recherche sur les Civilisations, 1989.

Roberts, Bryan R. *Cities of Peasants: The Political Economy of Urbanization in the Third World.* London: Edward Arnold, 1978.

Robinson, K. R. *Khami Ruins (Excavations 1947–1955).* Cambridge: Cambridge University Press, 1959.

Roche, Christian. "Ziguinchor et son passé." *Boletim Cultural da Guiné Portugesa* 28 (1973): 35–59.

Rodwin, Lloyd. *Cities of the Mind: Mirages and Themes of the City in the Social Sciences.* New York: Plenum Press, 1984.

Romero-Curtin, Patricia. "The Sacred Meadows: A Case Study of 'Anthropologyland' vs 'Historyland.'" *History in Africa* 9 (1982): 337–46.

———. "Laboratory for the Oral History of Slavery: The Island of Lamu on the Kenya Coast." *American Historical Review* 88, no. 4 (1983): 858–82.

———. "Where Have All the Slaves Gone? Emancipation and Post-Emancipation in Lamu, Kenya." *Journal of African History* 27, no. 3 (1986): 497–512.

Ross, Robert J. "Cape-Town (1750–1850): Synthesis in the Dialectic of Continents." In *Colonial Cities. Essays on Urbanism in a Colonial Context,* edited by Robert Ross and Gerard J. Telkamp. 105–21. Leiden: Martinus Nijhof for the Leiden University Press, 1985.

Rossi, Pietro, ed. *Modelli di Città. Strutture e Funzioni Politiche.* Torino: Einaudi, 1987.

Roussier, Paul. *L'établissement d'Issiny 1687–1702.* Paris: Larose, Publications du Comité d'Études Historiques et Scientifiques de l'AOF, 1935.

Ryder, A. F. C. *Benin and its Europeans, 1485–1897.* New York: Humanities Press, 1969.

Saad, Elias N. *Social History of Timbuktu. The Role of Muslim Scholars and Notables, 1400–1900.* Cambridge: Cambridge University Press, 1983.

Saison, B. "Azugi. Archéologie et histoire en Adrar mauritanien." *Recherche, Pédagogie et Culture* 9, no. 55 (1981): 66–74.

Salau, A. T. "The Urban Process in Africa. Observations on the Points of Divergence from the Western Experience." *African Urban Studies* 4 (1979): 20–27.

Sassoon, Hamo. "New Views on Engaruka, Northern Tanzania. Excavations Carried Out for the Tanzania Government in 1964 and 1966." *Journal of African History* 8, no. 2 (1967): 201–17.

Saunders, Christopher, ed. *Studies in the History of Cape Town*. 5 vols. Cape Town: Centre for African Studies, University of Cape Town, 1984.

Schwerdtfeger, Friedrich W. *Traditional Housing in African Cities. A Comparative Study of Houses in Zaria, Ibadan and Marrakech*. Chichester and New York: John Wiley and Sons, 1982.

Shaw, Thurstan L. *Igbo Ukwu. An Account of Archaeological Discoveries in Eastern Nigeria*. Evanston, Ill.: Northwestern University Press, 1970.

———. "Those Igbo Ukwu Radiocarbon Dates: Facts, Fictions and Probabilities." *Journal of African History* 16, no. 4 (1975): 503–17.

———. *Nigeria: Its Archaeology and Early History*. London: Thames and Hudson, 1979.

———. "Further Sight on Igbo-Ukwu, Including New Radio-Carbon Dates." *Proceedings*, 9th Panafrican Congress of Prehistory and Quaternary Studies, Jos, Nigeria, 1983.

Sheriff, A. *Slaves, Spices and Ivory in Zanzibar: Integration of an East African Commercial Empire into the World Economy, 1770–1873*. Athens: Ohio University Press, 1987.

———. *Zanzibar Stone Town*. Zanzibar: Gallery Publications, 1998.

———, ed. *The History and Conservation of Zanzibar Stone Town*. Athens: Ohio University Press, 1995.

Shinnie, P. L. *Meroe. A Civilization of the Sudan*. New York and Washington: Frederick A. Praeger, 1967.

Shinnie, P. L., and F. Y. Kense. Paper presented at Third International Meroïtic Conference, Toronto, 1977.

Shinnie, P., and P. Ozanne. "Excavations at Yendi Dabari." *Transactions of the Historical Society of Ghana* 6 (1962).

Shuval, T. *La ville d'Alger vers la fin du XVIIIᵉ siècle. Population et cadre urbain*. Paris: CNRS Éditions, 1998.

Sibrec, J. "A Quarter Century of Change and Progress: Antanarivo and Madagascar Twenty-five Years Ago." *Antanarivo Ann.* 12 (1888): 397–420.

Silverman, D. P., ed. *Ancient Egypt.* New York: Oxford University Press, 2003.

Sinou, Alain. *Comptoirs et villes coloniales du Sénégal - Saint-Louis, Gorée, Dakar.* Paris: Karthala, 1993.

———. *Ouidah une ville africaine singulière.* Paris: Karthala, 1995.

Sinou, Alain, and B. Oloudé. *Porto-Novo, Ville d'Afrique noire.* Paris/Marseille: Parenthèses/ORSTOM, 1988.

Siravo, F. *Zanzibar: A Plan for the Historic Stone Town.* Geneva and Zanzibar: Gallery Publications, 1996.

Siravo, F., and Ann Pulver. *Planning Lamu. Conservation of an East African Seaport.* Nairobi: National Museum of Kenya, 1986.

Sjoberg, Gideon. "The Pre-industrial City." *American Journal of Sociology* 60 (1955): 438–45.

———. *The Preindustrial City. Past and Present.* Glencoe, Ill.: The Free Press, 1960.

———. *Theory and Research in Urban Sociology.* New York: John Wiley and Sons, 1965.

Smith, Abdullah. "Some Considerations Relating to the Formation of States in Hausaland." *Journal of the Historical Society of Nigeria* 5, no. 3 (1970): 329–46.

Smith, Michael P. *The City and Social Theory.* Oxford: Blackwell, 1980.

Smith, Robert. "The Alafin in Exile: A Study of the Igboho Period in Oyo History." *Journal of African History* 6, no. 1 (1970): 57–77.

Southall, Aidan William. *Forms of Ethnic Linkage between Town and Country.* The Hague: Mouton, 1976.

———, ed. *Urban Anthropology. Cross-Cultural Studies of Urbanization.* New York: Oxford University Press, 1973.

Stevenson, R. C. "Old Khartoum, 1821–1885." *Sudan Notes and Records* 47 (1966): 1–38.

Stierlin, H. *L'architecture islamique.* Paris: PUF, 1993.

Summers, Roger. *Ancient Ruins and Vanished Civilizations of Southern Africa.* Cape Town: T. V. Bulpin, 1971.

Summers, Roger, ed. *Inyanga; Prehistoric Settlements in Southern Rhodesia. With contributions by H. B. S. Cooke, P. V. Tobias* ... [and others]. Cambridge, U.K.: Published for the Inyanga Research Fund at the University Press, 1958.

Sutton, J. E. G. "'Ancient Civilizations' and Modern Agricultural Systems in the Southern Highlands of Tanzania." *Azania* 4 (1969): 1–13.

———. "Dar es Salam: A Sketch of a Hundred Years." *Tanzania Notes and Records* 71 (1970): 1–20.

———. "Dawu—Radiocarbon Results." *Archaeology in Ghana* 3 (1987).

Tardits, C. *Le royaume Bamoum*. Paris: Éditions de la Sorbonne/Colin, 1980.

Thilmans, G. "Sur les objets de parure trouvés à Podor (Sénégal) en 1958." *Bulletin de l'IFAN-B* 39 (1977): 687.

Thilmans, G., and A. Ravisé. "Proto-histoire du Sénégal. II. Sinthiou Baré et les sites du fleuve." *Mémoire de l'IFAN* 91 (1980): 86–87.

Thomassey, P., and Raymond Mauny. "Campagnes de fouilles à Koumbi-Saley." *Bulletin de l'IFAN-B* 12, no. 2 (1951): 438–62.

Thornton, John K. "Early Kongo-Portuguese Relations: A New Interpretation." *History in Africa* 8 (1981): 183–204.

———. *Kingdom of Kongo. Civil War and Transition, 1641–1718*. Madison: University of Wisconsin Press, 1983.

Toynbee, Arnold. *Cities on the Move*. New York: Oxford University Press, 1970.

Ucko, Peter J., Ruth Tringham, and G. W. Dimbley. *Man, Settlement and Urbanism*. London: Duckworth, 1972.

Udo, Reuben K. "The Growth and Decline of Calabar." *Nigerian Geographical Journal* 10, no. 2 (1978): 91–106.

Usman, Yusufu Bala. "Some Aspects of the External Relations of Katsina before 1804." *Savanna* 1 (1972).

Van Dantzig, A., and B. Pridy. *A Short History of the Forts and Castles of Ghana*. Accra: Ghana Museums and Monuments, 1971.

Vanacker, Claudette. *Tegdaoust II. Fouilles d'un quartier artisanal*. Paris: Recherches sur les Civilisations, 1979.

Vansina, J. *The Children of Woot*. Madison: University of Wisconsin Press, 1978.

————. *Paths in the Rainforests: Toward a History of Political Tradition in Equatorial Africa.* Madison: University of Wisconsin Press, 1990.

Vernet, T. "Les cités-États swahili et la puissance omanaise, 1650–1720." *Journal des Africanistes* 72, no. 2 (2002).

Walter, B. J. "A Spatial Diffusion Perspective of Areal Growth in African Islamic Cities: The Example of Mombasa." *African Urban Notes* 7, no. 1 (1973): 95–109.

Weber, Max. *The City.* New York: Free Press, 1966. [Translated from Die Stadt. Begriff und Kategorien, 1921. In *Wirtschaft und Gesellschaft.*]

Welsby, Derek A. *The Kingdom of Kush. The Napatan and Meroitic Empires.* Princeton: Markus Wiener, 1998.

————. *The Medieval Kingdoms of Nubia: Pagans, Christians and Muslims along the Middle Nile.* London: British Museum Press, 2002.

Wheatley, Paul. "What the Greatness of a City Is Said to Be. Reflections on Sjoberg's 'Preindustrial City.'" *Pacific Viewpoint* 4 (1963): 163–88.

————. "The Significance of Traditional Yoruba Urbanism." *Comparative Studies on Society and History* 12, no. 4 (1970): 393–423.

————. "The Concept of Urbanism." In *Man, Settlement and Urbanism,* edited by Peter J. Ucko et al. London: Duckworth, 1972.

Wheeler, M. "The First Towns." *Antiquity* 30, no. 119 (1956): 132–36.

Whittlesey, D. "Kano: A Sudanese Metropolis." *Geographical Review* 27, no. 2 (1937): 177–99.

Whitty, Anthony. "A Classification of Prehistoric Stone Buildings in Mashonaland, Southern Rhodesia." *South African Archaeological Society Bulletin* 14 (1959): 57–70.

Wilks, Ivor. "The Northern Factor in Ashanti History: Begho and the Mande." *Journal of African History* 2, no. 1 (1961): 25–34.

Willis, J. *Mombasa, the Swahili and the Making of the Mijikenda.* Oxford: Clarendon Press, 1993.

Winters, Christopher. "Traditional Urbanism in the North Central Sudan." *Annals of the Association of American Geographers* 67, no. 4 (1977): 500–520.

————. "Urban Morphogenesis in Francophone Black Africa." *Geographical Review* 72 (1982): 139–54.

————. "The Classification of Traditional African Cities." *Journal of Urban History* 10, no. 1 (1983): 3–31.

Wirth, Louis. "Urbanism as a Way of Life." *American Journal of Sociology* 4 (1938).

Wirth, L. "Urbanism as a Way of Life." In *On Cities and Social Life. Selected Papers,* edited by L. Wirth and A. J. Reiss, 60–83. Chicago: University of Chicago Press, 1964.

Wright, M. *Consciousness and Protest among Slave Women in Central Africa, 1886–1911.* Madison: University of Wisconsin Press, 1983.

Yusuf, A. B. "A Reconsideration of Urban Conceptions: Hausa Urbanization and the Hausa Rural-Urban Continuum." *Urban Anthropology* 3 (1974): 200–221.

Zein, Abdul Hamid M. el-. *The Sacred Meadows: A Structural Analysis of Religious Symbolism in an East African Town* [Lamu]. Evanston, Ill.: Northwestern University Press, 1974.

# Index of Cities and Peoples

*Cities are in italics.*

*Abeokuta* 161, 174, 246, 248, 251, 253–54, 309, 328
*Abidjan* 70, 329
*Abomey* 159, 183, 185, 187–91, 264, 329, 358
Abomey (kingdom) 72, 142, 159, 167, 173–74, 179, 183, 190, 211, 358
*Abora* 153
Abotakyi 154
Abraman 16
Abu 101, 103, 249–50
Abu 'l-Bilma, see Bilma.
Abyssinia 171, 277, 283
*Accra* 149, 156, 229, 351
Accra (State of) 153
*Addis Ababa* 26, 261, 267, 272–75, 277, 328–29, 332, 338, 368–69
*Addis Alem* 274, 277
Adja (people) 183, 188
*Adowa* 270, 276, 332
Adrar of the Iforas 35, 102
*Adulia* 36
Adumangya 154
Afufu (state) 171
*Agades* 98, 103–6
*Ago* 162. See also *New Oyo.*
*Ago-Owu* 243
*Agoua* 151
Aïr 43, 45, 50, 102–5, 108, 337, 346
*Ajido* 249
Akan (people) 15, 116–17, 210, 254, 256, 294
*Akessim* 151
Akreijt (Dhar de) 42

Aku (people) 292, 298
*Akure* 160
Akyem (state) 153
*Al-Bilma* 101
*Al-Qasaba* 101, 345
*Alapinni* (district in Oyo) 250
Alima (Upper) 18
*Allada* 142, 188–90
Amhara (people) 271, 276
Amir 'Abdullah 34
*Anashan* 145
*Aneho* 174
Angola 80, 178, 284, 286–87
*Ankalas* 101
Ankobra (river) 115, 141, 147
Ankole (kingdom) 66, 72, 216, 218, 264, 320
*Anomabu* 176
Aouker (lake) 42
Apollonia Cape 153
Arabia 22, 36, 38–39, 41, 129, 201–2
*Arguin* 139–40, 142
Arivonimamo 15
Arlit 102, 105
Arna (people) 239
*Arugbo* 249
Asante (empire) 23, 25, 97, 115, 117, 167, 171–73, 176, 191–91, 196, 204, 211, 254–56, 327, 335, 356, 359, 367
Asante (people) 15, 117, 141, 172, 174, 190, 193, 195
*Asebu* 155
*Assode* 105
Assuan 33

413

Atbara River  34, 233
*Atebubu*  255
Awash (river)  273
*Awdaghust*  49, 51, 99–100, 108
Awori (people)  307
*Axim*  141, 147, 149
*Axum*  33, 36, 266
*Azelik*  103

*Badagry*  309
*Bagamoyo*  216, 220–25
Bagirmi  237
Baher Nägash  270
*Bahia*  138, 179, 289, 357
Bahr el Ghazal  13, 237
Bakuba  331
Baluchi  222, 226
*Bama*  238
*Bamako*  259, 329
Bambara (people)  14, 115, 307
Bambuk  115
Bamum (kingdom)  19, 75, 261, 320
Bamum (people)  14, 261–62, 264
*Banda*, see *Begho.*
*Bangui*  26
Bantu (people)  4, 31, 39–41, 52–53, 55, 65,
       68, 91, 133–34, 201, 216, 263, 297,
       318, 329, 341, 343
*Barolong*  228
*Batavia*  311, 313
*Bathurst*  137, 294, 329, 371
Batwa (people)  65
Bauchi (emirate)  242
*Begho* (present-day Banda)  115–117, 149,
       151, 153, 167, 327, 348
*Beira*  329
Benadir  39
*Benedugu*  47
Benguela Plateau  284
Benin (state)  19, 45, 137, 145, 153, 158–61,
       163, 166–169, 173–74, 178, 183, 188,
       307–8, 331, 336–37, 353–55, 357–58
*Benin City*  19, 45, 158–61, 163, 166–69,
       174, 183, 188, 307–8, 353, 355
Benue (river)  43, 167
Berber (people)  102, 104, 109–10
Bete (people)  14

*Bighu* (or *Begho*)  116
*Bigo*  66
*Bilma*  101, 241
*Birain*  24
*Biram*  118
*Birni*  236, 238, 349
*Birni N'Gazargamu*  106
*Birnin Gija*  123
*Bitu*  348
*Bobo Dioulasso*  25, 117, 191, 257, 259, 329,
       348
Boer  228
*Bonduku*  255, 257, 327
*Bonny*  247
*Bono–Mansu*  117, 348
Borgu (people)  160
Bornu  43, 91, 99, 102, 106–7, 117–20, 122,
       166, 230, 236–38, 241, 326, 346
*Bouna*  117, 229
Bourbon Island  213
*Brass*  247
*Brazzaville*  19, 329
Brong (people)  116, 348
*Buea*  263
Buganda (kingdom)  19, 66, 74, 211, 216,
       218, 264, 320, 343
*Bujumbura*  202, 360
*Bulawayo*  62
*Bundu*  229, 242
*Bunkeya*  214–15, 361
Bunyoro (kingdom)  66
*Bur Gao*  40
Bure  115
Burkina Faso  14
*Burmi–Zamfara*  238
Burundi (kingdom)  66, 68–70, 202, 320,
       342
Bushiri  221
Bushmen (people)  310–11
*Bussa*  167
*Busso*  237
*Bweyorere*  216

*Cabinda*  284
*Cairo*  6, 22, 92, 107–8, 230, 269, 279, 283,
       335, 369
*Calabar*  173, 247, 356, 366

*Calicut* 197
Cameroon 19, 75, 261–62, 320
*Cape, the,* see *Cape Town.*
*Cape Coast Castle* 145, 147, 149, 155, 176, 359
*Cape Town* 278, 310–11, 313–14, 316, 328, 341, 374–75
Cape Verde (islands) 139–42, 174, 181, 301, 305
Cayor 305
Chad 100, 166, 319, 326
Chad (lake) 33, 47, 118, 209, 237, 347, 364
*Chari* 237
Chokwe (people) 74
Chwezi (kingdom) 66, 320
*Cidade Velha,* see *Ribeira Grande.*
*Cobbe* 231
*Conakry* 329
Congo 8, 18, 32, 72–73, 79, 80, 82, 114, 151, 169, 209, 220, 223, 284, 318, 335, 342–44, 347, 370, 377
Congo (river) 22, 202, 353
*Cotonou* 5, 26–27, 188, 329

*Dabi* 123
Dahomey 13, 16, 182–83, 186, 191, 352–54, 356
*Dakar* 70, 302–3, 305, 307, 310, 329, 347, 357
*Dakka* 33–34
*Damer* 230–31, 233
Dande River 284
*Dar es Salaam* 221, 223–27, 328–29, 362–63
Dar-Kuti 237
Darfur 33, 230–31, 233, 283
*Daura* 118, 349
*Debarwa* 270
Denkyira (State) 193
*Denze* 237
*Derr* 230
*Dhlo-Dhlo* 62, 341
*Digsa* 270
*Dikwa* 237–38
*Dirani* 123
*Dirkou* 101
*Djenné* xv, 347 (see also Jenne-Jeno).

*Djibouti* 128, 275
Dogon 319
*Dongola* 34
Dra (Wadi) 110
Drakensberg Mountains 63
*Durban* 278, 329, 365, 374–75
*Duwa* 242

Ede 246, 249
Edo (Bini, people) 307–8
Efik (people) 247
Egba (people) 245–46, 252–53, 292, 307, 366
*Eguafo* (Great Kamenda) 16
Egypt 13, 33–36, 38–39, 50, 101, 110, 128, 231, 234, 280, 283, 338, 363, 369
Ekiti (country) 160
*Eko* 308
*Elesu* 250
*Elmina* 141–42, 144, 147–48, 229, 278, 327, 352
*Engaruka* 56–57
*Entebbe* 343
*Entoto* 273–74, 277
*Eruwa* 248
*Essina* 40
Ethiopia 14, 33, 36, 38–39, 72, 230, 261, 265–66, 268, 273, 277, 332, 368
Ewe (country) 257
Ewe (people) 174, 179, 183

Fante (people) 143, 153, 155, 176, 178, 352–53
*Faras* 34
*Fenoarivo* 15
Fernando-Po 300
*Fesu* 252
*Fez* 94, 109–10, 344
Fezzan 50, 101, 106–7, 112, 230, 237
*Filwoha* 272–73
Fon (people) 16, 174, 179, 181
*Fort Lamy* (N'Djamena) 329
*Fort Victoria* 14
*Fulah Town* 298
*Foumbam* 19, 72, 75, 261–64, 320
*Freetown* 229, 253, 278, 289, 291–94, 297–98, 300, 371–72

Fulani  xv, 107, 122, 124, 126, 163, 236,
    238–39, 241, 244, 364. *See also*
    Fulbe; Peul.
Fulbe  xv, 122, 124, 238–40, 242, 244,
    246, 261, 294, 307–8, 327. *See also*
    Fulani; Peul.
*Fundikira*  220
Funj (empire)  230, 233–34, 363
Futa-Jalon  292–93

Gabon  173, 300, 305
Gabou (kingdom)  173, 356
Galla (people)  128–30, 133, 197, 273, 276,
    283, 350
Gambia  137, 294
Gambia (river)  145
*Gana*, see Koumbi-Saleh.
Ganda (people)  73, 218
Ganda (kingdom)  19, 74, 76, 87, 218
*Gao*  40, 50, 91, 100, 102–5, 107–9, 112–14,
    166, 348
Gardafui (cape)  38
Garenganze (country)  214, 361
*Garumele*  106
*Gasabat Kawar*, see Kawar.
Gaye  237
*Gedi*  127, 129–30, 132
*Geebu*, see *Ijebu-Ode.*
*Gerri*  230
*Gezerani*  225
Gezira  278–79
*Ghadames*  104, 110
Ghana (empire)  26, 43, 50, 91, 97, 102,
    108, 115, 166, 180, 345, 348, 352–53
Goam  276
Gobir  103, 105, 118, 122, 238
Gold Coast  82, 143, 146, 152, 157, 167–68,
    171, 174, 176, 247, 257, 278, 304,
    309, 352–53, 359
*Gondar*  266–67, 269–73, 368
*Gonja*  41, 117, 241
Gonja (people)  192, 255
*Gorée*  141, 144, 174–75, 229, 278, 300–302,
    304–5, 307, 329, 373
Gun, see Adja.
Gran (people)  272
*Grand Bassam*  137

*Granville Town*  289
*Great Accra*  151, 153
*Great Komenda*  151
*Great Popo*  174
*Great Zimbabwe*  26, 55, 59, 64, 266, 335,
    341–42
Guinea  292, 305, 353, 358
Guinea-Bissau  174
Guinean Coast  139, 351
*Gwato*  247

*Halfaya*  231
*Hambarketolo*, see *Jenne-Jeno.*
*Harar*  128, 270
*Harare*, see *Salisbury.*
Hausa (kingdom)  24, 117-120, 126, 239,
    349
Hausa (people)  14, 97, 120, 124, 192-194,
    229, 244, 256-258, 309, 326, 348
Hima (people)  65–66, 320
Hottentots (people)  310-11
Hurutse (people)  64
Hutu (people)  65, 320

*Ibadan*  246–48, 251–52, 254, 328–29, 339,
    355, 366
Iddo Island  307
*Ife*  45, 158, 160–68, 246–49, 327, 329, 331,
    354–55, 366
Igbo (country)  10, 45
Igbo (people)  247, 292, 294
*Igbo-Ukwu*  45, 340
*Igboho*  25, 160
*Igbomosho*  25
*Ije*  158
*Ijebu*  168, 248
Ijebu (people)  158, 165, 246, 292, 307
*Ijebu-Ode*  159, 161
*Ikoyo*  25
*Ile-Ife*  160, 163, 165–66, 326
*Ilesha*  160, 164
*Ilira*  252
*Ilorin*  25, 244, 246
Inyanga (people)  57, 59, 341
*Irawo*  25
Ivory Coast  14–15, 115, 117, 137, 153, 208,
    255, 257, 353

*Iwere* 25
*Iwo* 246, 248

Jaga (people) 284
*Jega* 167
Jemaa 43
*Jenne* 26, 46–47, 49, 51, 91, 93, 96, 99–100,
103, 105, 107, 109–10, 112–15, 117,
151, 166, 191, 255, 259, 329, 340
*Jenne-Jeno* 26, 46, 47, 49, 51, 93, 96, 99
Jiji (people) 218–19
*Johannesburg* 328–29, 341, 365, 374
Jos Plateau 43, 333
Jula xv, 115–17, 120, 148, 151, 172, 191–92,
255, 257–59, 348

*Kabengo* 66
*Kairouan* 102
Kalahari 318
*Kalala* 101
*Kamenda (Great),* see Eguafo.
*Kampala* 19, 26–27, 66, 343
Kanem (kingdom) 91, 101–2, 106, 119,
236, 326, 346
Kanem-Bornu 91, 106, 346
*Kanembu* 236
*Kankan* 259, 293
*Kano* 91, 103, 118–20, 122–25, 166–67,
208, 229, 238–42, 255, 337, 349–50,
355, 364–65
Kanuri (people) 236, 347
Katanga 20, 25, 32, 67, 73, 209, 220, 225,
258
*Katsina* 91, 103, 118, 120, 122–23, 239,
349, 365
*Katunga,* see *Old Oyo; Oyo-Ile.*
*Kaw-Kaw,* see *Gao.*
*Kawa* 34
*Kawar* 43, 100–102, 107
Kazeh 220
*Kazimbe* 74
Kel Away (people) 105
Kenedugu (kingdom) 259, 367
Kenya 4, 39–40, 56, 223, 339, 351, 361
*Keta* 146, 174
*Khami* 62, 341

*Khartoum* 26, 35, 171, 209, 229, 231,
234–36, 278–83, 329, 338, 363,
369–70
Khoikhoi (people) 310
*Kibuga* 335, 342–43
*Kilwa* 39, 60, 127, 130–32, 198, 212, 215,
329, 350
*Kimberley* 63
*Kinshasa* (former *Leopoldville*) 8
*Kintampo* 255–57
*Kishi* 25
*Kiyange* 68
Koki 218
Koloko (people) 65
*Kolwezi* 74
*Kong* 116–17, 191, 241, 259, 367
Kongo (kingdom) 19–20, 77, 79–82, 87,
157, 284, 335, 343–44
Kongo (people) 77, 82–83, 335, 343–44
Kordofan 33, 230, 233–35
Kotoko (people) 237
*Koumbi-Saleh* 345. See also *Kumbi-Saleh.*
*Kumbi-Saleh* 50, 97, 100. See also
*Koumbi-Saleh.*
Kru (people) 292, 294
Kuba (kingdom) 82–83, 86–87
*Kukawa* 107, 236–37
*Kumasi* 26, 124, 141, 172–73, 183, 190–93,
195–96, 254, 327, 329, 331, 359, 367
Kuramo 159
*Kurrichane* 64
Kurru 34
Kush (kingdom) 33, 40, 338
*Kwaman* 153
Kwanza (river) 284

*Lagos* 8, 159, 168, 179–80, 229, 245,
252–54, 278, 298, 307–10, 328–29,
349, 353, 373–74
*Lamu* 40, 97, 129, 132–34, 222, 351
Lamu (island) 40, 127, 129, 223, 350, 360
*Leopoldville,* see *Kinshasa.*
Liberia 115, 117, 278, 289–90, 298, 337,
372
*Libreville* 26, 278, 328, 344
Liesbeek River 311
Limpopo River 59, 63

*Loango* 77, 80
*Lomé* 345
*Luanda* 80, 142, 277, 284–88
Luiche River 218
Lunda (empire) 20, 73, 319, 342, 375
Lunda (people) 67, 82
*Lungu* 242
*Lusaka* 26, 329

Madagascar 15, 39, 182, 313, 350, 358
*Mafikeng* 228
*Magdella* 267
Maiduguri 238
Makerere Hill 75
Malawi (lake) 215
Mali (empire) 50, 91–92, 107–10, 112, 115, 119–20, 154, 365
Mali (state) 35, 102, 242, 260, 340, 365
*Malindi* 129–30, 132, 197
Mande (country) 115, 167, 348
Mande (people) 115–16, 119, 167, 257, 348, 355
Manding (people) 109–10, 115, 257–58, 294, 327
*Manjaffa* 237
*Mankessim* 151, 153
*Mapungunbwe* 63
*Maqdishu*, see *Mogadishu.*
*Maradi* 239, 364
*Maranda (Marandet)* 50, 104
*Marrakech* 110
Maroon (people) 290, 293, 295, 297, 371
Masai (people) 56, 223
*Massawa (Massaouah)* 270
Matabele (people) 65, 341
Mauritania 31, 42
Mauritius Island 200
*Mayap* 263
*Mbanza-Kongo* 22, 77, 80–81, 329 (see also São Salvador).
Mbanza-Soyo 81
Mboamaji 225
Mbugu (people) 56
Mbulu 40
*Meknès* 110
Mengo Hills 75
Menouthias (island) 40–41

*Meroë* (present-day *Merowe*) 33–36, 38, 44, 67, 338
Mesurado Cape 299
Mfecane 56, 62–63, 65, 228, 243, 341, 365
*Mietta* 274
Mirambo 209–10, 220
*Mogadiscio,* see *Mogadishu.*
*Mogadishu* 39–40, 127–28, 132, 333, 351
*Mombasa* 127, 129–132, 137, 140, 197–98, 201, 204, 212, 222, 224, 278, 329, 350–51, 359
Monomotapa (Mutapa) 57, 60, 62, 64, 341. *See also* Inyanga.
*Monrovia* 278, 289, 298–300, 372
Moor (people) 215, 346
*Mopti* 100, 191, 259
Mosi (country) 110, 117, 257, 259, 348
Mosi (people) 14, 255, 257–58
Mouri 149, 155
*Mozambique* (city/island) 137, 140, 197–98, 200, 202, 204, 215, 278, 289, 359
Mozambique 27, 39, 57, 64, 127, 209, 286, 313, 370
Msiri (people) 209–10, 214
*Mubende* 66
*Mugera* 68
Murchinson Bay 74
*Muscat* 197, 201
*Musumba* 20, 22, 67, 73–74, 87, 319, 329, 342
Mutapa 57, 60, 130, 198, 200. *See also* Monomotapa.
*Mwembe* 215–16
Mzimima

*Nabulagala (Kasubi)* 75
*Nairobi* 4, 26, 329, 359, 362
*Nampula* 137
*Napata* 33–34, 338
Natal 63, 143, 228, 318, 329, 365, 375. See also *Port Natal.*
Natron (lake) 56, 240
Ndebele (country) 60, 62
Ndebele (people) 65
*New Oyo* 162, 245, 251
*N'Guigmi* 106

Nguni (people) 62, 204, 228, 341
*Niani* 50, 100
Nigeria 8, 19, 35, 43–45, 123, 158, 168, 178, 208, 238, 246–47, 333, 335–37, 340, 349–50, 354–55, 358, 364–66, 373–74
Niger River 120, 208, 247, 257–58
*Nikki* 255
*Niklas* 101
*Nikon*, see *Port Dunford.*
Nile 33–34, 230–31, 233–37, 273, 278, 282–83, 343, 362–64, 368
Nile, Blue 33, 230, 234, 273, 278
Nile, White 234, 278, 282–83
Ningi Mountains 242, 365
*Nioro* 45
*Njimom* 263
Njola 261
*Nkoje* 284
*Nkyenefo* 156
*Nok* 35, 43–45, 163, 166, 340
Nova Scotian (people) 290, 293–95
Nubia 33–34, 38, 230, 356, 363–64
Nume (people) 116
Nupe 160, 166–67, 298, 326
Nyamwezi 66, 209, 214, 216, 219–20, 224, 360, 362
*Nyanza* 69, 342
Nyasa (lake) 215, 226. *See also* Malawi (lake).
Nyasaland 223

*Offra-Jakin* 174
Ofin River 115
*Ogbomoso* 252
Oko Island 308
*Old Oyo* 25, 160–63, 166–67, 243–44. See also *Oyo-Ile.*
Oman 197–99, 201–2, 278
*Omdurman* 26, 234–35, 279, 283, 329
*Ondo* 158–59
Onitsha 45
Orange River 63
*Orile-Owu* 243
*Ormuz* 137, 201
Oromo (people) 132
*Oshogbo* 246

*Ouagadougou* 5, 229, 257–58, 328–29, 334
*Owu* 163, 243, 245, 248, 354, 365
*Owu-Ipole* 243
*Owu-Ogbere* 243
*Oyo* 24–25, 158–64, 166–67, 243–46, 248–52, 327, 354–55. *See also New Oyo; Old Oyo.*
*Oyo-Ile* 243. *See also Old Oyo.*
*Oyo, New*, see *New Oyo.*
*Oyo, Old*, see *Old Oyo.*

*Pangani* 41, 220, 223–24
Pate 129, 132, 351
Pemba Island 40, 81, 127, 131, 140, 201–3, 360
Peul (people) xv. *See also* Fulani; Fulbe.
Popo (people) 174, 292
*Port Dunford* 40
*Port Elizabeth* 314
*Port Gentil* 329
Port Harcourt 329, 366
*Port Natal (Durban)* 329, 365, 374–75. *See also* Natal.
*Porto Novo* 137, 173, 180, 182–83, 188, 190, 208, 211, 329
*Poto-Poto* (district of *Brazzaville*) 19
*Praia* 140
Pselchis, see *Dakka.*
Pyralees (islands), see Lamu (island).

*Rano* 24, 239
*Ras Hafun* 39, 338
Reunion Island 200
Rhapta 41, 339
*Ribeira Grande* (now *Cidade Velha*) 140
Rima River 238
Rivières du Sud 174
Rokel River 293
Rozwi (people) 62
*Rubaga* 75
*Rufisque* 307
Rwanda 19, 66, 69, 202, 216, 218, 320, 342

Saad-Din Island 128

Sahara 4, 6, 31, 35, 59, 92, 94, 97–98, 100–101, 103–4, 109, 112, 114, 116, 139, 233, 319, 337, 345–47, 355, 376

Sahel 4, 14, 33, 47, 51, 92, 98, 100, 103, 109–10, 115–16, 167, 171, 191, 208, 229, 242, 292, 324, 365

*Santo Antonio de Axim* 141. See also *Axim*.

*Saõ Jorge da Mina* 141, 278. See also *Elmina*.

*Saõ Salvador* 77–78, 80–81, 204, 284, 329

*Sakkwato* 238

*Salaga* 167, 191–92, 255–57, 327, 359

*Salisbury* (now *Harare*) 26, 350

Salt River 311

Samori 208, 257, 259

*Samun Dukiya* 44

Sandal (people) 104

Sankoré 110

Sanye (people) 40

*Sao* 141, 319

Saõ Salvador 77–78, 80–81, 204, 302, 329

Sarakolle (people) 307

*Sarapion* 40

Saro (people) 253, 309

*Sefuwa* 106

*Sega* 148

*Segu* 255, 259, 293, 307

*Segueding* 101

*Sekondi* 1025

Senegal 14, 26, 47, 115, 137, 173, 175, 208, 229, 278, 300–301, 303–7, 328, 348, 357, 372–73

Senegal (river) 139, 175, 302, 305

*Sennar* 33, 230, 233, 279, 363, 369

Shaka 62, 228, 365

Sheluk (people) 279

*Shendi* 230–31, 280

Shirazi (people) 39, 126, 130–31, 133, 198, 201–2, 224, 338, 350, 359

Shoa 272, 276

Shona (country) 26, 33, 57–58, 61–63, 67, 342

Shungawaya 39–40

Shuwa 236

Sierra Leone 139, 143, 252–53, 277–78, 289–90, 292, 294, 297–98, 304–5, 309, 337, 371

*Siguiri* 293

*Sikasso* 259–60, 367

*Soba* 230

*Sofala* 57, 60, 64, 73, 130–31, 198, 329

*Sokoto* 238–41, 244

Sokoto (sultanate) 208, 244, 364–65

Somali (people) 129, 270

Somalia 127, 132, 202, 338, 350

Songhai (empire) 14, 91–92, 104–5, 110–12, 114–15, 118–19, 123

Soninke (people) 110, 115, 258

South Africa 3, 55–56, 62–63, 143, 227, 278, 313–14, 317, 341, 363, 374, 377

Soyo 77, 80–81

*St. Louis* 26, 229, 278, 296, 300–301, 303–7, 328

*Suakin* 230

Sudan 13, 17, 26–27, 33, 36, 42, 46, 92–93, 96–97, 104, 109, 111, 171, 208–9, 229–35, 241, 244, 257, 260, 278–80, 283, 338, 347–48, 363–64, 367, 369–70

Swahili (people) 4, 14, 17, 40–41, 51, 73, 76, 91, 97, 126–30, 132–34, 170–71, 195, 198, 200–202, 204, 209–16, 218–27, 318, 339, 350–51, 359–61

*Tabora* 216, 218–20

*Tadmakka* 102, 346

*Tado* 183, 190

Tafilelt 110

*Takedda* 45, 102–3

*Takoradi* 148

Tana (lake) 267

*Tananarive* 15

Tanganyika (lake) 202, 216, 360

Tanzania 56, 209, 339, 362–63

*Taruga* 35

Taruga (valley) 44

Tassili n-Adjer 35

*Tatru* 101

*Tegdaust* 49, 340

*Teghaza* 110

*Teguidam-Tessoum* 103

*Teguidda,* see *Takedda.*
Teke Plateau 32
Temne (people) 289
*Tete* 215
Three Points (Cape of) 148
Tichitt 42–43, 59, 339
Tichitt (Dhar) 42, 339
Tigre 269, 276
Tigre (people) 271
*Timbo* 292
*Timbuktu* 17, 46, 91, 98, 100, 105, 107–16, 166, 241, 255, 257, 329, 347
*Tlemcen* 103, 110, 120
Togo 145, 174, 257
Tokpo 249
Transvaal 63–64, 318
Traore 259
*Tripoli* 110, 209, 237, 241, 348, 364–65
Tripolitania 101, 107
Tswana (people)
Tuareg (people) 103–5, 109, 346
Tuat 103, 110
*Tunis* 110, 345
Tutsi (people) 65, 320, 342

Uadaï 230, 236, 241
Uganda 26, 66, 320
*Ujiji* 202, 216, 218–19, 362
Unyanyembe 220
Uzaramo (country) 226

Victoria (lake) 14, 74, 218, 278
Volta (river) 115–17, 147, 152–53, 177, 192, 351, 367
Vudee 56

Waalo 305, 356, 372
Wadoe (people) 221
Wakamba (people) 221
*Walata* 104, 107, 109
Wangara (people) 115–16, 120, 123
*Warri* 247
Wazaramo (people) 221
*Whydah* 140, 142–144, 146, 159, 163, 167, 174, 179, 180, 188, 352
*Winneba* 148
Wolof (people) 14, 173, 294, 307

Yao (people) 209, 215–17, 361
*Yaounde* 329
Yarse (people) 258
Yemen 269
*Yendi-Dabari* 100, 167, 345
Yoruba (land) 10, 15, 19, 24–26, 98, 117, 145, 158–63, 167, 181, 183, 210–11, 229, 243–46, 248, 251–55, 307, 321, 326, 335, 354, 366, 373, 376
Yoruba (people) 13, 16, 19, 33, 157–58, 165–67, 178–79, 181, 188–90, 243–45, 247–49, 251, 277, 292, 296, 298, 308–9, 326–27, 354, 358, 365–66, 375–76
*Yuri* 255

Zambezi (river) 59, 63, 74, 215
*Zanzibar* 40, 91, 97, 127, 130–31, 140, 198, 201–4, 209–10, 212, 216, 219–20, 222–25, 278, 350, 359–62
Zaramo (people) 225-26
Zaria 118, 122, 167, 229, 242, 255
Zaria (=Zazzau) 24, 118
Zarma 103
*Zeila* 128
*Zimbabwe* 14, 20, 26, 32, 55, 37, 64, 57-65, 67, 73, 87, 105, 200, 266, 335, 341
Zimbabwe (kingdom) 32, 200
Zulu (people) 56, 63, 65, 69, 342, 365, 370
Zwangendaba 62

# About the Author

CATHERINE COQUERY-VIDROVITCH is Professor Emeritus of Modern African History at University of Paris-7-Denis-Diderot, and also taught in the State University of New York, Binghamton, Department of Sociology from 1981 to 2005. She was a visiting fellow at the Woodrow Wilson International Center for Scholars, Washington, D.C., in 1987 and at the Shelby Cullom Davis Center for Historical Studies, Princeton University, in 1992. Originally an economic historian, she has specialized in African comparative history, social urban change, and gender history. She has traveled to Africa every year since 1965, and has visited most African countries.

Catherine Coquery-Vidrovitch has trained a large number of French-speaking African historians in Paris and at African universities, and has published half a dozen books, some of which have been translated into English: *Afrique noire, permanences et ruptures (Africa: Endurance and Change South of the Sahara)* and *Les Africaines: Histoire des femmes d'Afrique noire du XIX<sup>e</sup> au XX<sup>e</sup> siècle (African Women: A Modern History)*. Besides the present book, a fourth one will soon be translated: *L'Afrique et les Africains au XIX<sup>e</sup> siècle (Africans in the Nineteenth Century)*. Her latest work to appear in French is the fifth (revised) edition of *L'Afrique noire de 1800 à nos jours* (with Henri Moniot). She has edited about twenty books on African studies and the Third World, and recently provided the introductions to two books on Urban History edited by Toyin Falola and Steve Salm, *African Urban Spaces in Historical Perspective* and *African Urban Culture: A History*. She is now preparing a book (in French) on German Blacks in the twentieth century, and another (in English, with Dale Tomich), on the historical process of the Atlantic World seen as a constantly changing, interrelated whole spanning three continents.

In 1999 Catherine Coquery-Vidrovitch received the African Studies Association's Distinguished Africanist Award. She is a member of the ICHS (International Conference of Historical Sciences) International Bureau.